Criminal Law Revision Committee

ELEVENTH REPORT
Evidence (General)

Presented to Parliament by the Secretary of State for the Home Department
by Command of Her Majesty

June 1972

LONDON
HER MAJESTY'S STATIONERY OFFICE

Reprinted 1980

Cmnd. 4991   £7.50 net

The estimated cost of the preparation of this report (including the expenses of the committee) is £5,296·88 of which £3,900 represents the estimated cost of the printing and publishing of this report.

CRIMINAL LAW REVISION COMMITTEE

GENERAL TERMS OF REFERENCE

The Criminal Law Revision Committee was set up on 2nd February 1959 by the then Home Secretary, Mr. R. A. Butler, " to be a standing committee to examine such aspects of the criminal law of England and Wales as the Home Secretary may from time to time refer to the committee, to consider whether the law requires revision and to make recommendations."

MEMBERS OF THE COMMITTEE

The Right Honourable Lord Justice EDMUND DAVIES, *Chairman*

The Right Honourable Sir Frederic SELLERS, M.C.

The Right Honourable Lord Justice LAWTON

Sir Donald FINNEMORE

The Honourable Mr. Justice JAMES

The Common Serjeant, Mr. J. M. G. GRIFFITH-JONES, M.C.

Professor Rupert CROSS

Professor D. R. SEABORNE DAVIES

Sir Kenneth JONES, C.B.E.

Sir Frank MILTON

His Honour Judge Malcolm MORRIS, Q.C.

Mr. A. C. PROTHERO

Sir Norman SKELHORN, K.B.E., Q.C.

Professor Glanville WILLIAMS, Q.C.

Mr. G. V. HART, *Secretary*

Miss B. R. PUGH, *Assistant Secretary*

NOTES

Lord Justice Edmund Davies succeeded Sir Frederic Sellers as chairman of the committee on 12th May 1969.

The late Mr. Justice Marshall was a member of the committee when the subject of the present report was referred to them and took part in their consideration of it until his death on 20th June 1966.

The late Sir Rodger (formerly Lord Justice) Winn was a member of the committee when the subject of the present report was referred to them and took part in their consideration of it until prevented by illness in the summer of 1970.

The late Mr. James Whiteside, O.B.E., was a member of the committee when the subject of the present report was referred to them and took part in their consideration of it until his death on 14th November 1971.

The above list of members does not include three members (Mr. J. B. R. Hazan, Q.C., Mr. David Napley and Mr. William Scott) who were appointed in November 1970 to be members for the references beginning with that on offences against the person.

TABLE OF CONTENTS

Page

Introduction 5

Scope of report 8

General principles 9

Interrogation of suspects; effect of silence; Judges' Rules (clause 1)... 16

Confessions (clause 2) 34

Admissibility of other conduct of accused tending to show disposition (clause 3) 47

Giving of evidence by accused (clauses 4 and 5) 65

Restrictions on cross-examination of accused (clause 6) 71

Admissibility of evidence and questions about accused's disposition or reputation (clause 7) 85

Limits of burden of proof falling on accused (clause 8) 87

Competence and compellability of spouse of accused (clause 9) ... 92

Cross-examination (clauses 10–14) 98

Privilege (clauses 15 and 16) 103

Corroboration, and directions to juries (clauses 17—21) 106

Evidence of children (clause 22) 121

Time at which evidence may be called (clause 23) 124

Various provisions relating to convictions and acquittals (clauses 24—26) 128

Institution of proceedings for perjury etc. (clause 27) 130

Duty of magistrates' courts to have regard to enactments about warnings to juries (clause 28) 130

Abolition of right to make evidence of document called for and inspected by an opponent (clause 29) 131

Hearsay evidence (clauses 30—41) 132

Opinion and expert evidence (clauses 42—44) 154

Matters on which no change is proposed by draft Bill:

    (i) communications to ministers of religion or medical practitioners 157

    (ii) evidence on commission 161

    (iii) judicial discretion to exclude evidence 162

    (iv) abolition of the oath 163

Other matters 166

Conclusion 166

Annex 1—Draft Criminal Evidence Bill 169

Annex 2—Notes on draft Criminal Evidence Bill 211

CRIMINAL LAW REVISION COMMITTEE
ELEVENTH REPORT
Evidence (General)

To the Right Honourable REGINALD MAUDLING, M.P., *Her Majesty's Principal Secretary of State for the Home Department.*

INTRODUCTION

1. On 25th September 1964 the then Home Secretary, Mr. Henry (now Lord) Brooke, asked us

> " to review the law of evidence in criminal cases and to consider whether any changes are desirable in the interests of the fair and efficient administration of justice; and in particular what provision should be made for modifying rules which have ceased to be appropriate in modern conditions."

2. On 14th November 1966 at the request of the then Home Secretary, Mr. Roy Jenkins, we submitted a separate report[1] with our recommendations on three matters included in this reference on which Mr. Jenkins was considering including provisions in the forthcoming Bill for the Criminal Justice Act 1967 (c. 80). These were the making of further provision for allowing evidence to be given by written statement, allowing formal admissions and requiring notice to be given of alibi defences. The recommendations were embodied in three draft clauses annexed to the report which, with minor modifications, became ss. 9, 10 and 11 of the Criminal Justice Act. The present report completes our study of evidence in criminal cases.

3. We began by sending a circular letter to a number of persons and bodies concerned in the administration or teaching of the law in which we asked for their views on the matters within the terms of reference. The letter referred in particular to the most important of those matters, including the admissibility of confessions by accused persons, evidence of their previous misconduct, the competence or compellability of the accused's spouse, corroboration and hearsay evidence. The chairman wrote in similar terms to all the lords of appeal and judges of the Supreme Court who were or had been concerned with the criminal law, to the judges of the Central Criminal Court and to a number of recorders and chairmen of quarter sessions. We had not sought opinions in this way before beginning work on previous references; but we thought it right to do so in this case because it seemed clear that greatly different views would be held on many of these questions. This was amply borne out by events, as will appear later. Moreover we could not have begun consideration of evidence for some time, because when it was referred we were fully occupied with the references on felonies and misdemeanours (which had been referred to us only six months before) and on theft and related offences. We could therefore afford to leave a reasonable time for the societies circularized to consult their members. The views expressed were of great help to us.

---

[1] 9th Report: Evidence (Written statements, formal admissions and notices of alibi) (Cmnd. 3145).

4. While these consultations were going on, the committee set up a sub-committee to consider the subject in the first instance under the chairmanship of the then chairman of the committee, Lord Justice Sellers. The other members were the present chairman, Mr. Justice Marshall (until his death on 20th June 1966), Mr. (now Lord) Justice Lawton, the Common Serjeant, Sir Kenneth Jones, Sir Frank Milton, Sir Norman Skelhorn and Professor Glanville Williams. In addition the sub-committee had the assistance of Professor Rupert Cross, Vinerian Professor of English Law in the University of Oxford, who was co-opted as a member and also attended the meetings of the full committee (of which he became a member in November 1970).

5. The committee also set up two groups of three members each to study the laws of criminal evidence in certain other countries. The first group, under the chairmanship of Lord Justice Winn, studied the laws of the United States of America. The other members were Mr. (now Judge) Malcolm Morris and Professor Williams. The second group, under the chairmanship of Mr. (now Lord) Justice Lawton, considered the laws of France and the Federal Republic of Germany. The other members were Sir Donald Finnemore and Mr. (now Mr. Justice) James. This group had the great advantage of personal consultation with a recently retired French judge and a serving German judge, who were good enough to come to London for visits of a few days each for discussions with the group. The French judge was M. Manfred Simon, a former public prosecutor, member of the Conseil d'Etat and judge of the Paris Court of Appeals. The German judge was Professor Werner Sarstedt, President of the Third (Berlin) Criminal Division of the Supreme Court of the Federal Republic of Germany and Professor of Law at the Free University of Berlin. Before coming to London the judges had considered two imaginary cases, prepared by Mr. Justice Lawton, designed to raise as many as possible of the kinds of questions which the committee would be considering in relation to English law. At the meetings in London the judges, after giving outline accounts of the relevant law and procedure in criminal trials, explained how the imaginary cases would be tried under their laws and answered a number of questions for the purpose of testing the comparative advantages of their system and the English system. The meetings were of great value and interest to the committee, although for reasons which will be given below the great differences between continental and English criminal procedure make few if any of the French and German rules, where they differ from the English rules, suitable for adoption in England.

6. Besides these consultations the committee obtained valuable material as to the working of the law in Canada from Professor J. Ll. J. Edwards and Professor Martin Friedland, of the University of Toronto, and Professor E. A. Tollefson, of the University of Saskatchewan. In particular Professor Edwards gave the committee a detailed memorandum, incorporating opinions by experienced practising lawyers, in reply to a question by the committee as to the effect of the Canadian rule (which is similar to that in the United States) that the accused, if he gives evidence, is liable to cross-examination on his record like an ordinary witness. Professor Friedland was present by invitation at one of the committee's meetings.

7. On two subjects—identification evidence and police investigations—the committee had the help of senior representatives of the police, who accepted invitations to attend meetings when one or other of these subjects was being

6

discussed. These were Mr. F. E. Williamson (one of Her Majesty's Inspectors of Constabulary), Mr. C. H. Cooksley (Chief Constable of Northumberland), Mr. W. J. Richards (Chief Constable of Manchester) and Commander D. B. S. Adams and the late Detective Chief Superintendent T. Butler (Metropolitan Police).

8. The sub-committee were able to begin work late in 1965 after the committee had received most of the observations eventually sent in response to the request referred to in paragraph 3 and had finished work on felonies and misdemeanours and were near the end of that on theft. At a series of meetings the sub-committee worked out proposals on most of the present subject. The second half of 1966 was mostly devoted to the special report referred to in paragraph 2. The three clauses annexed to that report were, as mentioned in it, prepared for the committee by Parliamentary Counsel. For the rest of the subject the committee had the services of Parliamentary Counsel from the spring of 1967, when the committee or sub-committee had made enough progress to justify the drafting of clauses to give effect to their views. From then till the summer of 1968 there were meetings both of the sub-committee and of the full committee as the latter considered the provisional conclusions of the former. After the summer of 1968 all the work was done in the full committee.

9. In May 1968 we again consulted the interested persons and bodies who had been consulted at the beginning as mentioned in paragraph 3. We had formed views, some nearly final and some very provisional, on the most important matters under consideration and we thought that, since some of these subjects were difficult and controversial, it would be desirable, before reaching final conclusions, to give those consulted the opportunity to express their opinions on the desirability or otherwise of making the changes which we were considering recommending. On this occasion we consulted all the judges of the Supreme Court. In fact the majority of the persons and bodies consulted agreed substantially with our provisional proposals on most matters except the admissibility of evidence of other misconduct of the accused, on which we ourselves were (and still are) sharply divided.

10. We wish to record our gratitude to all those with whom we had the benefit of the consultations referred to in the previous paragraphs. Our eventual conclusions, arrived at in the light of these consultations and after much discussion and reconsideration, are embodied in the draft Criminal Evidence Bill prepared for the purpose by Parliamentary Counsel and annexed to the report as Annex 1. Notes on the draft Bill follow as Annex 2.

11. At the same time as the subject was referred to us the then Lord Chancellor (Viscount Dilhorne) made a similar reference of the law of evidence in civil proceedings to the Law Reform Committee. The two committees kept in touch so far as possible on topics more or less common to both kinds of proceedings, which however do not include the most difficult topics on the criminal side, as these relate to the special position of the accused in criminal trials. Criminal trials inevitably differ radically from civil trials in that the greater importance of their outcome for the accused, at least in serious cases, necessitates special safeguards for his protection. This is so in particular in trials on indictment, where the issue is decided by a jury, whereas juries are exceptional now in civil trials. Moreover, the simpler and more expeditious

procedures which are obviously necessary in criminal cases, and the virtual absence of interlocutory criminal proceedings, make changes which are appropriate for one kind of trial inappropriate for the other. The Law Reform Committee have made four reports on evidence[1]. The recommendations in their three reports made before 1968 for changes in the law were substantially given effect to by the Civil Evidence Act 1968 (c. 64). The Law Reform Committee had informed the present committee of their intended recommendations so far as they were of common interest, and in fact the present committee's draft Bill includes provisions corresponding to most of those made by the Civil Evidence Act or included in the subsequent report, though on the largest matter (hearsay evidence) the present committee's recommendations differ substantially from the provisions in the Act. This is because of the great contrast referred to above between civil and criminal procedure.

SCOPE OF REPORT

12. We have examined all those parts of the law of criminal evidence in which we thought that changes were or might be desirable for the reasons given in the terms of reference or otherwise. We have not attempted to construct a statutory code covering the whole law, as we did of the law of theft and related offences[2]. This is because (apart from the great delay which it would cause) we are recommending some far-reaching changes and these will have to be considered before codification is possible. We have assumed that the work of codification will be for the Law Commission as part of their share in the codification of the criminal law. On several subjects we considered whether to recommend changes in the law but decided not to do so. These matters are referred to at the end of the report.

13. We have assumed (as we must under our terms of reference) that the essential features of English criminal trials will remain much as at present. In particular we have assumed—

(i) that the English " adversary " system will not be replaced by the continental " inquisitorial " system (in which there is a full judicial investigation of the whole case, including that for the defence, before the trial and at the trial the judge questions the accused from the report of the investigation);

(ii) that trial by jury will remain and that the judge will not (as for example in France) retire with the jury when they consider their verdict;

(iii) that magistrates will continue to try the great majority of criminal cases and that of these a very high proportion will be tried by lay justices.

If any changes are desirable in these respects, they must come after a full consideration of the whole system: they cannot be made piecemeal in legislation about evidence. An illustration will show how these assumptions have affected our consideration. In France and Germany practically all evidence

---

[1] 13th Report (April 1966). Hearsay Evidence in Civil Proceedings. Cmnd. 2964.
15th Report (September 1967). The Rule in *Hollington v. Hewthorn*. Cmnd. 3391.
16th Report (December 1967). Privilege in Civil Proceedings. Cmnd. 3472.
17th Report (October 1970). Evidence of Opinion and Expert Evidence. Cmnd. 4489

[2] 8th Report: Cmnd. 2977.

which is relevant is admissible. In England a good deal of relevant evidence is excluded because of the danger that it would be too prejudicial to the accused, and much of this will still be excluded if our proposals are accepted. A good deal of this might reasonably be made admissible if the judge retired with the jury, as he would be able to prevent them from giving undue weight to it.

GENERAL PRINCIPLES

14. Since the object of a criminal trial should be to find out if the accused is guilty, it follows that ideally all evidence should be admissible which is relevant in the sense that it tends to render probable the existence or non-existence of any fact on which the question of guilt or innocence depends. This is the only possible meaning of relevance for the purpose of any reasonable discussion of the law of criminal evidence. It also follows that ideally every person who can give relevant evidence should be a compellable witness. In practice there must be certain exceptions, and the most important and difficult of the questions with which we have been concerned has been whether or how far a particular exception is necessary. We refer to some of these below.

15. Relevant evidence may be excluded because experience shows—or has been thought to show—that to admit it might be too prejudicial to the accused. The most important example is evidence of other misconduct by the accused showing a disposition to commit offences, especially the kind of offence charged. Although this evidence may be highly relevant, it has in general been rejected because of fears that it might influence jurors or lay justices disproportionately against the accused with the result that they might pay too little attention to the weight of the evidence connecting him with the offence charged.

16. Certain kinds of evidence have been thought generally too unreliable to be admitted. One of the reasons for the rule that a confession of guilt by the accused, in order to be admissible in evidence, must be proved to have been made voluntarily is the danger that a confession obtained by means of a threat or inducement may be untrue. One of the reasons for the general inadmissibility of hearsay evidence has been the difficulty of testing the reliability of a hearsay statement when the maker is not in court to be cross-examined; and although we are proposing that hearsay evidence should be much more widely admissible, we have included restrictions to take account of this difficulty. Possible unreliability is also the reason for excluding the evidence of very young children and for the rules as to corroboration of evidence.

17. Even the most cogent evidence may be rejected because of the way in which it was obtained. A suggested reason (besides possible unreliability) why a confession is inadmissible unless proved to have been voluntary is the need to discourage the use of improper means to obtain confessions. However, English law may not have been consistent in this respect, as will be mentioned below[1]. It is admittedly questionable whether the object mentioned should be secured by restricting the admissibility of evidence rather than by disciplining those responsible; but we do not think that we can leave this object out of account, and we have had regard to it in our recommendations about the admissibility of evidence of confessions[2].

---

[1] Paragraph 56.
[2] Ibid.

18. Some evidence is excluded because its reception might confuse the issue of guilt or innocence by introducing too many side issues or might lengthen trials out of all proportion to the value of the evidence for the ascertainment of the truth. For example, although a witness may be cross-examined as to his conduct in order to impair his credibility, evidence is in general not admissible to prove the conduct if he denies it.

19. Lastly, evidence may be excluded for overriding reasons of policy not related to its value. The most important example is the rule that, with certain exceptions, the spouse of the accused either cannot give evidence for the prosecution at all or cannot be compelled to do so. At common law the spouse was in nearly all cases incompetent as a witness for the prosecution or for the defence. The preservation of marital harmony was only one of the reasons for this rule; but it has been the most important factor in deciding how far to go along the inroads which have been made into the rule in the last century or so. As will be seen, we are proposing to go well beyond these. Another exclusionary rule is for the protection of communications for the purpose of obtaining legal advice. Obviously if the accused's solicitor had to give evidence of what the accused told him when he consulted him about the charge, this would help the jury to make up their minds about his guilt; but equally obviously justice could not be properly administered unless people could speak freely when seeking legal advice.

20. We have referred[1] to the ideal that all available and relevant evidence should be before the court. We have throughout aimed at reducing the exceptions to admissibility under the present law. Over and over again judges have had to reject evidence which would obviously have been valuable for the ascertainment of the truth, and could not possibly have caused any injustice, because " on the authorities " it was inadmissible. Often appellate courts have been compelled, with expressed reluctance, to quash a conviction because of misreception of evidence. Sometimes judges have acceded to an appeal by the defence to admit in the interests of justice a piece of evidence which they felt they ought in law to reject. Several of us have had personal experience of such incidents. We have all read of others, both in reports of cases and, recently, in the forceful criticism of some existing restrictions which features in many of the answers to our requests for observations. Some of these cases are mentioned later in the report. There must also have been many occasions on which parties have refrained from seeking to adduce valuable evidence because they knew that it was bound to be ruled out as inadmissible. Our firm conclusion is that it is right to extend admissibility as far as is possible without the risk of injustice to the accused. The difficulty is to agree on how far this means. Apart from this general argument for greater admissibility the fact that criminal trials now take place in circumstances very different from those which prevailed when the more restrictive rules were adopted seems to us to justify relaxation of the rules. The changes are referred to in the next paragraph.

21. The scales used to be loaded against the defence in ways which it is difficult now to remember.

     (i) Trials were often conducted with indecent haste. Mr. Justice Hawkins in his " Memoirs " (chapter IV) quotes a trial at the Old

---

[1] Paragraph 14.

Bailey in the 1840's for pickpocketing which, although the accused pleaded not guilty and two witnesses were called, lasted altogether 2 minutes and 53 seconds. The evidence was all given in reply to leading questions. The accused seems to have remained silent apart from pleading not guilty; and the judge's intimation to him of his right to cross-examine the two witnesses consisted only of: " I suppose you have nothing to ask him?" and that of his right to address the jury only of: " Nothing to say, I suppose?" The summing up consisted of: " Gentlemen, I suppose you have no doubt? I have none ". The author thought that this case was "perhaps ... a high example of expedition ", but he said that trials after dinner lasted on the average four minutes. Nowadays there are few complaints that trials before judges and juries are too short.

(ii) Accused persons enjoyed far less legal representation in the past than now. Before the Trials for Felony Act 1836 (c. 114) in the case of felony the defending counsel could do little more than argue points of law and advise the accused what questions to ask witnesses. He could not address the jury. For years afterwards the accused was often unrepresented even in serious cases. An unrepresented defendant in a trial on indictment is now a rarity, and even then it is usually by his own choice. S. 2 of the 1836 Act for the first time gave the accused the right to have full legal representation at summary trials. Previously the magistrates always could (and sometimes did) refuse to allow advocates to appear at all. Legal aid is now applied for, and granted, in a high proportion of the more serious cases tried summarily.

(iii) It was not until the Criminal Evidence Act 1898 (c. 36) that the accused and his spouse were able in all cases to give evidence on oath (though for some years this had been allowed by statute in the case of certain offences). During the previous sixty years or so (in some cases earlier) the accused had been allowed to make an unsworn statement about the facts; but this could not be tested by cross-examination, so that the court and jury were deprived of the advantage of hearing the sworn evidence of the person who was in the best position to say what had happened on the occasion in question. Being able to give sworn evidence the accused has the opportunity to explain away, if he can, evidence which it might have been thought too dangerous to admit when he had not this opportunity.

(iv) There are now far greater rights of appeal against conviction. Before the Criminal Appeal Act 1907 (c. 23) a conviction on indictment could be questioned only on narrow legal grounds. Now the grounds of appeal include the wide one under s. 2(1)(a) of the Criminal Appeal Act 1968 (c. 19) " that the verdict of the jury should be set aside on the ground that under all the circumstances of the case it is unsafe or unsatisfactory ". Convictions have several times been quashed under this power when, although no fault could be found with the conduct of the trial, the Court of Appeal felt doubt about the correctness of the verdict, for example because there might have been a mistaken identification. The possibility of an appeal has long since made trials like that mentioned by Mr. Justice Hawkins unthinkable.

Admittedly serious irregularities still sometimes occur (nearly always because of a momentary aberration), but there is now the Court of Appeal or the Divisional Court to quash a resulting conviction and, if necessary, to criticize severely those responsible.

(v) The quality of juries and of lay magistrates has greatly improved. Several judges have said that they rarely find a bad jury nowadays. This improvement is no doubt owing to better education. Lay magistrates now receive proper training for their duties, and they are normally assisted by clerks who are legally qualified and experienced and are mostly employed full-time. Even before the Courts Act 1971 (c. 23) there had been a great improvement in the standard of trials at quarter sessions, especially since most courts had come to have legally qualified chairmen.

(vi) Criminals are far more sophisticated than they used to be. Petty criminals may be only a little less ignorant and feckless about defending themselves than was Mr. Justice Hawkins's pickpocket; but there is now a large and increasing class of sophisticated professional criminals who are not only highly skilful in organizing their crimes and in the steps they take to avoid detection but are well aware of their legal rights and use every possible means to avoid conviction if caught. These include refusal to answer questions by the police and the elaborate manufacture of false evidence.

The chief significance of these comparisons for present purposes is that strict and formal rules of evidence, however illogically they may have worked in some cases, may have been necessary in order to give accused persons at least some protection, however inadequate, against injustice. But with changed conditions they may no longer serve a useful purpose but on the contrary have become a hindrance rather than a help to justice. There has also been a good deal of feeling in the committee and elsewhere that the law of evidence should now be less tender to criminals generally. With the improvements mentioned it seems to us reasonable to expect that the right amount of weight will be given to some kinds of evidence previously rejected as likely to be too prejudicial to the accused.

22. Naturally the most important question for us has been how far the differences noted above which have taken place since the rules of evidence were evolved justify making the law less favourable to the defence. Equally naturally we ourselves, and those who sent us observations, have disagreed widely on this. In some cases the views differed according to the extent to which the person or body expressing the view thought that amendment of the law of evidence might have value in the fight against crime. Some attached great importance to this, holding that criminals are getting the better of the law, that wrong acquittals make them bolder and encourage others to follow their example and that the more the guilty are convicted the better hope will there be of winning the fight. Supporters of this view point to the steady increase in crime and to the notably high proportion of acquittals in contested trials on indictment. Others hold that this view is greatly exaggerated, that wrong acquittals are few and that the harm done by them is minute in comparison with the harm done by failure to detect offenders. This difference

of view applies specially to the question of the admissibility of other misconduct of the accused. Again, widely different views have been expressed in the committee and in the observations to them as to whether the present safeguards against wrong convictions are sufficient, insufficient or excessive. This applies especially to interrogations by the police, the requirements as to corroboration and the danger of mistaken identification. It is remarkable how some of our provisional proposals have been welcomed by distinguished lawyers as clearly desirable reforms and yet denounced by others, equally distinguished, as subversive of justice. Again, one lawyer may think that the law is right on one point but needs radical alteration on another while a second will take the opposite view on both points. We suspect—without meaning any disrespect—that one cause of these differences of opinion is that with many lawyers the supreme merit of our law of evidence persists as an article of faith until they see one of the rules resulting in a glaring case of injustice, and then they become wholeheartedly radical in respect of this rule.

23. Whatever the causes of these differences of opinion, we have, after considering all the views expressed to us on each topic, necessarily gone our own way in deciding what to recommend. Where we have been satisfied that a change ought to be made, we have recommended it, however eminent the opposition. Where we have disagreed among ourselves, we have acted as seemed best in each case; but fortunately on most topics we eventually reached general agreement. Where there have been disagreements on important questions of principle, this is shown in the report. Some of the recommendations on matters of detail have been made by majority decisions, but in general these cases are not specially mentioned.

24. Our main object, then, has been to go as far in getting rid of restrictions on admissibility of evidence as is possible in the " modern conditions " referred to in our terms of reference, in particular having regard to the changed conditions referred to above[1]. We have also aimed at reducing the gap between the amount of relevant evidence which could be given and the amount which is in fact given. This is done chiefly by provisions designed to discourage the accused from refraining from giving evidence if a prima facie case has been made out against him, by reducing the great restrictions as to the giving of evidence by the spouse of the accused and by abolishing certain privileges of refusing to answer questions. We justify the reforms which we recommend for this purpose not only because of the changed conditions to which we have referred but mainly on the ground that there is no clear reason why the restrictions should ever have existed. We are also proposing to remove or modify certain restrictions, imposed by the law or practice relating to corroboration, on the freedom of the jury or magistrates' court to decide the issue of guilt or innocence on their own assessment of the cogency of the evidence given by the principal witness to an offence, even if that evidence is not corroborated.

25. Another important object we have had has been to simplify the law within the limits set by the difficulty of the subject matter and the fact that we are proposing amendments and not codification. Simplicity is specially important for the law of evidence. It is important for the court, because a point of evidence frequently arises suddenly and without warning during a

---

[1] Paragraphs 20–21.

hearing and has to be disposed of without there being a proper opportunity to consult authorities. Moreover it is the duty of the court to raise any question of admissibility even if no party does so. Simplicity is more important still for the jury, in the sense that the judge should be able to direct them in a way which they can understand—and accept as reasonable—on how they should regard a piece of evidence. The present law requires judges to direct juries to achieve certain mental feats which some judges think impossible for any lawyers to achieve; and it is no answer to criticisms of this kind to say, as is sometimes said, that there is no difficulty in directing the jury in the way in which the courts have said they should be directed. There may be no difficulty in saying the right words: the question is what the jury make of them, and nobody can be sure of that. One judge who wrote to us said that in his opinion some of the rules of evidence are " practically incomprehensible to anybody but a trained lawyer " and that he was " sure most juries do not understand them ". We have also included provisions designed to simplify or get rid of particular rules which, though not specially difficult in themselves, seem to us to involve anomalies or unnecessary complications. It should be emphasized that provisions designed to simplify a complicated system of law cannot always themselves be expressed in simple terms. We have done our best for this purpose, but it is better to have provisions which may look difficult but will simplify the working of the law than provisions which look easy but which make or leave the law difficult and obscure. In certain cases we have included provision to enact the substance of a common law rule or the effect of a decision on the construction of an existing enactment. This is intended to simplify the law in that the authority for a proposition will be found in the Act instead of having to be sought in perhaps a number of reported cases. There are lawyers who prefer to work on the common law, perhaps because it is more familiar; but it cannot be seriously disputed that to have a statutory provision is more convenient. Moreover we expect, as mentioned above[1], that the law of criminal evidence will eventually be codified.

26. There are some other particular objects which we have had in mind throughout as desirable.

    (i) One should avoid as far as possible the need to interrupt a witness in order to stop him from breaking a rule of evidence. Lay magistrates' courts in particular are known to dislike interruptions of the natural course of evidence; and juries, when a witness has to be told not to mention this or that, often seem to become suspicious and think that something important is being kept from them. This applies specially in relation to hearsay and opinion evidence, and we hope that our recommendations will reduce the occasions for interruption.

    (ii) Where evidence is admissible, it should wherever possible be so for all purposes. Our recommendations on hearsay evidence will get rid of most of the cases where the judge has to tell the jury that evidence that a witness said such-and-such a thing is admissible not as evidence of the truth of what he said but only as showing consistency or inconsistency with his evidence given in court. This distinction must be confusing to juries. Again, evidence admissible against any of a number of co-accused ought to be admissible against them all. Our recommendations will go a long way to achieving this result.

---

[1] Paragraph 12.

14

(iii) The rules of evidence should be similar at trials on indictment and at summary trials. We have had a good deal of doubt from time to time whether to recommend a reform which, though suitable for a trial on indictment, might not be suitable for a summary trial, especially before lay justices. Magistrates' courts raise special problems, quite apart from absence of legal qualifications, in that, where a question arises whether a piece of evidence is admissible, magistrates have to hear the evidence before deciding the question. In fact we have not made any difference between the two kinds of trials except that we propose that in certain cases a party should have to give notice of intention to adduce hearsay evidence at a trial on indictment; but, as mentioned below[1], this is in accordance with recent precedent. We have considered all our other proposals with special reference to their application to magistrates' courts, and we are satisfied that they may be applied to those courts without modification.

27. We need hardly say that we have no wish to lessen the fairness of criminal trials. But it must be clear what fairness means in this connection. It means, or ought to mean, that the law should be such as will secure as far as possible that the result of the trial is the right one. That is to say, the accused should be convicted if the evidence proves beyond reasonable doubt that he is guilty, but otherwise not. We stress this, although it may seem obvious, because fairness seems often to be thought of as something which is due to the defence only. At least there seems to be an idea that the defence have a sacred right to the benefit of anything in the law which may give them a chance of acquittal, even on a technicality, however strong the case is against them. We disagree entirely with this idea. It seems to derive from an unwarranted extension of the principle that, in order that the accused should be convicted, the prosecution must prove their case and perhaps also of the convention that those appearing for the prosecution are not concerned to secure a conviction but only to present the case. As a result the habit has grown up of looking at a criminal trial as a kind of game to be played, according to fixed rules, between the prosecution and the defence; and since the defence are naturally likely to be the weaker (and the accused may very likely seem stupid and helpless), it seems to be expected that the prosecution will refrain from using all their strength and that the judge will take any opportunity to make the contest more even. A bold attempt to get the benefit of this fallacy was made by the defence in *McGregor*[2]. The accused was charged with receiving stolen jewellery. At the first trial the jury disagreed. At the second trial the prosecution called evidence that the accused had admitted, when giving evidence at the first trial, that he had had possession of the jewellery. He did not give evidence at the second trial, and he was convicted. He appealed on the grounds, among others, that evidence of what evidence he gave at the first trial was inadmissible and that, even if it was admissible, it was " unfair " to admit it. The Court of Appeal held that the evidence was clearly admissible (though it was interesting that neither counsel nor any member of the court could remember a case where this kind of evidence was given). As to the second ground Lord Parker C.J. observed[3]:—

---

[1] Paragraphs 241, 256.
[2] [1968] 1 Q.B. 371; 51 Cr. App. R. 338.
[3] At p. 377D; p. 340.

15

" Secondly, it is said that it was unfair. As the court understands it, [the counsel for the appellant] says it was unfair, because it no doubt did cut the ground from under his feet and prevented him from making a submission of no case. It is also said to be unfair in that really if the defendant were to stand any chance he would have to give evidence. In fact he gave no evidence at all. Unfair in that sense it may have been, but unfair in the general circumstances of the administration of justice it was certainly not."

We too have in mind fairness "in the general circumstances of the administration of justice." It is as much in the public interest that a guilty person should be convicted as it is that an innocent person should be acquitted.

CLAUSE 1: INTERROGATION OF SUSPECTS; EFFECT OF SILENCE; JUDGES' RULES

28. We propose to restrict greatly the so-called " right of silence " enjoyed by suspects when interrogated by the police or by anyone charged with the duty of investigating offences or charging offenders. By the right of silence in this connection we mean the rule that, if the suspect, when being interrogated, omits to mention some fact which would exculpate him, but keeps this back till the trial, the court or jury may not infer that his evidence on this issue at the trial is untrue. Under our proposal it will be permissible to draw this inference if the circumstances justify it. The suspect will still have the " right of silence " in the sense that it is no offence to refuse to answer questions or tell his story when interrogated; but if he chooses to exercise this right, he will risk having an adverse inference drawn against him at his trial[1].

29. Since one cannot tell for certain what effect it has on the jury when the accused tells a story in court which he did not mention to the police when questioned, the practical importance of the restriction on comment concerns what the judge may say in summing up. Briefly, he may invite the jury, in considering the weight which they should give to the accused's evidence, to take into account the fact that, by not mentioning his story to the police, he has deprived them of the opportunity of investigating it[2]. The judge may also, apparently, say simply that the jury may take the accused's failure to give his explanation into account when they are considering the weight to give to his evidence in court, without having to add that the reason for this is that he has deprived the police of the opportunity to check his story[3]. But in several cases, including *Hoare*[4] and *Sullivan*[5], it has been held that it is a misdirection to suggest that the jury may infer that the story told in court is false because, if it had been true, the accused would naturally have told it to the police when they questioned him. In some of the cases the comment by the judge which

---

[1] In relation to the trial the " right of silence " enjoyed by the accused means that the prosecution have the burden of proving his guilt, that he may refrain from giving evidence and that the prosecution may not comment on his omission to give it. Under our proposals discussed in paragraphs 110 to 113 below comment on the omission will be allowed and it will be permissible to draw adverse inferences from it. We do not propose to weaken in any way the principle that the prosecution have the burden of proving the guilt of the accused: in fact our proposals discussed in paragraphs 140 to 142 are intended to strengthen this principle in one respect.
[2] *Littleboy*, [1934] 2 K.B. 408; 24 Cr. App. R. 192.
[3] *Ryan* (1966), 50 Cr. App. R. 144, 148.
[4] (1966), 50 Cr. App. R. 166.
[5] (1967), 51 Cr. App. R. 102.

16

was held to have been a misdirection was made with reference to the accused's failure to give an explanation when cautioned as required by the Judges' Rules[1] or when told in the statutory form or words at the end of the case for the prosecution in the committal proceedings that he was not obliged to say anything[2]. In these cases the Court of Criminal Appeal pointed out that, as the accused was told that he was not obliged to say anything, it would be a trap for him if the jury were to be invited to draw an adverse inference from his silence. But we have no doubt that it is now established that the rule that an invitation to draw an inference of guilt from the accused's silence is a misdirection exists independently of any caution. For in *Ryan*, referred to above, the comment related chiefly to the failure of the accused, when apparently caught in the act of stealing and before any question of giving a caution arose, to give the explanation which he gave at his trial; and the court, after having referred to the authorities and " given the most careful consideration to the case ", decided that it fell on the right side of the line indicated above. The judgment contains no reference to any caution, and it seems clear that, had the court construed the comment as meaning that the jury might infer guilt from the accused's failure to tell his story, they would have held the comment to have been a misdirection[3]. Moreover, in the recent case of *Hall v. R.*[4], an appeal to the Privy Council from Jamaica, where the common law applied, Lord Diplock, giving judgment, said:

> " The caution merely serves to remind the accused of a right which he already possesses at common law."

30. In our opinion it is wrong that it should not be permissible for the jury or magistrates' court to draw whatever inferences are reasonable from the failure of the accused, when interrogated, to mention a defence which he puts forward at his trial. To forbid it seems to us to be contrary to common sense and, without helping the innocent, to give an unnecessary advantage to the guilty. Hardened criminals often take advantage of the present rule to refuse to answer any questions at all, and this may greatly hamper the police and even bring their investigations to a halt. Therefore the abolition of the restriction would help justice. One of our members, Sir Norman Skelhorn, argued for an amendment of the law for these reasons in his address " Crime and the Punishment of Crime: Investigation of Offences and Trial of accused persons " delivered at the Commonwealth and Empire Law Conference in Sydney in 1965. The present restriction on judicial comment was also strongly criticized by Salmon L. J. (as he then was) in giving the judgment of the Court of Appeal in *Sullivan*, referred to above[5]. The accused, who was convicted of smuggling watches from Switzerland, had refused to answer questions by Customs officers. The judge, in the course of his summing up[6], had referred to the refusal and gone on:

---

[1] E.g. in *Leckey*, [1944] K.B. 80; 29 Cr. App. R. 128.
[2] E.g. in *Naylor*, [1933] 1 K.B. 685; 23 Cr. App. R. 177.
[3] The headnote to *Ryan* suggests that the reason why the judge's comment was upheld was that it was " coupled with an indication that the defendant was under no obligation to given any explanation "; but although this was referred to in the judgment, there seems no doubt that the ground of the decision was that mentioned above. In most, if not all, of the recent cases where a comment was held to have been a misdirection it had been coupled with a similar indication.
[4] (1970), 55 Cr. App. R. 108, 112.
[5] Paragraph 29.
[6] (1967), 51 Cr. App. R. at pp. 104–5.

" Of course bear in mind that he was fully entitled to refuse to answer questions, he has an absolute right to do just that, and it is not to be held against him that he did that. But you might well think that if a man is innocent he would be anxious to answer questions. Now, members of the jury, that is what it really amounts to."

The Court of Appeal said with reference to this[1]:

" It seems pretty plain that all the members of that jury, if they had any common sense at all, must have been saying to themselves precisely what the learned judge said to them. The appellant was not obliged to answer, but how odd, if he was innocent, that he should not have been anxious to tell the Customs officer why he had been to Geneva, whether he put the watches in the bag, and so on."

Then, after referring to the authorities, the judgment went on to say that sometimes comment on the accused's silence was unfair but that there was no unfairness in this case. It then continued:

" The line dividing what may be said and what may not be said is a very fine one, and it is perhaps doubtful whether in a case like the present it would be even perceptible to the members of any ordinary jury."

The court held that they were compelled, in the existing state of the law, to hold that the judge's comment was a misdirection, but they dismissed the appeal under the proviso to s. 4(1) of the Criminal Appeal Act 1907 (c. 23) on the ground that " no possible miscarriage of justice occurred." We agree with the court's criticism of the present rule.

31. So far as we can see, there are only two possible arguments for preserving the present rule.

(i) Some lawyers seem to think that it is somehow wrong in principle that a criminal should be under any kind of pressure to reveal his case before his trial. The reason seems to be that it is thought to be repugnant—or, perhaps rather, " unfair "—that a person should be obliged to choose between telling a lie and incriminating himself. Whatever the reason, this is a matter of opinion and we disagree. There seems to us nothing wrong in principle in allowing an adverse inference to be drawn against a person at his trial if he delays mentioning his defence till the trial and shows no good reason for the delay. As to the argument that it is " unfair " to put pressure on a suspect in this way, what we said above[2] about fairness in criminal trials generally applies. Bentham's famous comment on the rule that suspects could not be judicially interrogated seems to us to apply strongly to the " right of silence " in the sense under discussion. He wrote[3]:

"If all criminals of every class had assembled, and framed a system after their own wishes, is not this rule the very first which they would have established for their security? Innocence never takes advantage of it. Innocence claims the right of speaking, as guilt invokes the privilege of silence".

[1] Ibid. p. 105.
[2] Paragraph 27.
[3] " Treatise on Evidence ", p. 241.

18

(ii) It has been argued that the suggested change would endanger the innocent because it would enable the police, when giving evidence, to suppress the fact that the accused did mention to them the story which he told in court. But we reject this argument for two reasons. First, we do not regard this possible danger as a good enough reason for leaving the law as it now is. Second, it is already permissible to draw an adverse inference from the fact that the suspect told a lie to the police or tried to run away; and (as mentioned above[1]) even silence can be taken into account in assessing the value of the evidence given by the accused in court. In neither of these cases is it considered a fatal objection that the police might say falsely that the accused told the lie or that he failed to tell his story.

32. We propose that the law should be amended so that, if the accused has failed, when being interrogated by anyone charged with the duty of investigating offences or charging offenders, to mention a fact which he afterwards relies on at the committal proceedings or the trial, the court or jury may draw such inferences as appear proper in determining the question before them. The fact would have to be one which the accused could reasonably have been expected to mention at the time[2]. The provisions for this purpose are in clause 1(1) and (2). We mention several matters of detail in paragraphs 33 to 39.

33. The clause applies to failure by the accused to mention " any fact relied on in his defence in [the] proceedings." We arrived at these words, after a good deal of discussion, as being precise enough for practical purposes and as precise as it seems possible to be without great elaboration. The words are intended to apply to any definite statement made by a witness at the hearing and supporting the case for the defence. The facts might include an alibi, belief that stolen goods were not stolen (on a charge of handling stolen goods), the defence to a charge of robbery that the accused was resisting an indecent assault by the prosecutor, consent (on a charge of rape) and (on a charge of indecency with a child) innocent association (for example, that the accused took the child into the bushes to show him a bird's nest).

34. The provisions of clause 1 referred to above apply to interrogation by the police or by other persons " charged with the duty of investigating offences or charging offenders " (subsection (2)). These words follow Rule VI of the Judges' Rules (1964), which the Court of Appeal said in *Nichols*[3] were intended to apply to " persons who are professional investigators other than police officers." These would include persons in public positions such as Customs officers (when carrying out these duties) and also, we think, privately employed investigators, including store detectives (to whom the application of Rule VI was assumed, without being decided, in *Nichols*). The new provisions do not apply where the accused has been questioned by a person other than any of these—for example, by the victim of the offence or a member of his family, by an eyewitness or by a person having no interest in the case. Nor do the provisions apply to situations where the accused was not being questioned but was taxed with his conduct by somebody who knew or strongly suspected that

---

[1] Paragraph 29.
[2] This is mentioned further in paragraph 35.
[3] (1967), 51 Cr. App. R. 233, 236.

the accused was the offender. The possibility of drawing adverse inferences from the silence of the accused, or even from an evasive or otherwise unconvincing denial, in cases of the kinds mentioned is, in our opinion, sufficiently allowed for by the common law. It is well settled that the silence or other reaction of a person when challenged about an offence may in some circumstances amount to an acknowledgment of his guilt (in which case evidence of it may be given under the common law rule as to informal admissions which is to be replaced by the Bill); but the admissibility of evidence of his silence or other reaction is not limited to where this can be regarded as an acknowledgment. For example, in _Christie_[1] Lord Reading said, with reference to the admissibility of evidence of a statement made in the presence of the accused:

> " It might well be that the prosecution wished to give evidence of such a statement in order to prove the conduct and demeanour of the accused when hearing the statement as a relevant fact in the particular case, notwithstanding that it did not amount either to an acknowledgment or some evidence of an acknowledgment of any part of the truth of the statement."

It is true that in _Hall_, mentioned above[2] (which related to silence on the part of the appellant when told by a police officer that his co-accused had said that the appellant was the owner of the drugs which were the subject of the charge), it was suggested[3] that it was only " in very exceptional circumstances that an inference may be drawn from a failure to give an explanation or a disclaimer "; but in the context the reference appears to be to " an inference that [the accused] accepts the truth of the accusation ". In any event we are convinced that there is no reason why the courts should not hold that in cases not covered by the clause it is permissible to draw inferences, of the kind provided for by the clause, whenever the circumstances are such that the inference should be drawn as a matter of common sense and justice. The special difficulty with which the clause is to deal has arisen only in relation to questioning by the police or, at most, by other " professional investigators " such as mentioned above, and we do not think it necessary to complicate the clause by providing for all the situations where such inferences should be allowed to be drawn. But lest it should be suggested that the making of a special provision as to inferences which may be drawn in the case of questioning by the police and the others mentioned was intended to exclude the possibility of drawing such inferences in other cases, subsection (3) provides that the provisions in the clause referred to above shall not prejudice the admissibility in evidence of the silence or other reaction of the accused under the existing law in circumstances to which the clause does not apply or preclude the drawing of inferences, permissible under that law, from such silence or other reaction. With this saving, we see no reason why the courts should not take at least as liberal a view of the inferences which may be drawn from a person's failure to exculpate himself to a private person, where it would be natural for him to do so, as from his failure to exculpate himself to a police officer.

35. The clause allows for the drawing of "such inferences ... as appear proper " from the failure of the accused to mention the fact relied on. What,

---

[1] [1914] A.C. 545, 565–6; 10 Cr. App. R. 141, 166.
[2] Paragraph 29.
[3] (1970), 55 Cr. App. R. at p. 112.

20

if any, inferences are proper will depend on the circumstances. In a straight-forward case of interrogation by the police where the accused has no reason for withholding his story (apart from the fact that he has not had time to invent it or that he hopes to spring it on the court at his trial) an adverse inference will clearly be proper and, we think, should be readily drawn. Obviously there may be reasons for silence consistent with innocence. For example, the accused may be shocked by the accusation and unable at first to remember some fact which would clear him. Again, to mention an exculpatory fact might reveal something embarrassing to the accused, such as that he was in the company of a prostitute. Or he may wish to protect a member of his family. It will be for the court or (with the help of the judge's direction) for the jury to decide whether in all the circumstances they are justified in drawing an adverse inference.

36. For the clause to apply to the accused's failure to mention a fact the fact will have to be one " relied on in his defence " at the hearing. The stage at which it will appear that the fact is relied on in the defence will depend on how the defence is conducted. Usually, we think, it will be sufficiently clear from the cross-examination of the witnesses for the prosecution whether a fact is being relied on in this way, and then the prosecution will be able to adduce evidence that the accused did not mention it when interrogated. It is true that sometimes the defence will be able to avoid showing this before the accused gives evidence at the trial (subject, in trials on indictment, to the requirement under s. 11 of the Criminal Justice Act 1967 (c. 80) to give notice of a defence of alibi). The prosecution will then be able to ask the accused in cross-exami-nation why he failed to mention this fact when interrogated; and if the court in its discretion under clause 23(1) gives leave, the prosecution will be able to call evidence to prove the failure. The clause enables inferences to be drawn at committal proceedings (for the purpose of determining whether to commit the accused for trial) as well as allowing them to be drawn at the trial (by the court, for the purpose of determining whether there is a case to answer, and by the jury or magistrates' court, for the purpose of determining whether the accused is guilty); but the clause will seldom have any application to committal proceedings, as it is unusual for the accused to reveal his defence at this stage.

37. The clause applies not only to the accused's failure to mention a fact during interrogation but also to his failure to do so on being charged (or officially informed—i.e. by a police officer or other person investigating the offence (subsection (2))—that he might be prosecuted. At first we were in favour of limiting the provision to the stage before the charge (or official information as mentioned above). This was because we felt that, once this stage was reached, the investigatory process should be regarded as at an end and the judicial process as having begun. Therefore it might be thought reasonable that the accused should be entirely free to decide that he should say no more to the police but only to his solicitor. After this stage further interrogation is generally not allowed. Rule III(*b*) of the Judges' Rules says:

" It is only in exceptional cases that questions relating to the offence should be put to the accused person after he has been charged or informed that he may be prosecuted. Such questions may be put where they are necessary for the purpose of preventing or minimising harm or loss to

21

some other person or to the public or for clearing up an ambiguity in a previous answer or statement."

But we have come to the conclusion (with one dissentient) that it would be artificial to make the new rule apply to silence immediately before the accused is charged but not to silence on his being charged. For on the assumption (on which the clause is based) that it is natural to expect an innocent person who is being interrogated to mention a fact which will exculpate him, it seems equally natural to expect him to do so when he is charged if he has not done so before. Sometimes indeed a suspect may deliberately refrain from mentioning a fact during the interrogations because this may embarrass him and may mention it only at the charge stage when he has seen that the police " mean business." If he really thought at the charge stage that it was now too late to mention a matter, it will be open to him to say so at his trial when he gives his explanation why he did not mention it before. Moreover, to draw a distinction at the charge stage would be artificial in another way. For if the accused has not mentioned the fact in question at this stage, he will presumably not have done so before, and it would be curious to give evidence that he said nothing during the interrogation and not go on to say whether he said anything when charged. If he has mentioned the fact during the interrogation, his omission to repeat it when charged will hardly ever have any significance.

38. Apart from these general arguments, there are two particular arguments for applying the clause to the accused's silence on being charged. The first is that this is consistent with police procedure; for in the ordinary course the officer who charges the accused will have had nothing to do with the investigations. Where a suspect has been interrogated and the officer in charge of the investigations thinks that there is a sufficient case to justify charging the suspect, he takes him before the station officer and puts the information before the latter. The station officer may accept the charge, or reject it and release the prisoner, or defer a decision pending further investigation (such as an inquiry into a statement by the accused, made in response to the officer's invitation, which, if true, would exculpate him). This power to delay preferring a charge is often used in drug cases, the suspect being released on bail pending a scientific analysis of the material in question. It might be suggested because of this procedure that the clause should apply only up to the stage immediately before the charge; but we do not think that one should draw so fine a distinction as this, and it would be awkward to frame a provision by reference to police procedure, as this is not statutory and therefore might change. The second reason for applying the clause to the charge stage is that occasionally a person is charged without any previous interrogation. It will be noted that the clause will not apply to the limited questioning which is allowed by Rule III(b) of the Judges' Rules after the accused has been charged[1].

39. At the trial, the clause allows the drawing of inferences not only for the purpose of determining whether the accused is guilty but also for that of determining whether there is a case to answer. It might be suggested that to allow inferences for the latter purpose is excessive, especially as the court may not know at this stage what is the accused's reason, if any, for not having mentioned the fact on which he is going to rely. But (although probably the question will seldom arise) we think it would be artificial to draw this distinction.

---

[1] See paragraph 37.

For the court, in considering whether there is a case to answer, has to consider whether the accused could properly be convicted on the evidence so far given; and it would be strange if the court, in considering for this purpose how much importance to attach to the fact that the accused is relying on a fact to exculpate him, were not to be allowed to treat his failure to mention this fact in the same way as might be done for the purpose of determining whether he is guilty. It would also be difficult to tell whether the court had wrongly taken account of the accused's silence in this way unless they were to say expressly, when ruling on the submission of no case, that they had taken it into consideration. In any event, if the court determines that there is a case to answer, the defence will have the opportunity to show, if they can, that no weight should be given to the accused's silence for the purpose of determining whether he is guilty.

40. Under the clause, in any case where an adverse inference may properly be drawn from the accused's silence, it will be permissible to treat his silence as corroboration of the evidence against him for any purpose for which corroboration is material[1]. Of course whether in any case silence can or will amount to corroboration will depend entirely on the circumstances, in particular on the nature of the inference drawn from the silence. This is secured by the provision in subsection (1) that silence may be treated as corroboration "on the basis of" inferences properly drawn from the silence. Further, in order to be capable of being corroborated by the accused's silence, the evidence will have to be evidence to which the silence is " material." The effect will be this: if (i) the existence of some fact can properly be inferred from the accused's silence, and (ii) proof of this fact by other means would be capable of being corroboration of the evidence against the accused, then his silence will be capable of being corroboration of that evidence.

41. Our decision to recommend that silence might count as corroboration was taken only after very full consideration. The following seem to us to be the arguments against allowing it to count as corroboration:

(i) To allow silence to give rise to an adverse inference is a strong measure, and it may be thought excessive to go further and in effect cause the safeguards provided by the rules as to corroboration to be dispensed with merely because the accused has failed to mention a fact on which he relies in his defence.

(ii) Since failure to mention a fact is something negative, it may be thought that it cannot be sufficiently direct to be rightly treated as corroboration for the purposes of the special requirements as to corroboration.

42. The following arguments have been put forward in favour of allowing silence to be corroboration:

(i) Once it is accepted that failure to mention a matter should be capable of giving rise to an adverse inference, it seems illogical that it should not be capable of amounting to corroboration. Evidence of the failure, having been made admissible, should be admitted for all purposes for which it is logically probative.

---

[1] If our proposals in paragraphs 185, 191, 195 and 208 are accepted, the present rules as to corroboration will be greatly modified, but corroboration will remain important for some purposes.

(ii) We think it artificial, especially in a statute, to provide that a particular kind of evidence which would naturally be regarded as capable of being corroboration should never be capable of being so.

(iii) Not to allow silence to amount to corroboration would involve the judge's having to direct the jury in a way which would require them to draw a distinction which most people would regard as artificial.

For example, if, on a charge of indecent assault, the defence is an alibi, and failure to mention the alibi to the police is capable of giving rise to an adverse inference but not of being corroboration, the judge will have to say something like this to the jury:

"You may think that no man who had been in the Pig and Whistle for the last hour before being stopped by the constable would have refused to answer the constable's question as to where he was and that in the circumstances his silence goes to show that, when he now tells you he did not assault the girl, he is not telling the truth. But even if you do think this, you must on no account regard his silence as going to show that the girl is telling the truth when she says he did assault her."

This would seem hardly to make sense. We have formed the view that the arguments for allowing silence to be capable of being corroboration outweigh the contrary arguments.

43. If our proposal to allow adverse inferences to be drawn from the accused's silence is accepted, it follows that the requirements of the Judges' Rules to caution a suspect must be abolished or replaced by different kinds of warnings or intimations. Rule II requires that the " first caution " should be given when the police officer " has evidence which would afford reasonable grounds for suspecting that [the person in question] has committed an offence "; and Rule III(a) requires that the " second caution " should be given when the suspect is " charged with or informed that he may be prosecuted for an offence ". Both cautions include the statement " You are not obliged to say anything unless you wish to do so " and the warning that anything said may be given in evidence[1]. The warnings included in the first and second cautions are, on the face of them, a discouragement to the suspect to make a statement and are therefore directly contrary to the provision in clause 1(1). But apart from this, whatever may have been desirable in the past, we think that there are serious objections to the requirements to administer these cautions.

(i) It is of no help to an innocent person to caution him to the effect that he is not obliged to make a statement. Indeed, it might deter him from saying something which might serve to exculpate him. On the other hand the caution often assists the guilty by providing an excuse for keeping back a false story until it becomes difficult to expose its falsity. In fact the caution seems to stem from the ancient fallacy to which we referred earlier[2] that " fairness " in criminal trials requires

---
[1] There is also a caution which must be given under Rule III(b) before any of the limited questioning which is allowed after the charge takes place; but what is said in this paragraph is not intended to apply to this caution, which will require special consideration when and if administrative directions are being prepared to replace the Judges' Rules in accordance with our recommendation in paragraph 46.
[2] Paragraph 27.

that a guilty person should not be allowed to convict himself too easily. In any event practised criminals have little respect for the caution. An illustration of this is in *Weaver*[1], where the two accused brothers, when spoken to by the police about their having obtained money by false pretences, proceeded immediately " in a light-hearted way " to address the officers in the terms of the caution.

(ii) It is illogical that, when the police have a duty to question persons for the purpose of discovering whether and by whom an offence has been committed, they should be required to tell a person being questioned that he need not answer. In particular, the first caution (under Rule II), which was introduced when the rules were revised in 1964, has been objected to on the ground that it interrupts the natural course of interrogation and unduly hampers the police, as there may be a good deal more information which they wish to get, perhaps involving other offences and persons, after the stage when they have " evidence which would afford reasonable grounds for suspecting that [the person being questioned] has committed an offence." Indeed there may be a strong temptation for police officers not to interrupt an interrogation at a critical point by administering a caution which may render the investigation fruitless.

As the cautions are not required by statute or by a rule of the common law, but only administratively, there is no need to make provision in the Bill to abolish the need for them. But as they have become so much a part of the procedure in police interrogations, we think it desirable to include a declaration of the absence of any legal requirement to give a caution. This we have done in clause 1(5).

44. On the other hand, the fact that adverse inferences may be drawn from the failure of the accused to mention a fact on which he is going to rely at his trial raises the question whether suspects should be warned, when being interrogated, of this danger to them. This does seem to us necessary, because the new rule makes a great change from the present law. No doubt the change will be given plenty of publicity; but it may be some time before it becomes known to all persons whom it is likely to affect. Clause 1(4) provides that the new provisions shall not apply as regards a failure to mention a fact if the failure occurred before the commencement of the Act; but even if the failure occurred soon after this, the defence might argue that, as the accused did not know of the change in the law, the judge should direct the jury, as now, that they should not treat the failure to mention the fact as any indication of guilt. On the other hand, any procedure introduced for warning suspects of the danger of remaining silent should avoid as far as possible the disadvantages of the present rules as to cautions. In particular one does not want to interrupt the natural course of interrogations or to have side issues as to whether the proper warning was given. Nor must the need to give a warning be made an excuse for using threats. We think that the best course would be that there should be an administrative requirement (of the kind shown below[2]) that,

---

[1] [1968] 1 Q.B. 353, 357 D; 51 Cr. App. R. 77, 80.
[2] Paragraph 46 (where it is recommended that the Judges' Rules should be replaced by administrative directions by the Home Secretary). These would include the requirement to give the proposed warning.

when the accused is charged (or officially informed that he may be prosecuted), he should be given a written notice to the following effect:

" You have been charged with [informed that you may be prosecuted for]—. If there is any fact on which you intend to rely in your defence in court, you are advised to mention it now. If you hold it back till you go to court, your evidence may be less likely to be believed and this may have a bad effect on your case in general. If you wish to mention any fact now, and you would like it written down, this will be done."

The reasons for suggesting that the notice should be given in writing are that this will provide a record that it was given and also that some suspects try to interrupt and otherwise obstruct police officers trying to give them oral notices. We do not wish to recommend that there should be any general requirement to warn suspects at an earlier stage of the interrogations, because this might have the disadvantages mentioned above which result from the present cautions and because in any case the circumstances are likely to differ so much that it is difficult to lay down any fixed procedure in this respect. The matter must depend on what is fair and proper in each particular case.

45. Our proposals that the first two cautions should be abolished[1] but that a warning should have to be given as to the effect of clause 1[2] involve the complete reconsideration of the Judges' Rules. The present rules were issued in January 1964 to replace the four rules originally issued in 1912 and the five added in 1918. The text of the present rules is given, together with an introductory note, in Appendix A to the Home Office Circular No. 31/1964 published by the Stationery Office. The introductory note summarizes the origin and history of the rules. In addition to the cautions the rules lay down certain requirements as to interrogation and the taking of statements. Appendix B contains administrative directions to the police on ancillary matters concerning interrogation and the taking of statements. The legal status of the rules was described as follows by A. T. Lawrence J. in giving the judgment of the Court of Criminal Appeal in *Voisin*[3]:

" In 1912, the judges, at the request of the Home Secretary, drew up some rules as guides for police officers. These rules have not the force of law, they are administrative directions the observance of which the police authorities should enforce on their subordinates as tending to the fair administration of justice. It is important that they should do so, for statements obtained from prisoners contrary to the spirit of these rules may be rejected as evidence by the judge presiding at the trial."

In practice it seems that nowadays, before the prosecution can adduce evidence of a statement obtained in breach of the rules, there must be a positive decision by the court to exercise its discretion in favour of admitting the statement. The introductory statement of the five " principles " which are declared to be unaffected by the rules says:—

" Non-conformity with these Rules may render answers and statements liable to be excluded from evidence in subsequent criminal proceedings."

In *Collier and Stenning*[4], Lord Parker C. J. said, with reference to the require-

---

[1] Paragraph 43.
[2] Paragraph 44.
[3] (1918), 13 Cr. App. R. 89, 96.
[4] (1965), 49 Cr. App. R. 344, 350.

ment in Rule III(*a*) to administer the second caution, that any evidence obtained in breach of the rule " will, subject to the discretion of the judge, be inadmissible." The legal status of the administrative directions in Appendix B, so far as concerns the law of evidence, has not been precisely laid down. Clearly a breach will not make evidence of a resulting statement inadmissible; but it seems from *Roberts*[1] that evidence of the statement might, because of the breach, be excluded in exercise of the general exclusionary discretion, though a breach of a requirement as to a matter of detail at least would presumably be regarded as less serious than a breach of a requirement of the rules themselves.

46. Apart from the fact that some of the requirements of the Judges' Rules are inconsistent with our proposals referred to in paragraph 44, the substance of the rules has been criticized in various respects, in observations sent to us and elsewhere, in particular in that they hamper the police in their investigations. But the existence of the rules has also been objected to strongly on the ground that restrictions on the way in which the police should interrogate persons should be imposed not by the judges but by the authority responsible for the police (in this case, by the Home Secretary) or, if the matter is important enough, by law. We all think this last criticism is justified, and many of those who have sent us observations (including judges) have expressed the same view. None of those who have sent us observations has argued, at any rate expressly, for keeping the rules as " Judges' Rules ", though many persons and organizations have argued for or against the substance of the rules in some form. There have been a very few suggestions that the rules or parts of them should be made statutory. We are against making any of the provisions statutory. We think that the right course would be for the rules to be replaced by administrative directions by the Home Office dealing, so far as is thought desirable, with the matters provided for in the rules, and that the approval of the judges to the issuing of the directions should be sought, and referred to in the directions when issued, in some such way as was done in the case of the present directions in Appendix B to the Rules. Evidence of a statement obtained by means of a breach of the directions should clearly remain admissible in law. Whether and to what extent the present practice as to excluding evidence of a statement in exercise of the general discretion, if the statement was obtained by a breach of the Judges' Rules, should apply to a statement obtained by a breach of an administrative direction (whether this is a direction replacing an existing rule or one replacing an existing direction) is a matter which we think should be left to be decided by the courts. In addition there will be the sanction of judicial criticism of those responsible for breaches and, in the case of breaches by the police, enforcement by their superiors.

47. We have considered, but do not favour, suggestions that provision (which would have to be statutory) should be made for interrogation of suspects before magistrates. The suggestions took various forms. The essential feature is that at a certain stage the suspect should be taken compulsorily before a magistrate and obliged to listen to questions. The questions, and the answers if any, would be admissible. On some versions of this scheme evidence of anything said during interrogations by the police before the suspect was taken before the magistrate would be inadmissible. This is the rule provided

---

[1] [1970] Crim. L.R. 464; *Times*, 4th May 1970.

for by the Indian Evidence Act of 1872. But any scheme which made inadmissible evidence of what was said during police interrogations would be inconsistent with the principle underlying our clause 1. Provision might be made for compulsory interrogation before a magistrate while still allowing evidence to be given of interrogations not in the presence of a magistrate. On this scheme the questioning would probably have to be done by the police, as the magistrate could hardly be expected to acquire all the knowledge of the case which would enable him to put the questions which the police might profitably put. It is claimed for the system that it would ensure beyond doubt the " fairness " of the interrogation and that disputes as to what was said in the course of it would be avoided. We do not think it has been, or could seriously be, claimed that the system would make it more likely that the person interrogated would tell the truth. The formality of the procedure would, we think, often defeat its own purposes and the person interrogated would be likely to refuse to answer questions—even those by the police preceding the interrogation before the magistrate. We believe that magistrates, stipendiary and lay, would be opposed to the system and would be very reluctant to undertake the work. In any event we doubt very much whether it would be possible to arrange for magistrates to be available at all the times at which the police might think it necessary to conduct an interrogation immediately in order to enable them to identify associates of the suspect or to take steps which might be necessary for the protection of persons or the recovery of property. Nor do we think it possible to be confident that even a statement taken from an accused person at a formal interrogation in the presence of a magistrate would be accepted by the defence at the court of trial without challenge, at any rate as to the form and manner of the questioning. If there were a dispute as to what was said during the interrogation or how it was conducted, it might be necessary for the magistrate to be called as a witness and cross-examined, and it seems to us undesirable that magistrates should be subjected to this inconvenience and possible embarrassment.

48. We have considered whether to recommend that provision should be made as to the use of tape recorders in criminal interrogation. This is partly because of their increasing use generally and their value when rightly used and partly because our proposal to allow adverse inferences to be drawn from a person's silence when interrogated makes it even more important to have a reliable account of the interrogation. The latter consideration applies strongly to evidence of confessions, which subject is dealt with in the next section of the report[1]. Tape recordings are specially useful to prove an overheard conversation, for example to prove a blackmailing threat or the offer of a bribe. They have also been used many times to prove a conversation between two persons charged with an offence. An example is *Ali and Hussain*[2], where two Pakistanis charged with murder made incriminating statements in a conversation in a Punjabi dialect after the police had hidden a microphone in the room. The advantage of a requirement to use tape recorders in interrogations would sometimes be great, because, if the recording was made in favourable conditions, the playing over of the tape in court would show clearly what was said and in what tone of voice. As a Canadian judge said,

---

[1] Paragraphs 53–69.
[2] [1966] 1 Q.B. 688; 49 Cr. App. R. 230.

" a tape recording ... is better evidence and more capable of correct interpretation by a jury than *viva voce* evidence or a written statement, since it reproduces not only the exact words of the accused but the inflection and tone of the voice as well, without the necessity of substituting another's interpretation "[1].

49. There are, however, certain possible disadvantages or difficulties, and there are substantial differences of opinion in the committee as to the extent of these and, consequently, as to what, if any, recommendations should be made. For convenience we first summarize the disadvantages or difficulties which the majority think would or might occur if tape recorders were required to be used on a large scale[2]. We follow this with a summary of the majority's recommendation that tape recorders should be used on an experimental basis[3]. After this we set out the view of the minority that tape recorders should be used more widely and on a regular and not an experimental basis and that the operation of clause 1 should be suspended until this is done[4].

50. For the reasons set out in this paragraph the majority of the committee hesitate to recommend that tape recorders should be brought into general use in interrogations at present. In their view this should not be done until experience of their use on an experimental basis as the majority suggest has shown that the difficulties mentioned in this paragraph, in particular the technical difficulties, can be overcome and that the use of recorders makes a sufficiently valuable contribution to the ascertainment of the truth concerning happenings at police interrogations without seriously impairing their efficiency.

(i) The police fear that criminal investigations would be hampered if interrogations had to be tape-recorded, because many criminals would refuse to answer questions. This would be partly because of the more inquisitorial atmosphere and partly because criminals are often ready to talk so long as no record is being made. When a written record is being made, a criminal will sometimes say something incriminating but add: " Don't take that down ". He feels that, so long as it is not taken down, he will be able to deny having said it or to pretend that the police misrepresented the effect of the conversation or put pressure on him.

(ii) A tape recording is not always a better way of showing what was said at an interrogation than a written record of the effect of the questions and answers. It may be fairer to the accused that he should write down his statement (as many prefer to do) or that the police should take it down for him, because then he can control what goes into the final version by asking for omissions, additions or alterations and by refusing to sign it until he is satisfied with it. In the course of interrogations all kinds of things may be said which would in any event have to be left out when the tape was played over. Examples are references to the accused's criminal record or to his associates and statements which are irrelevant or otherwise inadmissible in evidence. Arrangements can be made at the request of

---

[1] Limerick J. A. in *Colpitts* (1965), 47 C.R. 175.
[2] Paragraph 50.
[3] Paragraph 51.
[4] Paragraph 52.

the defence for parts not to be played over, just as arrangements are made for parts of an oral or written statement not to be put in evidence, but it might be more noticeable to the jury that part of a tape was not being played over and they might be more likely to suspect that something significant was being kept from them.

(iii) If the use of tape recorders became standard, evidence of an interrogation not tape-recorded might be regarded as inferior and so suspect. Yet it might in fact be very important and there might have been a good reason why it was not tape-recorded. For example a conversation when the accused was on the way to the police station could not in any case be required to be tape-recorded.

(iv) The quality of tape recordings varies greatly. One of our members tried a case of blackmail in which the recording of the conversation in question was almost unintelligible. In *Ali and Hussain*, mentioned above[1],

" the microphone did not always pick up clearly all that was being said "

and

" from time to time the recording was overlaid by street noises from the open window, in particular, those resulting from the bus stop just under the window[2]."

There was a trial within the trial lasting two and a half days during which it was argued that for this and other reasons the recording should not have been received.

(v) We have been informed that it is astonishingly easy to tamper with a tape so as to add to, alter or cut out something said, and that this can be done in a very short time and without leaving a trace of the interference.

51. The majority of the committee think that the subject of tape recorders is not one suitable to be dealt with in the proposed administrative directions. But they think that careful consideration should be given by the police, in conjunction with the Home Office, to the possibilities of a wider use of tape recorders than at present. In particular they would suggest that experiments should be made in order to see how far their use would be helpful. Admittedly there are possible objections to experiments in a matter of this kind, as this might encourage criminals whose statements were not tape-recorded to complain that, had this been done, it would have been fairer to them; but this possible disadvantage does not seem strong enough to outweigh the possible value of an experiment. If our suggestion is accepted, the question of safeguards against tampering and that of cost (which we believe may be considerable) can be fully considered.

52. A minority of three members would go further in this matter than the rest of the committee. So far as concerns interrogation outside a police station—for example, when the police are interviewing in his consulting room

---

[1] Paragraph 48.
[2] [1966] 1 Q.B. at p. 692E; 49 Cr. App. R. at p. 233.

a doctor who is suspected of performing illegal abortions—the minority are content with the recommendation of the majority that careful consideration should be given to the possibility of using tape recorders on an experimental basis. But in respect of interrogations in police stations the minority would go further. As mentioned in sub-paragraph (vi) below, they consider that statutory provision should be made for the compulsory use of tape recorders at police stations in the larger centres of population and that the operation of clause 1 should be suspended until this has been done. Their reasons are given below.

(i) That the police should be able to question suspects in custody is now generally thought to be necessary for the due administration of the law; but the practice is fraught with dangers. In the first place, there is the danger of the use of bullying and even brutal methods by the police in order to obtain confessions. Examples are the Sheffield case in 1963 and the Challenor case in 1964. These incidents are attributable to a small number of " black sheep " in the police force. However rare their occurrence may be, every effort should be made to erect safeguards against them. Our arrangements should not depend upon the good faith of everyone concerned in the administration of the law. Perhaps a provision for the electronic recording of interrogations would not always eliminate the use of " third degree " methods by officers who are tempted to use them; but the knowledge that a recorder is running during an interview would surely exercise a deterrent effect. It is of great importance for the police themselves that any public suspicion of their practices should be allayed. In America, misconduct by the police has been partly responsible for the alienation of sympathy of the public from the police, which leads the public to refuse to help the police with information, and so greatly increases the difficulty of enforcing the law. Also, every proven instance of third degree by the police, or credible allegation of it, increases the suspicion with which juries regard the ordinary confession, which in fact is very likely to be true and properly obtained.

(ii) The minority argue that the use of tape recorders may help to reduce the occasions on which the police are tempted to fabricate confessions. As with the use of violence, it is impossible to assess the extent to which the police at present commit perjury, but there is a widespread impression, not only among criminals, that in tough areas a police officer who is certain that he has got the right man will invent some oral admission (colloquially known as a " verbal ") to clinch the case. The Royal Commission on the Police, 1962, said in its report:

> " There was a body of evidence, too substantial to disregard, which in effect accused the police of stooping to the use of undesirable means of obtaining statements and of occasionally giving perjured evidence in a court of law "[1].

If the accused alleges that the evidence against him is perjured, he is not likely to be believed, and the mere making of the allegation by

---

[1] Cmnd. 1728, paragraph 369.

the accused in giving evidence enables the prosecution (under the present law[1]) to elicit damaging facts relating to his previous record.

(iii) Short of using violence and perjury, the police may get confessions by the use of various kinds of persuasion, which is all the more effective when the suspect is isolated from his friends. The present position is that the courts do not exclude evidence of confessions merely because they were obtained by questioning at night or in the small hours. In a murder case in 1963, the police started to question a suspect at about 2 a.m. and obtained a confession at 5.15 a.m.; the confession was admitted in evidence[2]. In 1962, a man was questioned in a Birmingham police station for 10½ hours and was in that time given only one cup of tea; a conviction obtained by means of the resulting confession was sustained on appeal, though on this occasion the appellate court spoke severely about the conduct of the police[3]. It is demonstrated from time to time that even ordinary questioning can produce false confessions, but the risk is greatly increased if oppressive methods are used. Often there is a conflict of evidence between the accused and the police as to the time and duration of questioning. Electronic recording might reduce the conflict, especially if a " speaking clock " were superimposed on the recording; and incidentally, this would make it much more difficult to tamper with the recording afterwards.

(iv) A more subtle danger lies in the way in which confessions are generally taken. Most written statements produced in evidence are not in the suspect's handwriting and absolutely in his own words. As a result of questioning, the police officer may write a narrative which is in part a blend of question and answer. The statement reads as though it was volunteered by the suspect; but in fact it may have consisted of a monosyllabic answer to a leading question asked by the officer with one or more subordinate clauses. Since the statement does not distinguish between question and answer, one cannot tell from the statement what facts were suggested to the suspect by the way in which the question was worded. And the written word does not reproduce the inflection of the voice upon which meaning may depend. One may not even be sure that the officer understood what the suspect said, or that the suspect understood the written statement when he read it through or had it read to him. His signature is not a guarantee that the written statement exactly reproduces what he said.

(v) The possibilities of error are multiplied if, as often happens, the statement is not reduced to writing at the time and signed by the suspect. The investigating officer may simply embody what he regards as the kernel of the suspect's statement in his notebook. This notebook will be entered up after the interview, and the note may represent only a very small part of a long interrogation. It may be months before the case is heard, and by that time the officer may have no memory of the interview beyond his written note. If there

---

[1] Clause 6(4) proposes to modify this rule: see paragraph 128.
[2] *Massey* (*Times*, 2nd November 1963).
[3] *Burgess* (*Times*, 6th March 1962).

are two or more investigating officers, they are allowed to agree their evidence together before writing up their notes; this practice was approved by the Court of Criminal Appeal in 1953[1]. The officers may even prepare a joint note. If they are inclined to stretch the case a bit against the accused, perhaps because he has a " record " and appears to them to be guilty, they know that they will be able to back each other up at the trial and will be virtually impregnable from attack. The agreed note destroys any small chance that the accused might otherwise have had to set one officer against the other.

(vi) The practical effect of clause 1 of the draft Bill will be to put a measure of compulsion upon suspects to answer questions, even when they are in custody. It will therefore give some kind of statutory sanction to the practice of police questioning. In the view of the minority, this step ought not to be taken without all proper safeguards having first been introduced, and the principal safeguard required is the recording of the voices of all those concerned in an interrogation in a police station. Therefore, in the view of the minority, the operation of clause 1 of the draft Bill should be suspended until such time as provision has been made for the electronic recording of interrogations in police stations in the major centres of population. These police stations would in due course be specified in statutory instruments, and statements made by suspected persons when under interrogation in a listed police station would not be admissible in evidence unless they had been recorded. In the view of the minority, this provision would often be to the advantage of the prosecution because the recording would help to answer unfounded objections to the genuineness of the confession. There would not generally be a need to play the whole of the recording in court; in most cases a transcript of the essential part would be sufficient; but it would be open to counsel for the defence to ask for the recording to be played when it was relevant—or indeed, the prosecution might wish to do so, since the way in which the accused told his story may itself convey a strong impression of authenticity. The argument that the recording may be tampered with[2] is, as the majority accept, not a decisive one. Even if it were true that the recording can be falsified and that no steps could be taken to counter this (which the minority do not believe), it is equally true that the police can, if so minded, falsify the entry in their notebooks upon which evidence of alleged admissions by the accused is now often founded. Moreover, recordings are at present admissible in evidence (for example, in blackmail cases) without its being suggested as a fatal objection that they can be falsified. As for the argument that the use of recorders would cause offenders to refuse to answer questions[3], there is reason to believe that in practice the existence of the recorder would soon be forgotten by the person who is under interrogation, particularly when it comes to be realised that the law as it is proposed to be

---

[1] *Bass*, [1953] 1 Q.B. 680, 686; 37 Cr. App. R. 51, 59.
[2] **Paragraph** 50(v).
[3] **Paragraph** 50(i).

established by clause 1 provides a powerful sanction for the answering of questions by the police. At present the Judges' Rules provide that all statements made by a person in custody must be written down at the time, and the use of electronic recording would hardly be more inhibiting for an offender than the sight of a police officer writing down what he is saying, though it is true that the Judges' Rules on this point are often neglected. Even if some suspects refuse to answer when they know they are being recorded, the loss of this evidence must be accepted as the price paid for an essential safeguard.

CLAUSE 2: CONFESSIONS

53. Evidence that the accused confessed to having committed the offence charged, or that he made an admission which goes towards proving that he committed it, is admissible, as an exception to the rule against hearsay, in order to prove that he committed the offence or that what he admitted occurred. Although the statement is hearsay, it is admissible because what a person says against himself is likely to be true. But the courts tended to regard alleged confessions by accused persons with some suspicion, and they laid down a special rule in order to ensure that the statement should have been voluntary. This is the rule summarized in principle (e) in the introduction to the Judges' Rules, which says that

> " it is a fundamental condition of the admissibility in evidence against any person, equally of any oral answer given by that person to a question put by a police officer and of any statement made by that person, that it shall have been voluntary, in the sense that it has not been obtained from him by fear of prejudice or hope of advantage, exercised or held out by a person in authority, or by oppression ".

In *Commissioners of Customs and Excise v. Harz and Power*[1] Lord Reid, in a speech with which all the other law lords agreed, treated this, as the Court of Appeal have recently remarked[2], as a correct statement of the law. We have no doubt that the rule applies only to admissibility on behalf of the prosecution and that an accused person may, in order to exculpate himself, give in evidence a confession alleged to have been made by his co-accused, regardless of the methods by which it was obtained.

54. Before the prosecution may give evidence of a confession at a trial on indictment they must prove to the satisfaction of the judge that the confession was voluntary in the sense mentioned above. In practice, if the defence wish to prevent the giving of the evidence, they tell the prosecution beforehand and the judge decides the issue of admissibility in the absence of the jury at what is known as a " trial within the trial ". Even if the defence do not contest the admissibility of the confession, the judge must still be satisfied that it was voluntary. For example, he may consider it right, before allowing evidence of a confession to go to the jury, to require to be satisfied about the circumstances in which it was made. This may be because of something in the depositions or because a police officer who is to give evidence of the

---

[1] [1967] 1 A.C. 760, 818, 821; 51 Cr. App. R. 123, 155, 159.
[2] *Prager* (1971), 56 Cr. App. R. 151, 160–161.

confession gave evidence at an earlier trial concerning the same or a related offence and his evidence was challenged. Sometimes the defence refrain from challenging the admissibility of a confession but seek to show, by cross-examination of the police officer at the trial proper, that the confession was not made voluntarily and therefore should not be believed; but even in this event the judge must still be satisfied of the voluntariness of the confession. At a summary trial the procedure is in principle similar; but here, save where it is possible for the magistrates' court to decide the issue of admissibility without hearing the terms of the confession, there is the complication, referred to in the general part of the report[1], that, if they hold the confession to be inadmissible, they must, having heard it, dismiss it from their minds. At trials on indictment challenges to the admissibility of a confession, and consequently the need to hold a trial within the trial, occur frequently, and trials within the trial often take up a great deal of time. We should have been glad to find a way of getting rid of the need for a trial within the trial if this were possible without causing injustice to the accused; but short of allowing all confessions to go before the jury to assess their reliability (which possibility is discussed below[2] but to which the majority of the committee are opposed) there is no way of doing this. In fact we do not propose that the procedure should be altered.

55. Two reasons have been given for this rule. The first is that a confession not made voluntarily may not be reliable. Persons who are subjected to threats, inducements or oppression may " confess " falsely; juries are peculiarly apt to attach weight to such a confession, even though the evidence of the threat, inducement or oppression is before them; consequently, they must be prevented from knowing of the confession. This makes it necessary for the judge to adjudicate (in the absence of the jury) upon the voluntariness of the confession, and if he finds it to have been involuntary he excludes it. The second reason is that the police must be discouraged from using improper methods to obtain a confession. This discouragement takes place by depriving them of the advantage of the confession for the purpose of obtaining a conviction. These two explanations of the law we may call the reliability principle and the disciplinary principle. To a large extent they suggest the same rules of exclusion, but not entirely. It would be possible to subscribe to either, or to both; in the latter case the confession would be excluded if it fell foul of either principle.

56. We have no doubt it is the reliability principle which historically underlies the law. This is in accordance with the authorities, and it is shown by the fact that, if the police discover some fact as the result of a confession which they have obtained by means of a threat or inducement, then, although evidence of the confession is inadmissible, evidence of the fact discovered is admissible. This applies, for example, to the discovery of a corpse or of stolen property. If the disciplinary principle were applied, one would have expected the evidence to be excluded in order to prevent the prosecution from taking advantage of the impropriety. The reliability principle was clearly stated in the early case of *Warwickshall*[3]. A woman was charged with being an accessory after the fact to theft and with receiving the stolen property.

---

[1] Paragraph 26 (iii).
[2] Paragraphs 62–64.
[3] (1783), 1 Leach 263.

She had confessed her guilt, and in consequence the property was found in her lodgings. The confession was rejected as having been obtained by promises of favour; and her counsel contended that " as the fact of finding the stolen property in her custody had been obtained through the means of an inadmissible confession, the proof of that fact ought also to be rejected; for otherwise the faith which the prosecutor had pledged would be violated, and the prisoner made the deluded instrument of her own conviction ". But the court rejected this argument, saying:

" It is a mistaken notion, that the evidence of confessions and facts which have been obtained from prisoners by promises or threats, is to be rejected from a regard to public faith: no such rule ever prevailed. The idea is novel in theory, and would be as dangerous in practice as it is repugnant to the general principles of criminal law. Confessions are received in evidence, or rejected as inadmissible, under a consideration whether they are or are not entitled to credit. A free and voluntary confession is deserving of the highest credit, because it is presumed to flow from the strongest sense of guilt, and therefore it is admitted as proof of the crime to which it refers; but a confession forced from the mind by the flattery of hope, or by the torture of fear, comes in so questionable a shape when it is to be considered as the evidence of guilt. that no credit ought to be given to it; and therefore it is rejected. This principle respecting confessions has no application whatever as to the admission or rejection of facts, whether the knowledge of them be obtained in consequence of an extorted confession, or whether it arises from any other source; for a fact, if it exists at all, must exist invariably in the same manner, whether the confession from which it is derived be in other respects true or false. "

This is broadly the law still. There is a good deal of obscurity as to how far the discovery of facts as a result of a confession may be linked in evidence with the fact that the confession was made (this question will be referred to later in connection with our recommendations on the subject[1]); but it is certain that the fact that a confession can be proved by extraneous evidence to be reliable does not make it admissible if it was not obtained voluntarily, as would be the result if the reliability principle were fully applied. The reliability principle does, however, apply in relation to a second confession. If a confession is obtained by a threat or inducement, but later, when the pressure is at an end, the accused repeats his confession, the second confession is admissible, even though the accused would very likely not have made it but for the fact that he was caused to make the first confession and he probably had no idea that the first confession would have been inadmissible in evidence[2]. The law has been criticized on the ground that it is illogical not to apply fully one or other of the two principles mentioned—either (i) to apply the reliability principle and admit in evidence the whole of a confession shown to be likely to be true in spite of the method by which it was obtained or (ii) to apply the disciplinary principle and exclude evidence of facts discovered as a result of the confession. But the majority of the committee think that there are sufficient practical reasons for accepting the mixture of the two

---

[1] Paragraphs 68–69.
[2] *Smith*, [1959] 2 Q.B.35; 43 Cr. App. R. 121. The facts are mentioned in paragraph 57.

principles as the basis of the law, and they would preserve the law in general with a relaxation of the strict rule that any threat or inducement makes a confession inadmissible and with alteration in certain matters of detail.

57. Any threat or inducement, however mild or slight, uttered or held out by a person in authority makes a resulting confession inadmissible. The authorities are firm that there is no exception even for trivial inducements. In *Northam*[1] a man on bail awaiting trial on charges of housebreaking was questioned by a police officer about another case of housebreaking and confessed to having played a minor part in it. Before confessing he had asked the officer whether it would be possible for the other offence to be taken into consideration at his forthcoming trial (instead of his being tried for it separately later) and the officer said that the police would have no objection. The Court of Appeal felt bound to quash the conviction because this amounted to an inducement. In giving judgment Winn L.J., after expressing satisfaction that this committee were studying the whole problem of voluntary confessions and admissions, said[2]:

" In these days it really does seem that the undoubtedly well-established doctrine of our law that persons who are minded to make a confession or admission to the police or other authorities must be very strictly safeguarded against any persuasion or inducement to make any such confession or admission is in some respects somewhat out of date. In these days the criminal classes are only too well aware of their position of virtual immunity in the hands of the police. It does seem that some of the present doctrines and principles have come down in our law from earlier times when the police of this country were not to be trusted, as they are now to be trusted in almost every single case, to behave with complete fairness towards those who come into their hands or from whom they are seeking information. It was then thought right, and no doubt then was right, to take an extremely strict position with regard to any favours or inducements which might be said to have been offered. "

The court referred to the fact that it was not the officer but the accused who initiated the idea of having the other offence taken into consideration, but said[3] that this " would be a very narrow footing on which to decide the present appeal ", and added[4]:

" It is not the magnitude, it is not the cogency to the reasonable man or to persons with such knowledge as is possessed by lawyers and others which is the proper criterion. It is what the average, normal, probably quite unreasonable person in the position of the appellant at the time might have thought was likely to result to his advantage from the suggestion agreed to by the police officer. The court realises that this is imposing yet one more clog upon the efficient performance by the police of their duties ".

The Court of Appeal followed this decision in *Zaveckas*[5], where they quashed a conviction because evidence was given at the trial of a statement which the

[1] (1967). 52 Cr. App. R. 97.
[2] At p. 102.
[3] At p. 103.
[4] At p. 104.
[5] (1969), 54 Cr. App. R. 202.

accused had made after he had asked a police officer " If I make a statement, will I be given bail now?" and the officer had simply answered " Yes ". Fenton Atkinson L.J., who gave the judgment, said that " on the issue of guilt it would seem a very plain case " and, after quoting the passage in Winn L.J.'s judgment in *Northam* quoted just above, expressed " some regret " that the conviction must be quashed. Other cases where it was held that evidence of confessions should have been excluded because of a threat or inducement which no one would have thought would cause a person to make an untrue confession were *Smith*[1] and *Cleary*[2]. In *Smith* a soldier was convicted by a court-martial of murder by stabbing another in a fight which developed between a number of soldiers at about 10 p.m. A sergeant-major paraded the company and made it clear to them that he would keep them on parade until he found out who were concerned in the fighting. After a time the accused stepped forward and said that he had done the stabbing. The Courts-Martial Appeal Court held that evidence of this confession was wrongly admitted because the sergeant-major's statement, though proper for the purpose of enabling inquiries to be started, was clearly a threat (and possibly also an inducement, in that it meant that the other soldiers might go to bed). (The appeal was dismissed because the accused made another confession next morning, after caution, when it was held that the effect of the sergeant-major's threat or inducement had been dissipated[3].) In *Cleary* the accused, aged twenty, was convicted of manslaughter after having been indicted, with two others, for capital murder committed in the course of theft. When he was being questioned by the police, he asked to see his father, and he and his father then had a private conversation, out of the hearing of the police officers, and afterwards, in their hearing, the father put his arm on the accused's shoulder and said: " Put your cards on the table. Tell them the lot . . . If you did not hit him, they cannot hang you ". The accused then made a statement admitting his part in the offence. If the father's statement amounted to an inducement for the purpose of the rule, the fact that it was made in the presence of the police officers without dissent by them made the confession inadmissible on any view. The trial judge considered that it was not capable of being an inducement because it did not go beyond " a mere exhortation to tell the truth "[4]. But the Court of Criminal Appeal held that the statement was capable of being an inducement and that, since the judge had (rightly, on the view which he took) omitted to direct the jury that it was for them " to decide whether in fact there was an inducement, and whether in fact the prosecution had proved that the appellant was not affected by the inducement "[5], the conviction must be quashed. In our opinion cases such as these show that the present rule is too strict and should be altered.

58. A threat or inducement, in order to make a resulting confession inadmissible, must have been uttered or held out by a " person in authority ". The existence of this condition was reasserted, after full argument, by the Privy Council in *Deokinanan v. R.*[6], an appeal from Guyana which fell to

[1] [1959] 2 Q.B. 35; 43 Cr. App. R. 121.
[2] (1963), 48 Cr. App. R. 116.
[3] This matter is referred to in paragraph 56.
[4] See paragraph 59.
[5] P. 121.
[6] [1969] 1 A.C.20; 52 Cr. App. R. 241.

be decided in accordance with English law. The Privy Council clearly doubted the justification for the rule as a matter of principle, but considered that the rule was well established. In giving judgment Viscount Dilhorne said[1]:

" The fact that an inducement is made by a person in authority may make it more likely to operate on the accused's mind and lead him to confess. If the ground on which confessions induced by promises held out by persons in authority are held to be inadmissible is that they may not be true, then it may be that there is a similar risk that in some circumstances the confession may not be true if induced by a promise held out by a person not in authority, for instance if such a person offers a bribe in return for a confession.

There is, however, in their Lordships' opinion, no doubt that the law as it is at present only excludes confessions induced by promises when those promises are made by persons in authority ".

The English courts have not thought it necessary to define precisely who are persons in authority for the purpose of the rule, though in *Deokinanan v. R.* Viscount Dilhorne quoted with approval[2] the statement by Bain J. in the Canadian case of *Todd*[3] that—

" A person in authority means, generally speaking, anyone who has authority or control over the accused or over the proceedings or the prosecution against him ".

Usually the person concerned has been a police officer investigating the offence. The question has arisen in a number of old cases in relation to persons affected by the offence, to members of their families or to the accused's employer, and some subtle distinctions were drawn. The rule has several times been applied to the owner of stolen property when there was a question of refraining from prosecuting the thief if he returned the property. A recent example is *Wilson and Marshall-Graham*[4], where Lord Parker C.J., in giving the judgment of the Court of Appeal, said that " in these days it would probably be impossible for him [the owner] to stultify a prosecution that had been brought or to prevent a prosecution that had not yet been brought from being instituted "[5]. In any event we consider that the existing distinction should be abolished. Apart from the fact that the concept of a " person in authority " seems to us an unnecessary complication of the law, we regard as decisive the point mentioned by Viscount Dilhorne in the former passage quoted from the judgment in *Deokinanan v. R.*, that the risk that an inducement will result in an untrue confession is similar whether or not the inducement comes from a person in authority. The abolition of this distinction will, as far as it goes, be a relaxation of the law in favour of the defence.

59. Two matters of detail relating to threats and inducements should be mentioned here. First, it is clear that a mere exhortation on religious or moral grounds to tell the truth does not make a resulting confession inadmissible. There must be a fear of prejudice, or hope of advantage, of a

---

[1] At p. 33; p. 250.
[2] *Ibid.*
[3] (1901), 13 Man. L.R. 364, 376.
[4] [1967] 2 Q.B. 406; 51 Cr. App. R. 194.
[5] At p. 415; p. 201.

temporal nature (though the line has sometimes proved difficult to draw). In *Reeve and Hancock*[1] two boys, one aged eight and the other a little older, were convicted of obstructing a railway train on the strength of their confession made in the presence of their mothers and a policeman after the mother of one had said: " You had better, as good boys, tell the truth ". The confessions were held admissible. This rule seems clearly right. Second, there was at one time an idea, which was mentioned in some textbooks and also in some cases, that the threat or inducement, in order to make a confession inadmissible, must relate to the charge or contemplated charge. But this was negatived in *Harz and Power*, mentioned above[2]. We see no reason to alter the effect of this decision; for although the kind of threat or inducement which might be thought most likely in fact to render a resulting confession unreliable would be one relating to the charge or contemplated charge (for example, a threat to charge a more serious offence or to make the case look worse for the accused or a promise not to prosecute, to prosecute for a lesser offence or to make the case seem less serious), a threat or inducement relating to a matter unconnected with the proceedings might be just as likely to make a confession unreliable or be just as improper a method of obtaining the confession.

60. The rule that a confession is inadmissible if it was obtained by " oppression ". as distinct from a threat or inducement, is a recent development in the law. The first mention of this, so far as we know, is in the statement by Lord Parker C.J., in *Callis v. Gunn*[3], of the general rule of inadmissibility, where he said, in relation to statements to the police and to alleged confessions, that it was—

> " a fundamental principle of law that no answer to a question and no statement is admissible unless it is shown by the prosecution not to have been obtained in an oppressive manner and to have been voluntary in the sense that it has not been obtained by threats or inducements. "

Judgment in this case was given on 15th October 1963, and it is interesting that the statement of this principle (quoted above[4]) in the introduction to the new Judges' Rules, which were issued in January 1964, closely follows the statement in *Callis v. Gunn*, including the reference to oppression. Since, as mentioned above[5], the statement in the Judges' Rules represents the law, it follows that oppression is now established as a separate ground of inadmissibility. Until recently the idea of oppression in this connection seems to have been still unfamiliar to lawyers; for when (after considerable discussion) we included " oppression " as a ground for inadmissibility in the provisional proposals sent out with our second circular[6], several of those who replied wrote as if the idea was a new one and expressed doubts as to the meaning. However, the scope of this ground of inadmissibility has since been considered by the Court of Appeal in *Prager*[7], where the court said:

---

[1] (1872), L.R.1 C.C.R. 362.
[2] Paragraph 53.
[3] [1964] 1 Q.B. 495, 501; 48 Cr. App. R. 36, 39.
[4] Paragraph 53.
[5] *Ibid.*
[6] Paragraph 9.
[7] (1971), 56 Cr. App. R. 151, 161.

" The only reported judicial consideration of ' oppression ' in the Judges' Rules of which we are aware is that of Sachs J. in *Priestley*[1], where he said:

> '...to my mind, this word in the context of the principles under consideration imports something which tends to sap, and has sapped, that free will which must exist before a confession is voluntary... Whether or not there is oppression in an individual case depends upon many elements. I am not going into all of them. They include such things as the length of time of any individual period of questioning, the length of time intervening between periods of questioning, whether the accused person had been given proper refreshment or not, and the characteristics of the person who makes the statement. What may be oppressive as regards a child, an invalid or an old man or somebody inexperienced in the ways of this world may turn out not to be oppressive when one finds that the accused person is of a tough character and an experienced man of the world.'

In an address to the Bentham Club in 1968, Lord MacDermott described ' oppressive questioning ' as—

> ' questioning which by its nature, duration or other attendant circumstances (including the fact of custody) excites hopes (such as the hope of release) or fears, or so affects the mind of the suspect that his will crumbles and he speaks when otherwise he would have stayed silent.'

We adopt these definitions or descriptions and apply them to the present case."

We considered whether to keep the idea of oppression as a separate ground of inadmissibility in addition to threats or inducements. There is clearly a case for treating all these kinds of conduct in the same way. But we are proposing, as will be mentioned[2], to limit the cases where a threat or inducement will make a resulting confession inadmissible, and we do not think it would be right, or acceptable to public opinion, to make any exception to inadmissibility where there has been oppression. We are in fact proposing to substitute " oppressive treatment of the accused " (undefined) for "oppression" as this ground of inadmissibility and we expect that the expression will be construed substantially as in the two definitions adopted in *Prager*.

61. We considered several possible ways of altering the law in order to get rid of what we regard as the excessive strictness of the rule as to admissibility of alleged confessions. The two courses advocated by members were—

  (i) to have no restriction on admissibility but allow all confessions to be proved before the jury or magistrates' court;

  (ii) to preserve the general rule that a threat, inducement or oppression makes a resulting confession inadmissible but to provide that this

---

[1] (1965). The ruling is reported in a note in 51 Cr. App. R. 1 on that case.
[2] Paragraph 65.

41

should not apply to all threats or inducements but only to those likely to produce an unreliable confession.

We discuss these courses in paragraphs 62 to 65. To anticipate, the majority favour course (ii). We considered also the possibility of substituting for the present ground of inadmissibility the general ground that the confession was obtained by " unfairness " or the like; but we did not favour a test of this kind, which we thought would produce too much uncertainty in its application as courts would be likely to take widely different views of what were " fair " methods of obtaining confessions. However, if the confession was obtained by means involving serious impropriety, it might be excluded by the court in exercise of its general discretion[1].

62. There are undeniably strong arguments based on logic, simplicity and convenience in favour of allowing all confessions to go before the jury or magistrates' court, leaving it to them to consider whether to give less weight, or no weight at all, to the confession because of the way in which it was obtained. As long ago as 1852, in *Baldry*[2], two judges at least of the Court for Crown Cases Reserved—Parke B.[3] and Lord Campbell C. J.[4]—suggested that this might have been the better rule, though accepting that it was then too late to adopt it. The chief argument in favour of this course is that, since the object of a criminal trial is to get at the truth, and since a confession may be true even if obtained by improper means, a confession should never be inadmissible merely because of the means by which it was obtained; for the result may be that a dangerous murderer may have to go free. The advantages of this course on the grounds of simplicity and convenience are obvious, in particular that it would get rid of the need for a trial within the trial. The course also avoids what some maintain is the illogicality of admitting evidence of facts discovered as a result of an inadmissible confession (though others maintain that the distinction is justified on the ground that the facts have their own cogency irrespective of how they were discovered, whereas it is too dangerous to act on the view that confessions may have their own cogency irrespective of the way in which they were obtained[5]).

63. Three members are in favour of adopting this course and discontinuing the special rules for so-called involuntary confessions. Their views (in addition to what is said above) are these. Abolition of the special rule for confessions would not remove any substantial protection for accused persons. The rule may perhaps have served a useful purpose at one time, particularly when accused persons could not give evidence; but it does so no longer. There is no reason to believe that the jury are prone to make an incorrect assessment of the reliability of an induced confession. Indeed, evidence of improper conduct by the police is likely to make the jury sympathize with the accused. In any case, there are many pieces of evidence that are only arguably relevant or arguably reliable, yet we do not prevent the jury from hearing them. Sometimes an induced confession may be manifestly true, because it may give a

---

[1] Paragraph 278.
[2] 2 Den. 430.
[3] At p. 445.
[4] At pp. 446–7.
[5] See paragraph 56.

42

circumstantial account that one cannot imagine to have been invented; and the judgment of reliability may be all the stronger if the confession is played over from a recording, when the exact tone of voice of the accused can be heard. A confession cannot rationally be excluded, on the ground that it may be untrue, if any reasonable person hearing the confession in the context of the general evidence would judge it to be true. The second possible ground of exclusion, the disciplinary principle, has more to be said for it; and certainly the minority would not wish to encourage the police to use improper means to obtain confessions. But if it comes out in evidence before the jury that such improper means have been used, this will go far to destroy the utility of the confession from the point of view of the prosecution, unless there is other convincing evidence rendering it credible. Also, police officers naturally dislike evidence being given in court of deceitful or overbearing conduct on their part. On the whole it seems to the minority unlikely that these natural sanctions against impropriety are substantially reinforced by the judge's excluding the confession altogether from the consideration of the jury.

64. The majority of us, while recognizing the advantages of this course, are against it for two reasons in particular. First, as to reliability, they think that, although in most cases the jury would be able to assess the weight to be given to an induced confession, there is still the danger that, in a case where the strength of the evidence on either side is about evenly balanced, the immediate effect on the jury of evidence of a confession might be too great to be undone, even with the help of the summing up, by the evidence of the way in which the confession was obtained. Second, as to the discouragement of improper methods of interrogation, the majority think that to remove all restrictions on admissibility of confessions on account of the use of improper methods to obtain them could not but operate, human nature being what it is, to encourage the police to resort on occasions to at least small improprieties.

65. The majority consider that the right course is for the rule as to inadmissibility of a confession on account of a threat or inducement to be limited to threats or inducements of a kind likely to produce an unreliable confession, but for inadmissibility on account of oppression to remain. After considering several possible variants we concluded that the rule should be that a threat or inducement (whether made by a person in authority or not) should render a resulting confession inadmissible only if it was " of a sort likely, in the circumstances existing at the time, to render unreliable any confession which might be made by the accused in consequence thereof ". The essential feature of this test is that it applies not to the confession which the accused in fact made but to any confession which he might have made in consequence of the threat or inducement. On this scheme the judge should imagine that he was present at the interrogation and heard the threat or inducement. In the light of all the evidence given he will consider whether, at the point when the threat was uttered or the inducement offered, any confession which the accused might make as a result of it would be likely to be unreliable. If so, the confession would be inadmissible. For example, if the threat was to charge the suspect's wife jointly with him, the judge might think that a confession even of a serious offence would be likely to be

unreliable. If there was a promise to release the accused on bail to visit a sick member of his family, the judge might think that this would be unlikely to render a confession of a serious offence unreliable but likely to do so in the case of a minor offence. We do not suggest that at the trial within the trial the evidence should stop short at the point where the threat was uttered or the inducement offered. For the judge will usually require evidence of the whole course of the interrogation in order to enable him to gauge the likely effect of the threat or inducement at this point, especially as there will usually be conflicting accounts of what happened at the interrogation. Even the terms of the confession may have to be considered. For although the fact that a particular confession seems clearly to be true will not make it admissible if the threat or inducement was of a sort likely to cause the accused to make an unreliable confession, yet evidence of the terms of the confession may throw light on the facts concerning the interrogation. As mentioned above, the provision will not apply to confessions obtained as a result of oppression. These will remain inadmissible.

66. Clause 2 contains the provisions to give effect to our proposals mentioned above. As at present, the rule of inadmissibility will apply only to confessions tendered by the prosecution (subsection (1)) and confessions will include informal admissions falling short of full confessions (subsection (6)). The main provisions are in subsections (2) and (3). Subsection (2) gives the defence the right to raise the issue in any event by representing that the confession " was or may have been made in consequence of oppressive treatment of the accused or in consequence of any threat or inducement ". Subsection (3) enables the judge to raise the issue himself. In either event the prosecution will have to prove beyond reasonable doubt the facts on which admissibility depends. Some questions of importance or difficulty arising on the clause are mentioned below, and certain other matters of detail are left to the note on the clause in Annex 2.

67. The fact that the judge has decided at the trial within the trial that the confession is admissible will not prevent the defence from cross-examining the witnesses for the prosecution, or themselves giving evidence, at the trial proper about the way in which the confession was obtained with the object of convincing the jury that they should pay no attention to it. Even if the same evidence is given as that given at the trial within the trial, this will not prevent the jury from taking a different view from that which the judge took at the trial within the trial—even on the question, for example, whether there was any threat or inducement. This is in accordance with the present law[1]. It would be wrong in our opinion to make any provision designed to require the jury to accept the judge's finding that a confession was not obtained in the ways mentioned, as this would be to usurp their function of deciding what weight to give to the confession. But the relevance of the issue for the jury will be only as to weight; and they will be under no obligation to disregard a confession, believed by them to be true, if it should so happen that (differing from the judge) they think that the test for admissibility was not satisfied. We have no doubt that the purpose for which the jury should consider the way in which a confession was obtained should be only that of

---

[1] *Murray*, [1951] 1 K.B. 391; 34 Cr. App. R. 203.

deciding what weight to give to it. This is the present law[1] and it will remain the law under the clause.

68. Subsection (5)(a) provides that the fact that evidence of a confession is inadmissible under the clause shall not affect the admissibility in evidence of any facts discovered as a result of the confession. This preserves the present rule (sometimes referred to as that of the " fruit of the poisoned tree ") that evidence of such facts is admissible. The rule was stated in the passage quoted above[2] from the judgment in the old case of *Warwickshall*. The principle was restated in two modern Privy Council cases in relation to evidence of facts discovered as the result of illegal searches—*Kuruma, Son of Kaniu v. R.*[3] and *King v. R.*[4]. In the former case Lord Goddard referred to the interesting fact that such evidence is inadmissible in the United States, perhaps because of a provision in their constitution. The judgment also mentioned the possibility that the evidence might be excluded under the general exclusionary discretion. Lord Hodson's judgment in the latter case contains what is perhaps the best statement of the ground on which evidence obtained in these ways might be rejected in the exercise of the general discretion. He said that the case in question was not " a case in which evidence has been obtained by conduct of which the Crown ought not to take advantage "[5]. We have no doubt that, in the interests of the detection of crime, the rule must be preserved. It would be too great an interference with justice to prevent the police from using any " leads " obtained from an inadmissible confession. For example, this would mean that, if the police have been led to arrest other persons involved in the crime who were named in the confession, no evidence could be given against these other persons, even though perhaps the police would eventually have discovered their guilt by other means. This would be too severe a restriction on the prosecution.

69. A more difficult question is whether, if the truth of an inadmissible confession is confirmed, wholly or in part, by facts discovered as a result of it, evidence of the confession, or of the part confirmed, should be made admissible. Examples are where an inadmissible confession of murder includes a statement that the offender had hidden the victim's body or the weapon with which he was killed in a particular place, or where a confession of theft includes a similar statement about the stolen property, and it is found there. The cases on this subject are nearly all old and are hopelessly in conflict[6]. The question is one of policy. We are opposed to any general provision for admissibility of evidence of statements contained in a confession on the ground that the truth of the statement is confirmed by the discovery of facts as a result of it. For this would mean that the judge, for the purpose of ruling on admissibility, would have to decide whether the confession, or the part in question, seemed to him likely to be true; and even though the judge's opinion would be provisional and would not be binding on the jury, it would probably be difficult for the jury not to be impressed by it. It was partly for a similar

---

[1] *Chan Wei Keung v R.*, [1967] 2 A.C. 160; 51 Cr. App. R. 257 (disapproving a suggestion to the contrary in *Bass*, [1953] 1Q.B. 680, 685; 37 Cr. App. R. 51, 57); *Ovenell*, [1969] 1 Q.B. 17; 52 Cr. App. R. 167; *Burgess*, [1968] 2 Q.B. 112; 52 Cr. App. R. 258.
[2] Paragraph 56.
[3] [1955] A.C. 197, 203–205.
[4] [1969] 1 A.C. 304; 52 Cr. App. R. 353.
[5] At p. 319 F; p. 365.
[6] See Cross on Evidence, 3rd edition, pp. 263–266.

45

reason that we decided to recommend making the admissibility of a confession depend on the likely effect of a threat or inducement in relation to a hypothetical confession and not in relation to the confession in fact made[1]. There are however two respects in which we think that it would be right to allow some reference to be made to an otherwise inadmissible confession.·

(i) The majority would allow evidence to be given that the discovery of the fact in question was made " as a result of " a statement made by the accused, even though this statement was inadmissible. Whether this is allowed at present is not clear. The cases are in conflict[2]. The strongest reported case—Berriman[3]—seems to be against this, but we believe that in practice it is common for the witness reporting the discovery to say that he made it " as a result of " something which the accused said. The majority think it reasonable to allow this[4].

(ii) We think it right that, if something in a confession shows that the accused writes, speaks or expresses himself in a particular manner, and this serves to identify him with the offender, so much of the confession as is necessary to show the characteristic referred to should be admissible for the purpose of showing it. A case where the accused was identified as the offender by a peculiarity of spelling was that of Voisin[5]. Voisin was convicted of the murder of a woman part of whose body had been found in a parcel in which there was also a piece of paper with the words " Bladie Belgium ". The accused had been asked by a police officer if he had any objection to writing down the two words " Bloody Belgian " and had said " Not at all " and written down " Bladie Belgiam ". The accused appealed unsuccessfully against his conviction on the ground, among others, that this writing ought to have been rejected as he had not been cautioned before being asked to write the words down. Here there was no question of an involuntary confession; but if in a case of this kind the words had been written in an inadmissible confession, it seems to us right that this part of the confession should be admissible for the purpose mentioned. The court would naturally ensure that no more was admitted than was necessary and that it was understood that the part admitted was admitted only for the purpose of identification and not as evidence of the truth of what was said in it.

The provisions for this purpose are in subsection (5)(b) and (c). We considered whether to provide also that a part of a confession should be admissible if it showed that the accused had some special knowledge which only the offender could have had. For example, the accused might have said that he broke into a house by breaking a particular window, and it might be found that this window was in fact broken. This would be cogent evidence; but granted the policy that the confession should be inadmissible, because

---

[1] Paragraph 65.
[2] See footnote 6 on p. 45.
[3] (1854), 6 Cox 388.
[4] A minority dissent on the ground that it is wrong that the jury should be informed indirectly of something of which it is thought that the interests of justice require that they should not be informed directly.
[5] [1918] 1 K.B. 531; 13 Cr. App. R. 89.

of the way in which it was obtained, as evidence that the accused broke the window, it seems to us too dangerous to admit this part of the confession for the purpose of connecting the accused with the offence by showing his special knowledge, as in practice this would be scarcely distinguishable from admitting the statement as evidence that the accused broke the window. The exclusionary provision in subsection (2) will leave no room for an argument, on the basis of the case law, that any part of a confession which is inadmissible under the provision is admissible for any special purpose other than those mentioned in subsection (5).

CLAUSE 3: ADMISSIBILITY OF OTHER CONDUCT OF ACCUSED TENDING TO SHOW DISPOSITION

70. The question how far evidence should be admissible to show that the accused has been guilty of misconduct other than the offence charged has proved far the most difficult of all the topics which we have discussed. This was fully expected, because not only is the existing law very difficult but the policy of this part of the law of criminal evidence is most controversial. We have mentioned earlier[1] that there have been great differences of opinion among those whom we consulted, and among ourselves, on these questions. The more radical changes of substance which were advocated (often strongly) in the committee or by others proved totally unacceptable to the majority. In the end, as will be seen, we have had to be content to recommend relatively minor, though still important, changes and a certain amount of codification in order to make the law simpler and more easily accessible. Some of the changes recommended have been accepted by some members only as a compromise and by others not at all.

71. The main provisions concerning other misconduct of the accused are in clauses 3, 6 and 7. Clause 3 deals mostly with evidence adduced by the prosecution, and clauses 6 and 7 with the special problems relating to where the accused gives evidence or claims to be of " good character "[2]. The present section of the report relates mainly to clause 3; but we mention first[3] some general considerations on the question of other misconduct of the accused, as these have a bearing on clauses 6 and 7 as well as clause 3. These considerations concern the relevance of his other misconduct for the purpose of proving his guilt and the question whether wider admissibility would be too prejudicial to him in the sense that too much attention would be paid to the misconduct and not enough to the facts connecting him with the offence charged. They also concern in particular the question how far the accused, if he gives evidence, can or should be treated like other witnesses, especially if his defence involves attacks on the conduct or veracity of the witnesses for the prosecution or he claims to be of " good character ".

72. Evidence of other misconduct of the accused tending to show that he has a disposition to commit the kind of offence charged may clearly be highly relevant in the sense of making it more probable that he committed the offence charged; and, as we said at the beginning[4], this is the sense in which

---

[1] Paragraphs 9, 22.
[2] Clauses 6 and 7 are separated from clause 3 because the intervening clauses 4 and 5 also relate to the giving of evidence by the accused.
[3] Paragraphs 72–77.
[4] Paragraph 14.

relevance must be understood for the purpose of the law of evidence. Obviously, if there is no other evidence at all to connect the accused with the offence charged, the fact that he has a disposition to commit this kind of offence is of no value. But if there is evidence to connect him with the offence, then evidence of disposition must be of greater or less value according to the circumstances. This may seem obvious, but it tends to be overlooked—no doubt partly because, when conduct of the accused showing bad disposition is inadmissible in evidence, it is sometimes referred to by lawyers as being " irrelevant ". A few examples will make it clear that this is a fallacy.

(i) A man in a crowd leaving a football match has his pocket picked. He identifies A, who was beside him at the time and is a total stranger to him, as the thief. A has ninety convictions for pickpocketing.

(ii) B is found in possession of a valuable piece of machinery taken from a construction site beside his house during the previous night. Charged with stealing, his defence is that he was woken up by heavy rain, remembered seeing the machinery in the open, got up, took it to his house for protection and was going to return it to the owners if only the police had not come so quickly. He has been convicted many times of theft.

(iii) A child complains that he has been indecently assaulted by a man in some bushes and identifies C, a stranger to him, as the offender. C admits taking him into the bushes but says that this was only to show him a bird's nest and that nothing wrong happened. C has a number of convictions for indecent assaults on children.

Whether or not it is right that evidence of the other offences should be admissible in these cases, there can be no doubt of their relevance. It would be a great strain on human credulity to be asked to suppose that so confirmed a pickpocket as A would have been wrongly pointed out as the thief or that B and C, with their history, would not have taken care, if innocent, to avoid laying themselves open to such obvious suspicion. Other cases where a disposition to commit offences of the same kind is of particular relevance are those of armed robbers, safe-blowers, arsonists and confidence tricksters.

73. The general rule, to be referred to in more detail below[1], is that evidence showing *only* that the accused has a disposition to commit the kind of offence charged, or crimes in general, is inadmissible for the purpose of showing that he committed the offence charged. As will be mentioned, there are important exceptions to this rule. We have had to consider whether the rule is right in general and, if so, whether the exceptions should be altered. The chief reason for restricting evidence showing disposition to commit misconduct is, as we mentioned earlier[2], the possible danger that it might have a disproportionate influence against the accused.

74. In considering the likely effect on juries of making evidence of other misconduct of the accused more widely admissible, there is the immediate difficulty that juries deliberate in private and jurors are instructed not to disclose what was said during their deliberations. Thus it cannot be told for certain what juries make of previous misconduct of the accused in the cases

---

[1] Paragraphs 78–85.
[2] Paragraph 15.

where evidence can be given of it or what they would make of it if it were more widely admissible. It is often possible to judge how jurors might regard such evidence from their visible reactions to particular pieces of evidence or from questions which they ask the judge, and innumerable stories have been told of disclosures by individual jurors of their reasons for convicting or acquitting in particular cases; but in the absence of research among ex-jurors the effect of evidence of the kind in question must remain very much a matter of speculation. On one important matter in particular there is obscurity. This is whether juries assume that, if the accused does not set up his good character, he has a criminal record. The inference may be obvious if one co-accused sets up his good character and another does not. In any event there is likely to be a juror who knows that in general the prosecution are not allowed to bring out the accused's criminal record unless he claims to be of good character. Obviously it is at least possible that the juror will have passed on his knowledge to the others, and as a result the jury may suppose that the accused has a worse record than he has. If juries do take this view, the implications may be serious. In the next two paragraphs we mention some indications as to the likely effect on juries of disclosing the accused's record.

75. On the one hand, it might be hoped that, especially with the improvements noted earlier[1] in the quality of juries, they should be able to put the accused's criminal record in proper perspective. In France the history of the accused, including his criminal record, is read out at the beginning of the trial. The purpose is to give the jury a picture of the accused. M. Simon[2], questioned closely about this, was clear that the jurors regarded their task as the mental exercise of evaluating the evidence for and against the accused and understood the part which his record should play in this exercise. Making due allowance for the fact that in France the judges retire with the jury[3], it seems difficult to believe that English jurors are so much less capable than French jurors of taking a balanced view of the accused's record that such strict precautions have to be taken as are taken to keep this from them. Sometimes juries have clearly thought that it would be helpful to them to know the accused's record. A judge of the Central Criminal Court told us of a case where, after he had concluded his summing up and the jury were about to retire, a juror stood up and said:

" Before we retire, my lord, may we be told if the defendant has any previous convictions? "

Judges have sometimes kept the jury in the box to hear the bad records of persons whom they had weakly convicted only of minor offences charged, and it was obvious that the jury felt that they had been cheated by not knowing the record. A judge told us that he had twice seen ten jurors turn angrily on two when the jury heard the accused's record read out after they had convicted only on a minor count. That some jurors try to give the proper weight to evidence of other misconduct is shown by the cases which some of us have seen where juries acquitted persons whose bad records were for some reason before them. The jury may exceptionally know of an offence committed by the accused although evidence of this was inadmissible for the prosecution.

---

[1] Paragraph 21(v).
[2] See paragraph 5.
[3] Paragraph 13.

Sometimes this happens because a witness has disclosed the matter inadvertently, in which case the judge has a discretion whether to discharge the jury and order a fresh trial. If he does not, he asks the jury not to treat the disclosure as evidence of the accused's guilt, though obviously they cannot dismiss it altogether from their minds.

76. As against this, some experienced defending lawyers take the view that juries do sometimes give undue weight to evidence of the accused's criminal record when for some reason it is disclosed during the trial; and great care is taken to avoid causing it to be disclosed. This attitude may even suggest that the mystery in which the law tries to shroud the accused's misdeeds has itself the harmful effect that, when one of them is somehow revealed, it is magnified out of all proportion to its probative value and may provide the jury with a short cut to a finding of guilt. We differ greatly among ourselves as to the extent of the danger that juries may be unduly affected by knowledge of other misconduct of the accused and, as will be seen, as to how far it is right to go in allowing this conduct to be disclosed.

77. The special problems concerning the position of the accused as a witness will be discussed below in relation to the changes in the law which we propose in clauses 6 and 7. At this point it is enough to refer to some general considerations related to the giving of evidence by the accused which must be kept in mind when considering how far evidence of the accused's misconduct should be admissible. Now that the accused is competent to give evidence, his evidence ought ideally to be regarded like that of any other witness in the case, whether a witness called for the prosecution or the defence; that is to say, it ought to be believed or not according to its apparent probability and according to how far the witness seems likely, from his history, to be telling the truth. This suggests that the accused, if he gives evidence, ought to be open to cross-examination about his past conduct in order to test his credibility in the same way as other witnesses. But this appears to clash with the doctrine underlying the general rule that evidence showing the accused's criminal disposition may not be adduced for the purpose of showing that he is likely to have committed the offence charged. Unless one is prepared (as some are) to abolish this rule, the question arises whether it is right to allow the prosecution to bring up against the accused, if he gives evidence, misconduct which it is thought wrong to allow them to bring up in the main part of their case. This again raises the question whether the misconduct ought to be taken into account for the purpose of judging the accused's credibility as a witness but ignored for the purpose of judging whether he is likely to have committed the offence charged, and whether it is in practice possible to differentiate between these two purposes. At present, if the accused gives evidence, he is in general protected against cross-examination about his previous misconduct (at least, if evidence of it is inadmissible otherwise) unless (i) he claims to be of good character, (ii) he makes imputations against the witnesses for the prosecution or (iii) he gives evidence against a person charged with the same offence. These exceptions all raise difficult questions, as will be seen. The subject is mentioned here because, when one is considering how far the prosecution ought to be able to adduce evidence of the accused's misconduct for the purpose of proving their case, it is material to keep in mind the fact that it will be necessary to consider also what, if any, further provision should be made for

admissibility of the misconduct if the accused gives evidence and, if he does, whether this should depend on the nature of his defence.

78. It is now necessary to try to summarize the common law rule as to when the prosecution may adduce evidence of other conduct of the accused tending to show a disposition to commit the kind of offence charged. This summary will relate only to evidence to be given by the prosecution in the main part of their case and before the accused comes to give evidence, and it will be assumed that the defence have not asked any questions of the witnesses for the prosecution designed to show that the accused is of good character. The common law rule is difficult to summarize because it is exceptionally complicated and because opinions differ greatly as to the effect of some of the decisions and as to whether the law is entirely consistent in itself. But it is not necessary to go into it in great detail, because, for reasons to be given later, we are recommending codifying the main part of the rule, which is done in subsections (1) and (2) of clause 3.

79. The best known judicial formulation of the common law rule is that of Lord Herschell L.C. in giving the judgment of the Privy Council in *Makin v. Attorney General for New South Wales*[1]:

> " It is undoubtedly not competent for the prosecution to adduce evidence tending to show that the accused has been guilty of criminal acts other than those covered by the indictment, for the purpose of leading to the conclusion that the accused is a person likely from his criminal conduct or character to have committed the offence for which he is being tried. On the other hand, the mere fact that the evidence adduced tends to show the commission of other crimes does not render it inadmissible if it be relevant to an issue before the jury, and it may be so relevant if it bears upon the question whether the acts alleged to constitute the crime charged in the indictment were designed or accidental, or to rebut a defence which would otherwise be open to the accused ".

The effect of these words was felicitously expressed by Lord Goddard C.J. in *Sims*[2]:

> " Evidence is not to be excluded merely because it tends to show the accused to be of a bad disposition, but only if it shows nothing more ".

The essence of the matter is that, if the other conduct can be related to the offence charged in some specific way so as to make it of particular relevance to an issue in the case, then the conduct may be admissible. Owing to the generality of the rule there is little more that can be done by way of summary than to give some illustrations of its working and to mention some of the kinds of cases where evidence showing bad disposition is admissible as being of special relevance.

80. As to the working of the rule, the court has to decide, first, whether the evidence tends to show that the accused has the disposition in question and, if so, whether it shows only a disposition to commit the kind of offence charged (or to commit crimes in general, including that charged). An example of a case where the evidence, though it showed a disposition to commit the kind of offence charged, was held to be inadmissible because it showed nothing

---

[1] [1894] A.C. 57, 65.
[2] [1946] K.B. 531, 537; 31 Cr. App. R. 158, 165.

more is *Brown, Smith, Woods and Flanagan*[1], where the Court of Criminal Appeal quashed a conviction of a joint offence of shopbreaking and larceny because evidence had been admitted of a similar offence which had been committed by one of the accused five days before the joint offence and of which he had pleaded guilty. It was argued for the prosecution that the earlier offence did not show merely that the offender had a disposition to commit shopbreaking but was admissible as being of particular relevance to the joint charge. This was on the ground that it tended to identify the perpetrator of the earlier offence with one of the perpetrators of the later offence in that (i) the former was committed five days earlier and twenty miles away, (ii) both offences were committed in the lunch-hour when the shopkeeper was away and (iii) in both cases the perpetrator got in by opening the door with a skeleton key. The court held that there were no peculiar features linking the two offences sufficiently for the purpose of the rule.

81. Three particular matters should be mentioned in connection with the working of the rule.

(i) An important practical result of its working is that, in a case where evidence of another offence by the accused is admissible as being of particular relevance to the offence charged, the fact that the accused committed the former offence cannot be established merely by proof that he has been convicted of it, but evidence must be given of the facts concerning it. This is because in the majority of cases a conviction would not be enough to show that the offence was particularly relevant to the offence charged. Whether evidence of the conviction may at present be given in conjunction with evidence of the facts is uncertain, as mentioned below[2], but we propose allowing it in future.

(ii) In deciding whether evidence of other conduct is sufficiently relevant to an issue in the case it is necessary to take account of the defence, because otherwise the issue may not be clear enough. It is also important that the issues should be clearly defined before the question of relevance is argued. But in order that evidence may be admissible on the ground referred to in Lord Herschell's speech in *Makin*[3] that it is relevant " to rebut a defence which would otherwise be open to the accused " it is not necessary that the defence should have been actually raised. It was for some time thought that this was necessary; but it is now established that it is sufficient that the defence is one fairly open to the accused[4].

(iii) Besides the defence, it is also necessary to have regard to the other evidence for the prosecution. In *Horwood*[5], O'Connor J., in giving the judgment of the Court of Appeal, expressed agreement with the following statement in Cross on Evidence[6]:

" It is also very important that due regard should be paid to the other evidence adduced or about to be adduced by the prosecution, for, in order to be admissible, evidence which incidentally shows

---

[1] (1963), 47 Cr. App. R. 205.
[2] Paragraph 97.
[3] See paragraph 79.
[4] *Harris v. Director of Public Prosecutions*, [1952] A.C. 694, 705; 36 Cr. App. R. 39, 52.
[5] [1970] 1 Q.B. 133, 139; 53 Cr. App. R. 619, 625.
[6] 3rd edition pp. 303–4.

bad disposition must be substantially relevant for some other purpose, and the degree of relevancy of such evidence may be greatly affected by the other evidence. If brother and sister are charged with incest, proof of their former incestuous association does more than show a tendency to commit incest, for it indicates the existence of a guilty passion between the two accused. Nevertheless, it is unlikely that such evidence would be admitted if the only other evidence in the case were that they lived in the same house and often went out together; but if there was evidence that they occupied the same bedroom, there is no doubt that evidence of their former association would be admitted to show that they committed incest in that room."

82. Some examples of cases where evidence showing disposition to commit the kind of offence charged is admissible because it has particular relevance are mentioned in this and the next three paragraphs. But it is important to note that the law does not restrict the cases of admissibility to defined categories. In *Harris*[1] Viscount Simon said:

" It is, I think, an error to attempt to draw up a closed list of the sort of cases in which the principle operates: such a list only provides instances of a general application, whereas what really matters is the principle itself and its proper application to the particular circumstances of the charge that is being tried ".

Evidence of conduct may be admissible because it shows a disposition to commit the kind of offence charged in a particular manner or according to a particular mode of operation. This occurs frequently in cases of obtaining property by deception where the criminal uses the same deception over and over again. It also occurs in cases of burglary where the offender uses a distinguishing method of getting into the premises. A remarkable instance of admissibility on the ground of similarity is *Smith*[2] (the " Brides in the Bath " case), where the accused was convicted of murdering a woman in her bath after he had gone through a ceremony of marriage with her and insured her life in his favour. In order to disprove his defence that her death was accidental evidence was admitted that two other " brides " of his had died in similar circumstances. In *Straffen*[3], where the accused was convicted of murdering a small girl by strangling her in very peculiar circumstances, evidence was admitted that he had confessed to strangling two other small girls a year before in almost exactly similar circumstances.

83. Evidence showing a disposition to commit the kind of offence charged in respect of the person in respect of whom the offence charged was committed may obviously be particularly relevant, and it is admissible, for example, in sexual cases such as that of incest mentioned in the passage from Cross on Evidence quoted above[4]. This occurred in *Ball*[5]. Evidence showing disposition may also be admissible as being particularly relevant in that it tends to identify the accused with the offender. This happened in *Thompson v. R.*[6],

[1] [1952] A.C. at p. 705; 36 Cr. App. R. at pp. 51–2.
[2] (1915), 11 Cr. App. R. 229.
[3] [1952] 2 Q.B. 911; 36 Cr. App. R. 132.
[4] Paragraph 81(iii).
[5] [1911] A.C. 47; 6 Cr. App. R. 31.
[6] [1918] A.C. 221; 13 Cr. App. R. 61.

where on charges of gross indecency with two boys evidence of possession by the accused of powder puffs and indecent photographs was held to have been rightly admitted in the special circumstances as showing a disposition to homosexual conduct. The special circumstances were that according to the evidence for the prosecution the offender, after committing the offences charged, made an appointment with the boys for three days later at a public lavatory. Meanwhile the police had been informed, and they kept watch with one of the boys at the lavatory, where the boy pointed out the accused on his arrival as the offender. As he denied that he was the person concerned, and as he and the person who made the appointment had the common feature of homosexuality, the disposition was obviously highly relevant in the circumstances. There have been dicta which suggest that a homosexual tendency is always admissible on a charge of a homosexual offence on the ground that it marks the possessor out from other persons. In particular, a passage in the judgment of Lord Goddard C.J. in Sims[1] seems, on a broad interpretation, to support this view of the law. But the judgment is consistent with the interpretation that the admissibility of the evidence in that case depended on the presence of special features common to the occasions in question, and later decisions strongly support this narrow view of the effect of the judgment[2]. The clause proposes to settle the law in this sense; for we regard it as wrong in policy that evidence of a homosexual tendency should be admissible as a matter of course, and irrespective of the circumstances, on a charge of a homosexual offence.

84. The rule that evidence showing a criminal disposition is admissible in order to identify the accused as the offender is an important one in practice and has been applied to evidence of possession of instruments for use in burglary even though not proved to have been used in the burglary in question[3]. It played an important part in two recent murder cases. In Morris[4] the accused was convicted of the murder of a small girl whom he had abducted and indecently assaulted. The Court of Appeal held that the trial judge had rightly allowed a charge of attempted abduction of another small girl and a charge of indecent assault on a third to be tried with the charge of murder because the evidence of those two offences was admissible on the charge of murder as tending to identify the accused with the murderer. This was because the circumstances of the attempted abduction were strikingly similar to those of the abduction of the murdered girl and because some indecent photographs of the girl indecently assaulted which were found in the accused's possession showed her in a position strikingly similar to that of the murdered girl's body immediately after it was found, and because all the offences had been committed in the same geographical area. In Twomey[5], where the victim's body showed that he had been the subject of homosexual relations and been attacked with great violence, evidence was held to have been rightly admitted of several incidents showing that the accused (who was proved to have been near the place of the murder at the relevant time and had also made a confession which he sought unsuccessfully to have excluded on the ground

---

[1] [1946] K.B. 531, 540; 31 Cr. App. R. 158, 168.
[2] See Cross on Evidence, 3rd edition pp. 319–320; Supplement p. 14.
[3] Reading (1965), 50 Cr. App. R. 98.
[4] (1969), 54 Cr. App. R. 69.
[5] [1971] Crim. L.R. 277.

that it was extorted by violence and oppression) was given to homosexual acts accompanied by violence.

85. Apart from cases of identification, evidence showing that the accused has a disposition to commit the kind of offence charged may be admissible as being specially relevant to disprove such matters as accident, ignorance, mistake, innocent association (in particular on a charge of a sexual offence) or some other innocent explanation of a particular act or the possession of some article. Evidence showing disposition is also admissible, by way of exception to the general exclusionary rule, under certain statutes, which will be referred to below[1].

86. The rule as to admissibility of conduct of the accused showing disposition to commit the kind of offence charged has been discussed at length in the committee. It has been criticized in three respects in particular:

(i) It is argued that a rule which says in effect that evidence showing something which is admittedly relevant (disposition) is in general inadmissible, but it is admissible if it is *specially* relevant, is illogical. The argument is that what is really important, as being of probative value, is the disposition itself. Therefore, it is said, the law ought to have based itself on the essential proposition that the fact that a person has committed the same kind of offence on another occasion is of probative value in proving that he committed the offence charged, whereas instead it has concentrated perversely on matters, such as similarity of method or identity of the victim, which are merely particular aspects of this essential proposition. It has been argued that there has never been a clear explanation of why, for example, evidence that the accused is a professional burglar should sometimes be inadmissible because it shows only disposition and sometimes admissible because it shows a system of conduct. If a burglar is charged with getting into a house by means of a ladder, why should evidence that he got into another house the same way be admissible but not evidence that he got into another house by climbing up the ivy? What really matters is that he is a burglar and not that he uses ladders. Similarity of method may increase the relevance of disposition, but absence of similarity does not alter the fact that disposition is relevant.

(ii) It is argued that the law is too strict in requiring close similarity between the offence charged and the other misconduct. An extreme instance is *Slender*[2], where the accused's conviction of obtaining money by falsely pretending that he needed it in order to spend the night in Cheltenham was quashed because evidence was admitted that, two days before, he had obtained money by falsely pretending that he needed it in order to travel from Cheltenham to get to work. It is generally recognized that the strict application of the rule has caused difficulty in cases involving fraud. Experience shows that fraudsmen commonly continue to commit frauds, but the prosecution are prevented from proving convictions for fraud by the

[1] Paragraph 101(vi).
[2] (1938), 26 Cr. App. R. 155.

requirement of close similarity and the fact that many criminals vary their methods according to circumstances.

(iii) The case law is complicated and sometimes in conflict. It has led to endless arguments in the courts and outside. A particular case where difficulty has been caused has been on the question, referred to above[1], as to the admissibility of evidence of homosexual conduct for the purpose of identifying the accused as the offender.

87. Those who defend the present rule in general argue, as to (i) in paragraph 86, that the rule, properly looked at, is not illogical, because the criterion for admissibility should be not only whether the evidence is of probative value but also whether there is a danger that to admit it might be too prejudicial to the accused. Accepting the proposition that evidence showing disposition to commit the kind of offence charged is of probative value, they say that, if it shows only this disposition, there is or may be the danger mentioned, but that, if the " particular aspects " referred to are present, then the probative value of the evidence outweighs its possibly prejudicial effect sufficiently to justify admitting the evidence. Those who take this view agree that the objections mentioned in (ii) and (iii) in paragraph 86 exist, but they do not think that these are serious enough to justify a radical change in the present law, and they hope that they will be largely got over by the restatement and relaxation of the law which we are recommending.

88. We considered a great many possible changes of the law, some of which we mentioned in the consultations in 1968[2]. Merely to mention anything like all the suggestions put forward, with their various combinations and modifications, would make this section of the report far too long. We therefore refer to only two radical proposals which some members have put forward but which the majority have rejected[3] and the compromise proposal which we ultimately adopted[4].

89. The first radical proposal was to give effect to the proposition enunciated in paragraph 86(i) that what is really of probative value is the fact that the accused has a disposition to commit the kind of offence charged. On this proposal, evidence of another offence by the accused would be admissible if it is the same, or an offence of the same class, as the offence charged. It would probably not be sufficient to provide that the evidence should be admissible if the offences were " similar ", " of the same character " or " of the same general character " or the like. This is because offences do not fall into clearly defined classes, so that there might be uncertainty whether a particular offence was one of the same kind as the offence charged and it would be left to the courts to work out what should be the classes for this purpose. For example, although rape and incest are both sexual offences, they differ for the purposes of the suggested rule in that rape ordinarily involves violence and incest ordinarily does not, so that a disposition to commit one may be of little probative value on a charge of the other. Again, robbery is partly an offence of violence and partly one of dishonesty. Therefore, if this proposal were adopted, it would probably be desirable to specify the classes of offences

---

[1] Paragraph 83.
[2] Paragraph 9.
[3] Paragraphs 89, 90.
[4] Paragraphs 91–101.

in the statute. Classes suggested were (i) offences involving violence (except murder, rape and indecent assault), (ii) rape and indecent assault, (iii) offences involving fraud or deception, (iv) offences involving abortion and (v) offences of damage to property. Perhaps on this scheme exceptions should be made in respect of some kinds of offences. The main arguments for this view are (i) the probative value of the evidence as mentioned, (ii) the importance in the public interest that criminals, especially dangerous criminals, should not escape conviction because juries are kept in ignorance of facts which are highly material to their decision and (iii) that the division of offences into defined classes would make the rule simple to operate. An illustration of the importance of (ii) is a case[1] of a man sentenced to death in 1947 for strangling a woman; the sentence was commuted and he was released in 1956 after nine years in prison. Nine years after his release, namely in 1965, he wounded with a kitchen knife another woman with whom he had been living. His defence was that he had brandished the knife only to frighten the woman and she had fallen upon it. The jury acquitted of wounding with intent to murder and convicted of wounding with intent to cause grievous bodily harm. Another possible outcome would have been that the jury, being unaware of his previous conviction, might have believed his tale of wishing only to frighten the woman and therefore had to acquit him; and it is argued that the public safety demands that in such a case the previous conviction of violence should be before the jury. But the majority of the committee were opposed to this proposal, because they thought it would be too great an extension of admissibility and would involve the danger of injustice owing to the prejudicial effect of the previous offences. Some members also think that it would undermine the confidence of the public in criminal trials and might be a discouragement to criminals to reform because of their sense of unfairness and the hopelessness of avoiding conviction, even when innocent, because of their record.

90. The second radical proposal was that the accused's previous convictions should be read out at the opening of the trial. Those who take this view are convinced that it is right in principle, and in the interests of justice, that the jury or the magistrates' court should know what, if any, previous convictions the accused has, and they think that the proposal mentioned would be the most satisfactory way of achieving this object. This proposal may seem drastic, but its supporters argue that it is in fact much less so than it seems. The purpose would be to provide the jury or magistrates' court with a picture of the accused to be used as a background to the evidence. The judge would direct the jury that the information should be treated, and the magistrates' court would treat it, not as evidence but merely for the purpose mentioned. In fact the procedure would be a modified version of the French procedure referred to earlier[2]. The record would not be allowed to be referred to again in the case unless (i) the defence so wished, (ii) evidence of the conduct involved was admissible under the ordinary law (as proposed to be amended) or (iii) the judge thought it right to mention the convictions for some reason in his summing up. If he mentioned them, this might be an emphatic injunction to disregard them altogether. The convictions to be mentioned should probably be limited to those relevant in a general way for the purpose of providing a picture of the accused—perhaps the range of convictions commonly taken into

[1] Mentioned in (1966) 130 J.P.N. 121.
[2] Paragraph 75.

account in passing sentence. It is claimed that this scheme would have the advantage of being less harsh to the accused than when his previous record is brought out by the prosecution in cross-examination in all its detail. It is also claimed that it would have the great advantage of uniformity which is lacking under the present law and will still be lacking if our proposals are adopted. The procedure would quickly be fully understood by juries as part of the normal procedure of the courts and so would not have the same allegedly devastating effect as when previous convictions are given in evidence. It would remove from those conducting the case for the prosecution or the defence the burden of deciding at what stage as a matter of tactics previous convictions should be before the court, if admissible. It would also relieve the trial judge of the burden of exercising a discretion as to whether the convictions should be admissible. More generally, it is argued that an accused person with a criminal record should have no more right to keep the jury or magistrates' court in the dark about his record than a criminal with a peculiarly evil appearance has to wear a mask at his trial. This proposal received some support in the committee and outside, but the majority regard it as far too great a departure from the present procedure and as even more open to the dangers mentioned at the end of the previous paragraph in the case of the proposal there discussed.

91. Our eventual proposal is—
   (i) to preserve the substance of the common law rule that evidence showing a disposition to commit the kind of offence charged is in general inadmissible but to relax it in one important respect, and
   (ii) to make fresh provision as to admissibility of evidence of previous convictions for the purpose of proving that the accused committed the misconduct in respect of which he was convicted.
We propose that the common law rule, as relaxed, should be made statutory.

92. The relaxation mentioned in paragraph 91 is to provide that, where the defence admit that the conduct in respect of which the accused is charged occurred (but deny that the accused was guilty of an offence in respect of it), then evidence of other conduct of the accused tending to show in him a disposition to commit the kind of offence charged should be admissible for certain particular purposes. The purposes would be (i) showing that the accused possessed the state of mind necessary to make him guilty in respect of that conduct, (ii) proving that the conduct was not accidental or involuntary or (iii) proving that there was no lawful justification or excuse for it. Stated shortly, the effect will be that, where the *actus reus* is admitted, evidence showing a disposition to commit the kind of offence charged will be admissible for the purpose of proving the existence of the necessary *mens rea* even if there is no similarity or other connection between the previous offence and the offence charged such as is necessary in order to make evidence of the former admissible under the general rule. Thus, if the accused is charged with obtaining property by deception and admits that he made the statement and that it was false, evidence of any previous offence of obtaining property by deception will be admissible, on the issue of dishonesty, even if the circumstances were quite different. We hope that this relaxation will be valuable in view of the considerable difficulty which the strictness of the present rule has caused in this

58

kind of offence (for example, in *Slender*[1]). In a similar case in future evidence of the earlier deception, whether or not it would still be held inadmissible according to the general rule as enacted[2], would be admissible under our proposal if the accused admitted (as Slender seems in effect to have done) the making of the false pretence. The same would apply to a case like that of *Fisher*[3], where a conviction of obtaining a pony and trap by false pretences concerning the state of the accused's family and bank account was quashed because evidence had been wrongly admitted concerning the obtaining of provender by false pretences with regard to the state of his business. Other kinds of cases where we should expect evidence, held to have been wrongly admitted under the present law, to be admitted under the proposal mentioned are *Harrison-Owen*[4] (where a conviction for burglary was quashed because the prosecution were directed to question the accused about convictions for housebreaking and larceny in order to rebut a defence that he entered the house in a state of automatism) and *Coombes*[5] (where the accused was convicted of an indecent assault on a married woman, he having admitted the conduct charged but not the indecent intent, and the conviction was quashed because the prosecution were allowed to cross-examine the accused about a conviction for indecently assaulting a girl of twelve five months earlier).

93. We are all satisfied that, on the assumption (as to which some members of the committee do not agree[6]) that the proposal summarized in paragraph 92 will prove to be of sufficient practical value to justify the additional complication in the law which it involves, it would be consistent with the interests of justice to enact the proposal. This is because we are all satisfied that, when the accused admits that the conduct in question occurred, then evidence that he committed the kind of offence charged, in however dissimilar circumstances, may add greatly to the significance of the other offences. If the defence deny that the conduct in question took place at all, it is generally thought[7] that the prejudicial effect of the other offences outweighs their probative value; but all agree that, if the defence admit that the conduct took place, then the probative value of the other offences justifies making them admissible in evidence notwithstanding their possibly prejudicial effect.

94. The reason why some members dispute the practical value of the proposal summarized in paragraph 92 is that criminals might soon decide to take care to avoid making any admission as to the conduct in question and thus letting in evidence of the other offences. But the majority are satisfied that the accused will be unlikely to be able to adopt this course when his real defence is that the conduct took place but was innocent. For example, in a case of obtaining property by deception it will be difficult to combine a defence that there was no intent to deceive with a denial of the making of the statement or of its falsity; and even if the defence do not say at the beginning that the conduct is admitted, it should be clear from the cross-examination of the witnesses for the prosecution whether this is so. Moreover, if the making of

---

[1] See paragraph 86(ii).
[2] This question is discussed in paragraph 101(i).
[3] [1910] 1 K.B. 149; 3 Cr. App. R. 176.
[4] (1951), 35 Cr. App. R. 108.
[5] (1960), 45 Cr. App. R. 36.
[6] See paragraph 94.
[7] This is, of course, not accepted by those who support the proposals discussed in paragraphs 89 and 90.

the statement is admitted, there is unlikely to be any issue as to its falsity. If the admission is not made till the accused gives evidence, then the prosecution will be able to adduce the evidence later, as is mentioned below[1]. In any event, even if it is sometimes not clear that the *actus reus* is admitted, we hope that the suggested provision will be valuable for the cases where this is clear.

95. Our fresh proposals as to evidence of previous convictions are that—

(i) where evidence of other misconduct is admissible under the general rule (in the absence of an admission of the *actus reus*), evidence of a conviction resulting from it should be admissible in conjunction with evidence of the facts concerning that misconduct;

(ii) where evidence of other misconduct is admissible because of an admission of the *actus reus*, evidence of a resulting conviction should be admissible by itself without the need to adduce evidence of the facts concerning the other misconduct.

96. Of the proposals about convictions summarized in paragraph 95 proposal (ii) is much the more important, and we deal with it first. We have mentioned[2] that evidence of a bare conviction of an offence cannot be given in order to prove that the accused committed the offence, and therefore to prove that the accused has a disposition to commit this kind of offence. This, as mentioned, is because a bare conviction does not reveal the facts of the offence sufficiently to indicate whether the disposition which caused the accused to commit it is of particular relevance for the proof of the offence charged. But since we are proposing that, where the *actus reus* is admitted, evidence showing a disposition to commit the kind of offence charged, irrespective of the circumstances, should be admissible for the particular purposes mentioned, we think it follows that evidence of a conviction by itself can safely be made admissible in these cases, because the conviction shows a disposition to commit that kind of offence. If in a particular case the court thinks that the evidence may be insufficiently probative for this purpose (or that for any other reason it ought not to be given), it can exclude the evidence in exercise of the general discretion.

97. As to proposal (i) in paragraph 95, it is uncertain whether evidence of a conviction of an offence is admissible in conjunction with evidence of the facts of the offence. It is curious that this should not be clear, but there is very little authority. In principle it seems that the evidence should be held admissible, because the reason given above why evidence of a bare conviction is inadmissible—that it does not show enough about the facts of the offence in question for the purpose of the present rule—does not apply. On the other hand, in practice, where evidence of misconduct is admissible under the general rule, it is always proved by evidence of the facts; and in *Porter*[3], where it was held that the accused had been rightly cross-examined about offences similar to that charged, and where he had himself introduced the fact that he was convicted of one of the offences, Avory J., in giving the judgment of the Court of Criminal Appeal, used language[4] which suggests (though not clearly) that it would have been irregular for the prosecution to have questioned the accused

---

[1] See the summary in paragraph 101(v) of clause 3(6).
[2] Paragraph 81(i).
[3] (1935), 25 Cr. App. R. 59.
[4] At p. 63.

about the conviction. In any event, we are satisfied that evidence of a conviction should be admissible in conjunction with evidence of the facts, because the latter evidence will reveal enough about the facts to show whether the offence is sufficiently relevant to be admissible and it seems unnatural that, when the prosecution prove that the accused committed the other misconduct, they should have to stop short of saying that he was convicted of it (if this was the case).

98. There are two advantages in making evidence of a conviction admissible for the prosecution where this can be done without injustice to the defence. The first is that it avoids the need to bring to court the witnesses to prove the other offence, which might be difficult or impossible to do even after a short lapse of time. Second, in cases of sexual offences it makes it unnecessary to subject the victim to the distress, and, especially if the victim is a child, to the possible psychological harm, of having to give evidence again about the offence.

99. Where proof of a conviction is admissible, this will be conclusive evidence that the accused committed the offence to which the conviction relates (though not of the details of the offence). There is very little direct authority on this, but we have no doubt that it follows from the rule that a party is estopped from denying the conclusiveness of a judicial decision on an issue in proceedings between the same parties (in this case, the Crown and the accused); and this proposition seems to be indirectly supported by *Bynoe v. Bank of England*[1]. In practice, where evidence of a conviction is admissible under certain statutes[2], it is treated as conclusive and no difficulty or injustice is said to result. We gave a great deal of thought to whether the accused should be enabled to dispute the correctness of a conviction admissible under our proposals, but we decided that this would be impracticable. For it might become the practice to try to obstruct proceedings by disputing the correctness of convictions of which evidence was admissible, and the result might be to cause chaos in criminal trials. The great majority of those whom we consulted in 1968[3] were firmly against allowing this.

100. It seems to us clearly convenient that the Bill, as well as making the changes mentioned above, should enact the general rule (which is being substantially preserved) as to admissibility of other conduct for the purpose of showing disposition. Not only should it be more convenient to be able to find the rule in statutory form but this will show clearly what is the fundamental principle by reference to which the changes proposed would operate. Apart from convenience, the restatement should have the advantage of enabling the courts to make a fresh start and take a less strict view of the requirement of similarity or other connection between the other conduct and the offence charged than the view they have felt obliged to take in the past. The aim of the Bill is to formulate a principle which the courts will be able to apply in accordance with the requirements of reason and common sense to the facts of each case without being hampered by decisions in previous cases.

101. The provisions to give effect to our proposals are in clause 3. They are summarized below[4].

---

[1] [1902] 1 K.B. 467.
[2] See paragraph 101(vi).
[3] Paragraph 9.
[4] Some matters of detail are left to be mentioned in the notes on the clause in Annex 2.

(i) Subsections (1) and (2) state the general rule as summarized above[1]. Subsection (1) contains the exclusionary rule where the evidence shows only a disposition to commit the kind of offence charged or a general disposition to commit crimes. Subsection (2) contains the rule that evidence showing a disposition to commit the kind of offence charged is admissible if the disposition is of particular relevance. The test is expressed by the requirement that the disposition which the other conduct tends to show " is, in the circumstances of the case, of particular relevance to a matter in issue in the proceedings ". Examples are given in paragraphs (a) to (c). We selected this way of expressing the test, after considering many other possible ways, as corresponding most nearly in substance to the way in which the matter is expressed in the authorities. The examples correspond generally to the illustrations given above of the working of the rule[2]. In paragraph (a) the provision that the evidence should be admissible if it is relevant as showing a disposition to commit the kind of offence charged " in a particular manner or according to a particular mode of operation resembling the manner or mode of operation alleged as regards the offence charged " will, we hope, be particularly useful for the purpose mentioned at the end of paragraph 100 of enabling the court to decide the question of admissibility according to a practical view of whether the resemblance is sufficient to make the disposition " of particular relevance " to the offence charged. Had this formulation been available when *Slender*[3] was decided, it is possible that the evidence of the other offence would have been held admissible under the existing law. By making the cases referred to in paragraphs (a) to (c) examples only the clause takes account of Lord Simon's warning in *Harris*[4] that " it is...an error to attempt to draw up a closed list of the sort of cases in which the principle operates ". We emphasize that subsection (2) does not say that evidence showing any of the matters mentioned will necessarily be sufficient proof of the disposition in question or that the disposition which it would prove will necessarily be of particular relevance for the purpose of admissibility. The latter question will depend on whether the disposition is of particular relevance " in the circumstances of the case ", including the nature of the defence and the other evidence for the prosecution[5]. The court will always consider whether the evidence of the other misconduct is sufficient for this purpose, and it will in any event be able, if it seems right, to exclude the evidence in exercise of the general discretion.

(ii) Subsection (3) makes evidence of the conviction of an offence, if given in conjunction with evidence of the facts of the offence, admissible for the purpose of proving that the accused committed that offence[6].

(iii) Subsection (4) contains the provision that, where the defence admit the *actus reus*, evidence showing a disposition to commit the kind of offence charged, even in dissimilar circumstances, should be admissible for the purposes referred to, which are specified in paragraphs (a) to (c)[7]. One matter should be mentioned on this. Paragraph (a) includes " recklessness " among the states of mind to prove which the evidence is to be admissible, but the

---

[1] Paragraph 79.
[2] Paragraphs 82–85.
[3] See paragraphs 86(ii), 92.
[4] Paragraph 82.
[5] See paragraph 81(ii) and (iii).
[6] Paragraphs 95(i), 97.
[7] Paragraph 92.

proviso to the subsection excludes " negligence " from this. This is because " recklessness " is used in two senses in the law—(i) the deliberate taking of an unjustified risk and (ii) gross negligence. In (i) it involves a state of mind, in (ii) not necessarily so. We think that evidence should be admissible under subsection (4) to prove recklessness in sense (i) but not in (ii). This is because, assuming that there can be a relevant disposition to commit an offence of gross negligence, we do not think that it would be right to make evidence showing a disposition to commit this offence in wholly dissimilar circumstances (and still less evidence of a bare conviction) admissible for this purpose. We make no provision to the effect that evidence of a disposition to act with negligence is admissible under the general rule stated in subsection (2). There is no English authority on whether such evidence is admissible under the common law rule, though there is authority that it is sometimes admissible under the corresponding American rule. By not limiting the cases of admissibility under subsection (2) to those specified in the examples the clause will leave it open to the courts to decide whether evidence showing a disposition to act negligently should be admissible in an appropriate case.

(iv) Subsection (5) makes evidence of a conviction admissible for the purpose of proving other conduct admissible under subsection (4), whether or not any other evidence of that conduct is given[1].

(v) Subsection (6) deals with the situation where the prosecution might wish to cross-examine the accused or any other witness for the defence, or to adduce evidence after the close of the prosecution, about any matter (including a conviction of the accused) which is admissible in evidence under the clause but of which they did not adduce evidence during their own case. This situation might occur for any of various reasons. The evidence might not have been admissible during the case for the prosecution because its admissibility arose only under subsection (4) as a result of an admission by the accused, or its admissibility might somehow have not become apparent until after the end of the case for the prosecution. Again, it might not have been reasonably practicable for the evidence to be adduced during the case for the prosecution (for example, if a witness to prove a conviction was not available because it was not expected that the conviction would be disputed). In these cases it seems reasonable that the prosecution should be able to cross-examine the accused or a witness for the defence or to call a witness themselves in order to prove the matter. The difficulty is that in *Rice*[2] the Court of Criminal Appeal expressed the view that there is " a general principle of practice...requiring that all evidentiary matter that the Crown intend to rely upon as probative of the guilt of a defendant...should be adduced before the close of the prosecution case if it be then available ". We do not wish to disturb this general rule of practice (the situation in *Rice* had nothing to do with the matters to which clause 3 relates), but it seems to us important that the principle should not be allowed to operate so as to prevent the prosecution from acting as mentioned above. Subsection (6) therefore provides that the prosecution shall have the right to cross-examine the accused or a witness for the defence as mentioned. and also to adduce the evidence as mentioned after the conclusion of their case, but that the latter right is to be exercised subject to the discretion of the

---

[1] Paragraphs 95(ii), 96.
[2] [1963] 1 Q.B. 857, 867; 47 Cr. App. R. 79, 85.

court as to the stage at which the evidence should be adduced. For example, the court might decide that the evidence should be adduced by interposing a witness during the evidence for the defence or that it should not be adduced until after all the witnesses for the defence have been called. On the other hand, the subsection will not give the prosecution any right to adduce evidence after the conclusion of their case when there was no valid reason for not adducing it earlier. In fact we propose that the principle stated in *Rice* should be made statutory[1] (subject to a discretion, the existence of which was recognized in *Rice* and stressed in the recent case of *Doran*[2]).

(vi) Subsection (7) contains two savings. Paragraph (*a*) saves the admissibility of evidence of any conduct of the accused which is relevant for a reason other than a tendency to show in the accused a disposition. For example, on a charge of robbery it may be relevant to prove that the accused had stolen a car which was used in the commission of the robbery in order to connect him with the robbery. The admissibility of the theft is not an exception to the general exclusionary rule stated in subsection (1), but it seems desirable to include an express saving in order to avoid misunderstanding. Paragraph (*b*) preserves admissibility of evidence of other conduct which is admissible under any enactment. There are three important enactments of this kind. First, s. 15 of the Prevention of Crimes Act 1871 (c. 112) makes evidence of the " known character " of the accused admissible for the purpose of proving a criminal intention in the case of certain vagrancy offences. We considered recommending that this provision should be repealed and the matter left to be governed by the clause; but the law as to vagrancy offences includes several peculiar features and is, we understand, likely to be reviewed, so we think it better to leave this matter to the review. Second, s. 1(2) of the Official Secrets Act 1911 (c. 28) makes a similar provision for the purpose of proving a " purpose prejudicial to the safety or interests of the State ". The offences under that section clearly involve special questions which cannot be satisfactorily dealt with in a review of the law of evidence. The third provision is in s. 27(3) of the Theft Act 1968 (c. 60), but we are proposing, as mentioned below. that this should be repealed.

(vii) Subsection (9) repeals s. 27(3) of the Theft Act 1968 mentioned above. S. 27(3) provides that on a charge of handling stolen goods evidence that the accused possessed, or was otherwise concerned in dealing with, goods stolen during the year preceding the offence charged, or that he has been convicted within the five years preceding the offence of theft or handling stolen goods. shall be admissible in certain circumstances in order to prove that the accused knew or believed the goods to which the charge relates were stolen. We think that this provision should be repealed. It seems inappropriate that there should be a special provision dealing with an offence like handling stolen goods side by side with the provisions of clause 3, especially as the limitation in the Theft Act according to which only convictions which occurred within the five years preceding the offence charged are admissible will not apply to the admissibility of convictions under the clause. We do not regard the fact that the provision was enacted so recently as a reason against repealing it, because it was enacted as part of the restatement of the law of theft which

---

[1] Clause 23. See paragraph 212.
[2] *Times*, 17th March 1972.

resulted from our 8th report and we made it clear in that report that the inclusion in the draft Bill annexed to it of the provision corresponding to s. 27(3) was subject to our consideration, on the present reference, of the desirability of preserving the provision[1].

CLAUSES 4–5: GIVING OF EVIDENCE BY ACCUSED

102. The accused may either give evidence on oath (or affirmation) or he may make an unsworn statement. In the latter case his evidence will not be subject to cross-examination. We mentioned early in the report[2] that it was not till the Criminal Evidence Act 1898 that the accused was able in all cases to give evidence on oath. The right to make an unsworn statement derives from the time when the accused was not allowed legal representation (except in misdemeanours), but for some years before 1898 the accused was allowed to make an unsworn statement about the facts whether or not he was legally represented. It might have been expected that, when the 1898 Act allowed him to give evidence on oath, it would have abolished the right to make an unsworn statement as no longer serving any useful purpose. Instead s. 1(h) expressly preserved the right. This was in keeping with the policy of the Act that pressure should not be put on the accused to take advantage of the new right to give evidence on oath—a policy to which effect was given by the provision in s. 1(b) that the failure of the accused to do so should not be made the subject of comment by the prosecution. As will be mentioned below[3], we think that the time has come to reverse this policy.

103. The legal status of an unsworn statement is that of a kind of inferior evidence—inferior in the sense that its value cannot be tested by cross-examination—to which the jury or magistrates' court may give such weight as they think fit[4]. The statement is made not from the witness box but from the dock. The practice of making an unsworn statement has declined. It is very seldom done now at trials on indictment, but it is still done sometimes in magistrates' courts. When it is done at a trial on indictment, this may be because the accused hopes that the jury will not appreciate the smaller value of the evidence. Moreover, if the accused has a criminal record, and wishes to make imputations against the character of the witnesses for the prosecution, it may be to his advantage to make an unsworn statement instead of giving evidence on oath; for in the latter case, but not the former, he will be liable to have his record brought out by the prosecution.

104. We are strongly of opinion that the right to make an unsworn statement about the facts instead of giving evidence on oath or affirmation should be abolished. Whatever justification there may have been for preserving the right in 1898, we think that nowadays the accused, if he gives evidence, should do so in the same way as other witnesses and be subject to cross-examination. It is not in the interests of justice that the accused should have the advantages, for what they may be worth, mentioned in paragraph 103. The present rule has another disadvantage in that, if the accused is unrepresented, the court should explain to him that he has the choice between giving evidence on oath or unsworn and the differences between these courses. Since in the great

---

[1] Cmnd. 2977, paragraph 158.
[2] Paragraph 21(iii).
[3] Paragraph 110.
[4] *Frost and Hale* (1964), 48 Cr. App. R. 284, 290–291.

majority of cases the accused, if he intends to give evidence, intends to do so on oath, the explanation is mostly unnecessary anyhow; and it has the practical disadvantage, in the case of an undefended person who is at all nervous, that just at the time when he has to make his defence and should be concentrating on this, he may be put off by the legal technicality of an invitation to consider doing something which he had no thought of doing. The persons and bodies whom we consulted[1] were almost unanimous in agreeing with our suggestion that the unsworn statement should be abolished, though a few expressed indifference because they thought the matter unimportant.

105. The necessary provision for this purpose is in clause 4(2). The subsection includes a provision saving the right of the accused, if not legally represented, to address the court or jury on any matter on which, if he had been legally represented, his counsel or solicitor could have done so on his behalf. This is only to ensure that the accused will be able to conduct his own defence in the ordinary way. The saving will not allow him to make statements of fact like a witness when addressing the court or jury as his own advocate. In practice it may be impossible for the court to prevent this altogether. But this is a difficulty inherent in any procedure which allows the accused to conduct his own defence; and if the accused is clearly abusing his right in this way, the court might think it right to check this by inviting him to go into the witness box and repeat on oath the statements of fact included in his speech.

106. The provision applies to committal proceedings as well as to trials on indictment and summary trials. In committal proceedings there is a complication in that Rule 4(7) and (8) of the Magistrates' Courts Rules 1968 provides that, after the completion of the case for the prosecution, the court shall ask the accused whether he wishes to say anything in answer to the charge and that whatever he says shall be put into writing. By subsection (4)—the only unrepealed provision—of s. 12 of the Criminal Justice Act 1925 (c. 86)[2] the statement may be " given in evidence " at the trial. This last provision seems curious in that it does not say what is to be the evidential effect of the statement. In *Morry*[3] the accused, who was a solicitor conducting his own defence, tried to take advantage of this procedure by making a speech lasting three hours and claimed that it should have all been taken down, presumably with a view to its being all read at the trial. The Court of Criminal Appeal held that the procedure was never intended for this purpose and that it was not necessary that every word which the accused said should be taken down. We think that the procedure may be a survival from the time when the jurisdiction of the justices was inquisitorial. In any event we see no reason for preserving it. We consider that in committal proceedings, as at trials, any statement which the accused may wish to make concerning the facts (as distinct from a submission to the court as to what they should decide) should be made on oath. We recommend therefore that, when the Magistrates' Courts Rules are being amended in accordance with our proposals (if adopted), Rule 4(7) and (8) should be amended accordingly or, if not required for any other purpose, revoked. Clause 4(7) repeals s. 12 of the Criminal Justice Act.

---

[1] Paragraph 9.
[2] As substituted by s. 131 of and Schedule 5 to the Magistrates' Courts Act 1952 (c. 55).
[3] (1945), 31 Cr. App. R. 19.

107. Clause 4(4) makes a minor change as to the order in which the accused should give evidence if other witnesses are called for the defence. In *Morrison*[1] counsel for the defence deferred calling the accused until after calling some alibi witnesses. When asked by Lord Alverstone C.J. in the Court of Criminal Appeal why he had done this, counsel argued that he had the right to do so and said, with what has been called " engaging frankness ", " Before calling the appellant I wished to know myself what these witnesses had to say "[2]. Lord Alverstone then said:

> " In all cases I consider it most important for the prisoner to be called before any of his witnesses. He ought to give his evidence before he has heard the evidence and cross-examination of any witness he is going to call ".

This statement of the law was reaffirmed by the Court of Appeal in *Smith*[3], though the court said that there were " rare exceptions, such as when a formal witness, or a witness about whom there is no controversy, is interposed before the accused person with the consent of the court in the special circumstances then prevailing ". The rule has however not always been obeyed, and some members of the committee question whether it is within the province of the courts, or right in policy, to impose any restriction on counsel for the defence as to the order in which he calls his witnesses. In civil cases there is no requirement that the parties should be called before their respective witnesses. Other members think that the rule is in general right because the interests of justice require that the accused should tell his story first and without having the advantage of being able to trim his evidence so as to accord with that of his witnesses. They argue that to allow the defence complete freedom in this respect would give it an advantage over the prosecution in that the witnesses for the prosecution are ordinarily kept out of court until they give their evidence whereas the accused must be in court all the time. The majority of the committee think that the rule is in general right, but all think that the rule (at least as stated in *Smith*) is too strict in confining the exceptional cases where the court may allow the defence to call other witnesses before the accused to cases of formal or uncontroversial evidence. They think that the court should be given a wider discretion. For example it may be convenient for the defence, and right on the merits, that a witness, perhaps the wife of the accused, who is to speak of some event which occurred before the events about which the accused is to give evidence should be allowed to do so before the accused is called. Clause 4(4), in accordance with this view, provides that the accused shall be called first " except in so far as the court in its discretion otherwise allows ".

108. One of the arguments adduced against the Bill for the Criminal Evidence Act 1898, which gave the accused the right in all cases to give evidence on oath, was that it was wrong that pressure should be put on him to do so. It was as a concession to this view that s. 1(*b*) prohibited the prosecution from commenting on the failure of the accused to give evidence. In fact the enactment of s. 1(*b*) was the result of an amendment moved by a private Member of Parliament at the committee stage in the House of Commons.

---

[1] (1911), 6 Cr. App. R. 159.
[2] At p. 165.
[3] (1968) 52 Cr. App. R. 224.

As at first moved the amendment would have forbidden comment by the judge as well. The Solicitor General (Sir R. Finlay) at first resisted the amendment altogether; but eventually he suggested that the prohibition should apply to the prosecution only because there were exceptional cases, " such as where the defence involved grievous reflections on the character of the prosecutor ", where it would be right for the judge to be able to comment. Sir R. Finlay thought that the limitation would show that it was only in " special circumstances " that comment should be made[1]. Just after the passing of the Act, counsel for the defence argued, in *Rhodes*[2], that the Act did not give the judge the right to comment; but this argument was naturally rejected by the Court for Crown Cases Reserved, when Lord Russell C.J. said that it was a " question entirely for the discretion of the judge " whether to comment[3]. But an unjustified or excessive comment can be the subject of appeal[4].

109. How far the judge can properly go in commenting on the failure of the accused to give evidence, and in particular in inviting the jury to draw adverse inferences against the accused from his failure to do so, is not altogether clear. In *Nodder* (1937) Swift J. began his summing up by reminding the jury that they had heard evidence from several witnesses as to where the murdered girl had been up to a certain time when the accused was with her but none from the accused, although he alone could have given evidence of where she was afterwards[5]. Nowadays comment is made much more sparingly. There even seems to be a tendency to stress the right of the accused not to give evidence[6], and, where the court does comment on his failure to do so, this is sometimes done almost apologetically. Yet it seems that the judge is in a much stronger position even under the present law, if he thinks fit, to invite the jury to draw an adverse inference from the failure of the accused to give evidence of some matter than he is to invite them to do so from failure to mention a matter when interrogated by the police. This is because, once a prima facie case has been made against him, it is clearly incumbent on the accused to rebut this by evidence if he can. In *Jackson*[7], Lord Goddard C.J., in giving the judgment of the Court of Criminal Appeal, said that " whatever may have been the position very soon after the Criminal Evidence Act 1898 came into operation...everybody now knows that absence from the witness-box requires a very considerable amount of explanation ". But the comment must not go so far as to suggest that failure to give evidence is enough to lead to an inference of guilt[8].

110. In our opinion the present law and practice are much too favourable to the defence. We are convinced that, when a prima facie case has been made against the accused, it should be regarded as incumbent on him to give evidence in all ordinary cases. We have no doubt that the prosecution should be

---

[1] Parliamentary Debates, 4th Series, Vol. 60, col. 662–674 (30th June 1898).
[2] [1899] 1 Q.B. 77.
[3] At p. 83.
[4] *Waugh v. R.*, [1950] A.C. 203. See paragraph 109.
[5] See Glanville Williams in " The Proof of Guilt ", 3rd edition, pp. 59–60.
[6] For example Devlin J. (as he then was) said in *Adams* (1957): " I hope that the day will never come when that right is denied to any Englishman "—an observation which, taken out of its context, has been much relied on by defending counsel as an excuse for omission to call the accused. See Glanville Williams in the passage immediately following the quotation in the previous footnote.
[7] (1953), 37 Cr. App. R. 43. 50.
[8] *Pratt* [1971] Crim. L.R. 234.

entitled, like the judge, to comment on his failure to do so. The present prohibition of comment seems to us wrong in principle and entirely illogical. Assuming that the point which might be made in commenting is valid, it must seem strange to the jury that the prosecution should not make it in their final speech; and if the judge then makes the point, he may seem like an extra prosecutor. Moreover, now that the final speech for the defence always comes after that for the prosecution, the defence will be in a position to make such reply as they can to comment by the prosecution. A few suggestions have been put to us that only the judge should be able to comment because the prosecution may not use enough discretion in doing so; but we do not think that this is a strong enough argument, especially when both the defence and the court will be able to put the matter in perspective. As to what may properly be included in a comment, we have no doubt that the same kinds of adverse inferences, such as common sense dictates, should be allowed to be drawn from the accused's failure to give evidence as those which we have proposed[1] should be allowed to be drawn from his failure to mention, when interrogated, a fact on which he intends to rely at his trial. In fact the argument for allowing this seems even stronger in the case of failure to give evidence. We would stress that our proposals depend on there being a prima facie case against the accused. Failure to give evidence may be of little or no significance if there is no case against him or only a weak one. But the stronger the case is, the more significant will be his failure to give evidence.

111. Similar considerations in our view apply to corroboration. At present the failure of the accused to give evidence is not allowed to be treated as corroboration[2]. We disagree with this rule. It seems to us clearly right that, when the prosecution have adduced sufficient evidence of a fact to be considered by the jury or magistrates' court, the failure of the accused to give evidence denying the fact should be capable of corroborating the evidence of it. Admittedly, if the case is one where corroboration is required by law and the prosecution have not enough corroborative evidence to adduce, they may be unable to start the proceedings, because they will not know whether the accused will or will not give evidence; but there may be other corroborative evidence, and failure to give evidence will add to this. In any event the question relates also to where corroboration, though desirable, is not required as a matter of law.

112. The changes which we propose in paragraphs 110 and 111 will, we hope, operate as a strong inducement to accused persons to give evidence. But we wish to go further still for this purpose. We propose that, once the court has decided that there is a case for the defence to answer (which the court is under a duty to consider even if the defence do not submit that there is no case), the court should tell the accused that he will be called on at the appropriate time to give evidence in his own defence and should tell him what the effect will be if he refuses to do so; and we propose that, when this time comes, the court should formally call on the accused to give evidence. The intimation by the court will leave the accused under no mistake as to what will be his position. This is particularly important if the accused is unrepresented. We think that the formal calling on the accused to give

---

[1] Clause 1.
[2] *Jackson* (1953), 37 Cr. App. R. 43 (mentioned in paragraph 109) at p. 48.

evidence, followed by his refusal, would have value in demonstrating to the jury or magistrates that the accused had the right, and obligation, to give evidence but declined to do so. Admittedly the introduction of these procedural requirements is not a necessary consequence of the proposed change in the law as to refusal to give evidence, and there is a risk that they may sometimes be overlooked; but our general opinion is that the value of the procedure will outweigh this objection.

113. The provisions for this purpose are in clause 5. The main provisions as to calling on the accused and the effect of his refusal to give evidence are in subsections (2) and (3). Apart from the fact that the suggested procedure will apply only where the court holds that there is a case for the accused to answer (subsection (1)(a)), we propose that there should be two exceptions. First, there is no need to tell the accused that he will be called on if he or his counsel or solicitor has already informed the court that he will give evidence (subsection (1)(b)), nor will it be necessary in this case to call on the accused formally to give evidence at the appropriate time. Second, the procedure will not apply if " it appears to the court that the physical or mental condition of the accused makes it undesirable for him to be called upon to give evidence " (subsection (1)(c)). The latter exception is to provide, in particular, for a case where there is a defence of insanity or diminished responsibility. In this case it would hardly ever be appropriate to comment adversely on the failure of the accused to give evidence. We propose that the provision as to the effect of refusing to be sworn should apply also to refusing without good cause to answer a particular question (subsection (3)(b)). The only cases where there will be a good cause will be (i) where the accused is entitled (under clause 6(1)) to refuse to answer a question about other misconduct which he has committed, (ii) where he is entitled to do so under any other enactment (for example his limited right under clause 15(2)(b) to refuse to answer on the ground that this might incriminate himself or his spouse, and the right of a person charged with the commission of an offence when he was aged twenty-one or over to refuse to answer a question, asked in breach of s. 16(2) of the Children and Young Persons Act 1963 (c. 37)[1], about an offence of which he was found guilty when under fourteen), (iii) where he is entitled to claim professional privilege (for communications with his solicitor) and (iv) where the court in its discretion excuses him from answering (for example, because the question is too oppressive). These cases are specified in subsection (5). In this connection we hope that, if the defence claim that the accused should not be called on to give evidence or to answer a particular question, and their claim depends on the ascertainment of any facts not already before the court, the court will require evidence to be given on oath in support of the claim. We stress this because sometimes counsel has been allowed to tell the jury of some fact said to justify the accused in not giving evidence. We think this is wrong and that any fact relied on in support of an objection should have to be proved by proper evidence. The right of the prosecution to comment on the accused's failure to give evidence will follow from the repeal, which we propose, of s. 1(b) of the 1898 Act.

---

[1] As to be amended by clause 46(2) of, and Schedule 1 to, the draft Bill.

CLAUSE 6: RESTRICTIONS ON CROSS-EXAMINATION OF ACCUSED

114. Clauses 6 and 7 of the draft Bill relate mostly to the extent to which the accused, if he gives evidence, may be cross-examined about misconduct other than the offence charged; but clause 7, which deals with the situation where the accused sets up his good character, applies where he does this by asking questions of other witnesses (for or against him) as well as where he gives the evidence himself. So far as concerns the giving of evidence by the accused himself, the matter is at present provided for by s. 1(f) of the Criminal Evidence Act 1898 (c. 36). For convenience this paragraph is quoted here, together with the closely related paragraph (e). The paragraphs run as follows:

" (e) A person charged and being a witness in pursuance of this Act may be asked any question in cross-examination notwithstanding that it would tend to criminate him as to the offence charged:

(f) A person charged and called as a witness in pursuance of this Act shall not be asked, and if asked shall not be required to answer, any question tending to show that he has committed or been convicted of or been charged with any offence other than that wherewith he is then charged, or is of bad character, unless—

(i) the proof that he has committed or been convicted of such other offence is admissible evidence to show that he is guilty of the offence wherewith he is then charged; or

(ii) he has personally or by his advocate asked questions of the witnesses for the prosecution with a view to establish his own good character, or has given evidence of his good character, or the nature or conduct of the defence is such as to involve imputations on the character of the prosecutor or the witnesses for the prosecution; or

(iii) he has given evidence against any other person charged with the same offence."

The draft Bill proposes to repeal these paragraphs and the greater part of the Act. The provisions corresponding to paragraph (f) are in clauses 6 and 7. The provision in paragraph (e), which takes away from the accused, if he gives evidence, the privilege against self-incrimination in respect of the offence charged, is dealt with in a later clause[1], but the paragraph is quoted here because it is linked with paragraph (f) in a way to be mentioned below[2].

115. When Parliament at last decided in 1898 to enable the accused to give evidence on oath in all cases, it had to decide how an accused person who had committed earlier offences, or was otherwise of bad character (in the ordinary sense of the word), should be treated if he gave evidence. There were, broadly, three possible courses[3]:

(i) He might be treated like an ordinary witness and so open to cross-examination about his other misconduct in order to show that his evidence should not be believed.

---

[1] Clause 15(2).
[2] Paragraphs 116–117.
[3] For convenience we refer to course (i) as the " ordinary witness " course, to course (ii) as the " full protection " course and to course (iii) as the " 1898 compromise ".

(ii) He might be protected from any cross-examination about misconduct otherwise inadmissible in evidence (unless he claimed to be of
good character) on the ground that to allow cross-examination on
this might be too prejudicial to a person in his position.

(iii) A compromise might be adopted.

S.1(f) adopted the compromise described below. Subject to a complication about
sub-paragraph (i) which will be mentioned[1], the accused is protected from
cross-examination about his previous misconduct unless (a) he claims to
be of good character, or (b) he makes imputations against the witnesses for the
prosecution, or (c) he gives evidence against another person charged with the
same offence. It is interesting to note that the 1898 compromise was adopted
only after a great deal of consideration. Bills to allow the accused to give
evidence had been introduced in one or other House of Parliament in many
years between 1877 and 1898. The first (1877) adopted the full protection
course. S. 523 of the draft code prepared by the Criminal Code Bill Commission in 1879 adopted the ordinary witness course, but with a proviso that
" so far as the cross-examination relates to the credit of the accused, the
court may limit such cross-examination to such extent as it thinks proper,
although the proposed cross-examination might be permissible in the case of
any other witness". Our own discussions have naturally centred on the choice
between these courses. We mention first some particular questions which
have arisen on paragraphs (e) and (f) of s. 1 of the 1898 Act and how we
propose that these matters should be dealt with in future[2]. We then discuss the
arguments for and against the various courses, ending this with the statement
of the majority's recommendation (a modification of the 1898 compromise)
and of objections to this by some members[3]. The construction of paragraphs
(e) and (f) has caused a good deal of difficulty over the years, and there have
been conflicting decisions. Difficulties on questions of detail are mentioned in
the notes on the provisions in the clauses which are intended to settle them
for the future.

116. There has been a total difference of judicial opinion on the fundamental
question of the relation between paragraphs (e) and (f). Eventually in *Jones v.
Director of Public Prosecutions*[4] the majority of the House of Lords (Viscount
Simonds, Lord Reid and Lord Morris of Borth-y-Gest) held that paragraph (e)
allows only questions tending directly to criminate the accused as to the
offence charged, and not questions tending to do so indirectly such as questions
about other misconduct of which evidence was admissible at common law.
That is to say, the question must relate directly to the offence charged, and it is
not enough that the other misconduct would have been admissible during the
case for the prosecution. On this view paragraph (f) allows questions which
tend indirectly to criminate the accused as to the offence charged, and questions
directed to his credibility as a witness, only if the case falls within one of the
three exceptions in paragraph (f). The minority (Lord Denning and Lord

---

[1] Paragraphs 116–117.
[2] Paragraphs 116–121.
[3] Paragraphs 122–131. We leave the questions on the provision in paragraph (f)(ii) as to
where the accused seeks to establish his own good character to the discussion of clause 7,
which deals with this situation.
[4] [1962] A.C. 635; 46 Cr. App. R. 129.

Devlin) considered that paragraph (e) allowed questions tending, whether directly or indirectly, to criminate the accused as to the offence charged and that paragraph (f) related only to questions directed to the credibility of the accused as a witness. The majority, however, held that the words "tending to show" in paragraph (f) meant tending to show for the first time, so that the prohibition in the paragraph would not be infringed if evidence of the conduct had already been given, whether by the accused himself (as happened in the case in question) or (when this was admissible at common law) by the prosecution. The minority disagreed with this view and considered that "tending to show" meant tending to show when regarded in isolation. The result was that all five members of the House of Lords held that the disputed question was admissible, but for different reasons.

117. Having regard to the difficulty which the 1898 Act caused in *Jones* it is clearly desirable to make fresh provision. We propose that the Bill should restate the law on both the points mentioned above in accordance with what we regard as the right policy. On the question of the relation between paragraphs (e) and (f) we have no doubt that the minority view gives the right result. We therefore propose that the accused, if he gives evidence, should be open to cross-examination about any misconduct of which evidence would have been admissible (in particular, under clause 3) during the case for the prosecution. On the question of "tending to show" in paragraph (f), we adopt the majority view, so that cross-examination of the accused about his misconduct will not be forbidden if the misconduct has already been mentioned at the trial. This result is secured by the combination of subsections (1) and (2) of clause 6. Subsection (1) contains the general prohibition of cross-examination "tending to reveal to the court or jury" the fact that the accused has committed other misconduct; subsection (2) removes the prohibition in relation to misconduct which is admissible in evidence as mentioned[1].

118. The construction of the word "character" in paragraph (f) (where it is used four times) has given a good deal of difficulty. For the purpose of the common law rules as to evidence of character the word means general reputation and not disposition[2]; but there has been much argument as to whether the word bears this meaning in paragraph (f). In *Stirland v. Director of Public Prosecutions*[3] Viscount Simon L.C., in a speech with which the other law lords concurred, expressed the view that in the term "good character" in the paragraph both the conception of good reputation and that of real disposition were "combined". This view is generally accepted, but in *Jones* (mentioned in paragraph 116) Lord Devlin expressed the view that the framers of the 1898 Act intended the word to have the meaning of "reputation"[4] and that the matter had still to be decided by the House of Lords[5]. The latest case in the House of Lords, *Selvey v. Director of Public Prosecutions*[6], seems still to leave the point open. We think that this ambiguity must be got rid of,

---

[1] Subsection (3) contains a provision, analogous to subsection (2), to remove the prohibition in relation to misconduct of one accused which is admissible on behalf of a co-accused for the purpose of showing that the latter is not guilty of an offence with which he is charged.
[2] *Rowton* (1865), Le. & Ca. 520.
[3] [1944] A.C. 315, 324–325; 30 Cr. App. R. 40, 52.
[4] [1962] A.C. at p. 699; 46 Cr. App. R. at p. 194.
[5] Ibid. at p. 709; p. 206.
[6] [1970] A.C. 304; 52 Cr. App. R. 443.

and we propose to drop the word " character " altogether and to say instead " disposition ", " reputation " or " credibility " (as a witness) according to the sense required in each case[1].

119. The provision in paragraph (f)(ii) that the accused is liable to be cross-examined about his other misconduct if " the nature or conduct of the defence is such as to involve imputations on the character of the prosecutor or the witnesses for the prosecution " has caused difficulty in cases where the making of imputations is a necessary part of the defence. It has been argued that this has the effect of depriving the accused of the protection given by the paragraph. This applies in particular where the defence is that on the occasion in question the accused was only defending himself against an assault by the prosecutor, as in *Brown*[2], or where he alleges indecent approaches by the prosecutor, as in *Flynn*[3] and *Selvey*[4]. Another kind of case is where the accused alleges that the police obtained a confession from him by a threat, as in *Cook*[5]. For a time a solution of this difficulty was provided by the discretion of the court to disallow the cross-examination. The practice is that the prosecution should seek the court's permission before cross-examining the accused as allowed by the paragraph, and the doctrine, stated by the Court of Criminal Appeal in *Flynn*, was that in a case where the imputation was a necessary part of the defence the court should in general exercise its discretion so as to disallow the cross-examination. But in *Selvey* the House of Lords held firmly that the wording of the paragraph was inconsistent with the existence of any such general doctrine[6]. Inevitably the courts have not attempted to give a complete definition of "imputations", though *Selvey* confirms the tendency of previous cases to treat an attack on the witnesses for the prosecution which is really only an emphatic denial of the charge as not coming within the paragraph. The case also confirms the decision of the Court of Criminal Appeal in *Turner*[7] that in a case of rape the defence of consent is not within the paragraph. The House of Lords regarded this case as *sui generis* (though it is difficult to see on what principle an exception can be read into the paragraph for one class of case where the defence necessarily involves an imputation on a witness for the prosecution).

120. The authorities are consistently to the effect that the purpose of cross-examination allowed by paragraph (f)(ii) is to show that the evidence given by the accused should not be believed[8], and there have been many statements in judgments to the effect that it is in the public interest that, where there is a conflict of evidence between the prosecution and the defence, and the defence make imputations against a witness for the prosecution, the jury or magistrates' court should know what kind of a person the accused is in order to enable them to judge whom to believe. This point was stressed by the Court of Appeal in *Sargvon*[9], and also in *Selvey* mentioned above[10]. But it is difficult

---

[1] In this we have adopted a suggestion made to us by Lord Devlin himself.
[2] (1960), 44 Cr. App. R. 181.
[3] [1963] 1 Q.B. 729; 45 Cr. App. R. 268.
[4] Mentioned in paragraph 118.
[5] [1959] 2 Q.B. 340; 43 Cr. App. R. 138.
[6] They also rejected an argument by the prosecution that there was no discretion at all to disallow cross-examination allowed by sub-paragraph (ii).
[7] [1944] K.B. 463; 30 Cr. App. R. 9.
[8] This was recently restated by the Court of Appeal in *Vickers*, [1972] Crim. L.R. 101.
[9] (1967), 51 Cr. App. R. 394.
[10] Paragraphs 118, 119.

to see how this purpose was served in *Morris*[1]. The accused appealed against a conviction of sexual intercourse with his stepdaughter aged eleven. At the trial the defence cross-examined the girl suggesting that she had stolen and had had sexual intercourse, and they cross-examined her mother suggesting that she had committed adultery. Because of this the judge allowed the prosecution to cross-examine the accused about a conviction of dishonesty. The Court of Criminal Appeal held that this was rightly allowed. There seems to have been no suggestion in the case that the accused's dishonesty was irrelevant to the question of his credibility (or his disposition). Whether it is sound in policy to allow cross-examination on the principle mentioned above, and in particular whether it is possible to treat the accused's misconduct as showing that he is not a person to be believed but not as showing also that he is a person likely from his criminal disposition to have committed the offence, are questions about which there has been much argument in and out of the committee. Some have argued strongly that the distinction is quite unreal and unlikely to be understood by a jury. However, the majority of the committee think that the distinction is a genuine one which can be applied in practice and, as will be mentioned, propose to make it the basis of the provision to replace this part of s. 1(f) of the 1898 Act.

121. The provision in s. 1(f)(iii) of the 1898 Act[2] allowing cross-examination of the accused about his other misconduct if he gives evidence against a person charged with the same offence has not given rise to anything like the same difficulty as the provision as to imputations; but it raises one important question of policy. In *Murdoch v. Taylor*[3] the House of Lords decided (upholding previous authorities) that the court has no discretion to prevent one co-accused from cross-examining another under this sub-paragraph (though it has a discretion to prevent the prosecution from doing so). The argument is that, if one of the accused gives evidence against another, he is, so far as the latter is concerned, to be treated as a witness for the prosecution and therefore open to cross-examination on his misconduct in order to show that he should not be believed. We discuss this below[4]; but we do not propose to alter the rule that there is no discretion to disallow the cross-examination, and we propose to restate the rule with a minor modification to be mentioned.

122. Leaving aside the situation where the accused sets up his own good character, and the situation where one co-accused gives evidence against another, the essential question, in choosing between the courses mentioned in paragraph 115, is whether it is right to keep in some form the provision in s. 1(f)(ii) of the 1898 Act that the accused is liable to cross-examination about his other misconduct if he makes " imputations on the character of the prosecutor or the witnesses for the prosecution ". This question has caused a sharp division of opinion in our discussions. The considerations summarized above[5] about the advantages and disadvantages of allowing evidence of other misconduct of the accused are in·general relevant here. In order to indicate the special problems involved in the rule about imputations, we set out next

---

[1] (1959), 43 Cr. App. R. 206.
[2] Quoted in paragraph 114.
[3] [1965] A.C. 574; 49 Cr. App. R. 119.
[4] Paragraph 132.
[5] Paragraphs 72–77. Paragraph 77 (referring briefly to the position of the accused as a witness) is specially relevant.

the arguments which have been put forward against the present rule allowing the accused to be cross-examined about his misconduct because he makes imputations[1], followed by the arguments put forward in favour of allowing this[2].

123. The arguments put forward against the present rule allowing the accused to be cross-examined about his misconduct, other than that involved in the offence charged, because he makes imputations against witnesses for the prosecution may be summarized in this way:

(i) When the law has drawn the line as to what evidence of other misconduct should be admissible during the case for the prosecution, it is entirely wrong that the line should be redrawn if the accused attacks the witnesses for the prosecution. For if relevant evidence is excluded during the case for the prosecution because it may be too prejudicial to the accused, it does not become any less prejudicial because the accused attacks the witnesses for the prosecution. Therefore the imputations rule is merely a case of tit for tat—penalizing the accused for the imputation by exposing him to admittedly prejudicial evidence. Whether or not it is right that there should be any special sanction to discourage a person being tried for an offence from making false imputations against the witnesses for the prosecution, the sanction should not be one which may well make it more likely that he will be convicted of the offence. Moreover the sanction applies whether or not the imputation is a necessary part of the accused's defence and even if it is perfectly true; and in the latter event the accused is doing nothing wrong in making the imputation[3].

(ii) If a witness for the prosecution is vulnerable to attack in respect of his conduct in a way which is relevant to an issue in the case or to his credibility as a witness, then it is wrong that the jury or magistrates' court should be left with the impression that he is a respectable and reliable witness. The interests of justice require that the accused should be free to bring out any matter which is material to the decision.

(iii) The law attaches great importance to allowing parties to legal proceedings freedom of speech in court. It is for this reason that the parties and witnesses are accorded absolute privilege in the law of defamation, which means that they can with impunity say things that are deliberately false and malicious. The reason is the paramount importance of not subjecting the parties and witnesses to any fear of consequences in respect of what they may say during the trial. This principle is here abandoned, but only for the accused in a criminal case, and only by way of imposing upon him the very questionable sanction above mentioned.

(iv) The rule involves at least two anomalies. First, if the accused makes an imputation against a person who was concerned in the events in

---

[1] Paragraph 123.
[2] Paragraph 124.
[3] This objection is further developed by the minority who oppose the proposed compromise: see paragraph 130(i).

question but who for some reason is not called as a witness (perhaps because he has since died or is too ill to be called), then, although there is no material difference between this situation and the situation where the person in question is called as a witness, the accused is not open to cross-examination under the rule. Second, there is the anomaly mentioned above[1] that the rule does not apply in a case of rape where the defence is one of consent.

(v) It is wrong that the admissibility of evidence, in so important a matter as this, should depend on the tactics of the defence. The legal advisers of the accused are in the invidious situation of having to choose between leaving the jury or magistrates' court in ignorance of the facts behind the evidence given by prosecution witnesses (facts that may greatly impair that evidence) and allowing the prosecution to introduce prejudicial evidence of the accused's convictions. Whether the accused is convicted or not may depend on the way in which this choice is made, but it is not one that legal advisers should be called on to make. A rule that operates in this way turns the criminal trial into a kind of game. In fact prisoners from time to time complain to the Home Office that they were wrongly convicted because they had to refrain from mentioning some matter, such as the fabrication of evidence, which their solicitors had advised them it would be too dangerous to bring out at the trial because this would result in their being cross-examined about their criminal records.

124. The arguments put forward for preserving, in some form at least, the rule about imputations may be summarized in this way:

(i) It is right, and in accordance with the interests of justice, that, where there is a conflict between the evidence of the accused and that of a witness for the prosecution, *and the accused attacks the witness*, the jury or magistrates' court, when deciding whom to believe, should know what kind of person the accused, as well as the witness, is[2].

(ii) The protection given to the accused by the Act by which he is in general immune from cross-examination about his other misconduct amounts to putting him, as a witness, in a more favourable position than other witnesses and therefore goes beyond what the interests of justice require. It is therefore reasonable—and not contrary to the interests of justice—that the accused should lose this protection. at least in some cases, if he attacks the witnesses for the prosecution.

(iii) If one accepts that it is not contrary to the interests of justice to deprive the accused of the protection in some circumstances, the fact that he attacks the witnesses for the prosecution is a circumstance justifying this, because it is contrary to the public interest that these witnesses should be exposed to what may be wholly unjustifiable attacks without the prosecution's being able to show from the accused's record whether he is likely to be telling the truth in making the attacks. It is pointed out that accused persons, if they have no real defence, often invent the most disgraceful stories about the police or

---

[1] Paragraph 119.
[2] This point has been made in many reported cases as mentioned in paragraph 120. For criticism by supporters of the full protection course see paragraph 130(ii).

other witnesses for the prosecution without the slightest justification and in the hope of causing the jury to have just enough doubt about the evidence for the prosecution to compel them to acquit. The police are often accused of inventing confessions, using violence, manufacturing evidence and other misconduct. Witnesses other than policemen are also often made the subject of damaging imputations. For example, it is not uncommon for a person charged with robbery to accuse the victim of having made indecent approaches to him. Witnesses for the prosecution would have a legitimate grievance if they had to listen to attacks of this kind, knowing that the prosecution were not free to show what kind of person the attacker was. This is particularly important for ordinary people, who might be more reluctant to come forward to give evidence on these terms. Opponents of the rule dispute this argument, as mentioned above[1], on the ground that objectionable methods of defence ought not to be punished by the admission of prejudicial evidence and that in any event the imputations may be true; but supporters of the rule argue that the importance, in the public interest, of checking abuses of the kind mentioned in this sub-paragraph is so great that the present sanction, which is the only practicable one, should in general be maintained.

(iv) To enable accused persons to attack the witnesses for the prosecution with impunity would alter the balance of criminal trials in favour of the defence in a way which would be dangerous, as well as being unacceptable to public opinion.

125. Members' views on whether to adopt one of the three courses mentioned above[2] (the "ordinary witness" course, the "full protection" course and the "1898 compromise"), or some other course, depend on their views of the validity and strength of the arguments summarized in the two previous paragraphs and, generally, on their views as to the extent to which evidence of the previous misconduct of the accused should be admissible. The majority support the 1898 compromise, but with an important modification, in favour of the defence, as mentioned below[3]. A minority who regard it as wholly unacceptable that evidence of misconduct by the accused which is inadmissible during the main part of the case for the prosecution should become admissible because the accused gives evidence (without claiming to be of good "character") naturally adopt the full protection course.

126. Another minority favour the ordinary witness course. They do so mainly on the general ground that it is right that the accused, if he gives evidence, should be treated like other witnesses so far as evidence of previous misconduct is concerned. This course, its supporters argue, is the one which would best conduce to the obviously desirable object that as much relevant evidence as possible should be before the court; in particular, where the issue depends on whether the evidence of a witness for the prosecution or that of the accused should be believed, the court or jury would no longer be in the dark on the important question of which witness is the more likely, from his

---

[1] Paragraph 123(i). Cf. paragraph 130(i).
[2] Paragraph 115.
[3] Paragraph 128.

past conduct, to be telling the truth. If the accused gives evidence (as he will be under pressure to do owing to clause 5), this course would have the beneficial effect that there would be nothing to restrain the defence from bringing out anything about the witnesses for the prosecution which ought, in the interests of justice, to be before the court or jury in order to enable them to estimate the value of the witnesses' evidence. The defence would no longer have to weigh the relative advantages of bringing out this matter and of concealing the accused's record. It is true that there would be nothing special to restrain the defence from making unfounded imputations against the witnesses; but this, in the opinion of those who support this course (like that of those who support the full protection course) is not a matter against which it is right to seek to provide by means of the law of evidence. Supporters of the ordinary witness course would be content not to widen the admissibility of evidence of other misconduct during the case for the prosecution, but they think it fairer that matter detrimental to the accused and inadmissible under the present law should not be brought out until the accused gives evidence (and even then only if it seems to the prosecution—and to the court—that the interests of justice require that the matter should be brought out). This procedure would enable the defence to bring out the matter in question in examination in chief in such a way as to present it in the least possible unfavourable light. On this view the jury or magistates' court would judge the evidence for the prosecution without having in mind the possibility that the accused had a bad record; and it would be only after it was decided that the evidence for the prosecution, regarded by itself, made out a case for the defence to answer that it would be permissible to adduce extra evidence of the accused's previous misconduct. This course would have the desirable result that, if the accused gave evidence, his position in relation to cross-examination about his other misconduct would be the same in all circumstances regardless of how he had conducted his defence and, in particular, that there would be no difference in this respect between the positions of two or more persons tried together. The course would also avoid the two anomalies mentioned above in relation to the present law[1] and the dilemma which confronts supporters of the other courses as to whether the court should have a discretion to prevent one co-accused from cross-examining another co-accused about his misconduct if the latter gives evidence against the former[2]. In addition to the advantages mentioned, the course would have the great advantage of simplicity.

127. But the majority are opposed to the ordinary witness course. Their basic objection is that they do not accept the proposition underlying this scheme—that the accused, if he gives evidence, should in all cases be treated exactly like an ordinary witness for the purpose of testing his credibility. The majority have also two particular reasons for opposing this course:

(i) They do not think that the fact that the accused gives evidence is sufficient (irrespective of the evidence he gives) to justify making admissible misconduct which is not admissible during the case for the prosecution. Although the majority accept the principle that the making of imputations against witnesses for the prosecution should

[1] Paragraph 123(iv).
[2] Paragraph 132.

in certain circumstances expose the accused, if he gives evidence, to cross-examination, for the purpose of testing his credibility as a witness, to which ordinary witnesses are subject[1], it is generally considered that it would be too prejudicial to allow cross-examination for this purpose in all cases where the accused gives evidence[2].

(ii) It is argued that the course would discourage accused persons from giving evidence and so frustrate the purpose of clause 5 that they should always do so if a prima facie case has been made out. The ordinary witness course is in accordance with the law in Canada and the United States. Opinions·differ as to the extent to which the rule operates there to deter accused persons from giving evidence, but there is no doubt that it does deter them in a great many cases. Many of the committee are convinced that to adopt the ordinary witness course would be inconsistent with the policy of clause 5, because the justification for clause 5 is that the accused, if innocent, should be willing to give evidence and face cross-examination on the facts, whereas, if the ordinary witness course were adopted, the reason why a person with a criminal record would be unwilling to give evidence might be not that he feared cross-examination about the facts but that he feared cross-examination about his record. (Supporters of the course urge, in reply, that in practice an innocent person would never be deterred from giving evidence for fear of having his record brought out, and that the real reason why a person did not give evidence, if a prima facie case was made out, would be much more likely to be that he had no real defence but hoped that the prosecution would fail for some reason other than the merits of the case.)

128. Our views on the question of imputations have, as already mentioned, remained irreconcilable. We eventually decided, by a majority, to recommend that, if none of the courses discussed above is found acceptable in policy, a suitable compromise would be to relax the present law in one respect in favour of the defence. Under the proposed compromise the present rule that the making of imputations against a witness for the prosecution allows the accused to be cross-examined about his other misconduct would be preserved in general but would be limited to where the " main purpose " of the imputation is " to raise an issue as to the witness's credibility ". It is also proposed that the court should not permit the accused to be asked a question in cross-examination about his misconduct unless of opinion that the question is " relevant to his credibility as a witness ". The essence of the scheme is that the main purpose of the attack by the defence on the witness for the prosecution must be to shake his credibility as a witness. Therefore, if the attack is

---

[1] See paragraph 124(i).

[2] Supporters of the ordinary witness course do not accept the view that evidence of other misconduct of the accused, when admissible in cross-examination, should be regarded as going only to his credibility as a witness, as it has to be regarded under the present law and as the majority hold that it should continue to be regarded under the proposed compromise (see paragraph 120). In their opinion all such evidence should be regarded both for this purpose and also for the purpose of showing whether the accused is more likely, because of his disposition, to have committed the offence charged. This view runs counter to that of the majority that no misconduct should be admissible for the latter purpose which is not admissible during the case for the prosecution.

necessary in order to put forward the defence, it will not expose the accused to any cross-examination to which he would not otherwise be exposed. For example, the scheme will enable a person charged with an assault to put forward with impunity the defence that the alleged victim himself attacked the accused and that the latter acted in self-defence[1]. Again, it will enable the accused to say that a policeman to whom he made a confession extorted it by violence or that a policeman " planted " some object on him, because in either case the object will be not merely to show that the witness is lying but will be to rebut the evidence for the prosecution. In each case it will be for the court to decide what is the " main purpose " of the imputation. The requirement that the proposed cross-examination should be relevant to the accused's credibility is a natural corollary of the requirement that the main purpose of the imputation should be directed to the credibility of the witness for the prosecution. The provisions for the proposed compromise are in clause 6(4).

129. The proposed compromise, in the opinion of the majority, represents a reasonable balance between the considerations for and against the present rule as summarized in paragraphs 123 and 124. Stated broadly, the principle underlying the proposed compromise is this. When the accused gives evidence, and the finding on an issue in the case depends on whether his evidence or that of a witness for the prosecution should be believed, it is in principle absurd that the witness and the accused should not each be subject to cross-examination about any misconduct which is relevant to his credibility as a witness. In the case of an accused with a criminal record the proposed compromise stomachs this by giving him a choice whether there shall or shall not be cross-examination to credit. What the majority do not accept is that a prosecution witness giving evidence on an issue concerning the accused's guilt or innocence should be subject to cross-examination to credit but that the accused, when he gives evidence on the issue, should not be subject to such cross-examination also. The justification for basing the provision on credibility depends on the view accepted by the majority, as mentioned above[2], that there is a real difference between bringing out the accused's misconduct for the purpose of discrediting him as a witness and bringing it out in order to show that he is likely, from his conduct, to have committed the offence. As mentioned, this is the view taken by the courts of the purpose of the cross-examination of the accused permitted by the present law, and this seems to the majority of the committee to justify preserving the principle.

130. The minority who favour the full protection course remain strongly opposed to the proposed compromise. It has the advantage, from their point of view, of curtailing the extent to which cross-examination of the accused to credit is allowed under the present law. But it still allows such cross-examination, and is open to all the objections to the present rule set out in paragraph 123 except that it gets rid of the second anomaly referred to in sub-paragraph (iv). In addition, the minority have put forward the following specific objections to the proposed compromise:

---

[1] For example, as in *Brown*, mentioned in paragraph 119. The fact that this defence cannot be put forward without letting in evidence of previous misconduct is probably the greatest difficulty under the present law for an accused with a criminal record.
[2] Paragraph 120.

(i) The majority agree that the prosecution should not be allowed to prove the accused's guilt by showing that he has committed other offences or is a shifty and untrustworthy person. Nor is he to be normally open to cross-examination to credit on these lines, because there is too great a danger that the jury may take account of the matter brought out as if it were relevant directly to the issue whereas its direct relevance is to the credibility of the accused in denying the charge. The point is, of course, that even a person who is utterly untrustworthy may be innocent of the offence charged against him. However, the majority propose that this line of cross-examination should be permissible if the accused attacks the credit of a prosecution witness (or that of a witness for a co-accused). This proposal can be justified only on the supposition that there is something wrong in the accused's behaving like this; but in fact the cross-examination may be perfectly proper, and of high importance[1]. Prima facie the prosecution witnesses speak as impartial witnesses to the truth; but the accused may wish to say, and be in a position to prove, that a witness has been convicted of perjury, or is a confidence trickster, or is a prostitute who is likely to want to stand well with the police. It seems to the minority to be altogether wrong that if he does this he should be subject to a line of cross-examination that is admitted to be prejudicial and is normally disallowed for that reason. The objection applies whether or not the cross-examination relates to an offence similar to that charged. For example, if the accused is charged with a sexual offence and gives evidence attacking the character of prosecution witnesses, he can (under the present law and under the majority's proposal) be cross-examined on his previous convictions for theft[2]. Equally, if the charge is for theft, he can be cross-examined on previous convictions for theft. The minority hold that in either case the cross-examination should be excluded, being either insufficiently relevant or too prejudicial.

(ii) The majority's recommendation seems to be based on the proposition that witnesses for the prosecution and the accused when giving evidence should be treated as on a par in respect of cross-examination to credit (though only when the accused's line of defence involves an attack on a prosecution witness)[3]. But there is a great difference. The issue before the court is whether the accused is guilty of the offence charged, and the credibility of witnesses is important only as bearing on this. As said before, the credibility of the witness for the prosecution is most material. But the credibility of the accused has not the same importance, because what the accused says in his own defence is naturally suspect in any case. What is important is not the accused's bare assertion but the extent to which his version of the facts may cast doubt upon the prosecution's version. It helps very little, in arriving at a just conclusion, to know that the accused is a

---

[1] The majority recognize that the imputation may be necessary for the defence and may be true (paragraph 123(i)). They justify the proposed compromise on the view that there should be cross-examination to credit for both sides or neither at the choice of the defence (paragraph 129).

[2] *Morris*, referred to in paragraph 120.

[3] See paragraph 124(i).

habitual liar, because in the circumstances in which he is placed even a normally honest person would be strongly tempted to lie, and would quite possibly do so[1].

(iii) If the accused does not give evidence, his counsel may with impunity cross-examine the prosecution witness to credit[2]. The sanction against it proposed by the majority operates only if the accused gives evidence. But the effect of clause 5 of the draft Bill will be to put great pressure on the accused to give evidence. If this virtually compels him to give evidence (in order to avoid the comment that may otherwise be made), he becomes open to prejudicial cross-examination by reason of the line of cross-examination previously undertaken by his counsel. The committee's other proposal will therefore increase the risk of injustice to the accused in the present connection.

(iv) At present the working of the law is ameliorated by the fact that the prosecution may themselves put in evidence the facts adverse to their witness's credit in order to save the accused from having to do so, or may refrain from exercising their right to retaliate if the accused does so. If the compromise proposal is now enacted after a full discussion of policy, the prosecution may feel that they are entitled to exercise their rights to the full, so that the position of the accused may sometimes be worse than it has been previously. In any case, it is not proper that the accused's protection should depend upon the good will of the legal advisers for the prosecution.

131. Since the principle underlying the proposed compromise is that the cross-examination must be relevant to the accused's credibility as a witness, it follows that, if he makes the imputation against a witness for the prosecution but does not himself give evidence, it will not be possible for the prosecution to adduce evidence of his other misconduct even for the purpose of showing that the witness against whom the imputation is made is likely to be telling the truth. This is in accordance with the 1898 Act, as exemplified in *Butterwasser*[3]. To many it is highly objectionable that the accused should be able to do this with impunity. The present rule also makes possible a particular abuse where there are two accused, A and B, and A has a bad record and B none. B makes the attack on the witnesses for the prosecution for the benefit of both A and himself, but A cannot be cross-examined on his record. We should have liked to find a way of preventing this abuse, and that exemplified in *Butterwasser*, but it is impossible to do so consistently with the principle that the purpose of the cross-examination is to show whether the witness attacked or the attacker is more likely to be telling the truth. The device employed in *Butterwasser* will, we hope, be effectually discouraged by the pressure which will be put on accused persons to give evidence by clause 5. For a reason similar to that mentioned above clause 6(4) does not reproduce the provision in s. 1(*f*)(ii) of

---

[1] The majority who support the proposed compromise do not agree with the argument in this sub-paragraph. While they do not contend that the accused, when giving evidence, should be regarded as altogether on a par with other witnesses (see paragraph 127), they are nevertheless convinced that cross-examination of the accused to credit is ordinarily likely to be helpful for the discovery of the truth and that juries (suitably directed) and magistrates can be relied on to appreciate that lying is not conclusive proof of guilt.
[2] See paragraph 131.
[3] [1948] 1 K.B. 4; 32 Cr. App. R. 81.

the 1898 Act allowing the cross-examination if the imputation is made against " the prosecutor " as distinct from " the witnesses for the prosecution "; but this is unimportant, as " the prosecutor " will nearly always give evidence. The subsection does, however, extend the rule to where the imputation is made against a witness for a person jointly charged with the person who makes the imputation. This seems a reasonable extension and justified on the principle on which the clause is based. The effect of the clause will be that, whether the imputation is made against a witness for the prosecution or against a witness for the co-accused (A), both the prosecution and A will be able to cross-examine the accused (B) who makes the imputation. This seems to us clearly right[1]. In particular the fact that the prosecution may have refrained from cross-examining B should not prevent A from cross-examining him, especially if the witness against whom the imputation is made is more favourable to A than to B.

132. The main question on s. 1(f)(iii) of the 1898 Act[2] is whether it is right to preserve the rule stated in *Murdoch v. Taylor*[3] that the court has no discretion to prevent one co-accused from cross-examining the other about the latter's misconduct if the latter gives evidence against the former. This situation presents a dilemma for all except those who favour the ordinary witness course, because for those who do not there is a choice between two evils. In favour of the present rule is the strong argument, relied on in *Murdoch v. Taylor*, that the accused (B) who gives evidence against the other (A) becomes, from A's point of view, like a witness for the prosecution and that A would certainly have a grievance if he were convicted on the evidence of a person (B) whom he was not allowed to question in order to show that he was so bad a person that his evidence should not be relied on. On the other hand there might be a case for giving a discretion to the court in order to enable it to do justice, as far as possible, in a case where A has, say, only one relevant conviction and B has twenty. Suppose A has given evidence that B committed the offence. B cross-examines A in order to show that A committed the offence and puts A's single conviction to him. B may then refuse to give evidence himself, in spite of clause 5, but may call witnesses to say that A committed the offence. A cannot put B's record to him, and it might be thought fairer that the court should be able to redress the balance by forbidding B to question A about his conviction. But the majority think that the present rule should be preserved as the lesser of two evils, because they think it unacceptable that it should be possible to prevent an accused person from bringing out the misconduct of another accused who has given evidence against him. In particular, they think it unsound to make the matter one of discretion, because this might lead to too much difference in the way in which the discretion was exercised. For different judges might take different views on the general question which of the two evils mentioned was the lesser one. Therefore subsection (5) preserves the present rule in the 1898 Act with a minor change. This is that the subsection applies whenever the two accused are jointly tried and does not require, as does the 1898 Act, that they should be charged with the same offence. The present rule has caused difficulty in cases where two persons are

---

[1] Whether the 1898 Act allows A to cross-examine B because B makes imputations against a witness for the prosecution was left open by the Court of Appeal in *Russell*, [1971] 1 Q.B. 151, 153 A-C, 155 D-E; 55 Cr. App. R. 23, 27–28, 31.
[2] Quoted in paragraph 114 and referred to in paragraph 121.
[3] See paragraph 121.

charged with offences arising out of the same transaction or series of transactions, as in *Roberts*[1] and *Russell*[2]. We see no reason why the rule should not apply to all cases where the accused are tried together.

CLAUSE 7: ADMISSIBILITY OF EVIDENCE AND QUESTIONS ABOUT ACCUSED'S DISPOSITION OR REPUTATION

133. S. 1(*f*)(ii) of the Criminal Evidence Act 1898[3] takes away the accused's immunity from cross-examination about his other misconduct if the accused " has personally or by his advocate asked questions of the witnesses for the prosecution with a view to establish his own good character, or has given evidence of his good character.. ". Also, if without giving evidence himself he calls a witness, or questions a witness for the prosecution, in order to establish his good character, the prosecution may by common law call evidence to refute his claim. It is clear that the prosecution should be able to do this, because the accused must not be allowed to claim a character to which he is not entitled. The only question for us is whether the rule is right in detail. On this a few questions have arisen of which the more important are referred to in paragraphs 134 and 135 and the others in the note on clause 7, which contains the new provision to deal with this matter.

134. As mentioned previously[4], it was held in *Rowton*[5] that the meaning of " character " for the purpose of the common law rule as to claims to be of good character is general reputation. This rule was criticized by Sir Fitzjames Stephen[6] because—

> " a witness may with perfect truth swear that a man, who to his knowledge has been a receiver of stolen goods for years, has an excellent character for honesty, if he has the good luck to conceal his crimes from his neighbours ".

The rule seems to be persistently ignored in practice, but Lord Goddard C.J. criticized this laxity in *Butterwasser*[7], when he said[8]:

> " Evidence of character nowadays is very loosely given and received, and it would be as well if all courts paid attention to a well-known case in the Court of Crown Cases Reserved, *Reg. v. Rowton*, in which a court of twelve judges laid down the principles which should govern the giving

---

[1] (1936), 25 Cr. App. R. 158.
[2] [1971] 1 Q.B. 151. The case is mentioned in a different connection in n. 1 on paragraph 131 (p. 84).
[3] Quoted in paragraph 114.
[4] Paragraph 118.
[5] (1865), Le. & C. 520.
[6] " Digest of the Law of Evidence " (12th edition) p. 201.
[7] Referred to in paragraph 131.
[8] [1948] 1 K.B. at p. 6; 32 Cr. App. R. at p. 85.

of evidence of character and of evidence in rebuttal of bad character. It was pointed out that the evidence must be evidence of general reputation and not dependent upon particular acts or actions ".

Since s. 1(*f*)(ii) of the 1898 Act applies to the situation where the accused has exercised his common law right to set up good character, one would suppose that "character" has the same meaning in that Act; but in any event we are satisfied that the rule should apply both to reputation and to disposition; and in the replacement of this part of s. 1(*f*)(ii) by clause 7, as in clause 6[1], we refer to "disposition or reputation" instead of "character".

135. There is an important question as to what should count as claiming to be of "good character" for the purpose of the rule. At present a person is treated as setting up his good character not only when he expressly claims this but also when he tries to achieve the same effect indirectly by evidence suggesting that he is a respectable person. For example, in *Coulman*[2] Swift J., during the argument in the Court of Criminal Appeal, gave as an instance of setting up character that of asking a man "whether he is a married man with a family, in regular work, and has a wife and three children". But the ingenuity of modern criminals has developed a practice of giving the impression that the criminal is a respectable person while avoiding taking any course which clearly enables the court to hold that the accused "has personally or by his advocate asked questions of witnesses for the prosecution with a view to establish his own good character, or has given evidence of his good character" within the meaning of paragraph (*f*)(ii). An example is provided by a case which was tried at the Central Criminal Court about three years ago. One of two men charged with conspiracy to rob (both had long criminal records) went into the witness box wearing a dark suit and looking as if he were a respectable business man. When asked by his counsel when and where he met his co-accused, he said: "About eighteen months ago at my golf club. I was looking for a game. The secretary introduced us". In another case the defence contrived to introduce evidence suggesting that the accused, who lived on crime, was negotiating for the purchase of a substantial property. We think that it would be useful to strengthen the law by applying the rule to the introduction of evidence "with a view to establishing directly or by implication that the accused is generally or in a particular respect a person of good disposition or reputation".

136. Clause 7 restates the law in accordance with the proposals in paragraphs 134 and 135. Subsection (1)(*a*) includes the words quoted in paragraph 135 to deal with cases of hinting indirectly that the accused is a respectable person. The clause also makes it clear that a co-accused, as well as the prosecution, may cross-examine the accused to rebut his claim to be of good disposition or reputation and may adduce evidence for this purpose. This is in accordance with the present law; and it is clearly right, because each of the two accused may be seeking to show that the offence was committed by the other.

---

[1] See paragraph 118.
[2] (1927), 20 Cr. App. R. 106, 108.

CLAUSE 8: LIMITS OF BURDEN OF PROOF FALLING ON ACCUSED

137. There are many cases where, in order that the accused may be acquitted, an issue must be raised in his favour on some particular matter. At common law this happens, for example, with insanity, self-defence, provocation (in murder) and duress. Many enactments provide, in one form or another, that the burden of proving certain matters should be on the defence. These usually relate to such matters as lawful authority or excuse for the possession of certain articles or some other matter which is likely to be within the special knowledge of the accused. For example, under s. 1(1) of the Prevention of Crime Act 1953 (c. 14) it is an offence for a person to have an offensive weapon with him in any public place " without lawful authority or reasonable excuse, the proof whereof shall lie on him ". Again, s. 30(2) of the Sexual Offences Act 1956 (c. 69) provides that, for the purpose of the offence under the section of knowingly living on the earnings of prostitution, a man who lives with, or exercises control over, a prostitute " shall be presumed to be knowingly living on the earnings of prostitution, unless he proves the contrary ".

138. When there is a burden on the accused, it is necessary to know whether the burden is a " persuasive " or an " evidential " burden. The difference between these burdens was explained by the Court of Criminal Appeal in *Gill*[1]. A persuasive burden means that the matter in question must be taken as proved against the accused unless he satisfies the jury (or magistrates' court), on a balance of probabilities, to the contrary. An evidential burden means that the matter must be taken as proved against the accused unless there is sufficient evidence to raise an issue on the matter but that, if there is sufficient evidence, then the prosecution have the burden of satisfying the jury (or magistrates' court) as to the matter beyond reasonable doubt in the ordinary way. The rule as to evidential burdens was stated in *Gill*[2] (a case concerning duress) as follows:—

> " The accused, either by the cross-examination of the prosecution witnesses or by evidence called on his behalf, or by a combination of the two, must place before the court such material as makes duress a live issue fit and proper to be left to the jury. But, once he has succeeded in doing this, it is then for the Crown to destroy that defence in such a manner as to leave in the jury's minds no reasonable doubt that the accused cannot be absolved on the grounds of the alleged compulsion ."

The words " a live issue fit and proper to be left to the jury " show that it is not enough for the defence merely to allege the fact in question: the court decides whether there is a real issue on the matter[3]. Therefore, when the burden is an evidential one, there is no need for the judge to mention the burden to the jury at all. If he decides that there is insufficient evidence to raise an issue on the

---

[1] (1963), 47 Cr. App. R. 166, 171–2.
[2] At p. 172.
[3] Cf. Lord Devlin's statement, in giving the judgment of the Privy Council in *Jayasena v. R.* [1970] A.C. 618, 623E, that in the case of a defence to a charge of murder (other than insanity or diminished responsibility): " Some evidence in support of such an answer must be adduced before the jury is directed to consider it; but the only burden laid upon the accused in this respect is to collect from the evidence enough material to make it possible for a reasonable jury to acquit. "

matter, he directs the jury that they must take the matter as proved against the defence. If he decides that there is sufficient evidence to raise an issue on the matter, he simply directs the jury in the ordinary way that it is for the prosecution to satisfy them on the matter beyond reasonable doubt. When, on the other hand, the burden is a persuasive one, the judge must direct the jury that, although on other matters it is for the prosecution to satisfy them beyond reasonable doubt, on the matter in question it is for the defence to satisfy them on a balance of probabilities.

139. It is now settled (after doubt in some cases) that all the common law burdens on the defence except that of proving insanity are evidential burdens. The burden of proving insanity is a persuasive one[1]. With the statutory burdens the matter depends on the terms of the particular enactment; but although there have been doubts in the past, we think that in the typical case, at least, of enactments of the type quoted in paragraph 137 it would now be held that the burden is a persuasive one. This seems to us to be in accordance with the reasoning in Lord Devlin's judgment in *Jayasena v. R.*[2]. Side by side with enactments relating to particular defences there is a general provision in s. 81 of the Magistrates' Courts Act 1952 (c. 55) that, " where the defendant to an information or complaint relies for his defence on any exception, exemption, proviso, excuse or qualification, ...the burden of proving the exception, exemption, proviso, excuse or qualification shall be on him ". In *Gatland v. Metropolitan Police Commissioner*[3] Lord Parker C.J. considered that this provision (which is descended from a provision in s. 14 of the Summary Jurisdiction Act 1848 (c. 43)) casts a persuasive burden of proof on the defence.

140. We are strongly of the opinion that, both on principle and for the sake of clarity and convenience in practice, burdens on the defence should be evidential only. This is subject to the two exceptions which we recommend in paragraph 141. Our reasons are given below.

   (i) In the typical case where the essence of the offence is that the offender has acted with blameworthy intent, and the defence which the accused has the burden of proving implies that he had no such intent but acted wholly innocently, it seems to us repugnant to principle that the jury or magistrates' court should be under a legal duty, if they are left in doubt whether or not the accused had the guilty intent, to convict him. For this is what the law requires. For example, in a case under the Prevention of Crime Act 1953[4] the accused's defence might be that somebody else put the weapon into his pocket or that he picked it up and was going to hand it to the police. The judge must direct the jury that, if they cannot decide on the evidence whether his story is more probable than not, they should convict. It may well be that this kind of situation does not occur at all commonly but that in practice the prosecution assume the burden of proving

---

[1] *Woolmington v. Director of Public Prosecutions*, [1935] A.C. 462, 475; 25 Cr. App. R. 72, 89.
[2] Mentioned in n. 3 on p. 87.
[3] [1968] 2 Q.B. 279, 286D.
[4] Mentioned in paragraph 137.

the whole case; for in our 6th report[1] we mentioned (in relation to a suggestion to create an offence with a persuasive burden on the accused) that " the experience of members of the committee in the case of similar provisions as regards existing offences suggests that in practice provisions of this kind are less efficacious than may have been hoped when they were enacted, because juries are sometimes unwilling to convict unless the prosecution leads evidence sufficient to rule out the defence ". But even if so, it seems to us undesirable that the possibility which we mentioned should continue to exist even in theory. If provisions of this kind have indeed little or no effect, the case for altering them seems, if anything, stronger. The course suggested would be in accordance with what Viscount Sankey L.C. in *Woolmington*[2] called the " golden thread " of the criminal law that " it is the duty of the prosecution to prove the prisoner's guilt ".

(ii) The change would be in general accordance with the principle in s. 25(3) of the Theft Act 1968 (c. 60) in relation to the offence of going equipped for stealing etc. In the corresponding offence under s. 28(2) of the Larceny Act 1916 (c. 50) of possession by a person of housebreaking implements " without lawful excuse (the proof whereof shall lie on such person) " the burden of proof was a persuasive one. By contrast s. 25(3) of the 1968 Act provides only that proof that the accused had with him " any article made or adapted for use in committing " a relevant offence " shall be evidence that he had it with him for such use ". This change was made in accordance with the recommendation in our 8th report[3]. As the typical offences in respect of which there are persuasive burdens on the defence are mostly comparable for present purposes with the offence of going equipped for stealing etc., it seems to us that consistency requires that the burdens in the case of the former offences should, like that in the case of the latter, be reduced from persuasive to evidential ones.

(iii) The change would also be in general accordance with the common law, which with the sole exception of insanity[4] has not found it necessary to impose any persuasive burden on the defence.

(iv) The real purpose, we think, of casting burdens on the defence in criminal cases is to prevent the accused, in a case where his proved conduct calls, as a matter of common sense, for an explanation, from submitting at the end of the evidence for the prosecution that he has no case to answer because the prosecution have not adduced evidence to negative the possibility of an innocent explanation. This applies especially to cases (such as those mentioned above[5]) where the defence relates to a matter peculiarly within the knowledge of the accused. (It used sometimes to be said that there was a general rule that in

---

[1] "Perjury and Attendance of Witnesses " (Cmnd. 2465) paragraph 17.
[2] [1935] A.C. at p. 481; 25 Cr. App. R. at p. 95.
[3] " Theft and Related Offences " (Cmnd. 2977) paragraphs 151–153.
[4] For the reasons given at the end of this paragraph we propose that the burden of proving insanity should also be made an evidential one.
[5] Paragraph 137.

such a case the burden of proving the matter was on the defence; but the existence of such a rule was negatived by the Court of Criminal Appeal in *Spurge*[1].) It seems to us that it is entirely justifiable to impose a burden on the defence for this purpose but that the purpose is sufficiently served by making the burden an evidential one.

(v) The change would get rid of the present need[2] for the judge to give the jury the complicated direction on the difference between the burden on the prosecution of proving a matter beyond reasonable doubt and that on the defence of proving a matter on a balance of probabilities. Many judges have said that they find it difficult or impossible to direct juries on this in a way which the jury are likely to find satisfactory or even intelligible.

We propose also that the burden of proving insanity as a defence should be made an evidential one. The present rule that it is a persuasive burden is, in our opinion, anomalous and open to most of the objections stated in this paragraph to the statutory persuasive burdens. Moreover, the burden on the defence of making good the similar defence of diminished responsibility, which is at present a persuasive burden[3], will become an evidential one if our proposals are adopted; and these two burdens should clearly be of the same kind. The great majority of those whom we consulted in 1968[4] were in favour of the proposed change. A few, however, opposed it, chiefly on the ground that it would be an unwarranted departure from the policy of Parliament in a number of enactments. But we do not regard this as sufficient to outweigh the arguments mentioned above.

141. We propose that there should be two exceptions to the provision discussed above:

(i) " *Third-party proceedings* ". In a few cases there is a special statutory procedure by which a person charged with a contravention of the statute is entitled to be acquitted if, among other things, he proves that the contravention was due to the act or default of another person who is brought before the court for the purpose of the proceedings, whereupon the latter may be convicted of the offence. The provision which we propose could not be applied to these enactments without modification; for under them proof by the accused that his contravention was due to the act or default of the third party apparently operates without more to cause the third party to be convicted, and this could not be allowed to follow from the discharge by the accused of an evidential burden. Therefore, to apply the principle underlying our proposal to these enactments would require an alteration of the scheme of the enactments—for example, by making the matter to be proved in order that the third party should be convicted different from the matter to be proved in order that the accused should be acquitted. This would involve a substantial reconsideration of the special procedure involved, which

---

[1] [1961] 2 Q.B. 205; 45 Cr. App. R. 191.
[2] Mentioned in paragraph 138.
[3] Homicide Act 1957 (c. 11) s. 2(2).
[4] See paragraph 9.

could not be undertaken as part of a review of the law of evidence or without consultation with the authorities concerned with the subject-matter of the enactments.

(ii) *Conviction of a person other than the accused.* We shall be recommending that, where the fact that a person other than the accused has committed an offence is relevant, the fact that that person has been convicted of it shall be admissible in order to prove that he committed it, and we shall be recommending also that he shall be taken to have done so unless the contrary is proved. This matter is discussed later[1], and for the reason to be given we shall be recommending that the burden on the accused of disproving the guilt of the other person should be a persuasive one.

142. Clause 8 is to give effect to our proposals[2]. We mention a few particular matters (leaving others to the note on the clause in Annex 2). Under subsection (1) the question whether a matter in issue should be taken as proved against the defence or the burden of proving it should be on the prosecution in the ordinary way will depend on whether " there is sufficient evidence to raise an issue with respect to that matter ". This is intended to correspond to the test as stated in *Gill*[3] whether there is sufficient material before the court to make the issue " a live issue fit and proper to be left to the jury ". There is no need, in our opinion, to be more precise than this, because this is a test to be applied by the court and not the jury and it is the test which courts have already to apply where there is an evidential burden[4]. Nor do we think that there will be a danger that magistrates', courts, for example, will accede too readily to a submission by the defence that they have discharged the evidential burden as expressed in these words. For the question whether they have done so will be one of law on which the prosecution can appeal to the High Court. For example, in *Hill v. Baxter*[5], a man charged with motoring offences gave evidence that he remembered nothing between the time when he left a certain place and the time of the accident and that he was " not conscious of what he was doing " after leaving that place. The magistrates accepted this evidence and a submission by the defence that it established a defence of automatism. But the High Court allowed the prosecutor's appeal on the ground that the evidence was insufficient to justify this. The clause naturally applies only to existing enactments; but subsection (3)(*a*) provides that it will apply to future enactments similarly " unless the contrary intention appears ". Subsections (4) and (5) make the exception for " third-party " proceedings.

---

[1] Paragraphs 217–219—in particular paragraph 219(i).
[2] The exception in respect of a conviction of a person other than the accused is made by clause 24(2).
[3] Quoted in paragraph 138.
[4] But the proviso to clause 2(4) ensures that the court will not be required to treat an issue as necessarily raised merely because of any matter favourable to himself which the accused has included in a confession proved under clause 2.
[5] [1958] 1 Q.B. 277; 42 Cr. App. R. 51.

CLAUSE 9: COMPETENCE AND COMPELLABILITY OF SPOUSE OF ACCUSED

143. The law as to the competence and compellability of the accused's spouse has developed in a haphazard way and, as a result, is anomalous and complicated. It is also obscure in some respects. Some of the rules are so curious that it is not surprising that they have sometimes been overlooked. We have no doubt that the law should be redrawn in accordance with what seems right in policy. We need therefore to refer only briefly to the existing law before discussing what the new law should be[1]. For simplicity it will be assumed that the accused is the husband, but the law is similar when the accused is the wife.

144. In general the accused's wife is incompetent to give evidence for the prosecution. This applies even if she and her husband have been judicially separated[2]. At common law the only clear exception is that she is competent and compellable in cases of personal violence against her[3]. The exact extent of this exception is doubtful, as the cases are in conflict. There are also possible exceptions in the case of treason and that of abduction (even if the accused has married the woman abducted). By various enactments, including s. 4 of the Criminal Evidence Act 1898 (c. 36) (which Act made the accused's wife, like himself, competent to give evidence on his behalf), the wife is competent for the prosecution in the case of a number of offences, but in these cases she is not compellable[4]. The most important offences are offences against the property of the wife, failure to maintain wife or children, many other offences relating to children (including cruelty), bigamy and most sexual offences against a third person (not including unnatural offences). If the wife herself brings the proceedings against her husband (which s. 30(2) of the Theft Act 1968 (c. 60) enables her to do for any offence except that the consent of the Director of Public Prosecutions is required for a prosecution for stealing or damaging her property), she is competent under that provision to give evidence against him.

145. The accused's wife is competent as a witness for him, under s. 1 of the 1898 Act, in all cases, but she is compellable for him only in cases where she is competent (and compellable) for the prosecution at common law. As mentioned above[5], the only clear case is that of violence against her. Comment by the prosecution (but not by the judge) on her failure to give evidence for her husband is prohibited by s. 1(b) of the 1898 Act.

146. The wife of the accused is competent to give evidence, again under s. 1 of the 1898 Act, for a person accused (and tried) jointly with her husband in all cases with her husband's consent. In the cases mentioned in paragraph

---

[1] What is said in this section of the report does not apply to proceedings on indictment for a nuisance to a highway or otherwise for the enforcement of a purely civil right. In these proceedings, which are criminal in form only, the spouse of the defendant is competent and compellable for any party, as in ordinary civil proceedings, under the Evidence Act 1877 (c. 14). But indictments for these purposes are now in practice obsolete, and therefore the Act no longer serves any useful purpose and the draft Bill proposes to repeal it.
[2] *Moss v. Moss*, [1963] 2 Q.B. 799; 47 Cr. App. R. 222.
[3] *Lapworth*, [1931] 1 K.B. 117; 22 Cr. App. R. 87.
[4] *Leach v. R.*, [1912] A.C. 305; 7 Cr. App. R. 158.
[5] Paragraph 144.

144 where the wife is made competent for the prosecution by s. 4 of the 1898 Act she is competent for the co-accused under that section, even without her husband's consent. In the cases where she is competent (and compellable) for the prosecution at common law she is probably also compellable for the co-accused.

147. How far the wife of the accused should be competent and compellable for the prosecution, for the accused and for a co-accused is in these days essentially a question of balancing the desirability that all available evidence which might conduce to the right verdict should be before the court against (i) the objection on social grounds to disturbing marital harmony more than is absolutely necessary and (ii) what many regard as the harshness of compelling a wife to give evidence against her husband. Older objections, even to competence, based on the theoretical unity of the spouses or on the interest of the accused's wife in the outcome of the proceedings, and in particular on the likelihood that his wife will be biased in favour of the accused, can have no place in the decisions as to the extent of competence and compellability nowadays. But the question of the right balance between the considerations of policy mentioned is one on which different opinions are inevitably—and sometimes strongly—held. The arguments relate mostly to compellability for the prosecution but, as will be seen[1], not entirely so. The argument for more compellability for the prosecution is the straightforward one that, if it is left to the wife to choose whether to give evidence against her husband, the result may be that a dangerous criminal will go free. The argument to the contrary is that, if the wife is not willing to give the evidence, the state should not expose her to the pitiful clash between the duty to aid the prosecution by giving evidence, however unwillingly, and the natural duty to protect her husband whatever the circumstances. It has been argued strongly in support of this view that the law ought to recognize that, as between spouses, conviction and punishment may have consequences of the most serious economic and social kind for their future and that neither of them should in any circumstances be compelled, against his or her will, to contribute to bringing this about. It is also pointed out that there is at least a considerable likelihood that the result of more compellability will be either perjury or contempt by silence. The particular provisions which we recommend are intended (in addition to simplifying the law) as a compromise between these views.

148. We have no doubt that the wife should be made competent as a witness for the prosecution in all cases. If she is willing to give evidence, we think that the law would be showing excessive concern for the preservation of marital harmony if it were to say that she must not do so. There is only one argument of any substance which we can think of against making the wife competent in all cases. This is that, as we are not proposing to make her compellable for the prosecution in all cases[2], it would be a mistake to make her competent without being compellable. The argument is that compellability saves her from the embarrassing choice between her duty to the public to give the evidence and her loyalty to her husband. It is said that, if her husband is convicted on her evidence, she can answer his reproaches by

[1] See paragraphs 153–154 (in relation to compellability on behalf of the accused spouse) and paragraph 155 (in relation to compellability on behalf of the accused spouse's co-accused).
[2] See paragraphs 149–152.

saying that she could not have avoided giving the evidence. But we do not think that much can be made of this argument. It may perhaps have some force in the case of a minor offence, but in the case of a serious offence it seems to us too subtle to be likely to be advanced by the wife or appreciated by her husband. We therefore do not think that competence and compellability on behalf of the prosecution should coincide. Moreover the great majority of those whom we consulted agreed that the wife should be competent in all cases; and there seems little if any reason why she should be competent in the case of some offences and not in that of others. Therefore clause 9(1) makes the wife competent for the prosecution (unless she is being tried jointly with her husband) in all cases.

149. How far the wife should be compellable for the prosecution is a more difficult question. We are in favour of maintaining the existing rule that she is compellable on a charge against her husband of violence to her. We considered an argument that in these days, when wives are so much less under the domination of their husbands, a wife should be made competent only, so that the choice whether to give evidence would be left to her. The result would no doubt be that in many cases it would depend on her whether there was a prosecution or not. We recognize the force of the argument that this would be right in policy, especially because the wife might think that by refraining from giving evidence she would have a better hope that her husband would treat her well in future. But on the whole we think that the public interest in the punishment of violence requires that compellability should remain. It is true that the wife may still refuse to give evidence even though compellable; but the fact that there is compellability should make it easier to counter the effect of possible intimidation by her husband and to persuade her to give evidence. In any event there does not seem to us to be any evidence that the present rule of compellability does any harm, so it seems safest to preserve it.

150. We in fact favour going further and making the wife compellable in the case of offences of violence towards children under the age of sixteen belonging to the same household as the accused. The seriousness of some of these cases seems to us to make it right to strengthen the hand of prosecuting authorities by making the wife compellable, especially as the wife may be in fear of her husband and therefore reluctant to give evidence unless she can be compelled to do so. In the case of violence towards the children compellability seems to us even more important than in cases of violence towards the wife herself. For although violence towards children may be easier to detect than violence towards the wife, it is likely to be harder to prove it in court against the spouse responsible, especially if the child is unable to give evidence. Another reason for giving the wife no choice whether to give evidence is that she may have been a party to the violence or at least have acquiesced in it, although it is not proposed to prosecute her. For similar reasons we think that the wife should be compellable on a charge of a sexual offence against a child under sixteen belonging to the accused's household. We considered an argument that this would be unnecessary because some of these offences may not be serious and it may be better for all those concerned, parent or child, that the offence should be overlooked than that it should be exposed in court and the offender punished, especially as the marriage might as a result be

94

broken up. It has been argued that for this reason it is better to leave it to the wife to judge whether she should give the evidence. On the other hand some sexual offences may have worse effects than all but the most serious offences of violence. On balance we concluded that it was right to draw no distinction in relation to compellability between sexual offences and offences of violence.

151. Our decision to recommend limiting compellability in respect of offences against children under sixteen to children of the same household as the accused was taken after a good deal of consideration as to whether compellability should apply to offences against any child under that age even if unconnected with the spouses. This would have the desirable effect of giving further protection to children, and the proposed limitation would exclude some cases where compellability might be thought desirable in any event—for example, if the offence was against a neighbour's child visiting the spouses' house or against a nephew or niece of the offender. But on the whole we think it excessive to extend compellability so far and to apply it, for example, to a common assault on a boy of fifteen having nothing to do with the family. Short of this it would be difficult to draw the line satisfactorily without great complication. Besides, part of the reason for applying compellability to offences against children of the household is that offences committed in the family may be harder to prove if the unoffending spouse is free to choose whether to give evidence, whereas in the case of an offence outside the family other evidence is likely to be available.

152. We do not think that the wife should be compellable for the prosecution in the case of offences other than those mentioned above. We need waste no time on the doubtful compellability under the present law in treason and abduction. It might be argued that the wife should be compellable in very serious cases such as murder and spying or perhaps in all serious cases of violence; but the law has never, except perhaps in treason, made the seriousness of an offence by itself a ground for compellability, and we do not favour doing so now. Therefore clause 9(3) provides expressly that the wife shall not be compellable except in the cases (mentioned above) specified in the subsection.

153. We have no doubt that the accused's wife should be made compellable for him in all cases. It is surprising that she should not be so now. The only possible argument against this seems to be that the wife ought not to be put into a position where she may have to choose between incriminating her husband and committing perjury. But this argument seems to us quite unacceptable in these days and in any event to have very little weight compared with the argument that the husband might feel a great grievance if he could not compel his possibly estranged wife to give evidence for him. No doubt the accused would prefer, if possible, to avoid calling his wife, if she was reluctant to give evidence, for fear that her evidence would be unfavourable to him because of the compulsion; but if she could in fact give true evidence which would be in his favour, he would probably think that, however reluctant she was to give evidence, the truth would emerge if she did so. Clause 9(2) makes the accused's wife compellable on his behalf in all cases (unless she is jointly charged and tried with him). This is contrary to proviso (a) to s. 30(3) of the Theft Act 1968 in the cases to which s. 30 applies; but, as mentioned in our report on theft and related offences[1], the corresponding provision in the draft

---

[1] Cmnd. 2977, paragraph 199.

Bill annexed to that report was included as an interim measure and pending our consideration of the general question of policy on this reference.

154. The prohibition in s. 1(*b*) of the 1898 Act of comment by the prosecution on the failure of the accused's spouse to give evidence should in our opinion be lifted. The case for this is not so obvious as is that for lifting the prohibition of comment on failure of the accused himself to give evidence[1]. In favour of lifting the former prohibition it is argued that, if the accused puts forward a defence which, if true, his wife would be able to corroborate by her evidence, and she is not called, it is natural that the prosecution should be able to comment on this just as they may on the failure of the defence to call somebody else who would have been able to corroborate his evidence if it was true. Also the prohibition is not one which one would expect to exist, especially in a reformed and modernized law of evidence, and there would be the danger that it might be forgotten and that a conviction might have to be quashed in consequence. Moreover in any event it seems right to continue to allow comment by the judge, because in a proper case the judge might think it right to advise the jury that in the circumstances they should not hold the failure against the accused although it might have seemed right to them to do so; and we are not in favour of prohibiting comment by the prosecution when comment by the judge is allowed. In favour of the present prohibition it is argued that inexperienced prosecutors might use their new freedom without sufficient discrimination (though the effect of this should be counteracted by the court). Another argument is that the real reason for the failure to call the wife might have been that the accused was afraid that, because she was being compelled to give evidence, she might deliberately be unhelpful to him. It was also pointed out that a practice might grow up of calling the wife unnecessarily in order to avoid adverse comment on failure to call her. We think that the arguments in favour of lifting the prohibition are the stronger. Clause 9(6) provides accordingly[2].

155. We recommend that the wife of accused A should be competent to give evidence on behalf of his co-accused B whether or not A is willing. At present A's consent is necessary under s. 1(*c*) of the 1898 Act. We do not think that A should have any right to prevent Mrs. A from giving evidence on behalf of B if she is willing. A more difficult question seems to be whether she should be compellable on behalf of B in all cases. In favour of making her so it is argued that the interests of justice require that B should be able to compel anybody not being tried with him to give evidence on his behalf and that the fact that the witness happens to be A's wife should make no difference, even though the result might be her incriminating A. Against this it is argued that, since the prosecution cannot call Mrs. A as a witness in order that she may incriminate

---

[1] See paragraph 110.

[2] The reason why clause 9(6) expressly abolishes the prohibition in s. 1(*b*) of the 1898 Act of comment on the failure of the accused's wife to give evidence, instead of leaving the prohibition to disappear, like that of comment on the failure of the accused himself to give evidence, with the repeal of the whole of s. 1 (as mentioned in the last sentence of paragraph 113), is that the right to comment on the failure of the accused himself to give evidence is a necessary consequence of the provision in clause 5 allowing adverse inferences to be drawn from his failure to do so, whereas clause 9 makes no provision for adverse inferences to be drawn from the failure of the accused's wife to give evidence. Therefore the proposal to abolish the prohibition of comment on the wife's failure involves a separate decision of policy which requires a positive provision.

A, it is wrong that they should be able to compel her to incriminate him by cross-examination if she is called by B. We think that the argument against compellability is the stronger. We considered a possible compromise by which Mrs. A should be compellable on behalf of B only if A consented. Then A could give his consent if Mrs. A could help B's defence without incriminating A. But on the whole we are opposed to this, because it might be procedurally awkward, and embarrassing for A's defence, if it were necessary to ask him in court whether he consented to his wife's giving evidence, especially if he agreed at first that she should do so but changed his mind before the time came to call her because of evidence given meanwhile. But we propose that Mrs. A should be compellable on behalf of B in any case where she would be compellable on behalf of the prosecution even though the result might be that she would incriminate A. Here the argument mentioned above against making her compellable for B in general does not apply; and although the general arguments for compellability on behalf of the prosecution (in particular the possibility of intimidation by the witness's husband) do not apply either, it seems wrong to deny to the co-accused a right which is given to the prosecution. Clause 9(3) provides accordingly.

156. We considered whether to provide that, if the spouses were judicially separated or were not cohabiting, they should be treated for the purpose of competence and compellability as if they were unmarried[1]. There is clearly a case for this, at least where they are judicially separated, for the law recognizes that for many purposes this is equivalent to a divorce. But it is difficult to draw a line for this purpose without complicating the clause (and the other provisions in the draft Bill where a similar question arises). For if there is to be an exception from the general rule in cases of judicial separation, it would seem logical to apply the exception to cases where there is a matrimonial order under the Matrimonial Proceedings (Magistrates' Courts) Act 1960 (c. 48) containing a provision under s. 2(1)(a) that the spouses should no longer be bound to cohabit, as this provision has the same effect as a judicial separation. But the inclusion or non-inclusion of such a provision in a matrimonial order depends very much on the circumstances of the case in question and may therefore be an inappropriate test for the purpose of compellability. Moreover, the parties often resume cohabitation even when there is a provision of the kind mentioned in the order; and, although this causes the order to cease to have effect under s. 7(2) of the 1960 Act, the provision would involve the side issue whether the spouses had resumed cohabitation. Again, if such a provision as suggested were to be included, it would be necessary to consider whether it should apply to orders made by courts outside England. We considered providing that the spouses should be treated as unmarried for the purpose of compellability if there were in existence any judicial order relating to the marriage and they were not cohabiting or if, irrespective of whether there was such an order in existence, they were in fact not cohabiting. But again this would involve the question whether they were cohabiting. On the whole we think that it is unnecessary to complicate the clause by any provision for these purposes. For if the parties are judicially separated or otherwise not cohabiting, and if there is little prospect that they will become reconciled, the spouse

---

[1] The effect would be to reverse the rule in *Moss v. Moss*, mentioned in paragraph 144, that even a judicial separation makes no difference in respect of competence and compellability.

in question is likely to be willing to give evidence; and if there is a prospect of reconciliation, it may be better to avoid the risk of spoiling this prospect by compelling the spouse to give evidence when he or she would not have been compellable in the ordinary case.

157. If the spouses have been divorced or if their marriage, being voidable, has been annulled, the former wife is incompetent to give evidence for the prosecution about a matter which occurred during the marriage, at least if she would have been incompetent to do so had the marriage still subsisted[1]. Presumably she is competent or compellable, as the case may be, if she would have been competent or compellable had the marriage subsisted, but there is no direct authority on this. In any event we are convinced that there is no good reason for keeping the present rule, and clause 9(4) proposes that, if the spouses are no longer married, they shall be compellable as if they had never been married.

CLAUSES 10–14: CROSS-EXAMINATION

158. In addition to our recommendations as to cross-examination of the accused we recommend that the law as to cross-examination generally should be amended in certain respects mentioned in the following paragraphs. The amendments relate to matters of detail and are mainly for the purpose of replacing with improvements provisions of the Criminal Procedure Act 1865 (c. 18). The relevant provisions of that Act apply to civil, as well as criminal, proceedings by virtue of s. 1; and if our recommendations are accepted, no doubt consideration will be given to making similar amendments in the civil law.

159. S. 6 of the 1865 Act begins by providing that—

" A witness may be questioned as to whether he has been convicted of any felony or misdemeanor, and upon being so questioned, if he either denies or does not admit the fact, or refuses to answer, it shall be lawful for the cross-examining party to prove such conviction... ".

It then goes on to provide in detail for the method of proving a conviction. The opening words allowing questions as to a conviction of " any felony or misdemeanour " are curiously wide, as they seem to mean that any witness may be questioned about a conviction of any offence however little it has to do with any issue in the case or with credibility as a witness. In fact the section was probably intended only to provide for the means by which a conviction which was admissible under the existing law might be proved if it was denied;

---

[1] *Algar*, [1954] 1 Q.B. 279; 37 Cr. App. R.200.

and the opening words were probably intended only as an introduction in order to indicate the subject of the section. This is suggested by the side-note —" Proof of conviction of witness for felony or misdemeanor may be given ". In practice it is difficult to see how cross-examination about a conviction which is relevant neither to an issue nor to the witness's credibility is relevant at all, and presumably in any case the court would effectually discourage cross-examination about such a conviction. It might therefore be thought unnecessary to include any provision corresponding to the opening words of the section quoted above; but since we are proposing that the provisions about proof of convictions should be replaced, it seems desirable to replace also the opening provision. We think that the new provision should be a general one to the effect that a witness (other than the accused[1]) shall not be asked any question as to his conduct on any occasion, or as to any charge, conviction or acquittal of any offence, unless this is relevant to any issue in the proceedings or to his credibility as a witness. Clause 10(1) provides accordingly.

160. We do not think it necessary or appropriate to attempt to define what should be the test for deciding whether a question to a witness other than the accused should be admissible on the ground that the fact to which it relates is relevant to his credibility as a witness. The view has been expressed to and in the committee that the only kinds of misconduct which are relevant for this purpose are those involving dishonesty or perjury. Others think that a serious offence of violence, for example, may be relevant on the ground that the fact that the witness has been guilty of an outrageous disregard of the standards of good behaviour is something which it is right to take into account when considering whether to believe him or a well-behaved witness on a matter in issue. There is no case law on the subject, though it seems that the tendency is to allow cross-examination to credit without any strict requirement that the conduct in question should show that the witness should not be believed. For example, in the divorce case of *Clifford v. Clifford*[2] Cairns J. (as he then was) held that the wife respondent, though charged only with cruelty, might be cross-examined as to adultery in order to discredit her as a witness. S. 6 of the 1865 Act was not referred to, but the judge said[3]:

" It has never, I think, been doubted that a conviction for any offence could be put to a witness by way of cross-examination as to credit, even though the offence was not one of dishonesty ".

The fact that a person has been charged with, or acquitted of, an offence might be relevant to his credibility as a witness if, for example, he denied that this was the case. We are satisfied that the extent to which the clause should apply should be left to be decided by the courts when the need arises, especially as the clause does not involve any substantial change in the way in which the law is applied at present.

161. S. 3 of the 1865 Act certainly requires thorough revision. It reads as follows:

" A party producing a witness shall not be allowed to impeach his credit by general evidence of bad character; but he may, in case the

---

[1] The position of the accused in this respect is dealt with in clauses 6 and 7.
[2] [1961] 3 All E.R. 231.
[3] At p. 232C.

witness shall in the opinion of the judge prove adverse, contradict him by other evidence, or, by leave of the judge, prove that he has made at other times a statement inconsistent with his present testimony; but before such last-mentioned proof can be given the circumstances of the supposed statement, sufficient to designate the particular occasion, must be mentioned to the witness, and he must be asked whether or not he has made such statement. "

The principle of the section is that in general a party calling a witness must be taken to be putting him forward as a person who intends to tell the truth to the best of his recollection. Therefore, if the witness gives unfavourable evidence, the party must not have a free hand to turn round and attack him as if he were a witness for the other side. Hence the opening provision which prohibits the party from impeaching the witness's credit by general evidence of bad character. This prohibition causes no difficulty, but after this the section has gone wrong. It proceeds to deal with the cases where it is right that a party should be able to refute the evidence of his witness if the witness has proved " adverse " to him; but at this point there is a " great blunder " in the drafting (to quote from the judgment of Cockburn C.J. in *Greenough .v. Eccles*[1]). In that case it was held that the condition that the witness should have proved " adverse " meant that it was not enough that he gave evidence unfavourable to the party calling him but that he must have proved " hostile " in the sense that he was unwilling to tell the truth. The intention was that, if the witness proved hostile in this sense, the party should be able to seek leave to cross-examine him about any statement which he had made inconsistent with his evidence as if he were a witness on the other side (because then there would be no danger that he would too readily say what the party calling him wanted him to say) and to call evidence of the making of the statement if the witness denied it[2]. To use the word " adverse " in this sense was obviously misleading, because it suggested that it was enough that the witness's evidence was unfavourable. But the " great blunder " to which Cockburn C.J. referred was more serious, because the section, read literally, appears to say that it is only when the witness proves adverse (in the sense of hostile) that the party calling him may contradict him by other evidence. In fact there was no need to make provision to allow a party to adduce evidence contradicting unfavourable evidence given by one of his witnesses, because this was naturally allowed by the common law. Otherwise there would have been the absurdity that, if a single witness gave evidence unfavourable to his party, the party would not be allowed to call his other witnesses who might give favourable evidence on the same point. However, the condition that the witness should have proved hostile is always treated as not applying to the right to contradict him by other evidence but only to the right to question the witness (with the leave of the court) about a previous statement inconsistent with his evidence. For these reasons alone it would be desirable to replace the section; but in our opinion it should as a matter of policy be further altered as mentioned below.

162. We are in favour of keeping the substance of the general prohibition of impeaching the credit of one's witness by general evidence of bad

---

[1] (1859), 5 C.B. (N.S.) 786, 806. The judgment related to the identically worded s. 22 of the Common Law Procedure Act 1854 (c. 125).

[2] Although ss. 3 and 4 are not clear on the point, their combined effect seems to be that what the party should ask leave for is (i) to cross-examine his witness about the previous statement and (ii) to prove this if the witness denies it and that leave, if given, embraces both.

" character ". There is a case for allowing a party to do this at least where it appears to the judge that the witness is trying to avoid helping the case of the party calling him. The justification would be that the witness is in effect like a witness on the other side. But it seems to us that it would be repugnant to principle, and likely to lead to abuse, to enable a party, having called a witness on the basis that he is at least in general going to tell the truth, to question him or call other evidence designed to show that he is a liar. To allow this might also have the danger that a party calling a witness with perhaps an old conviction for an offence might threaten to bring up the conviction if the witness gave unfavourable evidence. We concluded that the arguments for maintaining the prohibition were the stronger. Clause 11 therefore reproduces the prohibition in the form (consistent with clauses 6 and 7) of a prohibition of impeaching the witness's credibility by evidence tending to establish that he is a person of " bad disposition or reputation ".

163. Clause 11 makes no provision for a party to be allowed to call other evidence to contradict unfavourable evidence given by one of his witnesses. A provision[1] for this purpose is unnecessary because, as mentioned above[1], this is allowed by common law and the attempt to provide for it in s. 3 of the 1865 Act resulted in the " great blunder " pointed out by Cockburn C.J.

164. The rule established in *Greenough v. Eccles*[2] that it is only when a witness proves " hostile " to the party calling him that the party may cross-examine him under s. 3 of the 1865 Act about a statement made by the witness inconsistent with his evidence seems to us unsatisfactory in several respects. There is obscurity as to what the court may take into account in order to decide whether the witness has proved hostile; and it may be difficult for the court to decide this, especially if the witness, although he has in fact been induced to go over to the other side, takes care to give the impression that he is sympathetic to the party calling him and that it is only candour which prevents him from saying what would help that party. Moreover in practice the fact that a witness has made a statement inconsistent with his evidence given in court is commonly treated as sufficient to establish that he is a hostile witness in the sense required by s. 3 of the Act. The matter arises commonly when a person who has made a statement to the police incriminating the accused is persuaded to go back on his statement when he gives evidence. In *Fraser and Warren*[3] Lord Goddard C.J. said that, if in a criminal case counsel for the prosecution had a statement by a Crown witness contradicting his evidence at the trial that he was unable to identify the accused, he should at once show the statement to the judge and ask for leave to cross-examine the witness as a hostile witness. Although there may be little doubt but that a person who goes back on his statement in this way is indeed lying in order to prevent the accused from being convicted, it seems difficult to regard the inconsistency as sufficient in itself to show that the witness is a hostile witness in the sense of s. 3 of the 1865 Act. But in any event it seems to us right in policy that, if a witness either gives evidence adverse to the party calling him or gives evidence inconsistent with a statement which he has previously made, that party should be able to seek the leave of the court to cross-examine the witness as if he were

---

[1] Paragraph 161.
[2] Mentioned in paragraph 161.
[3] (1956), 40 Cr. App. R. 160.

a witness called by another party. Questions designed to show that the witness was a person of bad disposition or reputation would still be prohibited[1], but otherwise the ordinary rule as to what questions are permissible in cross-examination would apply. In particular the witness could be questioned about his previous inconsistent statement. As leave would be required, the court would have a discretion to disallow the cross-examination (as at present it can refuse leave to cross-examine a witness as being hostile), if it thought that leave was sought not for the purpose of eliciting the truth but for the purpose of harassing the witness or otherwise abusing the procedure. In a case where the witness has made a statement inconsistent with his evidence, it seems more likely to conduce to the discovery of the truth if the fact that the witness made the statement is before the court, because the previous statement may be the nearer to the truth and in any event is likely to affect the value of the evidence given in court; and it seems artificial to base the admission of the previous statement (as the law does in effect since *Fraser and Warren*) on the idea that the fact that the witness made it shows that he is now hostile. At present the previous statement, when admissible, is not evidence of the truth of the facts stated in it, but is admissible only in order to destroy the effect of the evidence given in court[2]; but we shall be proposing below[3] that it shall be admissible as evidence of the facts stated in it.

165. The provisions for enabling a party to cross-examine his witness on the ground that the witness has given evidence adverse to the party or has made a statement inconsistent with his evidence are in clause 11. The effect will be that, on the happening of either of these things, the party may apply to the court for leave to cross-examine the witness. If the court grants leave, this will apply once for all and the party will be free to ask any question (apart from a question designed to show that the witness is a person of a bad disposition or reputation) as in ordinary cross-examination, and it will not be necessary to obtain leave for the particular questions to be asked. The clause does not reproduce the requirement in s. 3 of the 1865 Act to draw the witness's attention to the occasion on which he is supposed to have made the previous inconsistent statement. This seems an unnecessary detail, as in practice it would be impossible to cross-examine about a previous statement without indicating the circumstances in which it was alleged to have been made.

166. S. 4 of the 1865 Act provides that, where a witness is cross-examined about a previous statement which he is alleged to have made inconsistent with his present evidence, and does not admit that he made it, the party cross-examining him may prove that he made it. The provision is necessary because otherwise by common law the denial would be final. This provision is restated by clause 12 without change of substance.

167. S. 5 of the 1865 Act provides that a witness may be cross-examined about a previous written statement by him without the need to show him the statement first but that, if it is intended to use the writing in order to contradict his evidence, his attention must first be drawn to the parts which are to be used for this purpose. The section provides also that the judge may require

---

[1] Cf. paragraph 162.
[2] *Golder* (1961), 45 Cr. App. R. 5, 9.
[3] Clause 33. Paragraph 257 refers.

the production of the writing for his inspection and may make such use of it for the purpose of the proceedings as he thinks fit. This section is the authority for the regular practice by which a witness who gives evidence inconsistent with a previous statement written by him or taken down from what he said is cross-examined about the discrepancy with a view to showing that his evidence is unreliable. The right was given by the almost identically worded s. 24 of the Common Law Procedure Act 1854, which was passed in order to get rid of the extraordinary rule laid down by the judges advising the House of Lords in *The Queen's Case*[1] as to how a witness should be cross-examined about inconsistencies between a written statement by him and his evidence in court. The rule required that the party must show the document to the witness before asking him whether he had made the statements contained in it. Even if the witness admitted that the document contained his statements, the cross-examining party was not allowed to read out parts of the document to him but, if he wished to show from any part of the document that the witness had contradicted himself, he had to put the whole document in as part of his evidence. Nor was he required to give the witness the opportunity to account for any discrepancies. The rule had many disadvantages. Clause 13 reproduces the effect of s. 5 of the 1865 Act without change of substance but with minor adaptations to fit the structure of the Bill.

168. The opening words of s. 6 of the 1865 Act[2] include the provision that, if a witness denies having been convicted of an offence, the conviction may be proved against him. Without this provision the denial would have been final. Clause 14 reproduces the provision and applies the right (in order to conform to clause 6 and to avoid any uncertainty) to a denial of having been charged with or acquitted of an offence and to denials by the accused when giving evidence as well as denials by other witnesses.

CLAUSES 15-16: PRIVILEGE

169. A witness in criminal proceedings (other than the accused) enjoys the ordinary privilege against self-incrimination. That is to say, he may decline to answer a question if there is (in the opinion of the court) a substantial danger that the answer would expose the witness to proceedings for a criminal offence or for the recovery of a penalty. We do not recommend that this rule should be changed. But there are two points on which the law is doubtful:

(i) whether the privilege extends to liability to proceedings under foreign law; and

(ii) whether the privilege applies to possible proceedings against the wife or husband of the witness as it applies to proceedings against the witness.

---

[1] (1820), 2 Brod. & Bing. 286.
[2] Quoted in paragraph 159.

There are considerations of policy in favour of a positive or negative conclusion on both points. But we need not go into these, because in the case of civil proceedings s. 14(1) of the Civil Evidence Act 1968 (c. 64) provides, as to (i), that the privilege shall apply only to liability to criminal proceedings under the law of a part of the United Kingdom and, as to (ii), that the privilege shall extend to proceedings against the wife or husband of the witness. These provisions were enacted on the recommendation of the Law Reform Committee in their 16th report[1], which recommendations were made with the concurrence of this committee. We have no doubt that the law in this respect in criminal proceedings should be similar to that in civil proceedings. Clause 15(1) therefore makes provision for this purpose corresponding to that in s. 14(1) of the Civil Evidence Act.

170. When the accused or his wife gives evidence, this raises special questions concerning the privilege against incrimination to which there are no corresponding questions in the law of civil evidence. Those questions depend partly on common law and partly on s. 1(e) and (f)(i) of the Criminal Evidence Act 1898. S. 1(e) clearly prevents the accused from claiming privilege in relation to a question directly incriminating him of the offence charged. But whether he may refuse to answer other incriminating questions is obscure. The question might arise in relation to (i) other offences which are directly or indirectly relevant as tending to show that the accused committed the offence charged or (ii) other offences which are relevant to his credibility as a witness. An example of (i) would be where the accused is charged with shoplifting in shop A, swears that he was not in the shop at the material time, is asked in cross-examination where he was and wishes to object to answer because the answer would show that he was in another shop committing a similar offence. An example of (ii) would be where the accused is charged with theft, has made imputations against a witness for the prosecution and then gives evidence, is asked in cross-examination whether he has not made a number of false tax returns and wishes to object because the answer would tend to incriminate him as to the tax returns. There is no direct authority on whether the objection would be upheld in either of these cases. This may be surprising, although the question would ordinarily not arise because the accused's claim of privilege would be likely to have very much the same effect as an admission. The answer to the question appears to depend on inferences from observations on the construction of s. 1(e) and (f) of the 1898 Act in *Maxwell v. Director of Public Prosecutions*[2], *Stirland v. Director of Public Prosecutions*[3] and *Jones v. Director of Public Prosecutions*[4]. But we need not go into this, because the matter is one of policy for the future. There is a case for allowing the privilege on the grounds that (i) the accused, if he gives evidence, should have the same privilege against incrimination in respect of other offences as any other witness has and (ii) in practice it is not important to take away the privilege, because the claim of privilege would, as mentioned above, be likely to be treated as an admission and because in any event the accused would scarcely be dealt with for contempt if he had no privilege but refused to answer. Another view is that, if the accused decides to give evidence, he should be

---

[1] Privilege in Civil Proceedings: Cmnd. 3472.
[2] [1935] A.C. 309; 24 Cr. App. R. 152.
[3] [1944] A.C. 315; 30 Cr. App. R. 40.
[4] [1962] A.C. 635; 46 Cr. App. R. 129.

treated as thereby submitting himself to cross-examination by means of any questions relevant directly or indirectly to whether he committed the offence charged or relevant to his credibility as a witness.

171. We favour a compromise by which the accused should have no privilege against self-incrimination in the case of questions about the offence charged or about any other offence which is admissible as tending directly or indirectly to show that he committed the offence charged but should have the privilege in respect of other offences which are relevant to his credibility as a witness. Therefore in the two examples suggested in paragraph 170 the accused could not refuse to say where he was at the time of the shoplifting, but could refuse to answer about the tax returns. To allow the privilege in the former case, even in theory, might make the law seem artificial, but it would seem reasonable to allow it in the latter case. But no privilege should, in our view, be allowed if the accused has claimed to be of good disposition or reputation, as mentioned in clause 7; for this would be inconsistent with the principle of that clause that the accused must not be allowed to mislead the court or jury by claiming a merit which he does not possess. The necessary provisions for the compromise are in clause 15(2)(a) and (b)(i). Since the division between offences which are relevant to the question whether the accused committed the offence charged and offences which are relevant to his credibility as a witness may not always be clear-cut, paragraph (b) provides that the test should be whether the question " in the opinion of the court is relevant solely or mainly to the accused's credibility as a witness ". The test will thus be similar to that which will govern the admissibility of cross-examination to credit under clause 6(4) on account of imputations against a witness for the prosecution.

172. On the same principles clause 15(2)(b)(ii) allows the accused no privilege against incriminating his wife except in relation to an offence going to his credibility as a witness. For example, if he was charged with burgling a house in which his wife worked as a servant and she had stolen the key and given it to him to get in with, and the key was found in his possession, it would be curious if he could refuse to say how he got the key because this would show that his wife stole it. The possibility of cross-examining the accused about an offence by his wife for the purpose of impairing the accused's credibility as a witness would seldom if ever occur (one would have to imagine that the accused has made imputations against a witness for the prosecution and is open to cross-examination about his association with his wife in her fraudulent activities); but if the situation did occur, it would be consistent with the protection which the clause gives the accused in relation to his own offences to give him the protection in relation to his wife's offences. Clause 15(3) makes corresponding provision, as seems right in policy, for where the accused's wife gives evidence.

173. Clause 16 abolishes certain unimportant privileges which exist in criminal proceedings and existed in civil proceedings until they were abolished in these by s. 16 of the Civil Evidence Act 1968. These are (i) the right to decline to answer a question or produce a document which would tend to expose the witness to a forfeiture or to produce a document of title to his land, (ii) the right to decline to disclose a communication made to the witness by

his wife during the marriage (there is no privilege against disclosing a communication made by the witness to his wife) and (iii) the right to decline to say whether marital intercourse did or did not take place between the witness and his wife during any period. We have no doubt that these privileges should be abolished in criminal proceedings also. In the case of communications between spouses there may be a case for preserving the privilege and extending it to communications made by the witness to his wife, and the former might be given the right to prevent the wife from disclosing the communication; but the abolition of this privilege, like that of the others mentioned above, in civil proceedings was in accordance with recommendations of the Law Reform Committee in their 16th report[1]. The committee had informed us of their proposal to make these recommendations and we had agreed with them. Moreover, it would in our view be undesirable that witnesses in criminal proceedings should enjoy greater privileges in these respects than witnesses in civil proceedings.

CLAUSES 17–21: CORROBORATION, AND DIRECTIONS TO JURIES

174. Although in general the evidence of a single witness, if believed, is sufficient to prove any issue relevant to the guilt of the accused, there are certain cases where corroboration is required by statute and there are other cases where the courts have held that the judge must give a warning to the jury that it is in general dangerous to convict on evidence of the kind in question unless it is corroborated. But in cases where the warning is required the judge may go on to direct the jury that they may nevertheless convict if they are satisfied that they can safely do so in the particular case. We summarize the law below and then give the reasons for the substantial changes which we recommend.

175. The statutory provisions requiring corroboration are those mentioned below.

(i) *Treason by compassing etc. the death, restraint etc. of the Queen or her heirs.* S. 1 of the Treason Act 1795 (36 Geo. 3 c. 7), which created this particular offence of treason, makes " the oaths of two lawful and credible witnesses " necessary for a conviction.

(ii) *Perjury.* A person cannot be convicted of an offence of perjury or subornation of perjury " solely upon the evidence of one witness as to the falsity of any statement alleged to be false " (Perjury Act 1911 (c. 6) s. 13).

(iii) *Unsworn evidence of children.* A person cannot be convicted on such unsworn evidence " unless that evidence is corroborated by some other material evidence in support thereof implicating him " (Children and Young Persons Act 1933 (c. 12) s. 38(1)).

(iv) *Personation at elections.* A person cannot be convicted of personation at elections " except on the evidence of not less than two credible witnesses " (Representation of the People Act 1949 (c. 68) s. 146(5)).

---

[1] Mentioned in paragraph 169.

(v) *Procuration etc.* A person cannot be convicted of certain sexual offences against women " on the evidence of one witness only, unless the witness is corroborated in some material particular by evidence implicating the accused " (Sexual Offences Act 1956 (c. 69) ss. 2(2), 3(2), 4(2), 22(2) and 23(2)). The offences are procuring a woman by threats or false pretences to have sexual intercourse with the offender, administering drugs to obtain or facilitate sexual intercourse, causing prostitution and procuring girls under twenty-one.

specific sexual offences

(vi) *Speeding.* A person cannot be convicted of speeding " solely on the evidence of one witness to the effect that in the opinion of the witness the person prosecuted was driving the vehicle at a speed exceeding a specified limit " (Road Traffic Act 1960 (c. 16) s. 4(2)).

Since these requirements are absolute, it follows that, at the end of the case for the prosecution, the accused must be acquitted (or not committed for trial) if the prosecution are unable to adduce corroborative evidence (or, in the case of (i) or (iv), a second witness).

176. The cases where the courts have laid down that the judge must give a warning of the danger of convicting on uncorroborated evidence are those of:—

(i) accomplices;
(ii) complainants in cases of sexual offences;
(iii) sworn evidence of children.

warning required.

In these cases the requirement to give the warning, having started as a rule of practice, has become a rule of law[1]. Since corroboration is not required as a matter of law, it follows that a conviction will not be quashed merely because of absence of corroboration; but if the judge does not give the warning, the conviction will be quashed, even if there is corroboration, unless the appeal can be dismissed in accordance with the proviso to s. 2(1) of the Criminal Appeal Act 1968 (c. 19) on the ground that " no miscarriage of justice has actually occurred ". A magistrates' court has the duty of taking into account, when considering its decision, all factors on which the judge would have directed the jury if the trial had been on indictment.

177. What is meant by corroboration for the purpose of these rules (both statutory and common law) was stated by Lord Reading C. J. in giving the judgment of the Court of Criminal Appeal in *Baskerville*[2]. Lord Reading said:

" We hold that evidence in corroboration must be independent testimony which affects the accused by connecting or tending to connect him with the crime. In other words, it must be evidence which implicates him, that is, which confirms in some material particular not only the evidence that the crime has been committed, but also that the prisoner committed it. The test applicable to determine the nature and extent

---

[1] *Davies v. Director of Public Prosecutions*, [1954] A.C. 378, 399; 38 Cr. App. R. 11, 32 (accomplices); *Trigg* (1963), 47 Cr. App. R. 94 (sexual offences); *Sawyer* (1959), 43 Cr. App. R. 187. 190 (sworn child).
[2] [1916] 2 K.B. 658, 667; 12 Cr. App. R. 81, 91.

of the corroboration is thus the same whether the case falls within the rule of practice at common law or within that class of offences for which corroboration is required by statute. "

Since corroboration, both that required by statute and that to be looked for under the common law rules, must be " independent testimony which affects the accused by connecting or tending to connect him with the crime ", it follows that a witness cannot corroborate himself; but evidence by another witness of a child's distress immediately after a sexual offence may corroborate the child's evidence[1]. We have already proposed that failure by the accused, when interrogated, to mention a matter of defence relied on at his trial should be capable of being corroboration[2] and similarly with refusal to give evidence at the trial when called on to do so[3]. Evidence of a fresh complaint by the victim of a sexual offence is not corroboration but is admissible only to show consistency of the victim's story (a distinction which has been much criticized as illogical and likely to cause bewilderment to a jury)[4]. A witness whose evidence requires corroboration, or in whose case corroboration has to be looked for under the common law rules, cannot be corroborated by a similar witness. Thus one accomplice cannot corroborate another. An unsworn child cannot corroborate another unsworn child; but the authorities are confused as to whether an unsworn child can corroborate a sworn child[5] or a sworn child an unsworn child.

178. The main reason for the rules as to corroboration is, obviously, that it has been thought that there is a danger that a person will be wrongly convicted in the absence of corroboration, of the warning or, in the case of some offences, of a second witness. In the case of perjury in judicial proceedings it has also been argued that without the requirement a person might be convicted when it was only a matter of oath against oath; but this argument does not seem to us a strong one, as there may be more than oath against oath when the falsity of the accused's evidence is corroborated although not by a second witness. The fact (when it is a fact) that the false statement in question was made on oath seems to have been seized on without much thought as an argument for the rule, whereas there are many cases where corroboration is not required but the decision depends on the choice between two pieces of sworn evidence.. In fact the historical reason for the rule is that perjury was originally punished in the Star Chamber, which usually required a second witness in the cases which it tried.

179. The committee has received a good deal of criticism of the law about corroboration. Many lawyers consider that there should be no special rules but that in every case it should be for the judge or magistrates' court to consider whether there are any circumstances relating to the particular witness which require that special care should be taken before convicting the accused on the strength of his evidence and, if so, that it should be for the judge to direct the jury accordingly. It is argued in particular that the present

---

[1] *Redpath* (1962), 46 Cr. App. R. 319.
[2] Clause 1(1); paragraphs 40–42.
[3] Clause 5(3); paragraph 111.
[4] If our recommendations on hearsay evidence are accepted, the complaint will become admissible as evidence of the facts stated in it (clause 31(1)(a)), but it will still not be corroboration of the victim's evidence in court (clause 36(5)(a)).
[5] The Court of Appeal has now held that he cannot: *Hester* (*Times*, 21st April 1972).

law is wrong in selecting particular kinds of evidence as requiring corroboration or a direction to the jury that it is dangerous to convict in the absence of corroboration. For the result, it is said, is to suggest that corroboration is always of little or no importance in the case of other kinds of evidence when in fact it may often be more so in some cases. For example, it is argued that in fact the evidence of an accomplice may be much less dangerous to rely on than the evidence of identification of the accused by a witness who had only a brief opportunity to see him or who, without being an accomplice, is a person of bad character. It is also argued that the law is too rigid in that it requires corroboration, or the giving of a warning, in all cases without exception where the issue depends on evidence of the kind in question and in not taking sufficient account of the fact that circumstances differ so much that in some of these cases corroboration may not be at all important.

180. The rules undoubtedly have the great disadvantage of being sometimes difficult to apply owing to technical distinctions, for example as to what kinds of evidence may be corroboration and as to whether a person is an accomplice. These difficulties have caused many mistaken rulings at trials and consequent quashings of convictions. One disadvantage in particular is that a conviction may have to be quashed if the judge directs the jury that a piece of evidence is capable of being corroboration but the Court of Appeal holds that it was not capable of being so. Clearly the conviction would have to be quashed if corroboration was required by statute and there was no other corroboration; but it may have to be quashed even in a case where only a warning was necessary, notwithstanding the fact that it was open to the jury to convict in the absence of corroboration. The conviction might have to be quashed in such a case (i) because the judge erroneously took the view that the evidence was capable of being corroboration, and therefore omitted to give the warning or (ii) because, even if the judge gave the warning out of caution, the Court of Appeal considered that the jury might have found that the evidence was corroboration, when in fact it was not, and so have thought that the danger referred to did not exist. This is the situation even if there is plenty of other evidence, because the verdict will not show whether the jury accepted the other evidence or convicted on the strength of the uncorroborated evidence. The strictness of the present law in these respects has often caused judges, out of caution, to follow too closely in their summing up the wording of the enactment requiring corroboration or the words used in a judgment; and as a result the jury may be confused or even get the impression that the judge intends to convey to them that they should not convict unless the evidence achieves moral certainty as distinct from proof beyond reasonable doubt.

181. The rules requiring the giving of a warning of the danger of convicting in the absence of corroboration have been the subject of special criticism. This relates to the requirement that the judge should refer to the " danger " of convicting. Although there is no fixed formula, the idea of danger must be included in the direction. Looked at from the point of view of the defence, it is said that the direction is absurd in that the judge, having warned the jury that it is dangerous to convict, may go on to say that they may nevertheless convict. It is true that the direction, looked at carefully, implies that it is in general dangerous to convict on evidence of the kind in question but that in the particular case there may be no danger; but the distinction is a subtle one,

and it is said that in practice the effect of adding that the jury may nevertheless convict is to take away much of the protection given by telling them of the danger of doing so. Looked at from the point of view of the prosecution, it is said that the direction provides an extra weapon for the defence in that counsel may urge on the jury the injustice of doing something which the judge is about to tell them it is dangerous to do.

182. It seems to us that there is a great deal of substance in many of the criticisms levelled against the rules as to corroboration. Some members would have liked to abolish all or most of the requirements altogether and replace them with a general provision enjoining judges to give a direction as to the special need for care in deciding whether to act on any particular piece of evidence if the circumstances of the witness required this. But the majority came to the conclusion that in some cases corroboration or a warning (of a different kind from the present) was necessary. We deal with the different rules in the following paragraphs, taking the rules in the order which seems most convenient.

183. We are strongly of the opinion that there should be no special rule about corroboration of the evidence of accomplices. Therefore little need be said by way of summary of the present law in addition to what was said above about corroboration generally. The classes of persons who are accomplices for the purpose of the rule were laid down by the House of Lords in *Davies v. Director of Public Prosecutions*[1]. These are (i) parties to the offence in question, (ii) handlers of stolen goods, in the case of thieves, and (iii) parties to another offence committed by the accused in respect of which evidence is admitted. The rule applies only to these persons when called by the prosecution and does not apply between two co-accused. But there is an increasing tendency in favour of a practice that the judge should give a warning to the jury of the need for special care before convicting on the uncorroborated evidence of a witness, whether a co-accused or a witness for the prosecution, who may have some purpose of his own to serve in giving evidence against the accused, although the witness may not be an accomplice in the strict sense; but it has been stressed that every case must be looked at in the light of its own facts[2]. It is for the judge to rule whether there is evidence that a witness is an accomplice for the purpose of the rule and, if there is, for the jury to find whether he is one[3]. The limited extent to which the rule applies seems to us in itself an objection to the rule, in particular in that it applies only to witnesses called by the prosecution. Also, as mentioned above[4], it is often difficult to decide whether a person is an accomplice of the accused in respect of the offence charged, and the difficulty is aggravated when there are several accused and several charges. But a more serious objection in our view is the fact that the rule applies in all cases merely because the witness is an accomplice and irrespective of the circumstances of the particular case. The reason for the rule is supposed to be the danger that the accomplice may be giving false evidence against the accused in order to minimize his own part in the offence or out of spite against the accused. But although it is clearly right that the

---

[1] [1954] A.C. 378, 400; 38 Cr. App. R. 11, 32–33.
[2] *Prater*, [1960] 2 Q.B. 464; 44 Cr. App. R. 83.
[3] *Davies*, quoted above, at pp. 401–402; pp. 34–35.
[4] Paragraph 180.

attention of the jury should be drawn to these possibilities, if they exist, there are many cases where there is no such possibility. For example, it may be obvious that the accomplice has no ill-feeling against the accused, and he may be repentant and clearly trying to tell the truth about his own part. There may also be many other cases where, in the circumstances, there can be no doubt but that the accomplice's evidence may be wholly reliable, yet the judge must still warn the jury that it is dangerous to rely on it.

184. In truth the idea that there is something about the evidence of accomplices so special as invariably to require a direction that it is dangerous to rely on the evidence is in our view very much in need of reconsideration. As long ago as 1836, when it was still only a rule of practice, and not one of law, that a special direction should be given as to the evidence of accomplices, Henry Joy, Lord Chief Baron of the Court of Exchequer in Ireland, published a book " On the Evidence of Accomplices ", in the course of which he wrote[1]:

> " How the practice which at present prevails, could ever have grown into a general regulation, must be matter of surprise to every person who considers its nature. Why the case of an accomplice should require a particular rule for itself; why it should not, like that of every other witness of whose credit there is an impeachment, be left to the unfettered discretion of the judge, to deal with it as the circumstances of each particular case may require, it seems difficult to explain. Why a fixed unvarying rule should be applied to a subject which admits of such endless variety as the credit of witnesses, seems hardly reconcileable to the principles of reason. But, that a judge should come prepared to reject altogether the testimony of a competent witness as unworthy of credit, before he had even seen that witness; before he had observed his look, his manner, his demeanour; before he had had an opportunity of considering the consistency and probability of his story; before he had known the nature of the crime of which he was to accuse himself, or the temptation which led to it, or the contrition with which it was followed; that a judge, I say, should come prepared beforehand to advise the jury to reject without consideration such evidence, even though judge and jury should be perfectly convinced of its truth, seems to be a violation of the principles of common sense, the dictates of morality, and the sanctity of a juror's oath. "

The view that the present requirement is wholly wrong is also in accordance with the views of the great majority of those who replied to our request for observations in 1968. One judge wrote:

> " Some accomplices clearly have the strongest motives for casting all or most of the blame on the accused, others have no possible motive for lying. It has always seemed to me that to give the required warning as regards the accomplice in the second class is wholly unnecessary and unfair to the accomplice ... In such cases I have given the warning required, but have gone on to point out that what weight the jury attach to such a warning is for them and that they will probably want to consider on the facts of the case they are trying whether the accomplice has any motive at all for lying ".

---

[1] Quoted by Glanville Williams in [1962] Crim. L. R. at p. 590.

185. In our opinion it should be a matter for the judge's discretion whether to give the jury a warning about convicting on the uncorroborated evidence of an accomplice (or, for the reasons given below[1], on the sworn evidence of a child in the case of an offence other than a sexual one). This result will be secured by the provision in clause 20(1) that (subject to any statutory requirements in the Bill or elsewhere about corroboration)—

" at a trial on indictment it shall be for the court to decide in its discretion, having regard to the evidence given, whether the jury should be given a warning about convicting the accused on uncorroborated evidence ".

The subsection goes on to provide that—

" any rule of law or practice whereby at such a trial it is in certain circumstances obligatory for the court to give the jury such a warning is hereby abrogated ".

The effect of the subsection, so far as accomplices are concerned, will be that it will be for the judge to consider whether the circumstances are such that a special warning should be given. For example, if it appears that the accomplice has a purpose of his own to serve in giving the evidence, it will be right to give an appropriate warning, but a warning will not be necessary if it is clear that there is no special reason to think that the accomplice may be lying. There will be no need to consider whether the witness is or is not an accomplice, but only what may be his motives in giving the evidence that he does; and it will be as if the principle stated in *Prater*, referred to above[2], was extended so as to swallow up the rule about accomplices. The provision in subsection (1) that the giving of a warning shall not be " obligatory " takes account of the possibility that in an appropriate case it may be right to give a direction in substance similar to that given at present in the case of accomplices. Although the judge will have a discretion, the exercise of the discretion will, as in ordinary cases of judicial discretion, be open to review on appeal, so that the Court of Appeal might quash a conviction on the ground that in the circumstances the evidence of an accomplice called for a particular direction. We see no reason to think that an innocent person will be any less protected against the danger of a wrong conviction on the evidence of an accomplice than he is under the present rule; and we hope that the inclusion of the provision will serve as a reminder of the need to consider the giving of a warning even in cases where a warning is not required under the present law. One matter of detail should be mentioned here. For the reasons to be given later[3], we are proposing that the rule that the evidence of one accomplice cannot corroborate that of another accomplice should be abolished by the general provision in clause 19(1).

186. The requirement to give a warning of the danger of convicting on the uncorroborated evidence of the complainant in the case of a sexual offence is a much more difficult matter than the requirement in the case of accomplices. We do not think that the former requirement should be simply abolished in reliance on the discretion provided for in clause 20(1) as summarized in paragraph 185. This is because the reason for the requirement

---

[1] Paragraph 208.
[2] Paragraph 183.
[3] Paragraph 194.

112

in sexual cases is quite different from that in the case of an accomplice. In sexual cases it is the danger that the complainant may have made a false accusation owing to sexual neurosis, jealousy, fantasy, spite or a girl's refusal to admit that she consented to an act of which she is now ashamed. In the case of an accomplice any special danger that there may be in relying on the witness's evidence is apparent from the fact that he is an accomplice or it can be easily made apparent by the defence. In the case of a sexual offence the danger may be hidden. Moreover the nature of the evidence may make the jury too sympathetic to the complainant and so prejudice them against the accused.

187. The foregoing reasons are in the opinion of the majority strong arguments for having some special requirement in respect of the evidence of complainants in sexual cases. The arguments to the contrary are the general objection mentioned above[1] to singling out particular kinds of evidence in this way and the inevitable difficulty of the law of corroboration. There are, however, different views in the committee as to how great the dangers mentioned in fact are. It is argued that, since many sexual offences are committed in circumstances in which corroboration is difficult or impossible to obtain, the result of having a requirement relating to corroboration may be that guilty persons will go unpunished. In any event there must be some cases where there can be no danger in relying on uncorroborated evidence. For example, in a case of an indecent assault on an elderly woman there may be no doubt that the assault occurred and the only question may be the identity of the offender. There may be great danger in relying on the evidence of identification (a matter discussed below[2]), but this is not because the offence is a sexual one.

188. In our opinion the best course is to enact separate rules as to corroboration of the evidence of a complainant in a sexual case according to whether the victim is aged fourteen or over or is under that age. We shall be recommending later[3] that, instead of the present rules as to when children should give evidence sworn or unsworn, children under that age should in all cases give their evidence unsworn and those over that age should give it sworn. Where the complainant is fourteen or over, we recommend that the judge should warn the jury that, if they find that the complainant's evidence is not corroborated, there will be a " special need for caution " before convicting the accused on that evidence. This provision is in clause 17(1). A direction to this effect will, we think, convey what is the real difficulty in sexual offences, and it will avoid preserving the seeming anomaly in the present law of directing the jury that there is a " danger " which nevertheless need not prevent them from convicting. What form the warning should take will be a matter for the judge to decide according to the circumstances. He may think it desirable to mention any of the possibilities referred to above[4] as making evidence unreliable which may be relevant in the case, or the warning might be in quite general terms. But clearly there should be no stereotyped formula, and clause 20(2)(a) expressly provides that the court shall not be required to use any particular form of words in giving the warning. In the case of a sexual offence against a child under fourteen we think that there should still be a requirement

---

[1] Paragraph 179.
[2] Paragraphs 196–203.
[3] Paragraph 206.
[4] Paragraph 186.

of corroboration. This is provided for in clause 17(2)[1]. Our particular reason for recommending a stricter rule in the case of offences against children under fourteen is the danger that the child's evidence may be unreliable because of susceptibility or fallibility of memory. In view of these recommendations we regard it as unnecessary to preserve the special provisions in the Sexual Offences Act 1956[2] requiring corroboration in the case of certain sexual offences. Therefore clause 19(4) proposes to repeal these provisions. As a result the question of corroboration in these offences will be left to be governed by the general provisions in clause 17.

189. We consider next the provision in s. 13 of the Perjury Act 1911 requiring corroboration in the case of an offence of, or akin to, perjury. The section reads as follows:

> " A person shall not be liable to be convicted of any offence against this Act, or of any offence declared by any other Act to be perjury or subornation of perjury, or to be punishable as perjury or subornation of perjury, solely upon the evidence of one witness as to the falsity of any statement alleged to be false. "

In considering the policy of this provision we distinguish between—

(i) perjury in judicial proceedings—that is to say, the offence under s. 1 of the Perjury Act and the kindred offence under s. 89 of the Criminal Justice Act 1967 (c. 80) (to which the requirement also applies) of wilfully making a false statement in a written statement tendered in evidence under s. 2 or s. 9 of the 1967 Act; and

(ii) the many other offences under the Perjury Act of making false statements, on oath, in statutory declarations or otherwise, but not in judicial proceedings.

These are dealt with in paragraphs 190 (read with 192) and 191 respectively.

190. The majority of us do not think that the requirement of corroboration in the case of perjury in judicial proceedings—(i) in paragraph 189—should be altogether abolished. As indicated above[3], the consideration that without corroboration it would be oath against oath is not in our view a sufficient justification for requiring corroboration. No doubt anything which would make it easier to secure the punishment of the many bad cases of perjury which are known to occur would be advantageous for the administration of justice; but we doubt whether the abolition, or (except in the respect mentioned below[4]) an alteration, of the requirement would have this effect. In any case the majority think that the requirement is still desirable, because to make a prosecution for perjury too easy might discourage persons from giving evidence. There would also, in the opinion of the majority, be the danger that the successful party to litigation might seek to have his opponent or the latter's witnesses prosecuted for perjury as a result of his evidence having been preferred to theirs (though the latter objection would mostly be got over

---

[1] Clause 17(2), read with clause 19(1), makes it plain that the unsworn evidence of a child complainant may be corroborated by the unsworn evidence of another child, thus altering the law as stated in *Hester*, referred to in paragraph 177 n. 5.
[2] Mentioned in paragraph 175(v).
[3] Paragraph 178.
[4] Paragraph 192.

by our proposal put forward below[1] that the consent of the Director of Public Prosecutions should be necessary for a prosecution for perjury in judicial proceedings). We therefore recommend that corroboration should still be required in respect of perjury in judicial proceedings (including the offence under s. 89 of the Criminal Justice Act mentioned in (i) in paragraph 189).

191. In the case of false statements, made otherwise than in judicial proceedings, to which the requirement in s. 13 of the Perjury Act applies as mentioned in (ii) in paragraph 189, we see no need to preserve the requirement. This is in accordance with the provisional view expressed by the Law Commission in their working paper[2] on perjury and kindred offences published, for the purpose of discussion, on 14th October 1970. The Law Commission said:

> " The numerous statutory offences of making false statements for various purposes (such as those in the Road Traffic Act 1960 (c. 16) and in social security legislation) do not impose a requirement of corroboration and it is difficult to understand why, for example, offences under s. 5 of the 1911 Act should be differently treated. It may be observed in this connection that graver offences punishable under the Theft Act, such as obtaining property or a pecuniary advantage by deception, which may also involve the commission of an offence akin to perjury, do not require corroboration. Our provisional view is, therefore, that the requirement of corroboration is unnecessary save in the special instance of perjury in judicial proceedings ".

We agree with this reasoning, and we recommend that the requirement of corroboration in s. 13 of the Perjury Act should be confined to perjury in judicial proceedings (and, in relation to them, that it should be amended as mentioned in the following paragraph).

192. The provision in s. 13 of the Perjury Act that a person is not liable to conviction " solely upon the evidence of one witness as to the falsity of any statement alleged to be false " differs from ordinary statutory provisions requiring corroboration and refers expressly to the evidence of one witness. The section is treated, rightly or wrongly, as requiring that a second witness should give evidence, from his own knowledge, of the falsity of the statement in question. It follows that it is not enough (as it would be if the section merely required the evidence to be corroborated) that a second witness should prove that the accused admitted the falsity of the statement. This seems to us unnecessarily restrictive; and we recommend that the difficulty should be got over by replacing the rule in s. 13 by a provision to the effect that the accused shall not be liable to be convicted on the evidence of one witness only as to the falsity of the statement in question unless the evidence is corroborated in some material particular by other evidence. This would bring the section into line with the ordinary provisions requiring corroboration. Clause 18 provides accordingly and, in accordance with what is said in the previous paragraph, applies only to perjury in judicial proceedings.

193. The provision in the Road Traffic Act 1960[3] preventing a conviction of speeding on the uncorroborated evidence of one witness of his estimate

---

[1] Paragraph 221.
[2] Published Working Paper No. 33 " Perjury and Kindred Offences ", paragraph 45.
[3] See paragraph 175(vi).

of the speed of a vehicle is clearly a special case, and we do not recommend that the provision should be altered.

194. We recommend the abolition of the rule that the evidence of one witness whose evidence requires corroboration, or in whose case a warning as to the danger of convicting on his evidence if uncorroborated is required, cannot be corroborated by the evidence of another witness who is in a similar position. A rule of this kind may seem logical at first sight, but we do not think that it is really so. For corroboration means " independent testimony which affects the accused by connecting or tending to connect him with the crime "[1]; and there seems no reason why the suggested corroborative evidence, being *ex hypothesi* relevant, admissible, independent and affecting the accused in the way mentioned, should not be allowed to count as corroboration. The fact that the suggested corroborative evidence, if it stood alone, would have been evidence of which corroboration would have been necessary or desirable is obviously a matter to be taken into consideration in estimating its weight; but this is quite different from saying that it is not to be accepted as corroboration at all. For example, where the witness whose evidence is to be corroborated (A) and the suggested corroborating witness (B) are both accomplices, and both, acting independently of each other, tell the same story with consistent details and are unshaken in cross-examination, it seems extraordinary that B's evidence should not be capable of corroborating A's; and it is still more extraordinary if a third accomplice gives similar evidence. The rule also has unfortunate results in cases of sexual offences against children. If the accused is charged with a number of indecent assaults on boys, it is a misdirection to tell the jury that, provided that they are satisfied that the boys did not collaborate to give false evidence, the evidence of one may be taken as corroborating that of another[2]. Yet it would be an extraordinary coincidence if the boys had all by chance picked on the accused to tell the same false story about him from spite or fantasy. In any case the total effect of the evidence could hardly fail to be convincing. Obviously if there is any possibility that the witnesses have collaborated in telling their stories, this may diminish the value of their evidence and an appropriate direction may be necessary; but this is a situation which may occur also with evidence in respect of which no rule as to corroboration applies, and even for example in the case of police witnesses. It seems to the majority of us that the evidence should be capable of counting as corroboration subject only to weight. Clause 19(1) provides accordingly.

195. We see no possible reason to preserve the provisions in the two enactments referred to above[3] requiring a second witness for a conviction of certain offences. Clause 19(2) and (3) therefore repeals these provisions.

196. We have been much concerned by the danger of wrong convictions on account of mistaken identification of the accused and as to whether to make any recommendations with a view to lessening this danger. We regard mistaken identification as by far the greatest cause of actual or possible wrong convictions. Several cases have occurred in recent years when a person has been charged or convicted on what has later been shown beyond doubt to have been mistaken identification. In some cases the actual offender has

---

[1] See paragraph 177.
[2] *Chandor*, [1959] 1 Q.B. 545; 43 Cr. App. R. 74.
[3] Paragraph 175(i) and (iv).

afterwards admitted his guilt. Convictions have also been quashed because of doubt as to the correctness of an identification. Some of these cases have naturally caused great public disquiet, and sometimes this has been temporarily allayed by reference to the fact that we are examining the subject of identification evidence. We regard this as one of the most important matters with which we have been concerned.

197. The subject is one on which it is more than usually difficult to make recommendations. This is because the danger of mistaken identification is one against which in the nature of things there can be nothing like a perfect safeguard, as verdicts must often depend on whether the jury or magistrates' court are satisfied with the witness's identification, and all those concerned—witnesses, judges, juries and magistrates—are fallible. There is also the difficulty that the identifying witness may very likely be obviously perfectly honest and his evidence is likely to seem entirely convincing. The best therefore that can be done is to reduce the danger of injustice in an area where the administration of the criminal law is particularly vulnerable to mistake; and we hope that our recommendations will contribute to this aim.

198. We deal first with the only proposal which we make for legislation. This is that there should be a statutory requirement that the judge should in certain circumstances warn the jury of the need for care in convicting on disputed evidence of identification. Three views were expressed on whether there should be a statutory provision. The first was that there should be a requirement of corroboration in all cases where the issue depends on the correctness of a disputed identification, at least if the accused was not already known to the witness and the witness had not taken the initiative in pointing the accused out to the police, or to some other person concerned, as the offender. There might also be other exceptions, or the judge might be given a discretion to dispense with the requirement of corroboration where to do so would be in accordance with the interests of justice. An example might be where the accused had refused to take part in an identification parade. The advocates of a requirement of corroboration regard nothing less than this as a sufficient safeguard. They argue in particular that evidence of identification is often much weaker than other kinds of evidence in respect of which corroboration is required and that the lack of a requirement in the former case gives the impression that corroboration is there less important. It is also argued, more generally, that a provision is called for in order to make the courts, the legal profession and juries aware of the seriousness of the danger. At the other end of the scale it is argued that no provision should be made requiring corroboration or the giving of a warning. In support it is argued that it would be a scandal if, for example, a burglar could not be convicted on what any jury would accept as the reliable evidence of a householder who had had a clear view of him. Moreover, a requirement of corroboration would enable the defence, if there was no corroboration, to submit that there was no case to answer, and therefore the accused would not have to give evidence when, had he done so, he would probably have been convicted as the result of a damning cross-examination. It is also pointed out that it is now much easier for the Court of Appeal to quash a conviction, in a case where there was a real possibility of mistaken identification, in exercise of their new power under s. 2(1) of the Criminal Appeal Act 1968 (c. 19) to quash a conviction on the ground

that " under all the circumstances of the case it is unsafe or unsatisfactory ". Some of those who are opposed to a requirement of corroboration are opposed also to a requirement that a warning should be given to the jury, because they are convinced that a warning would always be given in a proper case and because they consider it unhelpful to give statutory directions to judges as to how they should direct juries when circumstances differ so much from case to case.

199. The majority of the committee are in favour of a statutory requirement that the judge should give a warning of the special need for caution before convicting in reliance on the correctness of one or more identifications of the accused where the case depends wholly or substantially on this. They think that a requirement of corroboration would be excessive but that the danger of miscarriages of justice and the public disquiet make it desirable that there should be a statutory provision. Without this they do not feel sufficiently confident that a warning would be given in cases where in their opinion it should be given or that appellate courts would hold that this should be done. The Supreme Court of the Republic of Ireland in *The People v. Casey (No. 2)*[1], laid down in clear terms the necessity to give a warning in cases of this kind. Among other things the court said:—

> " In our opinion it is desirable that in all cases, where the verdict depends substantially on the correctness of an identification, [the jury's] attention should be called in general terms to the fact that in a number of instances such identification has proved erroneous, to the possibilities of mistake in the case before them and to the necessity of caution. Nor do we think that such warning should be confined to cases where the identification is that of only one witness. Experience has shown that mistakes can occur where two or more witnesses have made positive identifications. "

It seems to the majority of the committee desirable that some such direction as this should be given in situations of the kind in question. They regard it as doubtful whether English law would go so far at present; for in *Williams*[2] the Court of Criminal Appeal rejected an argument that there was an obligation to give such a direction, and in *Arthurs v. Attorney General for Northern Ireland*[3] (in which the accused was in fact well known to the witness) the House of Lords left for future consideration the question whether there was " need to lay down any rule for the guidance of courts " in cases where the accused was not known to the witness[4]. Before the decision in *Arthurs* a provision requiring the giving of a caution had been prepared to give effect to our views. We considered whether the decision in *Arthurs* made the provision unnecessary, but we thought it desirable to include it. The provision is in clause 21. It will be noted that it avoids referring to corroboration at all and expressly provides for the giving of the direction even when there is more than one identification. The clause is not limited to cases where the accused was previously unknown to the witness, because even where they are known to each other there may be a danger that the identification is mistaken—at least

---

[1] [1963] I.R. 33, 39–40.
[2] [1956] Crim. L.R. 833.
[3] (1970), 55 Cr. App. R. 161.
[4] At p. 169.

if the witness had only a limited opportunity to observe the offender. In a case where he had a good opportunity the direction would naturally be less strong. The clause provides that, as with the other requirements to give a direction, it shall not be necessary to use any particular form of words. It will be the duty of magistrates' courts to have regard to the need for caution in a case where the direction would have been called for had the trial been on indictment[1].

200. It would also help, in our opinion, to reduce the danger of convictions on mistaken identification if the police made it a practice in all cases to supply the defence with copies of any descriptions of the offender which any likely witness has given to them. This would assist the defence to challenge the value of the witness's identification of the accused. This proposal was discussed with the police representatives who came to one of our meetings, and they agreed that it would be desirable. They mentioned that even at present the witness's description would very likely be included in a statement of evidence served on the accused under s. 1 of the Criminal Justice Act 1967 for the purpose of committal proceedings and that in any event the description would always be supplied on request or (at least in some forces) in any case where identification was in issue. We recognize that this practice might sometimes enable the defence to secure an unjustified acquittal by over-insistence on discrepancies between the witness's original description and the appearance of the accused, because many people are very bad at describing appearances. Sometimes people mention only a particular feature of the offender which struck them. An informant who had been robbed might be frightened when giving his description and it might be unreliable as a result. In a murder case a witness described the murderer as being a person of seventeen or eighteen but later identified a man of forty-one, indisputably correctly, as the murderer. But none of our members or of the police representatives regard this possible danger as a reason for not making the recommendation. It would also, we think, be desirable that, where the circumstances allow, the police should ask an informant to write down or dictate his description as soon as possible and *before* being shown a photograph of the suspect. Because of the difficulty that many witnesses are bad at describing appearances we suggest that informants should be asked to complete a simple form giving the main features of the offender. We think it desirable that the practice should be laid down in administrative directions to the police, in which the details would be worked out.

201. We considered a suggestion designed to prevent as far as possible the situation which sometimes occurs in a case of disputed identification that the identifying witness points out the accused for the first time in court. Often this will be of little value because the witness may point to the accused merely because he is in the dock. The suggestion was that, in a disputed case of identification where the accused was a stranger to the witness and the witness did not take the initiative in pointing him out as the offender, the witness should not be allowed to give evidence identifying the accused in court as the offender unless he had first identified him at an identification parade. It might also be made a condition that the recommendations summarized above[2] as to supplying the defence with the witness's description of

---

[1] Clause 28; paragraph 222.
[2] Paragraph 200.

119

the offender should have been complied with. The court would have a discretion to allow the witness to identify the accused in court as the offender if there were some good reason for this. Examples would be where the accused refused to take part in a parade, where he had at first admitted his connection with the offence but afterwards denied it, where the witness was unable to attend a parade or where he attended it and recognized the accused but was afraid to point to him. In favour of this course it is argued that (apart from the weakness of identification in court) too many cases have occurred where for no good reason there was a failure to hold an identification parade or a witness identified the accused in the dock after failing to point him out at the parade. The majority of the committee, while agreeing strongly that in general it is right that a witness who is to identify the accused in court as the offender should be asked first to attend an identification parade, do not think that there should be a statutory requirement. They think that this would be too strict, as the matter must depend on the circumstances. If the evidence of the identifying witness would be so strong that a conviction would be inevitable, it seems to the majority wrong that the evidence should have to be excluded in all cases where there was no parade. Moreover, if the witness has positively identified the accused to the police soon after the offence (from a photograph or otherwise, for example in the street), there would be little purpose in holding a parade. In any event, unsuccessful identification parades (in the sense that there was no identification or a mistaken one) are so common —often because of the care with which they are conducted—that it would in our opinion be wrong to attach too much significance to them as a safeguard against the danger of wrong conviction on identification evidence. A police representative estimated the rate of success in London in 1968 as so low as one in eight, and he added that sometimes a witness who failed to point out a suspect told the police afterwards that he thought—in fact rightly—that somebody was the offender but he had said nothing because he was not sure. Two officials on the staff of one of our members took part in parades during our discussions. One took part in five parades and was twice picked out as the offender—once apparently for no better reason than that he was the shortest man on the parade and the offender was short. The other took part in three parades and was picked out once. If there was no good reason why an identification parade was not held, the defence can comment strongly on the failure to hold it; and courts have several times criticized such a failure or defects in the holding of the parades such as where the accused looked markedly different from the other members. In any event it would be impossible to define in a statute the kind of identification evidence which should not be allowed to be given in court. But clearly the warning which clause 21 requires to be given about the special need for caution before convicting on identification evidence ought to take particular account of the fact, if it is a fact, that the identifying witness had not pointed out the accused before giving his evidence.

202. We considered a dilemma which arises when the accused is first picked out by a witness from a photograph shown to him by the police. This happens, for example, when the police show the witness a number of photographs of persons who from his description are likely to include the offender. It is argued that the fact that the witness first identified the accused in this way greatly weakens the value of his evidence in court that the accused is the

offender, because there is the danger that the identification in court may be more from the photograph than from the witness's recollection of seeing the offender at the time of the offence. This is not always so, as the photograph may refresh the witness's memory of the offender's appearance, but it is difficult to dispute the existence of the danger. On the other hand, for the defence to bring out the fact that the accused was first identified from a photograph reveals the fact that the police possessed the accused's photograph and this implies almost certainly that he has a criminal record. The general effect of the present law is to present counsel for the defence with what may be a very difficult choice: either to reveal that the accused has a record or to allow the jury or magistrates' court to suppose that the witness for the prosecution has made an unassisted identification of the accused when in fact he has been shown a photograph. It was argued in the committee that the second course involves a greater danger of the conviction of an innocent person than the first and that, in order to minimize the danger and to take the decision out of the hands of a (possibly inexperienced) counsel for the defence, there should be a requirement that at trials on indictment the fact that the accused was first identified from the photograph should in all cases be mentioned to the jury by the prosecution. But the majority of the committee are opposed to this, because they do not agree that the possible weakness in the identification is necessarily more prejudicial to the accused than is the implication that he has a criminal record, and because they think that it must be left to the defence to estimate which is the greater danger. A possible way of resolving the dilemma which was suggested was that the judge should be informed, in the absence of the jury, that the accused was first identified from a photograph, so that the judge might give an emphatic warning to the jury about the need to consider carefully the strength of the identification evidence. But we do not favour this course, because we think that the principle must be adhered to that anything relevant to the jury's consideration of the case should be said in their presence. Moreover the proposal could not be applied to magistrates' courts, and the committee generally regard it as undesirable that the law of evidence in magistrates' courts should differ from that in the Crown Court.

203. We have two acknowledgments to make in connection with identification parades. First, the Home Office circular[1] which gave advice to the police on the practice as to these parades was issued in January 1969 during our discussions and after giving us an opportunity to consider a draft; and the final instructions took account of comments made during our discussions. Second, and more important, we were greatly impressed by the amount of work entailed for the police by the holding of identification parades and the way in which the police shouldered this burden with little public acknowledgment of its magnitude.

CLAUSE 22: EVIDENCE OF CHILDREN

204. There is no fixed age below which children are incompetent to give evidence on oath. In a case of doubt it is the duty of the court to question

---

[1] " Identification Parades " (No. 9/1969).

the child in order to determine whether he understands the nature and consequences of taking the oath. This was decided in *Brasier*[1], where a man was convicted of the rape of a girl under seven on the strength of evidence given by the girl's mother and another woman of what the girl told her and the girl herself did not give evidence. The twelve judges decided that the evidence was wrongly admitted as all evidence had to be given on oath. They said that the competence of children as witnesses " depends upon the sense and reason they entertain of the danger and impiety of falsehood, which is to be collected from their answers to questions propounded to them by the court ". But provision has been made by statute for the admission (in criminal cases only) of unsworn evidence by children. The present provision is in s. 38(1) of the Children and Young Persons Act 1933 (c. 12), which is as follows:—

> " Where, in any proceedings against any person for any offence, any child of tender years called as a witness does not in the opinion of the court understand the nature of an oath, his evidence may be received, though not given upon oath, if, in the opinion of the court, he is possessed of sufficient intelligence to justify the reception of the evidence, and understands the duty of speaking the truth . . . ".

The proviso contains the requirement of corroboration quoted above[2].

205. In our opinion the present rules, though they cause no serious difficulty, are unsatisfactory and should be replaced. The inquiry whether the child understands the nature of the oath, if carried out conscientiously, seems to us unrealistic; and the investigation sometimes made by the court as to whether the child believes in divine retribution for lying is really out of place when the question is whether he understands how important it is for the proceedings that he should tell the truth to the best of his ability about the events in question—in particular that he should not say anything against the accused which he does not really believe to be true and that he should say if he did not see something or does not remember it. For similar reasons the test in s. 38 of the 1933 Act whether the child " understands the duty of speaking the truth " seems inadequate; for even very young children understand this duty in a general way without necessarily understanding the particular importance of telling the truth in the proceedings. Some judges feel that the inquiry which they have to make sometimes verges on farce.

206. We think that it would be best to fix the age at and above which children should always give evidence on oath and below which they should always give it unsworn. This will provide a simple rule to apply and would also in our view be right in policy. The right age is very much a matter of opinion. We propose that it should be fourteen. At this age any normal young person should understand his duty when giving evidence, and his liability to prosecution if he gives false evidence, as well as does an adult, and he should also be free from the particular disadvantages (special susceptibility and fallibility of memory) of children's evidence. It may occasionally be obvious that a particular young person of fourteen or above is so retarded as to be unfit to give evidence, but here the problem is no different from that of a mentally subnormal adult. In the case of a child under fourteen there

---

[1] (1779), 1 Leach 199.
[2] Paragraph 175 (iii).

must be some test of fitness to give evidence. We recommend that, in order to meet the point made above[1] about the present test, the new test should be whether in the opinion of the court the child " is possessed of sufficient intelligence to justify the reception of his evidence and understands the importance of telling the truth in [the] proceedings ". This is provided for in clause 22(2). Since the test will be for the court to apply, it will be for it to decide what are the appropriate questions to put to the child. No provision is included in the clause to abolish the common law rule as to fitness to give evidence on oath, because, as indicated above, it will be taken that any normal person of fourteen or over is fit to do so.

207. At present, if a child gives false unsworn evidence such that, had the evidence been given on oath, he would have been guilty of perjury, he is punishable on summary conviction (assuming that he is of the age of criminal responsibility) under s. 38(2) of the Children and Young Persons Act 1933. Although the occasions for this are presumably rare, we think that provision should be made for such a case in the new law, because it would be wrong that a child should not be liable to be dealt with for a bad case of false evidence. One of our members tried a case where two boys of fourteen and fifteen were put up to swear to false alibis, and the boys might well have been below fourteen. But the form of the provision will have to depend on whether s.4 of the Children and Young Persons Act 1969 (c. 54), which raises the age of criminal responsibility from ten to fourteen, has come into force. As this is uncertain, clause 22(5) assumes that it will have done so and provides that the witness shall be treated for the purposes of Part I of the Act as guilty of an offence (and so liable to be dealt with in accordance with the non-criminal procedure for which Part I provides).

208. There remains the question of corroboration of children's evidence. As already mentioned, their unsworn evidence requires corroboration under s. 38 of the Children and Young Persons Act 1933[2] and a warning must be given of the danger of convicting on their sworn evidence[3]. We have already proposed that in the case of a sexual offence there should be a warning of the special need for caution before convicting on the uncorroborated evidence of a complainant of fourteen or over and that corroboration should be required if the complainant is under fourteen[4]. We considered whether any provision should be made as to corroboration of children's evidence in cases of non-sexual offences. In favour of doing so is the possible unreliability of their evidence for reasons mentioned above (susceptibility and fallibility of memory). On the other hand children are often very observant and, at least in non-sexual cases, often give very good evidence. More important, perhaps, is the fact that very young children are seldom required to give evidence except in sexual cases. We have come to the conclusion that in non-sexual cases there is no such danger in convicting on the uncorroborated evidence of children as to make it necessary to require corroboration or a warning about convicting on uncorroborated evidence. Accordingly, the present requirement of corroboration in s. 38 of the 1933 Act will disappear with the repeal of that section by clause 22(1), and the rule requiring the

---

[1] Paragraph 205.
[2] Paragraph 175(iii).
[3] Paragraph 176.
[4] Paragraph 188.

giving of a warning of the danger of convicting on children's sworn evidence will be abolished by clause 20(1)

CLAUSE 23: TIME AT WHICH EVIDENCE MAY BE CALLED

209. In connection with evidence of other misconduct of the accused[1] we referred to the rule of practice as stated in *Rice* that all evidentiary matter on which the prosecution intend to rely should be adduced before the close of their case if it is then available; and for the reason there given we proposed that the rule should be relaxed in the way provided by clause 3(6). Although there seems to be no express authority, the same rule applies to the defence in that, after they have closed their case and the speeches have begun, they require the leave of the court to call more evidence, though leave would no doubt be given in the interests of the accused if they showed a reasonable cause for not having called the evidence earlier. What is said above applies to the time before the jury or magistrates' court have retired. After that time the rule is much stricter, as mentioned below.

210. It is difficult to say how strict is the rule of practice that the prosecution should not be allowed to call evidence after the close of their case, because the authorities are in conflict. In *Frost*[2], Tindal C. J. said that it was only " if any matter arises *ex improviso*, which no human ingenuity can foresee, on the part of . . . a prisoner in a criminal case " that the prosecution may call fresh witnesses. The test, as there stated, is sometimes referred to as the " *ex improviso* rule ". Tindal C. J.'s statement of the rule seems to have more or less held the field till *Crippen*[3], where Darling J., in giving the judgment of the Court of Criminal Appeal, said[4]:

" We do not feel inclined to lay down the rule as strictly as Tindal C. J. did in *Reg. v. Frost*. We do not propose to adopt the language of Tindal C. J. The rule laid down in those terms may, we think, place an unfair burden on counsel for the prosecution in some cases . . . Assuming [the fresh evidence] to be admissible evidence, it then becomes a question for the judge at the trial to determine in his discretion whether the evidence, not having been tendered in chief, ought to be given as rebutting evidence ".

Between *Crippen* and *Owen*[5], Darling J.'s statement was disregarded in several cases in the Court of Criminal Appeal[6]. But the *Crippen* principle was reasserted by the Court of Criminal Appeal in *Owen*, where the court had the intervening cases as well as *Crippen* and the earlier cases in mind.

---

[1] Paragraph 101(v).
[2] (1839), 4 St. Tr. (N.S.) 85, 386.
[3] [1911] 1 K. B. 149.
[4] At p. 157. The passage in 5 Cr. App. R. 255, 265–266 is a little different.
[5] [1952] 2 Q. B. 362; 36 Cr. App. R. 16.
[6] These include *Harris*, [1927] 2 K.B. 587; 20 Cr. App. R. 86; *Liddle* (1928), 21 Cr. App. R. 3; and *Day* (1940), 27 Cr. App. R. 168. In none of these cases was the court's attention drawn to *Crippen*.

Lord Goddard C. J., in giving the reserved judgment of the Court of Criminal Appeal, said[1]:

" We may observe that the rule laid down by Tindal C. J. is probably in wider language than would be applied at the present day ".

But since this case the Court of Appeal have referred in at least two recent cases (*Tregear*[2] and *Cleghorn*[3]) to the " no human ingenuity can foresee " test in *Frost* in ways which suggest that they regarded the general rule of practice as going as far as that, though in both cases the court made it clear that the rule was only a rule of practice, and in *Tregear* the court upheld the decision of the judge to allow rebutting evidence. However, in the more recent case of *Milliken*[4], Winn L. J., in giving the judgment of the Court of Appeal, adopted Lord Goddard C. J.'s statement of the rule in *Owen* (re-marking that " it seems that sometimes these observations escape attention these days "). In the recent case of *Doran*[5] the Court of Appeal, after referring to several of the cases mentioned in this section of our report, said that it " [did] not regard a judge trying a criminal case as being limited, in the exercise of his discretion to allow fresh evidence, to cases where that evidence is strictly of a rebutting character ", though the court also " stressed that the calling of such evidence should be the rare exception rather than the common rule ". The " no human ingenuity can foresee " test is stated in Archbold[6].

211. In this state of the authorities it seems to us that it is desirable that the rule should be put on a statutory basis if it is to be preserved. The reasons for the rule, so far as evidence for the prosecution is concerned, are (i) that, since it is thought that fairness to the defence demands that they should be allowed to tell their story after the prosecution have told theirs, it would weaken this principle to allow the prosecution to give further evidence after that for the defence, and (ii) that it is untidy and inconvenient to sandwich defence evidence on some issues between parts of the prosecution evidence. In some cases to allow the prosecution to call a particular piece of evidence at a late stage might cause injustice to the defence because, coming as it did in isolation after the evidence for the defence and probably after argument as to whether it was so important that it should be admitted even at that stage, it might make a disproportionate impression on the jury. On the other hand, sometimes an important piece of information emerges only at a late stage. For example, we were told that in one case of robbery the accused gave evidence that at the time of the robbery he was coming out of a lavatory, but a member of the jury knew that the lavatory had been boarded up since well before that time, and as a result evidence to this effect was then called by the prosecution. In *Doran*, referred to above[7], two persons who happened to be present at a trial for handling stolen goods remembered, as a result of hearing some of the evidence for the defence, that they could give material evidence about the accused's disposing of some of the goods, and as a result the prosecution were allowed

---

[1] [1952] 2 Q.B. at p. 367; 36 Cr. App. R. at p. 20.
[2] [1967] 2 Q.B. 574, 581; 51 Cr. App. R. 280, 287.
[3] [1967] 2 Q.B. 584; 589; 51 Cr. App. R. 291, 295.
[4] (1969), 53 Cr.App. R. 330, 333–334.
[5] *Times*, 17th March 1972. The court followed its own decision in this respect in *Sillito and Badwal* (21st March 1972, unreported).
[6] 37th edition, paragraphs 554 and 1397.
[7] Paragraph 210.

by the judge to call them to give evidence after two witnesses had given eviden ce for the defence. The Court of Appeal upheld the judge's decision. It seems right that it should always be possible for a witness to give evidence of these kinds at any stage. The need to call evidence at a late stage might also arise on the part of the defence. If, for example, after the close of the case for the defence counsel for the prosecution in his final speech commented on the failure of the defence to call evidence on some matter, counsel for the defence might say that he had not expected this comment and that he could have called evidence on the point. It seems right that the court should have a discretion to allow this (in particular, if the counsel for the prosecution does not with-draw the point).

212. The better course, in our opinion, is to enact the rule so that all evidence to be given on behalf of either party shall be given before the conclusion of the party's case except in so far as the court in its discretion otherwise allows. We think it unnecessary, and undesirable, to specify the cases in which the discretion should be exercised, as it would be difficult to cover all the possible cases. Clause 23(1) provides accordingly. But the proviso makes an exception in the case of evidence of the accused himself. This is because it seems wrong that, if the accused refuses to give evidence when called on to do so at the appropriate time, he should be allowed to change his mind and do so after the defence have said that their case is closed. It seems that he must take the consequences of his refusal and not be allowed to retrieve his position after perhaps counsel for the prosecution or the court had made strong comments on his refusal to give evidence.

213. At trials on indictment there is a rule of practice, usually strictly insisted on, that after the summing up and the retirement of the jury no witness may be recalled, nor may a new witness be called, to give evidence whether at the request of the jury or otherwise; and it has been insisted on even though the defence were willing that the evidence should be given. The rule was laid down by the Court of Criminal Appeal in *Owen*[1], following a decision of the same court in *Browne*[2]. In *Owen* Lord Goddard C. J., giving the reserved judgment of the court, said[3]:

> " It is by no means uncommon for a jury to put a question to the presiding judge after he has concluded his summing up *and whether before or after they have retired*[4], and the usual practice is for the judge to tell the jury, if it is a fact, that no evidence on the point has been given and they must take it, therefore, that there is no evidence upon it, though, of course, if they ask a question upon which evidence has been given it is quite right for the judge to remind the jury of the evidence. We think this is the only safe practice, and it ought to be followed. The theory of our law is that he who affirms must prove, and therefore it is for the prose-cutor to prove his case, and if there is some matter which the prosecution might have proved but have not, it is too late, after the summing-up, to allow further evidence to be given, and that whether it might have been given by one of the witnesses already called or whether it would

---

[1] [1952] 2 Q.B. 362; 36 Cr. App. R. 16 (referred to also in paragraph 210).
[2] (1943), 29 Cr. App. R. 106.
[3] At [1952] 2 Q.B. pp. 368–369; 36 Cr. App. R. pp. 21–22.
[4] As to the words italicized see paragraph 214.

necessitate . . . the calling of a fresh witness. If this were allowed, it is difficult to see what limitation could be put upon it. A witness might be called who would then be open to cross-examination and the defence might then apply to call further evidence in answer ".

The principle stated in *Owen* has been applied in at least three recent cases[1] where the judge acceded to a request by the jury, after they had retired, to be allowed to see a person or a car involved in the case. The rule at summary trials[2] and appeals from them to the Crown Court[3] is less strict than that at trials on indictment.

214. Certain words are italicized in the quotation from *Owen* in paragraph 213 because in *Sanderson*[4], where a witness for the defence arrived late for the hearing and was allowed to give evidence after the summing up but before the jury retired, and the judge delivered a short supplementary summing up with reference to his evidence, the Court of Criminal Appeal distinguished *Owen* and held that in the circumstances there was no objection to the course taken, although it was " not a course one would wish to be taken often ", and dismissed the appeal against conviction. As a result, the statements in later cases of the rule in *Owen* are limited to where the jury have retired.

215. The Supreme Court of the Republic of Ireland regard the English rule as being too rigid. In *O'Brien*[5] the court held that there was a judicial discretion to allow a witness to be recalled at the jury's request. The judgment reviewed the previous English authorities (noting that there was some authority before *Owen* suggesting that the judge had a discretion to allow the evidence) and said[6]:

" The rule in *Owen*'s case has obvious advantages. It makes for tidiness and order. It is definite and easily operated ";

but concluded:

" In this country the proper rule is, in our view, that a trial judge has power in the exercise of his discretion to allow a witness to be recalled and to give evidence at any stage of the case before the jury agrees on a verdict. That discretion must, of course, be judicially exercised. The propriety of recalling a witness and of the questions addressed to him must to a great extent depend upon the course of the trial, the facts of the case, and other matters which can be fully and properly appreciated only by the trial judge himself. His discretion should therefore not be interfered with unless an injustice has resulted from its exercise ".

216. The arguments for and against the strict rule in *Owen* appear sufficiently from the quotations from that case and *O'Brien*. We prefer the more flexible Irish rule as being more convenient in practice. In particular it allows the judge to accede to a perfectly reasonable request by the jury such

---

[1] *Gearing* (1965), 50 Cr. App. R. 18; *Lawrence* (1968), 52 Cr. App. R. 163; *Nixon* (1968), 52 Cr. App. R. 218. In *Nixon* the Court of Appeal applied the proviso to s. 4(1) of the Criminal Appeal Act 1907 and dismissed the appeal because " the irregularity . . . took place with the express consent and at the express wish of the defence ".
[2] *Wood v. Leadbetter*, [1966] 2 All E.R. 114.
[3] *Phelan v. Back*, [1972] 1 W. L. R. 273; [1972] 1 All E.R. 901.
[4] (1953), 37 Cr. App. R. 32.
[5] [1963] I.R. 65.
[6] At pp. 79–80.

as those mentioned above[1]. Clause 23(2) accordingly makes the matter one for the discretion of the court. This will enable the court to allow a witness to be recalled and also to allow a new witness to be called. There seems no difference in principle between these cases. Here again, as in the case of the discretion under subsection (1) to allow a party to call evidence after the close of his case, it seems unnecessary and undesirable to specify the grounds on which the discretion should be exercised. No doubt the court will take into account in particular the danger mentioned above[2] that the jury might make too much of a particular piece of late evidence admitted on behalf of the prosecution. The rule will apply to summary trials as well as trials on indictment.

CLAUSES 24–26: VARIOUS PROVISIONS RELATING TO CONVICTIONS AND ACQUITTALS

217. S.11 of the Civil Evidence Act 1968 (c. 64) abolished the rule, generally referred to as the " rule in *Hollington v. Hewthorn* "[3], that a conviction of a criminal offence was inadmissible in civil proceedings as evidence of the fact that the person convicted committed the misconduct involved in the offence. The section, which adopted the recommendations of the Law Reform Committee in their 15th report[4], provides that in civil proceedings the fact that a person has been convicted of an offence at a court in the United Kingdom or by a court-martial shall be admissible to prove that he committed that offence. In civil proceedings other than proceedings for defamation the person convicted is to be taken to have committed the offence unless the contrary is proved. By s.13 the conviction is conclusive for the purpose of defamation proceedings. There are various ancillary provisions, including provision making the contents of indictments and other official documents containing the charge admissible for the purpose of identifying the facts on which the conviction was based and provision for proof of these documents.

218. There is no doubt that the principle of *Hollington v. Hewthorn* applies to criminal cases, although there is very little authority. For example, in *Turner*[5] " many of [the judges] appeared to think " that in a case of receiving stolen property the conviction of the thief " would not have been any evidence of her guilt, which must have been proved by other means ". This is always taken to be the law. In our opinion it is clearly right that convictions of persons other than the accused should be made admissible in criminal proceedings as evidence of the fact that the person convicted was guilty of the offence charged and that on proof of the conviction that person should be taken to have committed the offence charged unless the contrary is proved. Clause 24 provides accordingly. It seems quite wrong, as well as being

---

[1] Paragraph 213.
[2] Paragraph 211.
[3] [1943] K.B. 587.
[4] " The Rule in *Hollington v. Hewthorn* ": Cmnd. 3391.
[5] (1832), 1 Mood. C.C. 347, 349.

inconvenient, that the prosecution should be required to prove again the guilt of the person concerned. The clause will be helpful to the prosecution in various cases where the guilt of the accused depends on another person's having committed an offence. Examples are handling stolen goods, harbouring offenders and the offences under ss.4 and 5 of the Criminal Law Act 1967 (c. 58) of assisting offenders and concealing offences.

219. Two matters of detail should be mentioned in connection with clause 24:

    (i) Subsection (2) provides that, where a person other than the accused is proved to have been convicted of an offence, he shall be taken to have committed it " unless the contrary is proved ". Since the subsection also provides that clause 8 shall not have effect in relation to the subsection, the effect will be that, if the accused wishes to dispute the correctness of the other person's conviction, he will have to prove on a balance of probabilities (the ordinary burden of proof on the defence in criminal cases) that the conviction was wrong. We have no doubt that this result is right in policy and that it would be wrong for clause 8 to have effect in relation to clause 24 (2) and so reduce the burden of proof on the defence to an evidential one. For in a case to which clause 24 (2) applies the guilt of the other person will have been established by a judicial decision; and it would in our view be wholly inappropriate, and contrary to the interests of justice, that the mere fact that the accused was able to adduce some evidence fit for consideration that a subsisting conviction of another person was wrong should impose on the prosecution the burden of proving beyond reasonable doubt that the conviction was right. Moreover, what is perhaps the strongest argument for clause 8 is that it is wrong in principle that the jury or magistrates' court should have to convict the accused even if they are left in doubt as to an issue on which his guilt depends[1]; and this argument hardly applies where the issue is whether another person has committed an offence of which he has been duly convicted.

    (ii) There is no provision corresponding to the provision in s.13 of the Civil Evidence Act 1968 which makes a conviction conclusive for the purpose of an action for defamation. We regard it as unnecessary and undesirable to follow the Civil Evidence Act in this respect. For prosecutions for libel differ from civil actions in certain material respects. First, truth alone is not a defence to a criminal charge. Second, it is possible that in some circumstances an indictment will lie for libelling a deceased person. In any event prosecutions for libel are very rare; and in the unlikely event of an attempt by a person convicted of an offence to reopen the question of his guilt by means of criminal proceedings against somebody for referring to his having committed the offence it can hardly be supposed that a justice would see fit to issue a summons or that a judge would give leave to prefer a voluntary bill of indictment.

220. Clauses 25 and 26 contain ancillary provisions. Clause 25 contains provisions corresponding to the provisions in the Civil Evidence Act mentioned

---

[1] See paragraph 140(i).

above[1] for the admissibility of contents of indictments and other official documents. Clause 26 is a modernized provision for the proof of convictions and acquittals by means of the appropriate official documents. Details of these provisions are referred to in the notes on the clauses in Annex 2.

CLAUSE 27: INSTITUTION OF PROCEEDINGS FOR PERJURY ETC.

221. Clause 27 provides that proceedings for perjury in judicial proceedings[2] shall not be instituted except by or with the consent of the Director of Public Prosecutions. This restriction seems to us desirable for two reasons. First, perjury is an offence particularly related to the administration of justice, and it seems right that there should be a consistent policy as to prosecutions for the offence. Second, the relaxation by clause 18 of the requirement as to corroboration in proceedings for perjury might possibly have the effect of encouraging private prosecutions in cases where prosecutions would be wholly unjustified and improper (for example, in the cases suggested above[3] where a successful litigant might seek to prosecute his opponent for perjury). In consequence the clause also abolishes the power given to judges and other judicial authorities by s. 9 of the Perjury Act 1911 to order a prosecution for perjury which they consider to have been committed in proceedings before them. Orders for this purpose are very rarely made; and it seems in any event undesirable that the power should exist, because it involves the proposition that the authority in question has formed the opinion that the offence was committed, and this might be prejudicial to the accused. Moreover the authority before whom the perjury may have been committed may well not be in a position to judge whether sufficient corroboration will be available, and it is clearly unsatisfactory that the court or other authority should give a direction which the Director of Public Prosecutions may be unable for this reason effectually to carry out.

CLAUSE 28: DUTY OF MAGISTRATES' COURTS TO HAVE REGARD TO ENACTMENTS ABOUT WARNINGS TO JURIES

222. In the part of our report relating to corroboration and directions to juries we recommended that it should be the duty of judges to give, or to con-

---

[1] Paragraph 217.
[2] By perjury in judicial proceedings we mean the offences specified in head (i) in paragraph 189. These are the offences to which the requirement of corroboration is to be restricted by s.13 of the Perjury Act 1911 as substituted by clause 18.
[3] Paragraph 190.

sider the desirability of giving, directions to juries as to the special need for caution before convicting in certain circumstances[1]. At present in the cases where a judge is under an obligation to warn the jury of the danger of convicting on uncorroborated evidence (that is to say, in the cases of evidence of accomplices, complainants in sexual cases and the sworn evidence of children), magistrates' courts have the duty of directing themselves accordingly. It seems to us desirable that there should be a statutory provision to this effect in relation to the cases where a judge will have the duty under the new law as mentioned. Clause 28 provides accordingly.

CLAUSE 29: ABOLITION OF RIGHT TO MAKE EVIDENCE OF DOCUMENT CALLED FOR AND INSPECTED BY AN OPPONENT

223. There is an obscure rule, in civil cases at least, that, where party A calls for a document in the possession of party B and B produces the document without putting it in evidence, and A reads it, B can require A to put it in " evidence ". The rule was applied in the divorce case of *Stroud v. Stroud*[2]. We know of no instance of its being applied in criminal proceedings, but Wrangham J. in the case mentioned[3] expressly contemplated that the rule would apply to criminal proceedings. Probably any lawyer practising in the criminal courts would be surprised if the question arose of applying the rule there. There is no authority as to the exact purpose for which the document may be received in evidence—whether as evidence of the facts stated in it (in which case admissibility would be by way of exception to the rule against hearsay) or for some lesser purpose; but presumably it is the former purpose. How the rule would be applied where the document is one of a number in a file and party A reads part of the file it is difficult to forecast. In any event it seems to us very doubtful whether it is right that a party should be able to get a document before the court in this way when it may be impossible or difficult to find out who supplied the information contained in the document or what was his authority for doing so. The information might even have come from somebody incompetent to give evidence to the effect of the information. We considered whether to recommend preserving the rule, adjusting it to our proposals about hearsay evidence; but we came to the conclusion that, if the rule applies to criminal proceedings, it should do so no longer, because the benefit which it might confer in these proceedings is minute and it might work injustice, especially in a case such as suggested where the reliability of information contained in the document cannot be checked. Clause 29 therefore abolishes the rule so far as criminal proceedings are concerned.

---

[1] The relevant provisions are in clauses 17(1), 20(1) and 21.
[2] [1963] 3 All E.R. 539.
[3] At p. 541 H.

CLAUSES 30–41: HEARSAY EVIDENCE

224. We propose that large inroads should be made into the rule against hearsay comparable with, but different in important respects from, the inroads made into the rule in civil proceedings by the Civil Evidence Act 1968 (c. 64). This Act was passed in accordance with the recommendations of the Law Reform Committee in their 13th report[1]. Having regard to the Act and report, it is not necessary for our report to go fully into the law of hearsay before giving our recommendations; but for convenience we summarize the rule and refer to the arguments for and against allowing hearsay evidence in criminal proceedings.

225. We adopt the statement of the rule in Professor Cross's " Evidence "[2], as follows:

" Express or implied assertions of persons other than the witness who is testifying, and assertions in documents produced to the court when no witness is testifying, are inadmissible as evidence of the truth of that which was asserted ".

In its simplest application the rule has the effect that, if it is desired to prove that A was at a certain place at a certain time, a witness may not be called to say that B told the witness that A was there. In its more subtle applications the rule prevents a party from proving a fact by the production of a document recording the fact. The rule is subject to a large number of exceptions. Among the best known are informal admissions and confessions, declarations by deceased persons against interest or in the course of duty, dying declarations, statements in public documents and some statements admissible as being part of the " *res gestae* ". But there are many other exceptions, some by common law and some by statute. Some of the former are very obscure and ill-defined, and Professor Cross has pointed out that the admission of certain kinds of evidence " can only be explained on the footing that there are many more exceptions to the hearsay rule than is commonly supposed "[3]. In the draft American " Uniform Rules of Evidence " promulgated by the National Conference of Commissioners on Uniform State Laws in 1953, rule 63, which sets out the rule substantially to the same effect as above (except that it applies also to the previous statement of a witness who is testifying[4]), gives thirty-one exceptions supposed to exist at common law, many of them inapplicable to criminal law.

226. Two particular matters should be mentioned in relation to the rule:

(i) The rule as stated does not apply to previous statements of the witness who is testifying. But there is a kindred rule that it is not permissible for a witness, when giving evidence, to seek to strengthen his evidence by saying that he said the same thing on a previous occasion. The latter rule is subject to exceptions. It is very similar in its effect to the rule against hearsay, and it is sometimes confused with it. Our proposals, if adopted, will have the effect of getting rid

---

[1] Hearsay Evidence in Civil Proceedings: Cmnd. 2964.
[2] 3rd edition, p. 387.
[3] " Evidence ", 3rd edition, p. 453.
[4] See paragraph 226(i).

of this rule for all practical purposes and of merging what will be left of it with the residue of the rule against hearsay.

(ii) As shown in the statement of the rule against hearsay quoted above[1], it is only when the assertion in question is offered as evidence of the truth of what was asserted that the statement is inadmissible under the rule. If what is sought to be proved is not that what is contained in the statement is true but that the statement was in fact made, then the statement is not hearsay and the rule has no application. For example, the fact that somebody made a statement to the accused may be relevant in order to show the accused's state of mind and so to explain some conduct of his. Failure to draw this distinction has resulted in mistaken decisions. For example, in *Willis*[2], on a charge of stealing a drum of cable which had been loaded on to the accused's lorry, in his absence, by his foreman and a driver, the defence wished to prove that the reason why the accused had falsely told the police that he knew nothing about the drum was that his foreman had told the accused that he (the foreman) had not taken it. The trial judge held that the accused might not give evidence of what the foreman said to him, because this was hearsay; but the Court of Criminal Appeal held that it was not hearsay and that the accused should have been allowed to give the evidence in order to explain why he made the false statement.

227. The principal reasons why the rule against hearsay was established were (i) that the statement could not be tested by cross-examination of the maker and (ii) that the parties to the proceedings were incompetent to give evidence and so could not explain away the statement. In the nineteenth century, after the parties were made competent to give evidence, the justification for preserving the rule was put on the additional ground that laymen, whether jurors or magistrates, would be likely to give too much weight to hearsay evidence; but the statement sometimes made that this was the reason for the rule is historically incorrect.

228. The Law Reform Committee, in their report referred to above[3], quoted and considered the three arguments most commonly advanced for the hearsay rule, and they supported their proposals for allowing hearsay in civil proceedings by setting out five disadvantages of the rule. The three reasons for the rule are given in paragraph 7 as follows:

" (a) the unreliability of statements, whether written or oral, made by persons not under oath nor subject to cross-examination;

(b) the desirability of the ' best evidence ' being produced of any fact sought to be proved; and

(c) the danger that the relaxation of the rule would lead to a proliferation of evidence directed to establishing a particular fact ".

The five disadvantages of the rule are set out as follows in paragraph 40:

" First, it results in injustice where a witness who could prove a fact in issue is dead or unavailable to be called; secondly, it adds to the cost of

---

[1] Paragraph 225.
[2] (1959), 44 Cr. App. R. 32.
[3] Paragraph 224.

proving facts in issue which are not really in dispute; thirdly, it adds greatly to the technicality of the law of evidence because of its numerous exceptions. . . . ; fourthly, it deprives the court of material which would be of value in ascertaining the truth; and, fifthly, it often confuses witnesses and prevents them from telling their story in the witness-box in the natural way. "

In paragraphs 7–10 the committee argued that the reasons for the rule against hearsay evidence, in so far as they were valid, were insufficient to prevent the committee from recommending that such evidence should be made admissible subject to what the committee considered would be adequate safeguards. In particular they argued that it was impossible to generalize as to unreliability, as hearsay evidence might sometimes be wholly reliable, and that sometimes the " best " evidence available was hearsay. We agree with the Law Reform Committee both as to the insufficiency of the reasons for the rule excluding hearsay evidence and as to the disadvantages of the rule. In the following paragraphs we mention some considerations in amplification of these arguments and with particular reference to criminal proceedings. This is because, although hearsay evidence is now admissible generally in civil proceedings, it does not follow from this that it should be made admissible in criminal proceedings. In fact the Evidence Act 1938 (c. 28), which made the first general provision for admissibility of hearsay evidence, was limited (except in minor respects) to civil proceedings. The then Lord Chancellor (Lord Maugham), who introduced the Bill, would have been in favour of applying it to criminal proceedings also, but " thought it best to confine its operation for the main part to civil proceedings " because he feared opposition if it were extended to criminal proceedings[1].

229. We recognize that there is a case for preserving the rule against hearsay evidence in criminal trials. The principal arguments are related closely to the essential features of criminal trials as compared with civil trials. These are (i) the fact that in a criminal trial the evidence is mostly given orally, (ii) the fact that trials on indictment at least, once begun, are ordinarily continued without adjournments for further inquiries and (iii) the fact that there is little by way of preliminary proceedings (apart from committal proceedings). As a result jurors and spectators can follow the course of the trial and understand the issues without previous knowledge of the case. The high standard of proof required for a conviction (proof beyond reasonable doubt) is also an important consideration. Another argument which has much concerned us is the danger of manufactured evidence. Although this danger is not limited to the manufacture of evidence by the defence, it is perhaps greatest in the kind of case where a witness for the defence might give evidence that he heard somebody who must have seen the offence being committed, but who is said to be unavailable to give evidence, say something about the offence inconsistent with the guilt of the accused. We have no doubt that this is a real danger, and much of our discussion has been about how to provide against it; and we hope that the safeguards which we propose will go a long way to meet this danger even though it cannot be prevented altogether.

---

[1] " Observations on the Law of Evidence ": Canadian Bar Review, 1939, Vol. 17, pp. 475, 480.

230. Nevertheless the arguments against the present rule are in our opinion very strong. We also think that they have become a good deal stronger now than when the subject was referred to us. This is partly because the Civil Evidence Act 1968 has since been passed and partly because decisions of the courts have, as mentioned below, revealed serious objections to the rule. Our arguments for changing the rule are given in the following five paragraphs. We emphasize that these are in amplification of the arguments given by the Law Reform Committee in their report as quoted above[1].

231. There have been many cases where valuable evidence has had to be excluded owing to the present rule against hearsay. Perhaps the most remarkable recent case was that of *Myers v. Director of Public Prosecutions*[2]. The accused took part in a conspiracy involving buying wrecked cars with their log books, disguising stolen cars so as to make them conform with the log books of the wrecked cars and selling the stolen cars as renovated wrecks. In order to prove that the cars sold were the stolen ones and not the wrecked ones the prosecution called an officer in charge of the records of the manufacturers of the stolen cars to produce microfilms of the cards (since destroyed) filled in by workmen showing the numbers cast into cylinder blocks on the stolen cars, which numbers coincided with those on the cylinder blocks in the cars sold by the accused. The majority of the House of Lords considered that the admission of the records was a breach of the rule against hearsay because, as Lord Reid said[3], " the entries on the cards were assertions by the unidentifiable men who made them that they had entered numbers which they had seen on the cars ". In the older case of *Thomson*[4], where the accused was charged with using an instrument with intent to procure abortion, it was held that the defence might not adduce evidence that the woman concerned (who had since died from another cause) had said that she intended to procure her own miscarriage and evidence that she had told another woman that she had done so. In at least two recent cases[5] in which it was necessary for the prosecution to prove that the accused was driving a car at the time in question, the proof depended on the evidence of a witness who had noted the number of the car and given the number to another person to write down. In each case the other person wrote the number down, but the eye-witness had forgotten the number and had not seen what the other person had written. The person who wrote the number down gave evidence that he took it down from the eye-witness's dictation, but it was held that this was contrary to the rule against hearsay and the convictions were quashed. There have been many unreported cases where evidence had to be, or possibly ought to have been, rejected as being hearsay. One of our members tried a motorist on a charge of refusing a blood test without reasonable excuse. The motorist said that his doctor in Australia had told him that he should avoid all such punctures because he had a rare blood condition (Christmas disease) which made it dangerous for him to be pricked in any way. The accused's evidence that the doctor had given him the advice was inadmissible as evidence that the accused had the disease, but was admitted as evidence showing his state of mind, and therefore providing a reasonable

---

[1] Paragraph 228.
[2] [1965] A.C. 1009; 48 Cr. App. R. 348.
[3] At p. 1022; pp. 362–363.
[4] [1912] 3 K.B. 19; 7 Cr. App. R. 276.
[5] *Jones v. Metcalfe*, [1967] 1 W.L.R. 1286; [1967] 3 All E.R. 205; *McLean* (1967), 52 Cr. App. R. 80.

excuse for failing to provide a specimen of blood, on the principle mentioned above[1]; but it would have been more natural if the doctor's statement could have been admitted as evidence that the accused had the disease and the ground on which it was admitted might not have been available in some cases[2].

232. The present law has caused a good deal of trouble owing to the difficulty of deciding whether a statement is hearsay and, if so, whether it is admissible under any of the exceptions to the rule. The case of *Myers* mentioned above[3] is remarkable in that (i) all the members of the House of Lords held that the evidence in question was hearsay whereas the Court of Criminal Appeal considered that it was not, and (ii) two of the members of the House of Lords considered that the evidence was admissible by way of exception to the rule against hearsay but the majority considered that there was no existing exception by virtue of which the evidence could be admitted and that any new exceptions must be created by statute. Other difficulties are shown by the reference above[4] to the number and obscurity of the exceptions to the rule. Difficulty is also caused when evidence is given that a witness made a previous statement inconsistent with his evidence given in court. Evidence that the witness did so is admissible under s. 4 of the Criminal Procedure Act 1865 (c. 18); but it is admissible not in order to prove the truth of what was said in the previous statement (this would have been an exception to the rule against hearsay) but only in order to neutralize the effect of the evidence given in court by the maker of the statement. Many regard this as too subtle a distinction, and we agree. There is a comparable—and perhaps even subtler—distinction in relation to a complaint by the victim of a sexual offence. If the victim made the complaint soon after the offence, evidence by the victim or by another witness of the making of the complaint is admissible, but it is not admissible as evidence that the offence took place but only in order to show that the victim's evidence in court is consistent with his or her previous story and to negative consent. Evidence by the victim as to the complaint is admissible by way of exception to the rule mentioned above[5] against previous consistent statements. The admissibility of evidence by another witness as to the making of the complaint is not an exception to the rule against hearsay, because the evidence is admissible only for the purposes mentioned. But the need to direct the jury that they must not regard the terms of the complaint as evidence of the facts of which complaint was made, but only as showing that the victim's story in court is consistent with his or her previous statement and as negativing consent, is one which many regard as wholly unrealistic and difficult for a jury to appreciate. If our recommendations summarized below[6] with regard to hearsay are accepted, there will be no special rules concerning the admissibility of the terms of a complaint in a sexual case. Provided that the complainant gives evidence, they will be admissible as evidence of the facts complained of; and even if the complainant does not give evidence, they will still be admissible

---

[1] Paragraph 226(ii).
[2] A letter by the doctor to the accused to the same effect which the defence wished to produce was inadmissible to prove the disease; and it would still be inadmissible for this purpose under the draft Bill, if it was written after the accused was charged, because of clause 32(1): paragraph 237(iv).
[3] Paragraph 231.
[4] Paragraph 225.
[5] Paragraph 226(i).
[6] Paragraphs 236–237.

for this purpose provided that the appropriate conditions of admissibility are fulfilled. Under the present law the complaint is inadmissible if it was not made at the earliest reasonable opportunity or if it was made in answer to leading questions. The result of our recommendations will be that these matters will merely go to the weight of the evidence.

233. The opinion of the majority of the House of Lords in *Myers* that no more exceptions to the hearsay rule should be recognized by the courts makes it highly unlikely that there will be any further development of this branch of the law by case law. The majority urged full scale legislation after due consideration[1]. Lord Reid said[2]:

> " The only satisfactory solution is by legislation following on a wide survey of the whole field, and I think that such a survey is overdue. A policy of make do and mend is no longer adequate ".

Again, in *Jones v. Metcalfe*[3] Diplock L. J. (as he then was) said that the law as to hearsay " is a branch of the law which has little to do with common sense " and urged the need to reform the law on the lines of the Law Reform Committee's 13th report.

234. A substantial majority of those whom we consulted at the beginning of this reference were in favour of extending admissibility of hearsay evidence with appropriate safeguards. In our second request for observations (in 1968) we did not deal with hearsay evidence, because we had not sufficiently formulated our proposals on a number of points, and we referred to the topic only incidentally. We have little doubt that the majority of lawyers now favour substantial relaxation.

235. The fact that hearsay evidence is now widely admissible in civil proceedings under the Civil Evidence Act 1968 seems to us a fresh argument in favour of allowing such evidence in criminal proceedings. This is not only because it seems desirable in general that the law of evidence in civil and criminal proceedings should be as nearly alike as possible (though there are bound to be substantial differences) but because it would be particularly unfortunate if differences in the law were to lead to different results in proceedings relating to the same facts. For example, it is possible, in theory at least, that a person might be sued for fraud and be found not liable on the strength of hearsay evidence admissible under the Act of 1968 and yet be convicted of a criminal offence owing to the inadmissibility of similar evidence in criminal proceedings.

236. The scheme which we propose, stated shortly, is as follows:

(i) to make admissible any out-of-court statement if (*a*) the maker is called as a witness or (*b*) he cannot be called because he is dead or for one of the reasons mentioned later in this paragraph;

(ii) to make admissible statements contained in certain kinds of records if the information in the statement was supplied by a person having

---

[1] The Criminal Evidence Act 1965 (c.20), which makes records " relating to any trade or business " admissible in certain circumstances, was passed as an interim measure as a result of the decision in *Myers*.
[2] [1965] A.C. at p. 1022; 48 Cr. App. R. at p. 362.
[3] [1967] 1 W.L.R. at pp. 1290–1291; [1967] 3 All E.R. at p. 208.

personal knowledge of the matter in question and the supplier (a) is called as a witness, (b) cannot be called for one of the reasons referred to or (c) cannot be expected to remember the matters dealt with in the information;

(iii) to make special provision for the admissibility of information derived from computers;

(iv) to restate the rule as to admissibility of statements forming part of the *res gestae*;

(v) to provide that, subject to certain safeguards, out-of-court statements shall be admissible if the parties so agree;

(vi) to clarify the law by providing that hearsay evidence shall be admissible only under the provisions mentioned, under any other statutory provision or under the common law rules specifically preserved by the Bill. *Finality.*

The cases where an out-of-court statement is to be admissible on account of the impossibility of calling the maker as a witness are (a) where he is unavailable because he is dead, unfit to attend as a witness, abroad, impossible to identify or impossible to find and (b) where he is available but is either not compellable as a witness and refuses to give evidence or is compellable but refuses (in court) to be sworn. On the same principle, the prosecution will be able to give in evidence against one accused a statement made by another accused jointly tried with him, as the maker cannot be called for the prosecution.

237. Under our scheme admissibility of hearsay statements will be subject to a number of restrictions, of which the following are the most important:

(i) in the case of oral statements only first-hand evidence of the making of the statement will be admissible (unless the statement was made in giving evidence in court)[1];

(ii) a statement contained in a proof of evidence (including a proof incorporated in a record) given by a person who is called as a witness in the proceedings in question will not be admissible unless the court gives leave for this on the ground that in the circumstances it is in the interests of justice that the witness's evidence should be supplemented by the proof[2];

(iii) at a trial on indictment a statement will not be admissible by reason of the impossibility of calling the maker unless the party seeking to give it in evidence has given notice of his intention to do so with particulars of the statement and of the reason why he cannot call the maker[3];

(iv) a statement said to have been made, after the accused has been charged, by a person who is compellable as a witness but refuses to be sworn or by a person said to be abroad, impossible to identify or find, or to have refused to give evidence, will not be admissible at all (and there will be a similar restriction in the case of the supplier of information contained in a record)[4];

---

[1] See further paragraph 244.
[2] See further paragraph 239.
[3] See further paragraphs 240–242.
[4] See further paragraphs 240–242.

138

(v) a statement made by the wife or husband of the accused (not being tried jointly with the accused) will not be admissible on behalf of the prosecution unless the maker gives evidence for the prosecution or would have been a compellable witness for the prosecution[1].

238. The _purposes_ which we hope to achieve by this scheme are the following:

(i) to admit all hearsay evidence likely to be valuable to the greatest extent possible without undue complication or delay to the proceedings;

(ii) to ensure that evidence should continue to be given for the most part orally by allowing hearsay evidence only if the maker of the statement cannot be called or it is desirable to supplement his oral evidence[2];

(iii) to include necessary safeguards against the danger of manufactured hearsay evidence[3];

(iv) to follow the scheme of the Civil Evidence Act 1968 as far as the differences between civil and criminal proceedings allow[4].

Further comment on the purposes mentioned in (ii), (iii) and (iv) is made in the six following paragraphs. After this the proposed restriction mentioned in paragraph 237 (v) as to a statement made by the spouse of the accused is discussed[5].

239. The preservation of the principle of orality in criminal trials seems to us particularly important. We are not concerned to argue that the English system is the best system; but since this system is clearly going to be preserved in its essentials, it would be wrong to disrupt it by giving the parties complete freedom to choose between proving their case by oral evidence given by witnesses of the events in question and proving it by second-hand evidence of these events. To do so would alter the character of trials and be likely to confuse juries. The essence of our proposed scheme is to supplement the oral evidence by hearsay evidence which is likely to be valuable for the ascertainment of the truth and cannot be given because of the restrictions in the present law. In the case of a previous statement by a person who is called as a witness there is a special reason for proposing to make the statement admissible. It might be argued that, since the maker is giving evidence, there is no need to allow evidence to be given of what he said on a previous occasion. But assuming, as one must, that a person called as a witness in criminal proceedings is more likely than not to intend to try to tell the truth, it follows that what he said soon after the events in question is likely to be at least as reliable as his evidence given at the trial and will probably be more so. This may not always be the case, because the earlier statement may have been made in haste and perhaps under the influence of shock caused by the events in question, and the evidence given at the trial may be more carefully thought over; but at any rate, if there is a discrepancy, it is likely to be helpful to the court or jury to have both statements. In a case where the trial takes place long after the events in

[1] See further paragraph 245.
[2] See further paragraph 239.
[3] See further paragraphs 240–242.
[4] See further paragraphs 243–244.
[5] See paragraph 245.

question the earlier statement may be particularly valuable. Sometimes, for example, in a complicated fraud case the trial takes place years after the offence. But if the earlier statement is a proof of evidence, or a document of a similar nature, it seems desirable to make special provision in order to ensure that the proof or other document does not take the place of oral evidence. For even if the person taking the proof has not tried to get the witness to tell his story in the way most favourable to the party in whose interest it is taken, it is obviously likely that it will come out in this way; and therefore it would be wrong to enable the party calling the witness, say, simply to call him, show him the proof and put it in as his evidence. It is for this reason that we propose that the leave of the court should be necessary for the proof to be given in evidence. In the ordinary case the court would no doubt require the witness to give his evidence without the aid of any document (except such as may be used for refreshing memory); but if, for example, the witness is clearly unable to remember the events described in his proof, then the court will be likely to allow the proof to be referred to. Whether a document is in the nature of a proof of evidence will depend on the circumstances. Ordinarily, for example, a statement taken by the police for use as a written statement under s. 2 or s. 9 of the Criminal Justice Act 1967 will count as a proof for this purpose.

240. The need to provide for safeguards against the use of manufactured evidence caused us more difficulty than did any of the other questions relating to hearsay evidence. We have mentioned[1] this danger as one of the arguments against admitting hearsay evidence. Many of those who replied to our original request for observations expressed anxiety about this, as did several members during our discussion. We mentioned in particular the danger that the defence may seek to produce a statement, said to have been made by a person whom they are unfortunately unable to call as a witness, which, if true, would exculpate the accused. Apart from false alibis, there are several possible kinds of hearsay evidence which might be manufactured for this purpose. For example, there might be a statement by a supposed eye-witness of the offence describing the offender in a way totally inconsistent with his being the accused. Again, the statement might be that the maker himself committed the offence or that he had heard somebody else say that he had committed it or was about to do so. How far this danger exists is a matter of opinion. Some think that to admit hearsay evidence would not greatly increase the possibility of manufactured evidence which already exists with first-hand evidence: others think that the danger would be much greater. In our view it must be taken that the danger, although not great enough to require the rejection of any hearsay evidence exculpating the accused in a way such as suggested, or the rejection of hearsay evidence in general, is great enough to require and justify the imposition of the proposed restriction as to giving notice of intention to give the statement in evidence[2] and that as to statements made after the accused was charged[3].

241. The proposed requirement to give notice will enable the other parties to make inquiries as to the identity of the person supposed to have made the

---

[1] Paragraph 229.
[2] Paragraph 237(iii).
[3] Paragraph 237(iv).

statement, as to whether it is really impossible to call him and as to the contents of the statement. The purpose will be similar to that served by the requirement in s. 11 of the Criminal Justice Act 1967 (c. 80) to give notice of intention to adduce evidence of an alibi; and, as in the case of the notice last mentioned, the court will have a discretion to allow the statement to be given in evidence, if the interests of justice require this, even though notice has for some reason not been given. The proposed provision excluding altogether a statement supposed to have been made after the accused has been charged may seem drastic. But in our opinion it might well be too dangerous to allow such a statement to be given in evidence at all, even subject to the discretion of the court, because this might well encourage the defence to present such a statement in the hope that leave would be given. A further justification for these restrictions is the fact that at present, if a person makes a statement and then disappears, there is no power to allow the statement to be read out (save with consent under s. 9 of the Criminal Justice Act 1967). It is for the party who has obtained the statement to ensure that the maker is present to give evidence.

242. Some such safeguards as these seem to us particularly necessary in criminal proceedings because, owing to the rule that the accused cannot be convicted unless his guilt is proved beyond reasonable doubt, a false statement of a kind mentioned might be sufficient, if not to convince a jury, at least to raise a sufficient doubt in their minds as to the guilt of the accused. But with these safeguards we hope that the danger that tricks of the kind mentioned will succeed will be reduced to a point at which it can be accepted in the interests of allowing hearsay evidence which ought to be allowed. In the nature of things there can be no complete safeguard, just as there can be no complete safeguard against manufactured first-hand evidence. We considered going further and excluding altogether a statement made by an unidentified person or by a person who, though identified, could not be found. In the case of an unidentified person there would also be the argument that his credit as a witness could not be attacked. But although to make these further restrictions would decrease the danger of manufactured evidence, we do not think that they would be justified. For the case of an unidentified person does not seem to differ sufficiently for present purposes from the case, for example, of an identified person who has died. In the case of an identified person who cannot be found there may be a stronger argument because of the danger of his being kept out of the way. But we do not think it necessary to make even this restriction, especially as the person concerned might have given his statement to the prosecution and the defence might be keeping him out of the way.

243. We said[1] that one of our objects was to follow the scheme of the Civil Evidence Act 1968 as far as the differences between civil and criminal proceedings allowed. The special restrictions just referred to[2] naturally do not correspond to any provisions in the Act; but although the provisions in the draft Bill look very different from those of the Act, the scheme of both is in essence similar. For in both cases the object is that evidence as to facts in dispute should in principle be oral evidence, and it should be only where this is

---

[1] Paragraph 238(iv).
[2] Paragraphs 240–242.

unavailable or there is useful hearsay evidence to supplement the oral evidence that hearsay evidence should be allowed. The scheme of the Civil Evidence Act is that the party seeking to give a statement in evidence should give notice to the other parties, and the latter may by counter-notice object to its being given. If another party objects, the statement will not be admissible in evidence unless the maker is unavailable or the court gives leave. The purpose of the requirement in civil proceedings is to discourage litigants from offering hearsay evidence of a fact when direct evidence of the fact can be adduced without serious inconvenience or expense. This is secured by the system of notice and counter-notice. The system of notice and counter-notice is unsuitable for criminal proceedings in general, especially in the absence of interlocutory proceedings; and we hope that a similar result will be achieved by the requirements as to unavailability of the maker.

244. There is one particular respect in which our recommendations follow the Civil Evidence Act. This is the exclusion, as mentioned[1], of second-hand hearsay evidence. There are undoubtedly arguments for allowing even this, as it is possible that this evidence will sometimes be helpful. For example, if A has made a mental note of the number of a car involved in an offence and told B, B will be able to give evidence of what A told him; but if B has died or is unavailable, there may be nobody else who is in a position to give the number. On the other hand, to allow second-hand or remoter evidence of the making of a statement in all cases might let in very unreliable evidence. There would also be a greater danger of manufactured evidence if this was allowed. The committee generally came to the conclusion that, on balance, if would be safer to follow the Civil Evidence Act in restricting oral evidence of the making of a statement to first-hand evidence. In any event we thought it would be anomalous to allow second-hand and remoter hearsay evidence in criminal proceedings when it is not allowed in civil proceedings.

245. The proposal to restrict the admissibility of a statement made by the husband or wife of the accused[2] is a matter of policy comparable with the questions as to competence and compellability of the spouse discussed above[3]. On this our views differ. The majority think that to allow the prosecution to give in evidence a statement made by the spouse of the accused, in a case where the spouse does not give evidence or would not be compellable to do so, would be inconsistent with the policy that the spouse should in general have the right not to give evidence for the prosecution. It is argued, for example, that, if the police question the accused's wife about the receipt by him of stolen goods, she may say something which might incriminate the accused, although she could not be compelled to give evidence about this in court, and which she might regret saying. The police might tell her, truly, that she could not be compelled to give evidence against her husband, but omit to tell her that her statement might be given in evidence. In this and similar cases the majority think it wrong that the statement should be admissible. But a substantial minority think that the statement should be admissible because the

---

[1] Paragraph 237(i).
[2] Paragraph 237(v).
[3] Paragraphs 143–157.

principle of non-compellability is only that the wife should not be compelled to testify against her husband and does not require that something which she may have said out of court should not be admissible. The case where the spouse is tried jointly with the accused is dealt with later[1].

246. We considered a suggestion which has been made several times by legal writers and was put forward in some of the replies to our request for observations. This is that the problem of allowing useful hearsay evidence while excluding evidence which it would be too dangerous to allow should be solved by giving the court a discretion to admit otherwise inadmissible hearsay evidence. This course has the obvious attraction that the provision would be of the simplest. But we do not think it should be adopted, because it seems to us to involve four serious difficulties. First, with the differences of opinion about the value of hearsay evidence there would be bound to be large differences in practice between different courts. Second, there would be an almost inevitable tendency to allow hearsay evidence freely for the defence while restricting it when offered on behalf of the prosecution, and the committee generally are opposed to making distinctions between the parties in this way[2]. Third, it would make it much more difficult for the parties to prepare their case, because there would be no way of knowing in advance whether a court would allow a particular piece of hearsay evidence. Fourth, in summary trials the court would ordinarily have to hear the statement in order to decide whether to exercise the discretion to admit it. Nor do we think it right to confer any particular exclusionary discretion on courts in relation to hearsay evidence in addition to the general discretion which they enjoy at present to exclude evidence where, for example, they are of opinion that its prejudicial effect would outweigh its probative value. But there seems no objection to giving the limited discretion proposed above[3] to admit a statement in particular circumstances in the case of a previous statement made by a witness and in the case of failure to give notice of intention to give in evidence a statement by a person unavailable to give evidence.

247. We concluded, after considerable discussion, that the proposals mentioned above would provide the best way of allowing hearsay evidence which would be valuable while avoiding most of the difficulties inseparable from any general widening of the present law. Admittedly our proposals involve a certain amount of risk that unreliable evidence will be admitted and acted on; but there is much evidence other than hearsay evidence which is unreliable, and in our opinion it is better to accept the risk mentioned while providing such safeguards as can be provided without unduly restricting admissibility or complicating the law. We disagree strongly with the argument that juries and lay magistrates will be over-impressed by hearsay evidence and too ready to convict or acquit on the strength of it. Anybody with common sense will understand that evidence which cannot be tested by cross-examination may well be less reliable than evidence which can. In any event judges will be in a position to remind juries that the former is the case with hearsay evidence,

---

[1] Paragraph 252.

[2] The committee all recognize that there is a case in principle for wider admissibility of evidence on behalf of the defence than on behalf of the prosecution, but the majority are strongly of the opinion that the interests of justice require that the parties should in general be treated alike in this respect. Cf. paragraph 250.

[3] Paragraphs 239, 241.

143

and sometimes the judge may think it advisable to mention this to the jury at the time when the statement is admitted. On the other hand there is some hearsay evidence which would rightly convince anybody. Moreover, juries may have to consider hearsay evidence which is admissible under the present law, and there are other kinds of evidence which they may find it more difficult to evaluate than hearsay evidence—for example, evidence of other misconduct. It may also be objected that the provisions about hearsay evidence in the draft Bill are complicated. Admittedly this is so, and they may seem unduly complicated at first sight; but we believe that, if the provisions are adopted, the procedure as to the admission of hearsay evidence will be much less complicated than the provisions themselves look, and in any event we do not think it can be disputed that the provisions are much less complicated than is the present law.

248. The provisions to give effect to our recommendations are in clauses 30–41. Under them there will be several different grounds for admissibility, and the restrictions which apply to admissibility on some of the grounds will not apply to admissibility on some others. Clause 30 provides that a hearsay statement, to be admissible, will have to come under one or other of the clauses, under some other statutory provision or under one of the common law rules specifically preserved by clause 40. Thus there will be no room for an argument, based on the existing case law, in favour of admissibility of any other kind of hearsay evidence. Most of the clauses correspond very broadly to sections in Part I of the Civil Evidence Act 1968 for admissibility of hearsay in civil proceedings. Most of the substance of what we propose has already been shown; but certain matters of substance are mentioned below, and other matters of detail are referred to in the notes on the clauses in Annex 2.

249. Clause 31(1) contains the provision for admissibility of a statement in any of the cases mentioned above[1]—that is to say, where the maker is called as a witness or is unavailable to be called for any of the reasons mentioned or where the party seeking to give the statement in evidence cannot call the maker because he is not compellable to give evidence or, being compellable, refuses to be sworn. The case of competence without compellability will provide for a situation where one accused wishes to give in evidence a statement made by his co-accused or the latter's spouse (when not compellable) and a case where the maker is immune from legal process (for example a foreign diplomat).

250. We considered recommending that a hearsay statement should be made admissible in one other case, namely, that in which the maker is a very young child whose oral evidence would probably be held to be inadmissible under clause 22(2) if he were called as a witness. This situation raises a difficult question, which arose in an acute form in *Sparks v. R.*[2], an appeal to the Privy Council from Bermuda. The accused, a white man aged twenty-seven, was convicted of indecently assaulting a girl just under four, who was not called to give evidence. The trial judge held to be inadmissible, as being hearsay, evidence by the child's mother of a statement made to her by the child shortly after the assault that " it was a coloured boy ". The Privy Council held that this evidence was rightly rejected (but quashed the conviction on other grounds). Many lawyers regard it as contrary to justice that the law

[1] Paragraph 236(i).
[2] [1964] A.C. 964.

144

should have required the rejection of this evidence. On the face of it the inability of the defence to give in evidence a statement of this kind which, looked at by itself, would have exculpated the accused is obviously a grave defect in the law. On the other hand, had the statement been adverse to the accused, there would be a strong argument that it would be contrary to justice to allow the statement to be given in evidence for the prosecution when the child could not have given her evidence in court. A possible solution of the dilemma would be to make the statement, exceptionally, admissible on behalf of the defence but not on behalf of the prosecution; but the committee generally are opposed to this on the ground that the principle must be maintained that any evidence admissible for the defence must be admissible for the prosecution also.[1] This is one of the difficulties which may arise from time to time in the case of an offence against a very young child, and we think that it must be accepted. Fortunately this particular difficulty is one likely to occur very rarely. We think it would be even more rare for a party to tender in evidence the statement of a very young child who could not be called as a witness for any of the reasons stated in paragraph 236. If this were ever done, it would be open to the court either to hold the statement to be inadmissible on the ground that the fact stated was not one of which direct oral evidence by the maker would be admissible on account of his extreme youth when the fact stated was perceived by him, or else to treat the statement as one to which no weight should be attached both for that reason and because of the maker's extreme youth when the statement was made. No special provision for so remote a contingency is made in the Civil Evidence Act 1968, and we have not thought it necessary to make any such provision. Conversely, we have not thought it necessary to include a provision requiring the court to treat the hearsay statement of an older child as admissible. There is again no such provision in the Civil Evidence Act, and we think it better that, in each case, the court should be left to form its own opinion whether, in all the circumstances, the fact stated is one of which the child's direct oral evidence would have been admissible.

251. Clause 31(2) enables the prosecution to give in evidence a statement made by one accused (A) implicating another (B) who is being tried jointly with him. A special provision is necessary for this purpose, if it is accepted that it is right in policy to allow the prosecution to give the statement in evidence, because A is incompetent as a witness for the prosecution and because we do not propose that a person's incompetence as a witness should be a ground for the admissibility of his out-of-court statement. The provision involves a question of policy, and our decision to recommend it is a majority one. The majority think it right to make the provision on the ground that there are many cases where the interests of justice require that what any of the accused have said out of court about the part played by the others in the events in question should be before the court. For example, it often happens that, when A and B are charged jointly with an offence, A has made a statement implicating them both and B has made no statement; or again each may have made a statement seeking to throw the blame on the other. In the latter kind of case there may be much truth in both their statements, and their stories may be changed by the time of the trial. If there are discrepancies of this kind, it seems to the majority particularly desirable that the out-of-court statements

---

[1] See paragraph 246 and n.2 on it.

should be admissible in evidence in order that they may be compared with the makers' evidence at the trial. There are two additional arguments in favour of the majority view. First, if the maker of the statement in question should have died or become unavailable to give evidence in one of the ways mentioned, the statement will be admissible in any event. Second, to make the statement admissible (and so evidence of what is said in it) gets rid of the absurd situation which occurs under the present law that, when A has made a statement implicating himself and B, it is necessary to direct the jury that the statement is admissible in evidence against A but not against B. This is a subtlety which must be confusing to juries, and in reality they will inevitably take the statement into account against both accused. The minority are against this provision, because they consider that to admit the statement may be too prejudicial to the accused whom it implicates. This might be so in their opinion in a case, for example, where A was on any view deeply involved in the offence and is obviously a person whose statements cannot be relied on and, on the other hand, the other evidence against B is weak and he took at most a minor part in the offence. The majority consider that there is nothing so exceptional in this situation as to justify departing from the general principle that as much relevant evidence as possible should be before the court, and they think that courts should be relied on to ensure that the statement is given its proper weight. In any event the admissibility of the statement, if it is adverse to the maker, will be subject to the conditions in clause 2 as to the absence of oppressive treatment and of threats or inducements likely to make a confession unreliable.

252. In a case where a husband and wife are being tried jointly (with or without other persons) there is a question whether a previous statement made by (say) the wife implicating her husband should be admissible against him because the two are being jointly tried[1] or should be inadmissible for the reason (accepted by the majority in cases where the maker is not being tried[2]) that the parties are husband and wife. On this the committee generally take the view that, if it is accepted that statements by other persons jointly tried should be admissible, the fact that the spouses are being tried together should prevail and the statement should be admissible. They consider that the argument that it is desirable in the interests of justice that all statements by persons jointly tried should be admissible outweighs the argument for protecting the husband from the consequences of his wife's statement. A particular reason is that the opposite view involves the difficulty mentioned above[3] that it would be necessary to direct the jury that the wife's statement, though admissible against her (and against any third person being jointly tried with the spouses), is inadmissible against her husband.

253. Clause 31(5) contains the provision[4] making second-hand hearsay generally inadmissible except in the case of a statement made in giving evidence in other legal proceedings. In this case it seems clearly right to allow the statement to be proved by means of a transcript of the proceedings and not to require proof by a person who heard the evidence being given. The subsection is similar to s. 2(3) of the Civil Evidence Act.

[1] See paragraph 251.
[2] See paragraph 245.
[3] Paragraph 251.
[4] Discussed in paragraph 244.

254. Clause 31(6), which has no counterpart in the Civil Evidence Act, is a special provision intended to clarify the application of the hearsay provisions to a case where a person (A) makes an oral statement to or in the hearing of another (B) and B reduces the statement, or the substance of it, into writing. For example, A calls out the number of a car which he has seen being used as a getaway car after a robbery, or being involved in an accident, and B, perhaps a policeman or perhaps a member of the public, writes the number down, whether alone or together with other matter, in a document. Is the resulting statement in the document to count as having been made by A or only by B? The answer to this may be vital if it is necessary to prove that the car involved bore this number. At present, if A cannot be called as a witness, or cannot remember the number, there may be a fatal gap in the evidence, because B cannot give evidence of what A said[1]. Under the Bill, if A gives evidence or if one of the other conditions laid down in clause 31(1) in relation to the maker of a statement is satisfied, B's evidence of A's oral statement that this was the number of the car will be admissible in order to prove the number, and it will not be necessary to rely on the statement in the document. But if for some reason B is unavailable to give evidence, then proof of the number may depend on whether the statement in the document is admissible; and in any event it may be desirable to adduce this statement, because the fact that the number has been written down is likely to add weight to the statement that A called it out. If the statement in the document counts as having been made by A, then it will be admissible provided that one of the conditions referred to above in relation to A is satisfied. But if the statement has to be treated as having been made by B, then it will be inadmissible, because B had himself no knowledge of the number (and if nobody who heard A give the number of the car is available to give evidence that A did so, then it will be impossible to prove that he did so because of the general prohibition of second-hand hearsay by clause 31(5)). After considering two other possibilities, we concluded that it would be desirable to include an express provision to specify the circumstances in which a statement made orally by A and reduced into writing by B should count as having been made by A in the resulting document. It should do so, in our opinion, if A makes the statement in B's hearing and B reduces the statement, or its substance, into writing (i) " at the instance " of A and (ii) " at the time " when the statement was made " or reasonably soon afterwards ". If these conditions are satisfied, it seems to us justifiable and natural that the statement in the document should be treated as having been made by A and should therefore be admissible subject to the conditions for the admissibility of written hearsay statements. Clause 31(6) provides accordingly. The requirement that the statement should have been reduced into writing " at the time or reasonably soon afterwards " will enable the court to have regard to all the circumstances of the case, including even the nature of the document. For example, if a car number and no more were written down in anything other than the shortest possible time, the statement might well be excluded. On the other hand, if an illiterate old woman were to tell her son to write and tell the ex-lodger that he had left some things behind in his room, it might well be " reasonably soon afterwards " even if the son did not act " at her instance " until the next day.

---

[1] This was the situation which arose in *Jones v. Metcalfe* and *McLean*, mentioned in paragraph 231.

255. The other two courses which we considered (with variants) in relation to the case discussed in paragraph 254 where B takes down an oral statement made in his hearing by A were—

(i) to make no provision but leave it to the courts to say, as a matter of construction of the hearsay provisions in the Bill, when the statement in the document should be counted as A's; and

(ii) not to have any requirement that B should have taken the statement down " at the instance " of A.

Course (i) would have been perfectly reasonable, especially as this would be in accordance with the Civil Evidence Act, which does not include any clarificatory provision on the point; but we thought that a provision was desirable, for criminal proceedings at least, because in them admissibility is to depend so much on the fulfilment of certain conditions in relation to the maker of the statement. (In fact it is very probable that even without clause 31(6) the Bill would be construed in the way stated in that provision and that the Civil Evidence Act would be construed similarly.) The result of adopting course (ii) would have been that, if B had taken down the statement without any kind of request or hint from A, the written statement would or might be admissible as being A's statement. This would have meant going a long way to making second-hand written hearsay admissible. There would be at least two arguments for adopting this course. First, the fact that the statement is in a document decreases the danger of progressive inaccuracy resulting from oral repetitions; and in fact the circumstances may make it obvious that the danger does not exist. Second, if B had been available to give evidence, he would have been allowed to refresh his memory from the writing provided that he had made it at the time or reasonably soon afterwards. However, we concluded that it would be undesirable for the criminal law to go so much further than does the civil law in this respect. In making our decision we had it in mind that, when the whole law of civil and criminal evidence is eventually codified, it might be thought right to go further in admitting second-hand hearsay—in particular, written hearsay—than is at present proposed.

256. Clause 32 contains most of the restrictions described above[1] on the admissibility of hearsay evidence. These are (i) the exclusion of statements made after the accused was charged, (ii) the exclusion of certain statements by the spouse of the accused, (iii) the exclusion of a proof of the evidence given by a witness at the trial and (iv) the requirement of notice for hearsay evidence of a statement made by a person unavailable to give evidence. In view of what has been said before it is unnecessary to set out these provisions further, but one matter should be mentioned. The provisions relative to notice specify that the notice must be given within seven days of the end of the committal proceedings[2]. There is no provision requiring notice in the case of a summary trial. In this respect the clause follows the provision in s. 11 of the Criminal Justice Act 1967 as to notice of intention to set up an alibi. We considered whether it was necessary or desirable to make similar provision for summary trials, but concluded that it was not. First, it is important to keep the procedure in magistrates' courts simple. Secondly, there is not likely to be the same elaborate falsification of evidence as sometimes occurs in cases before the

---

[1] Paragraphs 237(ii)-(v), 239–243, 245.
[2] Clause 32(4).

higher courts. Thirdly, since the principal object of the requirement is to enable the prosecution to make the investigations referred to above, it is hoped that the same purpose will be achieved in summary proceedings by means of adjournment of the court.

257. Clause 33, which is similar to s. 3 of the Civil Evidence Act 1968, secures that a previous statement made by a witness will be admissible not only to support or impugn his credibility as a witness (as at present) but as evidence of the facts stated in it. The purpose of the clause is to do away with the situation in which a statement may be proved for one purpose, for example to show that a witness has contradicted himself, but is inadmissible as evidence of the facts stated. As previously mentioned[1], this is over-subtle, and it seems to us right that, as under the Civil Evidence Act, contradictory statements by the same person should confront one another on the same evidential footing.

258. Clause 34 gives effect to our recommendations for admissibility of evidence contained in records. The effect will be that if A, a person who has (or may reasonably be supposed to have had) personal knowledge of any matter, gives information about the matter to B, and B enters the information in any record which he compiles when acting under a duty or in the course of his trade, business, profession or occupation, or for the purposes of any paid or unpaid office held by him, the statement in the record will, subject to certain requirements, be admissible as evidence of any fact stated in it. The chief requirement will be that A (the person who originally supplied the information) is called as a witness or is a person who cannot be called because he is dead or for any of the other reasons specified in subsection (2) (which correspond to the reasons specified in clause 31(1)(b) and (c) in relation to the maker of an ordinary hearsay statement) or cannot be expected to remember the matters dealt with in the information. There will also be two restrictions corresponding to restrictions under clause 32 in the case of ordinary hearsay statements. First, in a case where the statement in the record contains information supplied by A after the accused was charged, and where it is claimed that A cannot be called as a witness, there will be a complete exclusion from admissibility in similar circumstances to those in which a non-record hearsay statement is to be excluded if made after the accused was charged[2]. Second, where the document containing the record consists of a proof of evidence to be given by A, and A is called as a witness, admissibility will depend on the leave of the court as in the case of a proof of evidence not being a record (which it will in fact ordinarily be)[3]. It will not be necessary that the information should be supplied directly by A to B (the compiler of the record), so long as each of the intermediaries was acting under a duty or in the course of his trade etc. as mentioned. The clause corresponds to s. 4 of the Civil Evidence Act 1968 except that (i) the requirement as to the impossibility of calling the supplier of the information and the exclusion of records containing information supplied after the accused was charged (which provisions are in accordance with the scheme of the Bill) have no counterparts in s. 4 of the Act and (ii), unlike the Act, the Bill does not require a party to give notice of his intention to give a record in evidence. There will be a certain amount of overlapping between

---

[1] Cf. paragraph 232.
[2] Clause 34(4). Cf. paragraph 237(iv).
[3] Clause 34(5). Cf. paragraph 237(ii).

clauses 31 and 34 in that sometimes a statement may be admissible under clause 31 subject to compliance with the requirement in clause 32 as to giving notice of intention to give the statement in evidence but the same statement, if it amounts to a record, will be admissible under clause 34 without the need to give notice. We considered whether to include provision to prevent this overlapping, but we are satisfied that it is unnecessary. The purpose of the requirement in clause 32 to give notice is to enable the other party to check, so far as possible, the reliability of the statement and the reasons why it is claimed that the maker cannot be called as a witness. But in order that a statement contained in a record should be admissible it will be necessary, as mentioned above, that the record should have been compiled by a person acting under a duty or otherwise in a responsible position as mentioned, and this fact seems to us to make the likelihood that the statement is reliable great enough to justify dispensing with the requirement to give notice of intention to give the statement in evidence. We agree with the views of the Law Reform Committee[1] as to the value of the requirement that the statement should have been made in the performance of a duty (in the broad sense indicated above) to record information. Clause 34 will supersede the Criminal Evidence Act 1965, which was passed as an interim measure in consequence of the decision in *Myers*, as mentioned above[2].

259. Clause 35 provides for the admissibility of statements produced by computers. The clause is similar to s. 5 of the Civil Evidence Act 1968 except in the respect mentioned below. Admissibility is subject to strict conditions, necessary in order to ensure that the information is reliable, as to the regular supply of information to the computer and to its proper working. The section in the Act did not derive from a recommendation of the Law Reform Committee, but was asked for by interested business and professional bodies. It seems to us desirable to include a similar provision in the Bill, because the increasing use of computers by the Post Office, local authorities, banks and business firms to store certain kinds of information will make it more difficult to prove certain matters, such as cheque frauds, unless it is made possible for this to be done from computers. The clause differs from s. 5 of the Act in that, while subsection (4) in both the clause and the section allows evidence by certificate in order to identify a document produced by the computer and to give particulars of its working, subsection (5) in the clause, which has no counterpart in the section, enables the court for special reason to require oral evidence to be given of these matters. Provision to this effect was unnecessary in civil proceedings, because rules made under the Act require a party desiring to give in evidence a statement produced by a computer to give notice with particulars of the persons concerned with the supply of information to the computer and its working and enable the other party to require oral evidence. The provision in subsection (5) of the clause seems desirable in the absence of a requirement to give notice and having regard to the higher standard of proof required for a conviction in criminal proceedings.

260. Clause 36 contains various supplementary provisions, mostly corresponding to provisions of s. 6 of the Civil Evidence Act 1968, relating to proof of documents, to the drawing of inferences, for the purpose of deciding

---

[1] 13th report, paragraph 16(*b*).
[2] Paragraph 233 n. 1.

admissibility, from the circumstances in which a statement was made and from the form and contents of a document, to the weight to be attached to admissible hearsay evidence and to preventing a hearsay statement made by a person from being used to corroborate evidence given in court by the maker of the statement. The clause also contains ancillary provisions referred to in the note in Annex 2.

261. Clause 37 substantially restates the common law rule as to the admissibility of a hearsay statement as forming part of the *res gestae*. The recent case of *Ratten v. R.*[1] (an appeal to the Privy Council from Australia) contains a valuable statement of the law as to this exception to the rule against hearsay. At the trial of the appellant for the murder of his wife the prosecution called a telephonist who said that at a time, identified as just before the killing, a woman, who in fact must have been the deceased, telephoned from the accused's number and said " Get me the police please " in a hysterical voice and sobbed. The Privy Council were satisfied that the evidence was admitted only as proof that the deceased made the telephone call (which the accused denied) and did so in a state of emotion or fear. But they also considered the case on the assumption, in accordance with the appellant's submission, that the words contained an element of hearsay in the sense that they were admitted as amounting to an assertion by the deceased that she was being attacked by the accused and that they might have been understood by the jury in this sense. On this assumption, Lord Wilberforce, who gave the judgment, analyzed the *res gestae* rule and held that the test was " not the uncertain one whether the making of the statement was in some sense part of the event or transaction "[2] but whether the statement was " made in such conditions (always being those of approximate but not exact contemporaneity) of involvement or pressure as to exclude the possibility of concoction or distortion to the advantage of the maker or the disadvantage of the accused "[3]. On this test the Privy Council were satisfied that the wife's words were admissible even as a hearsay statement to the effect mentioned. The test we propose is similar to that laid down in *Ratten*, though somewhat narrower. It is that the statement should be admissible if " it directly concerns an event in issue in [the] proceedings which took place in the presence, sight or hearing of [the maker] and it was made by him as an immediate reaction to that event ". Before *Ratten* the English decisions left it uncertain whether a statement admissible under the *res gestae* rule was admissible as evidence of the facts stated or only as explaining the events referred to; but the balance of authority seems to have been that it is admissible for the former purpose, and this is in accordance with the analysis in *Ratten*. In any event it seems to us clearly right that the statement should be admissible for this purpose, and the clause provides accordingly. As this is an independent ground of admissibility, the conditions and restrictions provided for in other clauses will not apply. The result will be that a statement, for example, made by a very young child, or an otherwise inadmissible statement made by the spouse of the accused, may be admissible under the clause if it was made as an immediate reaction to the event in question[4]. We considered whether the *res gestae* rule was worth preserving at all. Because of the wide provisions for

[1] (1971), 56 Cr. App. R. 18.
[2] P. 26.
[3] P. 29.
[4] This is probably in accordance with the common law: *Thompson and Ux' v. Trevanion* (1693), Skin. 402.

admissibility in clause 31 there will be very little scope for the application of clause 37. Its practical effect will be only to make admissible a statement such as mentioned by a very young child or by a spouse and perhaps occasionally to enable a party to adduce a statement without having to give notice under clause 32. It was suggested that these possibilities were insufficient to justify the complication involved in preserving a rule which has resulted in technical distinctions and which might continue to do so even as enacted. It was also suggested that the fact that a statement satisfied the test in clause 37 would be an insufficient justification for dispensing with the notice requirements which would have to be complied with if the statement did not fall within the clause. There is force in these arguments; and it is noteworthy that the Civil Evidence Act 1968 did not preserve the rule for civil cases. However, our general view is that the rule should be preserved as proposed because the clause might sometimes enable a party to adduce a statement which would be of genuine probative value and because it is hoped that the restatement will prove reasonably simple and workable.

262. Clause 38 provides for admissibility of hearsay statements by agreement of the parties. This may be useful for a case where a statement cannot be brought under any of the other heads of admissibility but the opposite party, while not necessarily admitting the correctness of the statement, is content that it should be admitted for what it is worth. The clause includes certain safeguards which we regard as necessary. It will not apply where any of the accused is unrepresented; for we regard it as too dangerous to allow an unrepresented person to consent to the admission of hearsay evidence when he may not appreciate the effect of the evidence on his case. It also seems safer to require that all the accused should be legally represented, as it may not be clear whom the statement will affect. Admissibility is also to be subject to the approval of the court, because there may be cases where the parties are content that a statement should be admitted but the court may consider that the interests of justice require that oral evidence on the matter should be given. For this reason, and in order to avoid the complication of a procedure involving the giving of consent in advance, the agreement will have to be made at the hearing. Otherwise the parties might agree beforehand that, because a particular matter was to be proved by means of hearsay evidence, a witness who was to have given oral evidence of the matter need not attend court or should be released. An agreement made during committal proceedings will not count for the purpose of the trial, at which a fresh agreement will be necessary.

263. Clause 39 provides for the admissibility of evidence as to the credibility of the maker of a hearsay statement which is admitted in evidence when the maker is not called as a witness. Broadly, it enables the parties to attack or support the maker's credibility as if the maker had been called as a witness except that *ex hypothesi* it is impossible to cross-examine the maker. The clause corresponds to s. 7 of the Civil Evidence Act 1968, but with one important difference. In the ordinary case where a person is called as a witness he may be cross-examined with a view to destroying his credibility as a witness but, in order not to raise side issues, a denial by the witness of a matter put to him in cross-examination in order to destroy his credibility is final in the sense that, although his denial need not be accepted by the jury or magistrates' court, the cross-examining party is not allowed to adduce evidence to refute his

denial. The principal exceptions are where the matter in question relates to bias on the part of the witness, a previous inconsistent statement made by him or his conviction of a criminal offence. In these cases a witness may be called to prove the matter in question. In the case of a hearsay statement there is a dilemma. If the maker of the statement had been guilty of discreditable conduct not resulting in a conviction, the other party might wish to give evidence of this; and since, if the maker had given evidence, he would very likely have admitted the conduct or his denial would not have been believed, the party against whom the hearsay statement is given in evidence might complain that, as the maker cannot be cross-examined, that party is at an unfair disadvantage. Against this, to allow unrestricted evidence of matter to the discredit of the absent maker of the statement might be very unfair to him and might lengthen the proceedings beyond what would be tolerable. S. 7 of the Civil Evidence Act resolves the dilemma in favour of excluding evidence of any matter as to which the maker's denial, had he been present and given evidence, would have been final. This is clearly defensible owing to the difficulties mentioned above and the fact that the lesser weight of hearsay statements would compensate for the lack of an opportunity to attack the maker's credit. However, we prefer the solution of allowing the evidence but subject to the leave of the court where the maker's denial would have been final. This should provide for the exceptional cases which might arise. Subsection (1)(*b*) provides accordingly.

264. Clause 40, which corresponds generally to s. 9 of the Civil Evidence Act 1968, saves the specified common-law exceptions to the rule against hearsay so far as these exceptions are relevant in criminal proceedings. But it includes certain provisions (referred to in the note in Annex 2) concerning admissions and evidence of reputation which differ from the provisions of s. 9 of the Act. A particular matter on which the clause makes no provision should be mentioned. This is the admissibility in evidence of things said at an identification parade. Evidence is commonly given that A (the victim of an offence or an eye-witness) pointed out the accused at the parade as the offender or that he failed to do so. Sometimes the evidence is given by A himself, sometimes by a policeman present at the parade. Assuming that the accused says nothing in reply to the accusation amounting to an admission of guilt, the admissibility of the evidence must be by virtue of an unformulated exception to the rule mentioned above[1] against previous consistent statements (in the case of evidence by A) and to the rule against hearsay (in the case of evidence by the policeman); but the law on this topic seems to have developed without special consideration of these rules. In *Christie*[2], where the accused had been convicted of an indecent assault on a boy of about five, the boy had pointed out the accused as the offender, not at an identification parade but at a confrontation (to which the same principles would apply) with the accused in the presence of the boy's mother and a policeman. At the trial the boy gave unsworn evidence about the assault and said that the accused committed it, but he was not questioned about his statement at the confrontation. His mother and the policeman gave evidence of the boy's statement at this. All the members of the House of Lords who gave opinions were clear that evidence by the boy that he pointed out the accused would have been admissible, but they differed

---

[1] Paragraph 226(i).
[2] [1914] A.C. 545; 10 Cr. App. R. 141.

on whether, as the boy had not given this evidence, the evidence by the mother and the policeman was admissible. There was no discussion of whether the boy's own evidence might have been inadmissible because of the rule against previous consistent statements, and the discussion as to the admissibility of the evidence of the mother and the policeman that the boy pointed out the accused was not related expressly to the rule against hearsay. But in any event we do not regard it as necessary to deal with the matter in the Bill. Since at present the rules against previous consistent statements and against hearsay apply in principle, and the evidence is admitted by virtue of exceptions to them, it seems right that the evidence should in future be admissible by virtue of the provisions in the Bill or not at all. The only case in which evidence admissible at present might become inadmissible as a result of the Bill, and for which it might be thought desirable to make provision, seems to be the case where a very young child has pointed out the accused at the parade. But to make special provision for this case would in the committee's view be inconsistent with the decision, taken for the reason given above[1], not to make a general provision for the admissibility of statements by very young children. Moreover, the particular difficulty which arose in *Christie*, that the boy did not give evidence about his statement at the confrontation, is a difficulty which will seldom occur.

265. Clause 41, which corresponds to s. 10 of the Civil Evidence Act, contains definitions for the purpose of the provisions concerning hearsay evidence.

CLAUSES 42–44: OPINION AND EXPERT EVIDENCE

266. The Law Reform Committee in their 17th report[2], published in October 1970, recommended the enactment of certain provisions about opinion and expert evidence. These provisions are contained in the draft clauses in Annex 2 to the report which were prepared by Parliamentary Counsel to give effect to their recommendations[3]. Apart from some important procedural matters, relevant to civil proceedings only[4], the provisions which the committee recommend involve only minor changes in the law, but they include useful simplifications. With the exception mentioned, we are satisfied that there would be value in enacting similar provisions for criminal proceedings and that this is a subject on which it is desirable that the law in the two kinds of proceedings should be in accord. In fact the two committees kept in touch with each other during their discussions on these subjects before the Law Reform Committee made their report, and all the recommendations relevant to criminal proceedings were in substance agreed between them. As these topics are dealt with in the Law Reform Committee's report, it is unnecessary to go into them fully here, but they are summarized in the five following paragraphs with reference to the relevant provisions in the draft Bill and the draft clauses prepared for the Law Reform Committee.

---

[1] Paragraph 250.
[2] Evidence of Opinion and Expert Evidence. Cmnd. 4489.
[3] A Civil Evidence Bill in terms of the Law Reform Committee's draft clauses, but with small differences, was introduced in the House of Commons on 20th December 1971.
[4] This refers to the provisions of clause 2 of the Law Reform Committee's draft clauses concerning rules of court with respect to expert reports and oral expert evidence.

267. Clause 42 of the draft Bill provides that the provisions of Part II of the Bill for admissibility of hearsay statements of fact shall apply, with the necessary modifications, to hearsay statements of opinion. The effect will be that, in a case where it would be permissible for A, if he were called as a witness, to express his opinion on a matter, evidence by B that A expressed the opinion out of court will be admissible subject to fulfilment of the appropriate conditions in relation to A. These will be the same as the conditions—as to unavailability to give evidence or otherwise—which would have to be fulfilled under Part II in order that B should be able to give evidence that A made some statement of fact. The clause corresponds to clause 1 of the Law Reform Committee's draft clauses[1].

268. Clause 43(1) provides that the opinion of an expert witness shall be admissible on any " relevant matter " on which he is qualified to give expert evidence. By virtue of subsection (3) " relevant matter " will include " an issue in the proceedings in question ". The purpose is to make it certain that the witness may express his opinion even on the ultimate issue which the court or jury have to decide. There have been judicial dicta that this is not to be allowed because it means that the witness is usurping the function of the court or jury; but the modern tendency is to allow this much more freely than in the past. This is natural, because it would often be artificial for the witness to avoid, or pretend to avoid, giving his opinion on a matter merely because it is the ultimate issue in the case and because his opinion on the ultimate issue may be obvious from the opinions which he has already expressed. Thus in *Director of Public Prosecutions v. A. & B. C. Chewing Gum Ltd.*[2] Lord Parker C. J. said:

> " I cannot help feeling that with the advance of science more and more inroads have been made into the old common law principles. Those who practise in the criminal courts see every day cases of experts being called on the question of diminished responsibility, and although technically the final question ' Do you think he was suffering from diminished responsibility? ' is strictly inadmissible, it is allowed time and time again without any objection ".

In the light of this it seems to us that it would now probably be held that the prohibition no longer exists. In any event we are satisfied that it should be done away with. It will follow that there will be no objection to asking the witness directly what is his opinion on the ultimate issue. This is in accordance with the views of the Law Reform Committee[3], and clause 3(1) of their draft clauses makes the corresponding provision for civil proceedings.

269. Before deciding to include the provision in clause 43(1) described in the previous paragraph we gave special consideration to whether it would be right that the provision should apply in respect of one particular class of case. This is the case of proceedings for an offence under s. 2 of the Obscene Publications Act 1959 (c. 66) of publishing an obscene article. The admissibility of expert evidence in these proceedings was before the courts in at least three recent cases—the *A. & B. C. Chewing Gum* case referred to in the previous paragraph, *Calder & Boyars Ltd.*[4] and *Anderson*[5]. These show that in ordinary cases

---

[1] See Law Reform Committee's 17th report, paragraph 23.
[2] [1968] 1 Q.B. 159, 164E.
[3] 17th report, paragraph 63.
[4] [1969] 1 Q.B. 151; 52 Cr. App. R. 706.
[5] [1972] 1 Q.B. 304; 56 Cr. App. R. 115.

expert evidence is inadmissible on the question whether an article is " such as to tend to deprave and corrupt " for the purpose of the test of obscenity laid down by s. 1 (as distinct from the question whether the publication is " justified as being for the public good " on one of the grounds mentioned in s. 4(1) in relation to the defence provided for by that section, on which question expert evidence is admissible under s. 4(2)), but that expert evidence is admissible on the former question in special cases where the subject-matter is such that expert knowledge is called for. The *A. & B. C. Chewing Gum* case was a special case, because the question was about the effect which the " battle cards " which were to be sold with packets of bubble gum would have on children of various ages from five upwards who would buy the packets. The Divisional Court held that this was a question on which expert witnesses experienced in child psychiatry was admissible. The principle is that in ordinary cases jurors and magistrates are as capable as anybody else of judging the likely effect of a publication, so that in these cases expert evidence is irrelevant and therefore inadmissible, but in special cases such as that mentioned, as Lord Parker C. J. said[1], " any jury and any justices need all the help they can get ". We are confident that, in cases where expert evidence is admissible, it is right, for the reason indicated by Lord Parker in the previous paragraph, that an expert witness should be allowed to give his opinion on the ultimate question whether the article is " such as to tend to deprave and corrupt ". Indeed it seems as artificial to allow the witness to describe the effect which an article would have on a child without saying in terms (when this is the case) that it would tend to deprave and corrupt as it would be to allow a witness to answer questions directed to each of the separate ingredients involved in the defence of diminished responsibility but to forbid him to answer the question " Do you think he was suffering from diminished responsibility? ". We are therefore satisfied that there is no reason why the provision should not apply to offences of publishing an obscene article as to other offences. But as there has been a good deal of misunderstanding about the admissibility of expert evidence in proceedings for offences relating to obscene publications, we think it desirable (though not necessary in law) that the clause should make it clear that the new provision is to apply only where expert evidence is admissible on the topic in question under the ordinary rules. This will be done by the provision in subsection (4) which provides that " Nothing in this section shall be taken to affect any rule of law as to the topics on which expert evidence is or is not admissible ".

270. Clause 43(2) is a declaratory provision that a statement of opinion by a non-expert witness on a " relevant matter ", " if made as a way of conveying relevant facts personally perceived by him, is admissible as evidence of what he perceived ". Again, by virtue of subsection (3), " relevant matter " will include " an issue in the proceedings in question ". We have no doubt that this is the present law, but it seems desirable for the statute to be explicit. The Law Reform Committee in their 17th report[2] pointed out that, although the fact that a non-expert witness is of the opinion that such and such is the case is not evidence that this is the case, yet the fact that his evidence describing an event which he perceived may take the form of an expression of opinion does not prevent its being evidence of this event. For example, as the committee pointed out, if a witness of an accident says that " there was nothing the

---

[1] [1968] 1 Q.B. at p. 165A.
[3] Paragraphs 4–6.

driver could do to avoid the accident ", this " may be the most vivid, as it is often the most natural, way of conveying...an accurate impression of the event which the witness is describing ". The committee argued from this, rightly in our opinion, that it would be wrong to stop a witness from giving his evidence in this way on the ground that he is expressing his opinion on the very issue which has to be decided. The enactment of the subsection will make it clear that the witness should be allowed to do so. The subsection will not allow a witness to say, for example, " in my opinion the accused was driving negligently " or " in my opinion the accused was guilty (or not guilty) ", because neither of these would be a " way of conveying relevant facts personally perceived " by the witness; nor would it allow an advocate to ask the witness to give his opinion on a matter. We are satisfied that it can be safely left to the courts and the legal profession to prevent any attempt to abuse the provision by, say, coaching an intelligent witness so that he will insinuate an expression of opinion into his evidence, seemingly spontaneously, in the hope that the jury will be induced to treat the fact that the witness took a certain view of the facts as a reason for them to take the same view. The corresponding provision in the Law Reform Committee's draft clauses is in clause 3(2).

271. Clause 44 makes two provisions about proof of foreign law. Subsection (1) declares that a witness suitably qualified to do so is competent to give evidence about the law of a country outside England and Wales irrespective of whether or not he is entitled to practise there. The purpose is to get rid of a supposed requirement, derived from statements in the old case of *Bristow v. Sequeville*[1] but not now insisted on, that the witness must be entitled to practise in the other country. We agree with the Law Reform Committee[2] that any such restriction is unnecessary. The remainder of the clause provides that a finding by an English court on a question of foreign law shall be prima facie evidence of that law and will thus avoid the present need, which follows from the rule that a question of foreign law is one of fact, to prove the matter again in later cases[3]. Questions of foreign law naturally occur very seldom in criminal proceedings in comparison with their occurrence in civil proceedings; but they may occur sometimes in the former. For example, in a prosecution for bigamy there may be a question whether a foreign marriage is valid; and in a prosecution for handling in England goods stolen abroad it is necessary under s. 24(1) of the Theft Act 1968 to prove that "the stealing...amounted to an offence where and at the time when the goods were stolen ". The provisions referred to in this paragraph correspond to those in clause 4 of the Law Reform Committee's draft clauses.

MATTERS ON WHICH NO CHANGE IS PROPOSED BY DRAFT BILL

(i) *Communications to ministers of religion or medical practitioners.*

272. We have no doubt that the only kind of professional privilege which English law allows is that of legal adviser and client (as to which we do not recommend any change). Although there is no conclusive decision, the over-

---

[1] (1850) 5 Ex. 275.
[2] 17th report, paragraph 19.
[3] Ibid., paragraph 64.

whelming weight of authority, both judicial and in books on the law, is to this effect[1]. This was also the view of the Law Reform Committee in their 16th report[2], published in December 1967; and since then it has been supported by the judgment of Baker J. (as he then was) in *Pais v. Pais*[3]. The two committees kept in touch with one another in considering whether to recommend legislation to confer a privilege in respect of any other professional relations, as is mentioned in the Law Reform Committee's report[4]. Both committees were satisfied that the only relations in respect of which there was any case for conferring the privilege were those of communications with ministers of religion and those of communications with medical practitioners; but after considering the question at considerable length both committees concluded that they should not recommend that the privilege should be conferred[5]. Our views are given in the four following paragraphs.

273. There are two arguments, both entitled to the highest respect, for conferring a privilege for communications to a minister of religion. The first is that it is in the interests of religion, morality and society generally that a person who is willing to confide in a minister about his wrongdoing or his wicked propensities should be encouraged to do so in the hope that the minister will be able to persuade him to lead a better life and that a person will be more ready to confide in the minister if there is no danger that the minister will be compelled to reveal the confidence in legal proceedings. The second argument is that to confer the privilege would be in accordance with the wish of the church leaders. In particular the Archbishop of Canterbury represented to the Law Reform Committee, and through them to us, that the creation of an absolute statutory privilege for penitential communications might remove a constitutional obstacle to a new canon on confessions which the Convocations of the Church of England desired to make. To confer the privilege would also avoid the possibility of a conflict, such as has very occasionally arisen, between the duty imposed on a priest by the rules of his church to keep secret a confidence (in particular one made during confession) and his legal duty to obey a requirement to reveal the confidence in court. This would ensure that a judge should not be in the embarrassing position of having to decide whether to punish a priest for refusing to disobey a rule of his church.

274. But the great majority of the committee, while fully sympathizing with the arguments above, are opposed to recommending the conferment of a privilege in respect of these communications. Their main reason is that there should be no restriction on the right of a party to criminal proceedings to compel a witness to give any information in his possession which is relevant to the charge, unless there is a compelling reason in policy for the restriction, and that the arguments for the proposal are not strong enough for this purpose. No serious difficulty has arisen for a great many years, and the majority are

---

[1] In the Republic of Ireland, Gavan Duffy J. held in *Cook v. Carroll*, [1945] I.R. 515, that a Roman Catholic priest had the right to refuse to reveal a statement made to him in his character as a priest, and irrespective of the wishes of the person who made it. The decision was based partly on the common law but also took account of the " special position " of the Roman Catholic Church as recognized in the constitution.

[2] Privilege in Civil Proceedings. Cmnd. 3472.

[3] [1971] P. 119, 120G–122B.

[4] Paragraph 53.

[5] Law Reform Committee's 16th report, paragraphs 46–47 (priest and penitent); 48–52 (doctor and patient); 54 (other confidential relationships).

satisfied that the prosecuting authorities and the courts would always be able to prevent a clash such as mentioned above. In a case where the accused had told a minister of religion that he had committed the offence charged—or, say, that he had a propensity to commit an offence of this kind—it would be exceptional for the prosecution to know of the communication, and there would have to be a strong reason for the prosecution to seek to compel the minister to give evidence about the communication or for the court to insist that he should give the evidence. On the other hand, it might occasionally happen that one of two accused persons had confessed to a minister that he alone, and not his co-accused, committed the offence. Even if any minister of religion felt able to stand by and let a possibly innocent person be convicted when the minister was in a position to exculpate him by giving evidence, we should not wish to recommend legislation which would allow this. It is possible, therefore, that any provision which might be enacted should apply only to information given by the accused about his own conduct. We have no doubt that the legislation would have to secure that the minister should be compellable to give evidence about a disclosure which the person who made it was willing to have disclosed[1]. Whether the minister should be free (so far as the law is concerned) to give the evidence without the consent of the person who made the disclosure is a more difficult question, and the fact that it would arise is an additional reason for our preference for not legislating but for leaving it to the courts and prosecuting authorities to deal with any case which might arise in practice.

275. But in this connection we should refer to a doubt which has been expressed in the committee about part of the Law Reform Committee's argument for not recommending that a statutory privilege should be conferred. The committee said that it was the policy of the common law " to limit to a minimum the categories of privileges which a person has an absolute right to claim, but to accord to the judge a wide discretion to permit a witness, whether a party to the proceedings or not, to refuse to disclose information where disclosure would be a breach of some ethical or social value and non-disclosure would be unlikely to result in serious injustice in the particular case in which it is claimed "[2]. In support of the statement that the judge has a wide discretion the committee referred to *Attorney-General v. Clough*[3] and *Attorney-General v. Mulholland*[4], which related to claims by journalists to be allowed to refuse to disclose their sources of information. The committee relied a good deal on the argument that conferring a statutory privilege might have the undesirable effect of narrowing the area in which the courts would feel able to exercise their discretion in favour of protecting confidential relations[5]. But although some of the statements in *Mulholland* at least are clearly in favour of the existence of a discretion, some members of the present committee have serious doubts whether the statements, if they are right for civil proceedings, have any general application to criminal proceedings. In criminal proceedings it is now established that the court has a general discretion to exclude evidence in order to prevent injustice to the defence[6]; but whether a judge could ever excuse a

---

[1] This would be contrary to the rule in *Cook v. Carroll* mentioned in n. 1 on p. 158.
[2] 16th report, paragraph 1.
[3] [1963] 1 Q.B. 773.
[4] [1963] 2 Q.B. 477.
[5] 16th report, paragraphs 1, 47.
[6] The exclusionary discretion will be preserved by clause 45(8): see paragraph 278.

witness from answering a relevant question asked by the defence in a criminal case on the ground that this would be a breach of a confidence reposed in the witness seems to some members highly questionable. But be this as it may, the majority are confident that any serious difficulties can be avoided, as mentioned above, even in the absence of an exclusionary discretion.

276. The arguments for and against conferring a privilege in relation to communications with a medical practitioner are broadly—though not entirely —similar to those for and against conferring a privilege in relation to communications with a minister of religion. Therefore it is unnecessary to go fully over the ground in relation to medical practitioners. But in their case there is a difficult question as to what should be the scope of the privilege if given. The privilege might be a wide one which would allow the doctor to refuse to give evidence (without the patient's consent) about any communication made to him by the patient in confidence, even one concerning a physical ailment or injury or, perhaps, even about the facts of any treatment given. The argument for this is that the public interest requires that a person should seek medical advice when this is necessary and that he should be able to speak freely to his doctor, even about something embarrassing or discreditable, without the danger that the doctor might have to give evidence about this in court. But we think that, even if any privilege were given, it would be wrong to go as far as this. To do so might exclude information which it was important in the interests of justice to have before the court. For example, it would be a scandal if a criminal who had been injured when blowing a safe or committing a robbery could prevent the doctor who had attended him from revealing what the criminal told him about how he came by his injury. There would be a stronger case for giving a narrower privilege according to which a person who had told a doctor practising psychiatry, in confidence, about an offence which he had committed, or a criminal propensity to which he was subject, for the purpose of obtaining advice or treatment which might help him to avoid committing offences in future, could object to the doctor's giving evidence about this. It is undoubtedly desirable that a person should consult a doctor for this purpose; and it can be argued that the possibility that this would bring about a reform in the conduct of the person in question is a good enough reason for conferring the privilege. The British Medical Association, in a memorandum sent to the Law Reform Committee and ourselves, argued in favour of conferring a medical privilege and said that, while the possibility of a conflict between medical and legal obligations applied to all physicians, " the dilemma is most acute in the field of psychiatry ". They added:

> " If a psychiatrist is to assist his patient, and in criminal cases possibly to assist the court to the best of his ability, it is essential that his interviews with his patient should be free and frank. In the course of such frank discussions matters may be brought to light which, whilst relevant to the mental state of the person concerned, will be gravely prejudicial to his interest, if the doctor is, as now, compelled to report them in open court ".

When we discussed this question, the general view was that the privilege, if given, should be the narrower one mentioned above, although it might sometimes be difficult to decide whether the case was a psychiatric or an ordinary medical one. For example, an unsophisticated person might consult a general practitioner about a problem about which a more sophisticated person would consult a psychiatrist, or a doctor might see that what a patient thought was a physical condition was in fact the result of psychological disturbance. In any event, we thought that some exceptions would have to be made. An example would be where the accused called the doctor as a witness in order to make out a defence of insanity, diminished responsibility, or some other defence depending on his mental state, and the prosecution wished to cross-examine the doctor in order to rebut the defence. However, in the end we decided, by a large majority, that for reasons similar to those in relation to ministers of religion —in particular the unlikelihood that any difficulty would arise in practice— we should not recommend that any privilege should be conferred in relation to medical practitioners.

(ii) *Evidence on commission*

277. We considered, but rejected, the idea of proposing legislation to allow evidence to be taken, in the United Kingdom or abroad, for use in criminal proceedings in England and Wales. Theoretically, this seems to be allowed in criminal, as well as civil, proceedings under the Evidence by Commission Act 1859 (c. 20) read with s. 3 of the Evidence by Commission Act 1885 (c. 74), but in fact commissions are not issued for this purpose in criminal cases in England and Wales[1]. There are a few cases in which depositions taken by a justice of the peace may be read at the trial; and under s. 691 of the Merchant Shipping Act 1894 (c. 60) evidence taken by a British court outside the United Kingdom or by a British consul in respect of an offence may in certain circumstances be read at the trial in England if the witness cannot be found in the United Kingdom, but in criminal cases the accused must have been present when the evidence was taken[2]. But apart from the theoretical possibility under the 1859 Act there is no procedure by which the assistance of foreign courts can be invoked to obtain oral evidence or procure documents in the possession of persons subject to the jurisdiction of the other court for use in criminal proceedings in England. In our original request for observations we included the question whether there should be provision for this. Only a very few of those who replied expressed any views on this matter, and of those who did some thought that this should be allowed only in respect of formal or undisputed evidence, which is now provided for by the provisions in ss. 2, 9 and 10 of the Criminal Justice Act 1967 allowing proof by written statement or by formal admissions. We decided that, in any event, we should not recommend that provision should be made for obtaining oral evidence on commission, because this would open the door too wide to the danger that evidence might be introduced at a late stage which could not be adequately tested. We considered a procedure by which a court should be able to issue a request for the production of a document in the possession of a person within the jurisdiction of a foreign court, because difficulties have occasionally happened in this respect; but in the end we decided that it was unnecessary to recommend making any provision for this purpose. This was chiefly because very little trouble has been experienced in these respects and because of the possible delays which the introduction of the procedure might cause, especially if the foreign court had difficulty in obtaining the document in good time. If serious difficulty occurs in future, no doubt the matter will be reconsidered.

---

[1] Archbold, Criminal Pleading, Evidence and Practice, 37th edition, paragraph 1250.
[2] There is a similar provision in s. 5 of the Tokyo Convention Act 1967 (c.52) in respect of offences on aircraft.

(iii) *Judicial discretion to exclude evidence*

278. We considered whether to include provision defining the extent of the judicial discretion to exclude admissible evidence and stating the grounds on which it should be exercised; but we decided against this for the reasons given below. The rules and practice as to an exclusionary discretion began to develop comparatively recently; for in 1914, during the argument in *Christie*[1], the Earl of Halsbury said that he " must protest against the suggestion that any judge has the right to exclude evidence which is in law admissible, on the ground of prudence or discretion, and so on ". But after this it was said in several cases that the court has a discretion to exclude cross-examination of the accused as to his previous misconduct and convictions when the cross-examination is allowed by s. 1(*f*)(ii) of the Criminal Evidence Act 1898 but the court considers that it would be unduly harsh to the accused. Eventually, in *Selvey v. Director of Public Prosecutions*[2], the House of Lords decided, after full argument, that the existence of the discretion was by then firmly established (though it has since been argued strongly[3] that the proposition that the discretion exists derives from a series of obiter dicta unsupported by authority and so often repeated that the case to the contrary went by default). Other situations in which the courts have said that the question of exercising the exclusionary discretion arose or might have arisen in criminal proceedings include cases of evidence obtained illegally[4] or by a breach of the Judges' Rules[5] or where the accused was misled as to the purpose for which he was providing the evidence[6]. The court has no discretion to prevent one co-accused from cross-examining another about his misconduct or convictions as allowed by s. 1(*f*)(iii) of the 1898 Act (to be replaced by clause 6(5)) when the latter has given evidence against the former[7]; and doubts have been expressed in the committee as to whether there is any discretion to exclude evidence in order to protect confidential relations[8]. We considered an argument that either the general discretion should be abolished and the law amended so as to make the evidence inadmissible in those cases (including, on one view, cases where the evidence was obtained illegally) where it was thought right in policy that it should be excluded or at least to define, for the sake of uniformity, the criteria on what the discretion should be exercised. But our general view is that the existence of the discretion is valuable in that it enables the courts to exclude evidence in cases, difficult to foresee and define, where its introduction would clearly be undesirable in the particular circumstances, and that it is best to leave it to the courts to lay down any general principles on which the discretion should be exercised. Clause 45(8) therefore preserves the existing discretion in general terms. An example of a case where the discretion might be exercised might be where the prosecution tries to insist on their right to cross-examine the accused about an isolated offence committed many years before the offence charged. Under the Bill, as at present, a refusal by the court to exercise its discretion to exclude evidence will be open to review on appeal.

---

[1] 10 Cr. App. R. 141, 149.
[2] [1970] A.C. 304; 52 Cr. App. R. 443. See paragraph 119.
[3] " Judicial discretion to exclude prejudicial evidence ": article by Mr. Bernard Livesey in (1968) 26 Cambridge Law Journal 291–309 (especially pp. 296–301).
[4] Paragraph 68.
[5] Paragraphs 45–46.
[6] *Payne* (1963), 47 Cr. App. R. 122.
[7] *Murdoch v. Taylor*, [1965] A.C. 574: 49 Cr. App. R. 119. See paragraphs 121, 132.
[8] Paragraph 275.

(iv) *Abolition of the oath*

279. We considered whether to recommend that witnesses in criminal proceedings should no longer take the oath but should make a declaration in the appropriate form undertaking to tell the truth. The great majority are strongly of the opinion that this change should be made. Their reasons are given in paragraph 280. A minority are strongly opposed to the change for the reasons given in paragraph 281. The reason why we have not included a provision to this effect in the draft Bill is that the question is obviously an important one of general policy going beyond the criminal law. In particular it would hardly be thought right to abolish the oath in criminal proceedings only while keeping it in civil proceedings. We were informed that the Law Reform Committee decided to make no recommendation about the oath in civil proceedings because they regarded the question as a social rather than a legal one. We agree that this is a good reason for not making a recommendation, but we think it right to express our opinion for two reasons. First, assuming that it is in fact right to replace the oath, this is one of those kinds of reform which may never happen unless bodies in favour of making it express their opinion on appropriate occasions, and a general review of criminal evidence is in our opinion an appropriate occasion. Second, three of our recommendations directly concern the oath. These are the abolition of the accused's right to make an unsworn statement[1], the provision for calling on the accused to give evidence[2] and the fixing of fourteen as the lowest age for giving evidence on oath[3]. If the witness's oath is replaced by a declaration, the law of perjury would be applied to false evidence given after a declaration as it applies to false evidence on oath or affirmation; and it might be thought right that the declaration should include an acknowledgment by the witness of his liability to be prosecuted for perjury if he told an untruth in giving his evidence.

280. The reasons why the majority consider that the oath should be replaced by an undertaking to tell the truth are given below[4]:

(i) The oath is a primitive institution which ought not to be preserved unless there is a good reason for preserving it. Its use has been traced back to times when man believed that a verbal formula could itself produce desired results, as in the case of the curse. Curses were operative magic performances, and the oath was a conditional self-curse. With the growth of religious belief it was thought that God was the executor of man's oath. He was believed to respond to its magic. The oath was an imprecation to heaven calling upon the supernatural powers to bring disaster on the speaker if he uttered falsehood. This was the basis of the Anglo-Saxon system of compurgation, which rested on the belief that the taking of a false oath brought automatic supernatural punishment. This view of the oath lasted for a surprisingly long time. A judicial expression of the traditional view of the oath is to be found as late as 1786 in *White*[5],

---

[1] Clause 4(2).
[2] Clause 5.
[3] Clause 22(2).
[4] We emphasize that not all the minority (or all the majority) accept the validity of all the arguments given in this paragraph.
[5] Leach 430.

where at a trial at the Old Bailey for horse-stealing a man was rejected as a witness because he " acknowledged that he had never learned the catechism, was altogether ignorant of the obligations of an oath, a future state of reward and punishment, the existence of another world, or what became of wicked people after death ". The court said " that an oath is a religous asseveration, by which a person renounces the mercy, and imprecates the vengeance of heaven, if he do not speak the truth; and therefore a person who has no idea of the sanction which this appeal to heaven creates, ought not to be sworn as a witness in any court of justice ". However, in 1817 Bentham attacked the traditional view with his usual vigour. He pointed to the " absurdity, than which nothing can be greater ", of the supposition that " by man, over the Almighty, *power* should be exercised or exercisable; man the legislator and judge, God the sheriff and executioner; man the despot, God his slave "[1].

(ii) It might be said that, although the original purpose of the oath is no longer relevant, it nevertheless has value now in that it serves to call the attention of a witness who believes in God to the fact that, if he tells a lie, he will incur the divine displeasure. But if this is its justification, it is curious that it is only in the case of lying in certain official proceedings that the citizen has his attention called to his assumed belief in divine retribution. We do not draw attention to this possibility for any other purpose of law enforcement.

(iii) There have already been large inroads into the practice of taking the oath. Originally, non-believers were prevented from taking the oath because this would have involved practising a kind of deception on the state. Eventually, however, concern for the promotion of trade brought about a change of attitude and infidels were allowed to take the oath and so to testify in legal proceedings. The Oaths Act 1838 (c. 105) for the first time allowed persons other than Christians and Jews to be sworn in such form as the witness might declare to be binding on him. In effect this involved an abandonment for these persons of an inquiry into their beliefs as to the hereafter. S. 3 of the Oaths Act 1888 (c. 46) declares that, where an oath has been duly administered, " the fact that the person to whom the same was administered had, at the time of taking such oath, no religious belief, shall not for any purpose affect the validity of such oath ". The same Act introduced the affirmation as an alternative to the oath. But affirmations were allowed only for those who declared that they had no religious belief or that their religious belief prevented them from taking an oath. Cases have occurred in which persons who could not bring themselves within either of these requirements, nor state what form of oath was binding on them, had their evidence rejected altogether. It is no longer considered a fatal objection to receiving the evidence of a child that he does not understand the nature of an oath. The last stage has been the Oaths Act 1961 (c. 21), which empowers the court to require a witness to affirm instead of taking the oath if it would not be " reasonably practicable without

---

[1] " Swear Not at All " pp. 3–4.

164

inconvenience or delay " to administer the oath to him in the way appropriate to his religion. In passing this Act Parliament recognized that there is nothing wrong in requiring a person to give evidence without being sworn even though he has a religious belief and it is not contrary to this to take an oath. It seems difficult, therefore, to see why this should not apply to all witnesses.

(iv) To many people it is incongruous that the Bible should be used, and the Deity invoked, in giving evidence of such matters as, for example, a common motoring offence. In evaluating evidence, little attention is paid to the mere fact that it has been given on oath. In any case it is probable that many witnesses who in fact have no religious belief take the oath because they do not wish to call attention to themselves or because they fear that the impact of their evidence will be weakened if they depart from the customary oath.

(v) If it is right to regard it as incongruous to require ordinary witnesses to take the oath, this is specially inappropriate in the case of the accused. The accused, if guilty (and sometimes even if not), is under an obvious temptation to lie. Our proposals involve putting pressure on him to give evidence, and it may seem to many excessive to require him to take a religious oath as well.

(vi) There would be a good case for keeping the oath if there were a real probability that it increases the amount of truth told. The majority do not think that it does this very much. For a person who has a firm religious belief, it is unlikely that taking the oath will act as any additional incentive to tell the truth. For a person without any religious belief, by hypothesis the oath can make no difference. There is value in having a witness " solemnly and sincerely " promise that he will tell the truth, and from this point of view the words of the affirmation are to many at least more impressive than the customary oath. The oath has not prevented an enormous amount of perjury in the courts. A witness who wishes to lie and who feels that the oath may be an impediment can easily say that taking an oath is contrary to his religious belief.

We need hardly say that we have no wish to offend any religious feelings, nor do we see why anything said above should do so. Moreover, the replacement of the oath by some form of declaration has been advocated several times recently in legal periodicals and in two of the observations sent to us, and the arguments in the periodicals do not seem to have provoked any arguments to the contrary. In 1968 the Magistrates' Association at their annual meeting voted by a narrow majority (140–130) that the oath sworn in magistrates' courts should be replaced by a simple promise to tell the truth[1]. In July 1970 the Memorandum of the Council of the Law Society on Oaths, Affirmations and Statutory Declarations recommended that " the present forms of oaths, affirmations and statutory declarations should be abolished and replaced by a single, non-religious form of promise or declaration for use on all occasions where formality is required ". In any event, whether the oath is kept or replaced, we hope that steps will be taken to ensure greater solemnity when a witness swears or makes the declaration. In our opinion it may be desirable

---

[1] " The Times ", 12th October, 1968.

that the oath or declaration should always be administered by the judge or presiding magistrate, as is the practice in Scotland. If it is decided to abolish the witness's oath, the question of the jurors' oath will require consideration; for if the jurors took the oath and the witnesses made a declaration, this might suggest that the witnesses' duty was less important than the jurors'. We express no opinion as to the abolition or preservation of other oaths.

281. The minority are strongly opposed to the replacement of the witness's oath by a declaration. They recognize that there is force in the arguments for this as set out in the previous paragraph; but they do not find any of them convincing. In their opinion there are many persons to whom the oath, administered properly and in complete silence, serves to bring home most strongly the solemnity of their obligation to tell the truth and to be careful about what they say in giving their evidence.

OTHER MATTERS

282. We received a good many other proposals for changing the law in addition to the matters discussed above. We considered them all, and it is only in order to avoid unduly lengthening the report that we do not mention them all in it. Some subsidiary matters are referred to in the notes in Annex 2. We wish only to refer to two matters here. First, we would repeat and emphasize the fact that we have not been concerned to codify the law of criminal evidence[1]. We mention this in particular because there are matters on which the law might be improved in the course of codification but which concern civil proceedings also. An example is the complicated provisions for the proof of documents, which might well be reduced to a much smaller number. Second, some of the provisions in the draft Bill will have the result that evidence will be admissible which at present is inadmissible altogether or is admissible only for more limited purposes. Therefore the courts may consider it desirable that judges should give particular directions to the jury as to how they should treat some kinds of newly admissible evidence—in particular, hearsay. For this purpose judges may think it desirable to give juries directions at the time when the evidence is given instead of waiting for the summing up. This might apply also to questions of corroboration. Directions are sometimes given in this way at present, but it may be desirable to extend the practice considerably because of the Bill. If so, it will be important to ensure that the direction, if not repeated in the summing up, appears on the record in order that it may be clear, in the event of an appeal, that the direction has been given.

CONCLUSION

283. Finally, we should like to express our appreciation of the work of those who have assisted us. Our deliberations over the years and the preparation of our reports have imposed a heavy burden on our secretary, Mr. G. V. Hart. We wish to record our deep gratitude to him for the outstandingly efficient manner in which he has discharged his duties and the unfailing patience and

---

[1] See paragraph 12.

good humour he has displayed even when we have been at our most disputatious. His contribution to the work of the committee during the thirteen years he has served us as secretary has been a major one.

284. Our warmest thanks are also due to Mr. G. L. J. Engle, of Parliamentary Counsel, who has rendered invaluable help by the preparation of numerous drafts to give effect to proposals which have been the subject of frequent changes in the course of our deliberations. We are greatly indebted to him for the guidance he has given to us on questions of drafting and for the care and skill with which he produced the draft Bill appended to our report.

EDMUND DAVIES, *Chairman.*
FREDERIC SELLERS.
FREDERICK LAWTON.
DONALD FINNEMORE.
ARTHUR EVAN JAMES.
MERVYN GRIFFITH-JONES.
RUPERT CROSS.
KENNETH JONES.
FRANK MILTON.
MALCOLM MORRIS.
A. C. PROTHERO.
NORMAN J. SKELHORN.
GLANVILLE WILLIAMS.

G. V. HART, *Secretary.*
BARBARA R. PUGH, *Assistant Secretary.*

30th May 1972.

Note.—Professor D. R. Seaborne Davies has not thought it right to sign this report because he was obliged by other duties to be absent from most of the meetings when the committee considered the subjects dealt with in it.

ANNEX 1

DRAFT CRIMINAL EVIDENCE BILL

ARRANGEMENT OF CLAUSES

PART I

PROVISIONS AS TO VARIOUS MATTERS

Provisions having special reference to the accused

Clause
1. Circumstances in which inferences may be drawn from accused's failure to mention particular facts when questioned, charged etc.
2. Confessions.
3. Admissibility of other conduct of accused tending to show disposition.
4. Giving of evidence by accused.
5. Accused to be called upon to give evidence at trial.
6. Restrictions on cross-examination of accused.
7. Admissibility of evidence and questions about accused's disposition or reputation.
8. Limits of burden of proof falling on accused.

Competence and compellability of spouse of accused

9. Competence and compellability of spouse of accused.

Cross-examination

10. Restrictions on cross-examination of witness other than an accused.
11. Circumstances in which party may cross-examine his own witness.
12. Right of cross-examining party to prove witness's previous inconsistent statement.
13. Use of document containing previous inconsistent statement of cross-examined witness.
14. Right of rebuttal where cross-examined witness denies having been convicted etc.

Privilege

15. Privilege against incrimination of self or spouse.
16. Abolition of certain privileges.

Corroboration, and directions to juries

17. Corroboration in proceedings for sexual offences.
18. Corroboration in proceedings for perjury etc.
19. Abolition of certain requirements as to corroboration.

Clause

20. Directions to juries about convicting on uncorroborated evidence.
21. Directions to juries about reliance on disputed identification of accused.

Evidence of children

22. Evidence of children.

Other matters

23. General rule, and court's discretion, as to time at which evidence may be called at trial.
24. Conviction as evidence of commission of offence by person other than the accused.
25. Provisions supplementary to ss. 3 and 24.
26. Manner in which certain United Kingdom convictions and acquittals may be proved.
27. Institution of proceedings for perjury etc.
28. Duty of magistrates' courts to have regard to enactments about warnings to juries.
29. Abolition of right to make evidence of document called for and inspected by an opponent.

PART II

HEARSAY EVIDENCE

30. Hearsay evidence to be admissible only by virtue of this Act and other statutory provisions or certain rules of law.
31. Admissibility of out-of-court statements as evidence of facts stated.
32. Restrictions on admissibility of statements by virtue of s. 31.
33. Witness's previous statement, if proved, to be evidence of facts stated.
34. Admissibility of certain records as evidence of facts stated.
35. Admissibility of statements produced by computers.
36. Provisions supplementary to ss. 31 to 35.
37. Admissibility of statements made as immediate reaction to events in issue personally witnessed.
38. Admissibility of hearsay evidence by agreement of the parties.
39. Admissibility of evidence as to credibility of maker etc. of statement admitted under certain provisions of Part II.
40. Saving for certain common-law exceptions to rule against hearsay.
41. Interpretation of Part II.

PART III

OPINION AND EXPERT EVIDENCE

42. Application of Part II to statements of opinion.
43. Admissibility of expert opinion and certain expressions of non-expert opinion.
44. Evidence of foreign law.

170

PART IV

MISCELLANEOUS AND GENERAL

Clause

45. General interpretation and savings.
46. Minor and consequential amendments, and repeals.
47. Short title, extent and commencement.

SCHEDULES:

Schedule 1—Consequential amendments of enactments.
Schedule 2—Repeals.

DRAFT OF A BILL TO

Amend and, in part, restate the law of evidence in relation to criminal proceedings; to amend section 129C of the Naval Discipline Act 1957; and for connected purposes.

Be it enacted by the Queen's most Excellent Majesty, by and with the advice and consent of the Lords Spiritual and Temporal, and Commons, in this present Parliament assembled, and by the authority of the same, as follows:—

PART I

PROVISIONS AS TO VARIOUS MATTERS

Provisions having special reference to the accused

Circumstances in which inferences may be drawn from accused's failure to mention particular facts when questioned, charged etc.

1.—(1) Where in any proceedings against a person for an offence evidence is given that the accused—

(a) at any time before he was charged with the offence, on being questioned by a police officer trying to discover whether or by whom the offence had been committed, failed to mention any fact relied on in his defence in those proceedings; or

(b) on being charged with the offence or officially informed that he might be prosecuted for it, failed to mention any such fact,

being a fact which in the circumstances existing at the time he could reasonably have been expected to mention when so questioned, charged or informed, as the case may be, the court, in determining whether to commit the accused for trial or whether there is a case to answer, and the court or jury, in determining whether the accused is guilty of the offence charged, may draw such inferences from the failure as appear proper; and the failure may, on the basis of such inferences, be treated as, or as capable of amounting to, corroboration of any evidence given against the accused in relation to which the failure is material.

(2) Subsection (1) above shall apply in relation to questioning by persons (other than police officers) charged with the duty of investigating offences or charging offenders as it applies in relation to questioning by police officers; and in that subsection " officially informed " means informed by a police officer or any such person.

(3) Nothing in subsection (1) or (2) above shall in any proceedings—

(a) prejudice the admissibility in evidence of the silence or other reaction of the accused in the face of anything said in his presence relating to the conduct in respect of which he is charged, in so far as evidence thereof would be admissible apart from those subsections; or

(b) be taken to preclude the drawing of any inference from any such silence or other reaction of the accused which could be drawn apart from those subsections.

(4) Subsections (1) and (2) above shall not apply as regards a failure P<small>ART</small> I to mention a fact if the failure occurred before the commencement of this Act.

(5) It is hereby declared that a police officer or other person who suspects a person of having committed an offence is not required by law to caution him before questioning him in relation to the offence.

2.—(1) In any proceedings a confession made by the accused may be Confessions. given in evidence by the prosecution in so far as it is relevant to any matter in issue in the proceedings and is not excluded by the court in pursuance of subsection (2) or (3) below.

(2) If, in any proceedings where the prosecution proposes to give in evidence a confession made by the accused, it is represented to the court that the confession was or may have been made in consequence of oppressive treatment of the accused or in consequence of any threat or inducement, the court shall not allow the confession to be given in evidence by the prosecution (whether by virtue of this section or otherwise) except in so far as the prosecution proves to the court beyond reasonable doubt that the confession (notwithstanding that it may be true)—

(a) was not obtained by oppressive treatment of the accused; and

(b) was not made in consequence of any threat or inducement of a sort likely, in the circumstances existing at the time, to render unreliable any confession which might be made by the accused in consequence thereof.

(3) In any proceedings where the prosecution proposes to give in evidence a confession made by the accused, the court may of its own motion require the prosecution, as a condition of allowing it to do so, to prove with respect to the confession the matters mentioned in paragraphs (a) and (b) of subsection (2) above.

(4) Where in any proceedings a confession is received in evidence by virtue of the foregoing provisions of this section, it shall by virtue of this subsection be admissible as evidence of any fact stated therein and of any matter dealt with in any opinion expressed therein, including any fact or matter favourable to the accused:

Provided that at the trial of any person for an offence the court shall not be required to treat an issue as having been raised with respect to any matter by reason only of evidence favourable to the accused which is admissible by virtue of this subsection.

(5) The fact that a confession is wholly or partly excluded in pursuance of subsection (2) or (3) above shall not affect the admissibility in evidence—

(a) of any facts discovered as a result of the confession; or

(b) as regards any fact so discovered, of the fact that it was discovered as a result of a statement made by the accused; or

(c) where the confession is relevant as showing that the accused speaks, writes or expresses himself in a particular way, of so much of the confession as is necessary to show this about him.

(6) In this section " confession " includes any statement wholly or partly adverse to the accused, whether made to a person in authority or not and whether made in words or otherwise.

Admissibility of other conduct of accused tending to show disposition.

3.—(1) Subject to the provisions of this section, in any proceedings evidence of other conduct of the accused shall not be admissible for the purpose of proving the commission by him of the offence charged by reason only that the conduct in question tends to show in him a disposition to commit the kind of offence with which he is charged or a general disposition to commit crimes.

In this section " other conduct of the accused " means conduct of the accused other than the conduct in respect of which he is charged.

(2) In any proceedings evidence of other conduct of the accused tending to show in him a disposition to commit the kind of offence with which he is charged shall be admissible for the said purpose if the disposition which that conduct tends to show is, in the circumstances of the case, of particular relevance to a matter in issue in the proceedings, as in appropriate circumstances would be, for example—

(a) a disposition to commit that kind of offence in a particular manner or according to a particular mode of operation resembling the manner or mode of operation alleged as regards the offence charged; or

(b) a disposition to commit that kind of offence in respect of the person in respect of whom he is alleged to have committed the offence charged; or

(c) a disposition to commit that kind of offence (even though not falling within paragraph (a) or (b) above) which tends to confirm the correctness of an identification of the accused by a witness for the prosecution.

(3) Where in any proceedings evidence of any other conduct of the accused is admissible by virtue of subsection (2) above for the purpose of proving the commission by him of the offence charged, and the accused has in respect of that other conduct been convicted of an offence by or before any court in the United Kingdom or by a court-martial there or elsewhere, then, if evidence tending to establish the conduct in question is given by virtue of that subsection, evidence that he has been so convicted in respect of it shall be admissible for that purpose in addition to the evidence given by virtue of that subsection.

(4) In any proceedings where the conduct in respect of which the accused is charged is admitted in the course of those proceedings by or on behalf of the accused, evidence of other conduct of the accused tending to show in him a disposition to commit the kind of offence with which he is charged shall be admissible for any of the following purposes, namely—

174

(a) to establish the existence in the accused of any state of mind (including recklessness) proof of which lies on the prosecution; or

(b) to prove that the conduct in respect of which the accused is charged was not accidental or involuntary; or

(c) to prove that there was no lawful justification or excuse for the conduct in respect of which the accused is charged,

notwithstanding that the other conduct is relevant for that purpose by reason only that it tends to show in the accused a disposition to commit the kind of offence with which he is charged:

Provided that no evidence shall be admissible by virtue of this subsection for the purpose of proving negligence on the part of the accused.

(5) If in any proceedings evidence of any other conduct of the accused is admissible by virtue of subsection (4) above for any purpose mentioned in that subsection, evidence that he has in respect of that other conduct been convicted of an offence by or before any court in the United Kingdom or by a court-martial there or elsewhere shall (notwithstanding anything in subsection (3) above) be admissible for that purpose, whether or not any other evidence of that conduct is given.

(6) If at the trial of a person for an offence the court is satisfied with respect to any matter which is admissible in evidence by virtue of subsection (2), (3), (4) or (5) above that the admissibility of that matter did not arise or become apparent until after the conclusion of the prosecution's case or that it was not reasonably practicable for evidence of that matter to be given before the conclusion of that case, then, notwithstanding any rule of practice—

(a) any person who gives evidence for the defence may be cross-examined about that matter; and

(b) subject to any directions by the court as to the time when it is to be given, evidence of that matter may be given on behalf of the prosecution after the conclusion of the prosecution's case.

(7) Nothing in the foregoing provisions of this section shall prejudice—

(a) the admissibility in evidence in any proceedings of any other conduct of the accused in so far as that conduct is relevant to any matter in issue in the proceedings for a reason other than a tendency to show in the accused a disposition; or

(b) the operation of any enactment (whether contained in this Act or in any other Act, whenever passed) by virtue of which evidence of other conduct of the accused, or evidence of his conviction of an offence, is or may become admissible in any criminal proceedings.

(8) The provisions of section 25 of this Act apply for the purposes of this section.

(9) Section 27(3) of the Theft Act 1968 (admissibility, where a person 1968 c. 60. is being proceeded against for handling stolen goods, of evidence that

he has acted in certain ways with respect to stolen goods or has been convicted of theft or of handling stolen goods) shall cease to have effect.

Giving of evidence by accused.

4.—(1) In any proceedings the accused shall be competent to give evidence on behalf of himself or any person jointly charged with him, but shall not be compellable to do so.

(2) In any proceedings the accused shall not be entitled to make a statement without being sworn, and accordingly, if he gives evidence, he shall do so on oath and be liable to cross-examination; but this subsection shall not affect the right of the accused, if not represented by counsel or a solicitor, to address the court or jury otherwise than on oath on any matter on which, if he were so represented, counsel or a solicitor could address the court or jury on his behalf.

(3) If at a trial on indictment the accused is the only person whom the defence intends to call as a witness to the facts of the case, he shall be called immediately after the close of the evidence for the prosecution.

(4) Subject to subsection (3) above, at the trial of any person for an offence the accused, if he gives evidence, shall be called as a witness before any other evidence is called for the defence except in so far as the court in its discretion otherwise allows.

(5) Subject to subsection (6) below, it is hereby declared that if, in the case of a trial on an information or indictment whereby two or more persons are jointly charged, any of those persons as a result of pleading guilty or for any other reason is not, or is no longer, liable to conviction at that trial, that person is compellable to give evidence for the prosecution or on behalf of any person who is liable to conviction at that trial.

(6) Without prejudice to section 9(5) of this Act, subsection (5) above does not apply in the case of a person who is not, or is no longer, liable to conviction at the trial in question if that person is the husband or wife of a person who is liable to conviction at that trial.

1925 c. 86.

(7) Section 12 of the Criminal Justice Act 1925 (admissibility at trial of statement made by accused in proceedings before examining justices in answer to the charge) shall cease to have effect.

Accused to be called upon to give evidence at trial.

5.—(1) At the trial of any person for an offence the following provisions of this section shall apply unless he pleads guilty, except that subsection (2) shall not apply if—

    (*a*) the court holds that there is no case to answer; or

    (*b*) before any evidence is called for the defence, the accused or counsel or a solicitor representing him informs the court that the accused will give evidence; or

    (*c*) it appears to the court that the physical or mental condition of the accused makes it undesirable for him to be called upon to give evidence.

(2) Before any evidence is called for the defence, the court shall tell the accused that he will be called upon by the court to give evidence in

his own defence and shall tell him in ordinary language what the effect of this section will be if, when so called upon, he refuses to be sworn; and thereupon or, if the court in the exercise of its discretion under section 4(4) of this Act allows the defence to call other evidence first, after that evidence has been given, the court shall call upon the accused to give evidence.

(3) If the accused—

    (a) after being called upon by the court to give evidence in pursuance of this section, or after he or counsel or a solicitor representing him has informed the court that he will give evidence, refuses to be sworn; or

    (b) having been sworn, without good cause refuses to answer any question,

the court or jury, in determining whether the accused is guilty of the offence charged, may draw such inferences from the refusal as appear proper; and the refusal may, on the basis of such inferences, be treated as, or as capable of amounting to, corroboration of any evidence given against the accused.

(4) Nothing in this section shall be taken to render the accused compellable to give evidence on his own behalf, and he shall accordingly not be guilty of contempt of court by reason of a refusal to be sworn in the circumstances described in subsection (3)(a) above.

(5) For the purposes of this section a person who, having been sworn, refuses to answer any question shall be taken to do so without good cause unless—

    (a) he is entitled to refuse to answer the question by virtue of section 6(1) of this Act or any other enactment, whenever passed, or on the ground of privilege; or

    (b) the court in the exercise of its general discretion excuses him from answering it.

(6) In relation to the trial of a child *for homicide* the foregoing provisions of this section have effect subject to section 22(3) of this Act.

6.—(1) Where in any proceedings the accused gives evidence, then, subject to the provisions of this and the next following section, he shall not in cross-examination be asked, and if asked shall not be required to answer, any question tending to reveal to the court or jury— Restrictions on cross-examination of accused.

    (a) the fact that he has committed, or has been charged with or convicted or acquitted of, any offence other than the offence charged; or

    (b) the fact that he is generally or in a particular respect a person of bad disposition or reputation.

(2) Subsection (1) above shall not apply to a question tending to reveal to the court or jury a fact about the accused such as is mentioned

in subsection (1)(*a*) or (*b*) above if evidence of that fact is (by virtue of section 3 of this Act or otherwise) admissible for the purpose of proving the commission by him of the offence charged.

(3) Where, in any proceedings in which two or more persons are jointly charged, any of the accused gives evidence, subsection (1) above shall not in his case apply to any question tending to reveal to the court or jury a fact about him such as is mentioned in subsection (1)(*a*) or (*b*) above if evidence of that fact is admissible for the purpose of showing any other of the accused to be not guilty of the offence with which that other is charged.

(4) Subsection (1) above shall not apply if—

(*a*) the accused has personally or by his advocate asked any witness for the prosecution or for a person jointly charged with him any question concerning the witness's conduct on any occasion or as to whether the witness has committed, or has been charged with or convicted or acquitted of, any offence; and

(*b*) the court is of the opinion that the main purpose of that question was to raise an issue as to the witness's credibility;

but the court shall not permit a question falling within subsection (1) above to be put to the accused by virtue of this subsection unless of opinion that the question is relevant to his credibility as a witness.

(5) Subsection (1) above shall not apply where the accused has himself given evidence against any person jointly charged with him in the same proceedings.

Admissibility of evidence and questions about accused's disposition or reputation.

7.—(1) In any proceedings the accused may—

(*a*) personally or by his advocate ask questions of any witness with a view to establishing directly or by implication that the accused is generally or in a particular respect a person of good disposition or reputation; or

(*b*) himself give evidence tending to establish directly or by implication that the accused is generally or in a particular respect such a person; or

(*c*) call a witness to give any such evidence;

but where any of these things has been done, the prosecution may call, and any person jointly charged with the accused may call or himself give, evidence to establish that the accused is a person of bad disposition or reputation, and the prosecution or any person so charged may in cross-examining any witness (including, where he gives evidence, the accused) ask him questions with a view to establishing that fact.

(2) Where by virtue of this section a party is entitled to call evidence to establish that the accused is a person of bad disposition or reputation, that party may call evidence of his previous convictions, if any, whether or not that party calls any other evidence for that purpose; and where by

178

virtue of this section a party is entitled in cross-examining the accused to ask him questions with a view to establishing that he is such a person, section 6(1) of this Act shall not apply in relation to his cross-examination by that party.

8.—(1) Where by virtue of any rule of law or existing enactment there falls on the accused in any proceedings any burden of proof with respect to a matter relevant to his guilt or innocence, then, subject to subsection (4) below—

(a) unless there is sufficient evidence to raise an issue with respect to that matter, that matter shall be taken as proved against him; but

(b) if there is sufficient evidence to raise an issue with respect to that matter, the court or jury, in determining whether he is guilty of the offence charged, shall decide by reference to the whole of the evidence whether the prosecution has proved that matter against the accused, drawing such inferences from the evidence as appear proper in the circumstances.

(2) Subsection (1) above shall have effect not only in relation to enactments saying in terms that proof of any matter is to lie on the accused, or that it shall be for the defence to prove (or show, or satisfy the court or jury of) any matter, or providing for a presumption adverse to the accused that can be displaced by proof (or evidence) of the contrary, or the like, but also in relation to any enactment, however framed or worded, whereby there falls on the accused a burden of proof of whatever nature or extent.

(3) In this section " existing enactment " means any enactment passed before this Act; but—

(a) in any enactment other than an existing enactment, provisions relating to the burden of proving any matter in proceedings shall, unless the contrary intention appears, be construed as having the like effect as those provisions would have by virtue of this section if they were contained in an existing enactment; and

(b) this section shall apply in relation to provisions contained in an instrument made under an Act of Parliament as it would apply if those provisions were enacted in that Act (and were or were not " existing enactments " accordingly).

(4) This section shall not affect the operation or construction of the enactments mentioned in subsection (5) below; nor shall it affect that of any other enactment (whether an existing enactment or not, and however framed or worded) which provides for a person charged with an offence to prove certain matters for the purpose of absolving himself from that charge, if—

(a) one of the matters which it requires him to prove for that purpose is that the offence was actually committed by some other person brought before the court, or that its commission was due to the act or default of some other person so brought; and

(b) on proof of some or all of the matters in question that other person is liable to be convicted of an offence.

(5) The enactments referred to in subsection (4) above are—

<table>
<tr><td>1950 c. 28.</td><td>(a) section 71(6) of the Shops Act 1950;</td></tr>
<tr><td>1952 c. 60.</td><td>(b) section 5(1) of the Agriculture (Poisonous Substances) Act 1952:</td></tr>
<tr><td>1955 c. 16
(4 & 5 Eliz. 2).</td><td>(c) section 113(1) of the Food and Drugs Act 1955;</td></tr>
<tr><td>1961 c. 34.</td><td>(d) section 161(1) of the Factories Act 1961; and</td></tr>
<tr><td>1963 c. 31.</td><td>(e) section 27(1) of the Weights and Measures Act 1963.</td></tr>
</table>

Competence and compellability of spouse of accused

Competence and compellability of spouse of accused.
9.—(1) In any proceedings the wife or husband of the accused shall be competent to give evidence for the prosecution or on behalf of the accused or any person jointly charged with the accused:

Provided that, subject to subsection (5) below, the wife or husband of the accused, if jointly charged with the accused, shall not be competent to give evidence for the prosecution.

(2) In any proceedings the wife or husband of the accused shall (unless jointly charged with the accused) be compellable to give evidence on behalf of the accused.

(3) In any proceedings the wife or husband of the accused shall (unless jointly charged with the accused) be compellable to give evidence for the prosecution or on behalf of any person jointly charged with the accused, where—

(a) the act or any of the acts constituting the offence charged consists of an assault on or a threat of violence to the wife or husband of the accused or a person who was at the material time a member of the same household as the accused and under the age of sixteen; or

(b) the offence charged is a sexual offence alleged to have been committed in respect of a person who was at the material time a member of the same household as the accused and under that age,

but, subject to subsections (4) and (5) below, the wife or husband of the accused shall not otherwise be compellable to give evidence for the prosecution or on behalf of a person jointly charged with the accused.

(4) In any proceedings a person who has been but is no longer married to the accused shall be compellable to give evidence as if that person and the accused had never been married.

(5) It is hereby declared that if, in the case of a trial on an information or indictment whereby a husband and his wife are jointly charged, one of them as a result of pleading guilty or for any other reason is not, or is no longer, liable to conviction at that trial, that one of them—

(*a*) is compellable to give evidence on behalf of the other; and

(*b*) in a case falling within subsection (3) above, is compellable to give evidence for the prosecution or on behalf of any person jointly charged with the other.

(6) So much of proviso (*b*) to section 1 of the Criminal Evidence Act 1898 as precludes the prosecution from commenting on the failure of the wife or husband of the accused to give evidence shall cease to have effect. 1898 c. 36.

Cross-examination

10.—(1) In any proceedings a witness other than any person charged therein shall not in cross-examination be asked, and if asked shall not be required to answer, any question as to his conduct on any occasion or as to whether he has committed, or has been charged with or convicted or acquitted of, any offence unless his conduct on that occasion or the fact that he has committed, or has been charged with or convicted or acquitted of, that offence, as the case may be, is relevant to an issue arising in the proceedings or to his credibility as a witness. Restrictions on cross-examination of witness other than an accused.

(2) Where, at a trial on an information or indictment whereby two or more persons are jointly charged, any of those persons gives evidence, then, if as a result of pleading guilty or for any other reason he is not, or is no longer, liable to conviction at that trial, subsection (1) above shall apply to him as it applies to a person not charged in the proceedings.

11. In any proceedings the party calling a witness shall in no circumstances be allowed to impeach his credibility as a witness by evidence tending to establish that he is a person of bad disposition or reputation; but, subject to that restriction, where in any proceedings a party calls a witness who— Circumstances in which party may cross-examine his own witness.

(*a*) gives evidence adverse to that party; or

(*b*) gives evidence which is inconsistent with a statement made by the witness on a previous occasion,

that party may, with the leave of the court, cross-examine him as if he were a witness called by another party.

12. If in any proceedings a witness, on being cross-examined about a statement, inconsistent with his present testimony, which he is alleged to have made on a previous occasion, does not distinctly admit having made it, the cross-examining party may adduce evidence to show that the witness did in fact make it. Right of cross-examining party to prove witness's previous inconsistent statement.

13.—(1) Where in any proceedings it is permissible to cross-examine a witness about a statement inconsistent with his present testimony, being a statement made by him in a document in writing or made by him and reduced into writing— Use of document containing previous inconsistent statement of cross-examined witness.

(*a*) he may be cross-examined about the statement without being shown the document containing it; but (*b*) if it is proposed to use that document for the purpose of showing that he has contradicted himself, then, before it is so used, his attention must be called to those parts of the document which are to be used for that purpose.

(2) Where in any proceedings a witness is cross-examined about a statement inconsistent with his present testimony, being a statement such as is mentioned in subsection (1) above, the court may at any time during the proceedings require the document to be produced for its inspection, and may thereupon, notwithstanding anything in subsection (1)(*b*) above, make such use of it for the purposes of the proceedings as the court thinks fit.

(3) The foregoing provisions of this section shall, with the necessary modifications, apply in relation to a statement contained in a document other than a document in writing as they apply in relation to a statement contained in a document in writing; and for the purposes of those provisions, as applied by this subsection, any reference to a document or part of a document shall, if the court so directs, be treated as, or as including, a reference to a copy of that document or part authenticated in such manner as the court may approve.

(4) In this section " document " and " copy " have the same meaning as in Part II of this Act.

Right of rebuttal where cross-examined witness denies having been convicted etc.

14. Where in any proceedings a witness (including, where he gives evidence, the accused) on being asked in cross-examination any question which it is permissible to ask him as to whether he has been charged with or convicted or acquitted of any offence either denies or does not admit that he has been charged with that offence or, as the case may be, convicted or acquitted thereof, the cross-examining party may bring evidence to prove that the witness has been so charged, convicted or acquitted.

Privilege

Privilege against incrimination of self or spouse.

15.—(1) Subject to the provisions of this section, in any proceedings the right of a person to refuse to answer any question or produce any document or thing if to do so would tend to expose that person to proceedings for an offence or for the recovery of a penalty—

(*a*) shall apply only as regards criminal offences under the law of any part of the United Kingdom and penalties provided for by such law; and

(*b*) shall include a like right to refuse to answer any question or produce any document or thing if to do so would tend to expose the wife or husband of that person to proceedings for any such criminal offence or for the recovery of any such penalty.

(2) Where the accused gives evidence in any proceedings—

(*a*) the accused shall not be entitled to refuse to answer a question or produce a document or thing on the ground that to do so would tend to prove the commission by the accused of the offence charged; and

(*b*) except as regards any question, document or thing which in the opinion of the court is relevant solely or mainly to the accused's

182

credibility as a witness (not being, in the case of a question, one asked by virtue of section 7 of this Act), the accused shall not be entitled to refuse to answer a question or produce a document or thing on the ground that to do so would—

PART I

(i) tend to expose the accused to proceedings for some other offence or for the recovery of a penalty; or

(ii) tend to expose the wife or husband of the accused to proceedings for an offence or for the recovery of a penalty.

(3) Where a person being the wife or husband of the accused gives evidence in any proceedings, that person––

(a) shall not be entitled to refuse to answer a question or produce a document or thing on the ground that to do so would tend to prove the commission by the accused of the offence charged; and

(b) except as regards any question, document or thing which in the opinion of the court is relevant solely or mainly to that person's credibility as a witness, shall not be entitled to refuse to answer a question or produce a document or thing on the ground that to do so would tend as mentioned in subsection (2)(b)(i) above.

(4) Any reference in this section to proceedings for the recovery of a penalty includes a reference to civil proceedings therefor.

16.—(1) The following rules of law are hereby abrogated in so far as they apply to criminal proceedings, that is to say— *Abolition of certain privileges.*

(a) the rule whereby, in any legal proceedings, a person cannot be compelled to answer any question or produce any document or thing if to do so would tend to expose him to a forfeiture; and

(b) the rule whereby, in any legal proceedings, a person other than a party to the proceedings cannot be compelled to produce any deed or other document relating to his title to any land.

(2) Section 3 of the Evidence (Amendment) Act 1853 (which provides that a husband or wife shall not be compellable to disclose any communication made to him or her by his or her spouse during the marriage, and which was repealed by section 16(3) of the Civil Evidence Act 1968 except in relation to criminal proceedings) shall cease to have effect. *1853 c. 83.* *1968 c. 64.*

(3) In section 43(1) of the Matrimonial Causes Act 1965 (which provides that the evidence of a husband or wife shall be admissible in any proceedings to prove that marital intercourse did or did not take place between them during any period, but that a husband or wife shall not be compellable in any proceedings to give evidence of the matters aforesaid), the words from " but a husband or wife " to the end of the subsection (which were repealed by section 16(4) of the Civil Evidence Act 1968 except in relation to criminal proceedings) shall cease to have effect. *1965 c. 72.*

Corroboration, and directions to juries

17.—(1) Where at the trial on indictment of a person charged with a sexual offence evidence is given by the person in respect of whom the *Corroboration in proceedings for sexual offences.*

183

offence is alleged to have been committed, then, unless subsection (2) below applies, the court shall warn the jury that, if they find that the evidence of that person is not corroborated in some material particular by evidence implicating the accused, there will be a special need for caution before convicting the accused on the evidence of that person only.

(2) Where, in the case of proceedings for a sexual offence, the person in respect of whom the offence is alleged to have been committed was at the material time a child, the accused shall not be convicted of the offence on the evidence of that person only, unless that evidence is corroborated in some material particular by evidence implicating the accused.

Corroboration in proceedings for perjury etc.
1911 c. 6.

1967 c. 80.

18. For section 13 of the Perjury Act 1911 (corroboration) there shall be substituted the following section—

" 13. A person shall not be liable to be convicted of—

   (*a*) an offence under section 1 of this Act or an offence which under any enactment is declared to be punishable as perjury; or

   (*b*) an offence under section 89(1) of the Criminal Justice Act 1967 (false written statements tendered in evidence in criminal proceedings by virtue of section 2 or 9 of that Act); or

   (*c*) an offence consisting of attempting to commit an offence falling within paragraph (*a*) or (*b*) above or of inciting or attempting to incite another to commit an offence so falling,

on the evidence of one witness only as to the falsity of any statement alleged to be false or any proposed statement which it is alleged would have been false if made, unless that evidence is corroborated in some material particular by other evidence."

Abolition of certain requirements as to corroboration.
1795 c. 7 (36 Geo. 3).

1949 c. 68.

1956 c. 69.

19.—(1) Any rule of law or practice whereby in criminal proceedings the evidence of one witness is incapable of corroborating the evidence of another witness is hereby abrogated.

(2) In section 1 of the Treason Act 1795 (penalty for compassing etc. the death, restraint etc. of the Queen or her heirs) the words " upon the oaths of two lawful and credible witnesses " shall be omitted.

(3) Section 146(5) of the Representation of the People Act 1949 (which, on a charge of personation, makes the evidence of at least two witnesses necessary for certain purposes) shall cease to have effect.

(4) In each of the following sections of the Sexual Offences Act 1956, namely—

   (*a*) sections 2 and 3 (procurement of woman by threats or by false pretences);

(b) section 4 (administering drugs to obtain or facilitate intercourse);

(c) section 22 (causing prostitution of women); and

(d) section 23 (procuration of girl under 21),

subsection (2) (by virtue of which a person cannot be convicted of an offence under the section in question on the uncorroborated evidence of a single witness) shall cease to have effect.

20.—(1) Subject to the provisions of section 17 of this Act and any other enactment relating to the corroboration of evidence in criminal proceedings, at a trial on indictment it shall be for the court to decide in its discretion, having regard to the evidence given, whether the jury should be given a warning about convicting the accused on uncorroborated evidence; and, accordingly, any rule of law or practice whereby at such a trial it is in certain circumstances obligatory for the court to give the jury such a warning is hereby abrogated.

(2) At a trial on indictment the court shall not be required to use any particular form of words—

(a) in giving the jury the warning required by section 17(1) of this Act or any other warning about convicting the accused on uncorroborated evidence; or

(b) in directing the jury as to the effect of section 17(2) of this Act or of any other enactment, whenever passed, under which corroboration is necessary.

21. Without prejudice to the general duty of the court at a trial on indictment to direct the jury on any matter on which it appears to the court appropriate to do so, where at such a trial the case against the accused depends wholly or substantially on the correctness of one or more identifications of the accused which the defence alleges to be mistaken, the court shall warn the jury of the special need for caution before convicting the accused in reliance on the correctness of the identification or identifications, but in doing so shall not be required to use any particular form of words.

Evidence of children

22.—(1) The following provisions of this section shall apply with respect to the evidence of children in criminal proceedings; and section 38 of the Children and Young Persons Act 1933 (evidence of children of tender years) shall cease to have effect.

(2) A child shall not be sworn as a witness in any proceedings; but a child may give evidence otherwise than on oath in any proceedings if in the opinion of the court he is possessed of sufficient intelligence to justify the reception of his evidence and understands the importance of telling the truth in those proceedings.

(3) In relation to the trial of a child *for homicide* section 5 of this Act shall have effect subject to the modification that for references to being

and refusing to be sworn there shall be substituted respectively references to agreeing and refusing to give evidence; and, without prejudice to section 5(1)(*a*) to (*c*) of this Act, section 5(2) shall not apply at such a trial unless the evidence of the accused is capable of being received under subsection (2) above.

(4) If the evidence of a child, though not given on oath, is otherwise taken and put into writing in accordance with the provisions as to the taking of depositions contained in rules made under section 15 of the Justices of the Peace Act 1949, that evidence shall be treated as a deposition within the meaning of those provisions.

1949 c. 101.

(5) If a person whose evidence is received under subsection (2) above wilfully gives false evidence in such circumstances that he would, if the evidence had been given on oath, have been guilty of perjury, *he shall be treated for the purposes of Part I of the Children and Young Persons Act 1969 as guilty of an offence.*

1969 c. 54.

(6) Where—

(*a*) a written statement by a child is tendered in evidence under section 2 or section 9 of the Criminal Justice Act 1967 (which relate to the admissibility of written statements in committal proceedings and in proceedings other than committal proceedings respectively); or

1967 c. 80.

(*b*) a statement made in writing by or taken in writing from a child is tendered in evidence under section 27 of the Children and Young Persons Act 1963 (evidence of children in committal proceedings for sexual offences),

1963 c. 37.

the extent to which the statement is admissible in evidence by virtue of that section shall be determined on the assumption that oral evidence by him could be received under subsection (2) above.

(7) Where the age of any person at any time is material for the purposes of any provision of sections 42 and 43 of the Children and Young Persons Act 1933 (which relate to the taking and admissibility of depositions of children and young persons), his age at that time shall for the purposes of that provision be deemed to be that which appears to the justice of the peace concerned or, as the case may be, the court to be his age at that time.

1933 c. 12.

Other matters

General rule, and court's discretion, as to time at which evidence may be called at trial.

23.—(1) Subject to the provisions of section 3(6) of this Act and of any other enactment relating to the time when any evidence may be given, at the trial of any person for an offence any evidence given on behalf of the prosecution or an accused shall be given before the conclusion of that party's case except in so far as the court in its discretion otherwise allows:

Provided that an accused shall not be allowed to give evidence on his own behalf after the conclusion of his case unless he did so in the course of that case.

(2) In the exercise of its discretion under this section the court may allow evidence to be given at any time before the delivery of the verdict or, at a summary trial, the decision of the court, and accordingly at a trial on indictment may do so after the conclusion of the summing-up or after the jury have retired, and at a summary trial may do so after the court has retired to consider its decision.

(3) Where at the trial of a person for an offence the court has indicated that in the exercise of its discretion under this section it will allow evidence of any matter to be given on behalf of a party after the conclusion of that party's case, any person who, whether before or after that evidence is given, gives evidence on behalf of any other party may, notwithstanding any rule of practice, be cross-examined about that matter.

(4) At the trial of any person for an offence the power of the court to call a witness may be exercised at any time before the delivery of the verdict or, at a summary trial, the decision of the court.

24.—(1) In any proceedings the fact that a person other than the accused has been convicted of an offence by or before any court in the United Kingdom or by a court-martial there or elsewhere shall be admissible in evidence for the purpose of proving, where to do so is relevant to any issue in those proceedings, that that person committed that offence, whether or not any other evidence of his having committed that offence is given.

Conviction as evidence of commission of offence by person other than the accused.

(2) In any proceedings in which by virtue of this section a person other than the accused is proved to have been convicted of an offence by or before any court in the United Kingdom or by a court-martial there or elsewhere, he shall be taken to have committed that offence unless the contrary is proved.
Section 8 of this Act shall not have effect in relation to this subsection

(3) Nothing in this section shall prejudice—

  (a) the admissibility in evidence of any conviction which would be admissible apart from this section; or

  (b) the operation of any enactment whereby a conviction or a finding of fact in any proceedings is for the purposes of any other proceedings made conclusive evidence of any fact.

(4) The provisions of section 25 of this Act apply for the purposes of this section.

25.—(1) Where evidence that a person has been convicted of an offence is admissible by virtue of section 3 or 24 of this Act, then, without prejudice to the reception of any other admissible evidence for the purpose of identifying the facts on which the conviction was based, the contents of any document which is admissible as evidence of the conviction, and the contents of the information, complaint, indictment or charge-sheet on which the person in question was convicted, shall be admissible in evidence for that purpose.

Provisions supplementary to ss. 3 and 24.

(2) Where in any proceedings the contents of any document are admissible in evidence by virtue of subsection (1) above, a copy of that document, or of the material part thereof, purporting to be certified or otherwise authenticated by or on behalf of the court or authority having custody of that document shall be admissible in evidence and shall be taken to be a true copy of that document or part unless the contrary is shown.

(3) Nothing in any of the following enactments, that is to say—

1948 c. 58.

    (a) section 12 of the Criminal Justice Act 1948 (under which a conviction leading to probation or discharge is to be disregarded except as therein mentioned);

1949 c. 94.

    (b) section 9 of the Criminal Justice (Scotland) Act 1949 (which makes similar provision in respect of convictions on indictment in Scotland); and

1950 c. 7 (N.I.).

    (c) section 8 of the Probation Act (Northern Ireland) 1950 (which corresponds to the said section 12) or any corresponding enactment of the Parliament of Northern Ireland for the time being in force,

shall affect the operation of section 3 or 24 of this Act; and for the purposes of the said sections 3 and 24 any order made by a court of summary jurisdiction in Scotland under section 1 or section 2 of the said Act of 1949 shall be treated as a conviction.

(4) Nothing in section 3 or 24 of this Act shall be construed as rendering admissible in any proceedings evidence of any conviction other than a subsisting one.

Manner in which certain United Kingdom convictions and acquittals may be proved.

26.—(1) Where in any proceedings the fact that a person has in the United Kingdom been convicted or acquitted of an offence otherwise than by a court-martial is admissible in evidence, it may be proved by producing a certificate of conviction or, as the case may be, of acquittal relating to that offence, and proving that the person named in the certificate as having been convicted or acquitted thereof is the person whose conviction or acquittal thereof is to be proved.

(2) For the purposes of this section a certificate of conviction or of acquittal—

    (a) shall, as regards a conviction or acquittal on indictment, consist of a certificate, signed by the clerk of the court where the conviction or acquittal took place, giving the substance and effect (omitting the formal parts) of the indictment and of the conviction or acquittal; and

    (b) shall, as regards a conviction or acquittal on a summary trial, consist of a copy of the conviction or of the dismissal of the information, signed by the clerk of the court where the conviction or acquittal took place or by the clerk of the court, if any, to which a memorandum of the conviction or acquittal was sent;

and a document purporting to be a duly signed certificate of conviction or acquittal under this section shall be taken to be such a certificate unless the contrary is proved.

(3) References in this section to the clerk of a court include references to his deputy and to any other person having the custody of the court's records.

(4) The method of proving a conviction or acquittal authorised by this section shall be in addition to and not to the exclusion of any other authorised manner of proving a conviction or acquittal.

27.—(1) This section applies to the following offences, namely—

    (a) offences under section 1 of the Perjury Act 1911 (perjury) and offences which under any enactment are declared to be punishable as perjury;

    (b) offences under section 89(1) of the Criminal Justice Act 1967 (false written statements tendered in evidence in criminal proceedings by virtue of section 2 or 9 of that Act);

    (c) offences consisting of attempting to commit an offence falling within paragraph (a) or (b) above or of inciting or attempting to incite another to commit an offence so falling.

(2) Proceedings for an offence to which this section applies shall not be instituted except by or with the consent of the Director of Public Prosecutions; and accordingly section 9 of the Perjury Act 1911 (which confers power on various authorities to direct a prosecution for perjury) shall cease to have effect.

28. At the summary trial of a person for an offence the court shall have regard to all such enactments as would or might in comparable circumstances at a trial on indictment require the court to warn the jury of a special need for caution before convicting the accused.

29. Where in any proceedings a party calls for and inspects a docu- ment which is in the possession or power of an opposing party or of a witness called by an opposing party, his doing so shall not of itself entitle the opposing party to make the document evidence in the proceedings.

HEARSAY EVIDENCE

Hearsay evidence to be admissible only by virtue of this Act and other statutory provisions or certain rules of law.

30.—(1) In any proceedings a statement other than one made by a person while giving oral evidence in those proceedings shall be admissible as evidence of any fact stated therein to the extent that it is so admissible by virtue of any provision of this Act or any other statutory provision, or by virtue of any rule of law mentioned in section 40 of this Act, but not otherwise.

(2) In this section " statutory provision " means any provision contained in, or in an instrument made under, this or any other Act, including any Act passed after this Act.

Admissibility of out-of-court statements as evidence of facts stated.

31.—(1) In any proceedings a statement made, whether orally or in a document or otherwise, by any person shall, subject to this and the next following section and to section 2 of this Act, be admissible as evidence of any fact stated therein of which direct oral evidence by him would be admissible, if—

(*a*) he has been or is to be called as a witness in the proceedings; or

(*b*) being compellable to give evidence on behalf of the party desiring to give the statement in evidence, he attends or is brought before the court but refuses to be sworn; or

(*c*) it is shown with respect to him—

(i) that he is dead, or is unfit by reason of his bodily or mental condition to attend as a witness; or

(ii) that he is beyond the seas and that it is not reasonably practicable to secure his attendance; or

(iii) that, being competent but not compellable to give evidence on behalf of the party desiring to give the statement in evidence, he refuses to give evidence on behalf of that party; or

(iv) that all reasonable steps have been taken to identify him, but that he cannot be identified; or

(v) that, his identity being known, all reasonable steps have been taken to find him, but that he cannot be found.

(2) Subject to section 2 of this Act, in any proceedings in which two or more persons are jointly charged, a statement made, whether orally or in a document or otherwise, by any of the accused may be given in evidence by the prosecution as evidence of any fact stated therein of which direct oral evidence by the maker would be admissible, notwithstanding that the maker has not been and is not to be called as a witness in the proceedings; and any statement given in evidence by virtue of this subsection shall be admissible as evidence of any such fact in relation to each of the accused.

190

(3) Where in any proceedings a statement has been received in evidence by virtue of paragraph (*a*) of subsection (1) above on the footing that the maker of it is to be called as a witness in the proceedings, then, if he is not subsequently so called, the statement shall not be admissible by virtue of that paragraph, and (unless it is or becomes admissible otherwise than by virtue of that paragraph) shall be disregarded accordingly.

(4) Where in any proceedings a deposition of a child or young person is received in evidence by virtue of section 43 of the Children and Young Persons Act 1933 on the ground that his attendance before the court would involve serious danger to his life or health, subsection (1) above shall apply to any statement made by him otherwise than in the deposition as if he had been shown to be unfit by reason of his bodily or mental condition to attend as a witness.

(5) Where in any proceedings a statement which was made otherwise than in a document is admissible by virtue of this section, no evidence other than direct oral evidence by the maker of the statement or any person who heard or otherwise perceived it being made shall be admissible for the purpose of proving it, and nothing in section 2 or 9 of the Criminal Justice Act 1967 or any other enactment passed before this Act shall render a written statement admissible for that purpose:

Provided that if the statement in question was made by a person while giving oral evidence in some other legal proceedings (whether civil or criminal), it may be proved in any manner authorised by the court.

(6) Where a person makes an oral statement to or in the hearing of another person who, acting at the instance of the maker of the statement, reduces it (or the substance of it) into writing at the time or reasonably soon afterwards, thereby producing a corresponding statement in a document, the statement in the document shall be treated for the purposes of this section (and sections 32, 36 and 41 so far as they have effect for the purposes of this section) as having been made in the document by the maker of the oral statement, whether or not it would be so treated apart from this subsection.

32.—(1) A statement shall not be admissible in evidence in any proceedings by virtue of subsection (1)(*b*) or subsection (1)(*c*)(ii), (iii), (iv) or (v) of section 31 of this Act if it was made after the earliest time when any of the following things was done in relation to the accused or, where two or more persons are jointly charged, in relation to any of the accused, that is to say—

    (*a*) he was charged with any offence in respect of the conduct constituting the offence with which he is charged; or

    (*b*) he was officially informed that he might be prosecuted in respect of that conduct; or

    (*c*) he was served with a summons issued against him under section 1 of the Magistrates' Courts Act 1952 in respect of that conduct.

In this subsection " officially informed " means informed by a police officer or by a person (other than a police officer) charged with the duty of investigating offences or charging offenders.

(2) A statement made by a person who is the wife or husband of the accused shall not be given in evidence on behalf of the prosecution by virtue of section 31(1)(*a*) of this Act unless the maker gives evidence for the prosecution; and a statement made by a person who is (or was at the time of that person's death) the wife or husband of the accused shall not be given in evidence on behalf of the prosecution by virtue of section 31(1)(*c*) unless the maker is (or would if living be) compellable to give evidence for the prosecution by virtue of section 9(3) or (4) of this Act.

(3) Where a document setting out the evidence which a person could be expected to give as a witness has been prepared for the purpose of any pending or contemplated proceedings, whether civil or criminal, then in any criminal proceedings in which that person has been or is to be called as a witness a statement made by him in that document shall not be given in evidence by virtue of section 31(1)(*a*) of this Act without the leave of the court; and the court shall not give leave under this subsection in respect of any such statement unless it is of the opinion that, in the particular circumstances in which that leave is sought, it is in the interests of justice for the witness's oral evidence to be supplemented by the reception of that statement or for the statement to be received as evidence of any matter about which he is unable or unwilling to give oral evidence.

(4) At a trial on indictment a statement shall not without the leave of the court be given in evidence by virtue of section 31(1)(*c*) of this Act on behalf of a party to the proceedings unless, before the end of the prescribed period, a notice complying with such of the requirements set out in subsection (5) below as are applicable has been served by or on behalf of that party on each of the other parties to the proceedings.

In this subsection " the prescribed period " means the period of seven days from the end of the proceedings before the examining justices or, where two or more persons are being jointly tried, from the end of the proceedings before the examining justices in respect of whichever of them was last committed for trial.

(5) The requirements referred to in subsection (4) above are as follows:—

    (*a*) the notice must state on which of the grounds mentioned in section 31(1)(*c*) of this Act it is claimed that the statement is admissible and, if the ground stated is that mentioned in section 31(1)(*c*)(iv) or (v), must give particulars of the steps taken to identify or find the maker;

    (*b*) in the case of a statement made otherwise than in a document, the notice must state whether it was made orally or in some other (and, if so, what) manner, and must also state—

        (i) the time and place at which the statement was made; and

        (ii) the name of the maker of the statement, if known, and (unless he is dead) his address, if known; and

        (iii) the name and address of a person who heard or otherwise perceived the statement being made; and

(iv) the substance of the statement or, if it was made orally and the actual words used in making it are material, the words so used;

(c) in the case of a statement made in a document, the notice must contain or have attached to it a copy of that document, or of the material part thereof, and must state the following matters, that is to say—

(i) the matters mentioned in paragraph (b)(i) and (ii) above; and

(ii) if the maker of the document is not the same person as the maker of the statement, the name of the maker of the document, if known, and (unless he is dead) his address, if known,

in so far as those matters are not readily apparent from the document or part in question.

(6) A notice required by subsection (4) above to be served on any person may be served—

(a) by delivering it to him or to his solicitor; or

(b) by addressing it to him and leaving it at his usual or last known place of abode or place of business or by addressing it to his solicitor and leaving it at his office; or

(c) by sending it in a registered letter or by the recorded delivery service addressed to him at his usual or last known place of abode or place of business or addressed to his solicitor at his office; or

(d) in the case of a body corporate, by delivering it to the secretary or clerk of the body at its registered or principal office or sending it in a registered letter or by the recorded delivery service addressed to the secretary or clerk of the body at that office.

33.—(1) Where in any proceedings—

(a) a previous inconsistent statement made by a person called as a witness in those proceedings is proved by virtue of section 12 or 13 of this Act; or

(b) a previous statement made by a person called as aforesaid is proved for the purpose of rebutting a suggestion that his evidence has been fabricated,

Witness's previous statement, if proved, to be evidence of facts stated.

that statement shall by virtue of this subsection (and notwithstanding anything in section 31 or 32 of this Act) be admissible as evidence of any fact stated therein of which direct oral evidence by him would be admissible.

(2) Nothing in this Act shall affect any of the rules of law relating to the circumstances in which, where a person called as a witness in any proceedings is cross-examined on a document used by him to refresh his memory, that document may be made evidence in those proceedings; and where a document or any part of a document is received in evidence

in any such proceedings by virtue of any such rule of law, any statement made in that document or part by the person using the document to refresh his memory shall by virtue of this subsection (and notwithstanding anything in section 31 or 32 of this Act) be admissible as evidence of any fact stated therein of which direct oral evidence by him would be admissible.

Admissibility of certain records as evidence of facts stated.

34.—(1) Without prejudice to section 35 of this Act, in any proceedings a statement contained in a document shall, subject to this section, be admissible as evidence of any fact stated therein of which direct oral evidence would be admissible, if—

(a) the document is, or forms part of, a record compiled by a person acting under a duty from information which was supplied by a person (whether acting under a duty or not) who had, or may reasonably be supposed to have had, personal knowledge of the matters dealt with in that information and which, if not supplied by that person to the compiler of the record directly, was supplied by him to the compiler of the record indirectly through one or more intermediaries each acting under a duty; and·

(b) the condition specified in subsection (2)(a) below or the condition specified in subsection (2)(b) below or any of the conditions specified in subsection (2)(c) below is satisfied as regards the person who originally supplied the information from which the record containing the statement was compiled.

(2) The conditions referred to in subsection (1)(b) above are the following, namely—

(a) that the person in question has been or is to be called as a witness in the proceedings;

(b) that the person in question, being compellable to give evidence on behalf of the party desiring to give the statement in evidence, attends or is brought before the court but refuses to be sworn;

(c) that it is shown with respect to the person in question—

(i) that he is dead or is unfit by reason of his bodily or mental condition to attend as a witness; or

(ii) that he is beyond the seas and that it is not reasonably practicable to secure his attendance; or

(iii) that, being competent but not compellable to give evidence on behalf of the party desiring to give the statement in evidence, he refuses to give evidence on behalf of that party; or

(iv) that all reasonable steps have been taken to identify him, but that he cannot be identified; or

(v) that, his identity being known, all reasonable steps have been taken to find him, but that he cannot be found; or

(vi) that, having regard to the time which has elapsed since he supplied the information and to all the circumstances, he cannot reasonably be expected to have any recollection of the matters dealt with in the statement.

(3) Section 31(3) of this Act shall apply to a statement received in evidence by virtue of subsection (2)(*a*) above as it applies to a statement received in evidence by virtue of section 31(1)(*a*).

(4) A statement shall not be admissible in evidence in any proceedings by virtue of subsection (2)(*b*) or subsection (2)(*c*)(ii), (iii), (iv) or (v) above if the person who originally supplied the information from which the record containing the statement was compiled did so after the earliest time when any of the following things was done in relation to the accused or, where two or more persons are jointly charged, in relation to any of the accused, that is to say—

(*a*) he was charged with any offence in respect of the conduct constituting the offence with which he is charged; or

(*b*) he was officially informed that he might be prosecuted in respect of that conduct; or

(*c*) he was served with a summons issued against him under section 1 of the Magistrates' Courts Act 1952 in respect of that conduct. 1952 c. 55.

In this subsection " officially informed " has the same meaning as in section 32(1) of this Act.

(5) Where a document setting out the evidence which a person could be expected to give as a witness has been prepared for the purpose of any pending or contemplated proceedings, whether civil or criminal, and that document falls within subsection (1)(*a*) above, then in any criminal proceedings in which that person has been or is to be called as a witness a statement contained in that document shall not be given in evidence by virtue of subsection (2)(*a*) or (*c*)(vi) above without the leave of the court; and the same restrictions shall apply with respect to the giving of leave under this subsection as apply under section 32(3) with respect to to the giving of leave under section 32(3).

(6) Any reference in this section to a person acting under a duty includes a reference to a person acting in the course of any trade, business, profession or other occupation in which he is engaged or employed or for the purposes of any paid or unpaid office held by him.

35.—(1) In any proceedings a statement contained in a document produced by a computer shall be admissible as evidence of any fact stated therein of which direct oral evidence would be admissible, if it is shown that the conditions mentioned in subsection (2) below are satisfied in relation to the statement and computer in question.

Admissibility of statements produced by computers.

(2) The said conditions are—

(*a*) that the document containing the statement was produced by the computer during a period over which the computer was used regularly to store or process information for the purposes of any activities regularly carried on over that period, whether for profit or not, by any body, whether corporate or not, or by any individual;

(b) that over that period there was regularly supplied to the computer in the ordinary course of those activities information of the kind contained in the statement or of the kind from which the information so contained is derived;

(c) that throughout the material part of that period the computer was operating properly or, if not, that any respect in which it was not operating properly or was out of operation during that part of that period was not such as to affect the production of the document or the accuracy of its contents; and

(d) that the information contained in the statement reproduces or is derived from information supplied to the computer in the ordinary course of those activities.

(3) Where over a period the function of storing or processing information for the purposes of any activities regularly carried on over that period as mentioned in subsection (2)(a) above was regularly performed by computers, whether—

(a) by a combination of computers operating over that period; or

(b) by different computers operating in succession over that period; or

(c) by different combinations of computers operating in succession over that period; or

(d) in any other manner involving the successive operation over that period, in whatever order, of one or more computers and one or more combinations of computers,

all the computers used for that purpose during that period shall be treated for the purposes of this Part of this Act as constituting a single computer; and references in this Part of this Act to a computer shall be construed accordingly.

(4) In any proceedings where it is desired to give a statement in evidence by virtue of this section, a certificate doing any of the following things, that is to say—

(a) identifying the document containing the statement and describing the manner in which it was produced;

(b) giving such particulars of any device involved in the production of that document as may be appropriate for the purpose of showing that the document was produced by a computer;

(c) dealing with any of the matters to which the conditions mentioned in subsection (2) above relate,

and purporting to be signed by a person occupying a responsible position in relation to the operation of the relevant device or the management of the relevant activities (whichever is appropriate) shall be evidence of any matter stated in the certificate; and for the purposes of this subsection it shall be sufficient for a matter to be stated to the best of the knowledge and belief of the person stating it.

(5) Notwithstanding subsection (4) above, in any such proceedings as are therein mentioned the court may for special cause require oral evidence to be given of any matter of which evidence could ordinarily be given by means of a certificate under that subsection.

(6) If any person in a certificate tendered in evidence in any proceedings by virtue of subsection (4) above intentionally makes a statement material in those proceedings which he knows to be false or does not believe to be true, he shall on conviction on indictment be liable to imprisonment for a term not exceeding two years or a fine, or both.

(7) For the purposes of this Part of this Act—

    (a) information shall be taken to be supplied to a computer if it is supplied thereto in any appropriate form and whether it is so supplied directly or (with or without human intervention) by means of any appropriate equipment;

    (b) where, in the course of activities carried on by any individual or body, information is supplied with a view to its being stored or processed for the purposes of those activities by a computer operated otherwise than in the course of those activities, that information, if duly supplied to that computer, shall be taken to be supplied to it in the course of those activities;

    (c) a document shall be taken to have been produced by a computer whether it was produced by it directly or (with or without human intervention) by means of any appropriate equipment.

(8) Subject to subsection (3) above, in this Part of this Act " computer " means any device for storing and processing information, and any reference to information being derived from other information is a reference to its being derived therefrom by calculation, comparison or any other process.

36.—(1) Where in any proceedings a statement contained in a document is admissible in evidence by virtue of section 31, 34 or 35 of this Act, it may be proved by the production of that document or (whether or not that document is still in existence) by the production of a copy of that document, or of the material part thereof, authenticated in such manner as the court may approve. Provisions supple- mentary to ss. 31 to 35.

(2) For the purpose of deciding whether or not a statement is admissible in evidence by virtue of section 31, 34 or 35 of this Act, the court may draw any reasonable inference from the circumstances in which the statement was made or otherwise came into being or from any other circumstances, including, in the case of a statement contained in a document, the form and contents of that document.

(3) In relation to a statement made by a child sections 31(1)(*b*) and 34(2)(*b*) of this Act shall each have effect as if for the reference to his refusing to be sworn there were substituted a reference to his refusing to give evidence.

(4) In estimating the weight, if any, to be attached to a statement admissible in evidence by virtue of section 31, 33, 34 or 35 of this Act regard shall be had to all the circumstances from which any inference can reasonably be drawn as to the accuracy or otherwise of the statement and, in particular—

(*a*) in the case of a statement falling within section 31(1) or (2) or 33(1) or (2) of this Act, to the question whether or not the statement was made contemporaneously with the occurrence or existence of the facts stated, and to the question whether or not the maker of the statement had any incentive to conceal or misrepresent the facts;

(*b*) in the case of a statement falling within section 34(1) of this Act, to the question whether or not the person who originally supplied the information from which the record containing the statement was compiled did so contemporaneously with the occurrence or existence of the facts dealt with in that information, and to the question whether or not that person, or any person concerned with compiling or keeping the record containing the statement, had any incentive to conceal or misrepresent the facts; and

(*c*) in the case of a statement falling within section 35(1) of this Act, to the question whether or not the information which the information contained in the statement reproduces or is derived from was supplied to the relevant computer, or recorded for the purpose of being supplied thereto, contemporaneously with the occurrence or existence of the facts dealt with in that information, and to the question whether or not any person concerned with the supply of information to that computer, or with the operation of that computer or any equipment by means of which the document containing the statement was produced by it, had any incentive to conceal or misrepresent the facts.

(5) For the purpose of any enactment (whenever passed) requiring evidence to be corroborated or regulating the manner in which un-corroborated evidence is to be treated—

(*a*) a statement which is admissible in evidence by virtue of section 31 or 33 of this Act shall not be capable of corroborating evidence given by the maker of the statement; and (*b*) a statement which is admissible in evidence by virtue of section 34 of this Act shall not be capable of corroborating evidence given by the person who originally supplied the information from which the record containing the statement was compiled.

(6) In deciding for the purposes of section 31 or 34 of this Act whether or not a person is fit to attend as a witness, a court may act on a certificate purporting to be a certificate of a duly registered medical practitioner.

37.—(1) In any proceedings a statement made by a person otherwise Admissibility than in a document shall be admissible as evidence of any fact stated of therein if— statements
made as
(*a*) it directly concerns an event in issue in those proceedings which immediate reaction to took place in the presence, sight or hearing of that person; events in and issue personally
(*b*) it was made by him as an immediate reaction to that event. witnessed.

(2) Where in any proceedings a statement is admissible by virtue of this section, no evidence other than direct oral evidence by the maker of the statement or any person who heard or otherwise perceived it being made shall be admissible for the purpose of proving it, and nothing in section 2 or 9 of the Criminal Justice Act 1967 or any other enactment 1967 c. 80. passed before this Act shall render a written statement admissible for that purpose.

(3) Section 36(5) of this Act shall apply to a statement which is admissible in evidence by virtue of this section as it applies to a statement which is admissible in evidence by virtue of section 31.

38.—(1) If, as regards any statement contained in a document or Admissibility made by a person otherwise than in a document, the parties to any of hearsay evidence by proceedings agree at a hearing that for the purpose of those proceedings agreement the statement may be given in evidence, then, unless the court otherwise of the directs, the statement shall in those proceedings and in any proceedings parties. arising out of them (including any appeal or retrial) be admissible as evidence of any fact stated therein:

Provided that such an agreement—

(*a*) shall not enable a statement to be given in evidence by virtue of this section on behalf of the prosecution if at the time when the agreement is made the accused or any of the accused is not represented by counsel or a solicitor; and

(*b*) if made during proceedings before a magistrates' court inquiring into an offence as examining justices, shall be of no effect for the purpose of any proceedings on indictment or any proceedings arising out of proceedings on indictment.

(2) Where in any proceedings a statement contained in a document is admissible by virtue of this section, it may be proved by the production of that document or (whether or not that document is still in existence) by the production of a copy of that document, or of the material part thereof, authenticated in such manner as the court may approve.

(3) Where a statement is given in evidence by virtue of this section but might have become admissible in evidence by virtue of section 31 or 34 of this Act, section 36(5) of this Act shall apply to it as if it were admissible by virtue of section 31 or 34 as the case may be.

Admissibility of evidence as to credibility of maker etc. of statement admitted under certain provisions of Part II.

39.—(1) Where in any proceedings a statement made by a person who is not called as a witness in those proceedings is given in evidence by virtue of section 31 of this Act—

(*a*) any evidence which, if that person had been so called, would be admissible for the purpose of destroying or supporting his credibility as a witness shall be admissible for that purpose in those proceedings; and

(*b*) as regards any matter which, if that person had been so called, could have been put to him in cross-examination for the purpose of destroying his credibility as a witness, being a matter of which, if he had denied it, evidence could not have been adduced by the cross-examining party, evidence of that matter may with the leave of the court be given for that purpose.

(2) Where in any proceedings a statement made by a person who is not called as a witness in those proceedings is given in evidence by virtue of section 31 or 37 of this Act, evidence tending to prove that, whether before or after he made that statement, that person made (whether orally or in a document or otherwise) another statement inconsistent therewith shall be admissible for the purpose of showing that that person has contradicted himself.

(3) Subsections (1) and (2) above shall apply in relation to a statement given in evidence by virtue of section 34 of this Act as they apply in relation to a statement given in evidence by virtue of section 31 of this Act, except that references to the person who made the statement and to his making the statement shall be construed respectively as references to the person who originally supplied the information from which the record containing the statement was compiled and to his supplying that information.

(4) Section 31(6) of this Act shall apply for the purposes of this section as it applies for the purposes of section 31.

(5) Section 33(1) of this Act shall apply to any statement proved by virtue of subsection (2) above as it applies to a previous inconsistent statement made by a person called as a witness which is proved as mentioned in paragraph (*a*) of section 33(1).

40.—(1) Nothing in this Part of this Act shall prejudice the admissibility in proceedings of any statement which, apart from the provisions of this Part of this Act, would by virtue of any rule of law mentioned in subsection (2) below be admissible as evidence of any fact stated therein. PART II

Saving for certain common-law exceptions to rule against hearsay.

(2) The rules of law referred to in subsection (1) above are the following, that is to say any rule of law whereby in any proceedings—

    (*a*) an admission adverse to the accused made—

        (i) by an agent of the accused acting within the scope of his authority; or

        (ii) by a person engaged with the accused in a common enterprise, if made in pursuance of their common purpose; or

        (iii) by one person to another where the maker is a person to whom the other was referred by the accused for information,

    may be given in evidence against the accused for the purpose of proving any fact stated in the admission;

    (*b*) published works dealing with matters of a public nature (for example, histories, scientific works, dictionaries and maps) are admissible as evidence of facts of a public nature stated therein;

    (*c*) public documents (for example, public registers, and returns made under public authority with respect to matters of public interest) are admissible as evidence of facts stated therein;

    (*d*) records (for example, the records of certain courts, treaties. Crown grants, pardons and commissions) are admissible as evidence of facts stated therein;

    (*e*) evidence of a person's reputation is admissible; or

    (*f*) evidence of reputation or family tradition is admissible for the purpose of proving or disproving the existence of any public or general right or of identifying any person or thing,

or whereby in any proceedings involving a question of pedigree or in which the existence of a marriage is in issue evidence of reputation or family tradition is admissible for the purpose of proving or disproving pedigree or the existence of a marriage, as the case may be.

(3) The words in which any rule of law mentioned in subsection (2) above is there described are intended only to identify the rule in question and shall not be construed as altering that rule in any way.

(4) In this section " admission " includes any representation of fact, whether made in words or otherwise.

41.—(1) In this Part of this Act—

    " computer " has the meaning assigned by section 35 of this Act;

    " document " includes, in addition to a document in writing—

        (*a*) any map, plan, graph or drawing;

(b) any photograph;

(c) any disc, tape, sound-track, or other device in which sounds or other data (not being visual images) are embodied so as to be capable (with or without the aid of some other equipment) of being reproduced therefrom; and

(d) any film, negative, tape or other device in which one or more visual images are embodied so as to be capable (as aforesaid) of being reproduced therefrom;

" film " includes a microfilm;

" statement " includes any representation of fact, whether made in words or otherwise.

(2) In this Part of this Act any reference to a copy of a document includes—

(a) in the case of a document falling within paragraph (c) but not (d) of the definition of " document " in the foregoing subsection, a transcript of the sounds or other data embodied therein;

(b) in the case of a document falling within paragraph (d) but not (c) of that definition, a reproduction or still reproduction of the image or images embodied therein, whether enlarged or not;

(c) in the case of a document falling within both those paragraphs, such a transcript together with such a still reproduction; and

(d) in the case of a document not falling within the said paragraph (d) of which a visual image is embodied in a document falling within that paragraph, a reproduction of that image, whether enlarged or not;

and any reference to a copy of the material part of a document shall be construed accordingly.

(3) For the purposes of this Part of this Act a protest, greeting or other verbal utterance may be treated as stating any fact which the utterance implies.

Part III

Opinion and Expert Evidence

Application of Part II to statements of opinion.

42.—(1) Subject to the provisions of this section, Part II of this Act, except section 35, shall apply in relation to statements of opinion as it applies in relation to statements of fact, subject to the necessary modifications and in particular the modification that any reference in that Part to a fact stated in a statement shall be construed as a reference to a matter dealt with therein.

(2) Section 34 of this Act, as applied by subsection (1) above, shall not render admissible in any proceedings a statement of opinion con-

tained in a record unless that statement would be admissible in those proceedings if made in the course of giving oral evidence by the person who originally supplied the information from which the record was compiled; but where a statement of opinion contained in a record deals with a matter on which the person who originally supplied the information from which the record was compiled is (or would if living be) qualified to give oral expert evidence, section 34 of this Act, as applied by subsection (1) above, shall have effect in relation to that statement as if so much of subsection (1) of that section as requires personal knowledge on the part of that person were omitted.

43.—(1) Where a person is called as a witness in any proceedings, his opinion on any relevant matter on which he is qualified to give expert evidence shall be admissible in evidence.

(2) It is hereby declared that where a person is called as a witness in any proceedings, a statement of opinion by him on a relevant matter on which he is not qualified to give expert evidence, if made as a way of conveying relevant facts personally perceived by him, is admissible as evidence of what he perceived.

(3) In this section " relevant matter " includes an issue in the proceedings in question.

(4) Nothing in this section shall be taken to affect any rule of law as to the topics on which expert evidence is or is not admissible.

Admissibility of expert opinion and certain expressions of non-expert opinion.

44.—(1) It is hereby declared that in criminal proceedings a person who is suitably qualified to do so on account of his knowledge or experience is competent to give expert evidence as to the law of any country or territory outside the United Kingdom, or of any part of the United Kingdom other than England and Wales, irrespective of whether he has acted or is entitled to act as a legal practitioner there.

Evidence of foreign law.

(2) Where any question as to the law of any country or territory outside the United Kingdom, or of any part of the United Kingdom other than England and Wales, with respect to any matter has been determined (whether before or after the passing of this Act) in any such proceedings as are mentioned in subsection (4) below, then in any criminal proceedings (not being proceedings before a court which can take judicial notice of the law of that country, territory or part with respect to that matter)—

(a) any finding made or decision given on that question in the first-mentioned proceedings shall, if reported or recorded in citable form, be admissible in evidence for the purpose of proving the law of that country, territory or part with respect to that matter; and

(b) if that finding or decision, as so reported or recorded, is adduced for that purpose, the law of that country, territory or part with respect to that matter shall be taken to be in accordance with that finding or decision unless the contrary is proved:

Provided that paragraph (*b*) above shall not apply in the case of a finding or decision which conflicts with another finding or decision on the same question adduced by virtue of this subsection in the same proceedings.

(3) Except with the leave of the court, a party to any proceedings shall not be permitted to adduce any such finding or decision as is mentioned in subsection (2) above by virtue of that subsection unless, before the hearing at which he seeks to adduce it, written notice that he intends to do so has been served on each of the other parties to the proceedings.

(4) The proceedings referred to in subsection (2) above are the following, whether civil or criminal, namely—

    (*a*) proceedings at first instance in any of the following courts, namely the High Court, the Crown Court, a court of quarter sessions, the Court of Chancery of the county palatine of Lancaster and the Court of Chancery of the county palatine of Durham;

    (*b*) appeals arising out of any such proceedings as are mentioned in paragraph (*a*) above;

    (*c*) proceedings before the Judicial Committee of the Privy Council on appeal (whether to Her Majesty in Council or to the Judicial Committee as such) from any decision of any court outside the United Kingdom.

(5) For the purpose of this section a finding or decision on any such question as is mentioned in subsection (2) above shall be taken to be reported or recorded in citable form if, but only if, it is reported or recorded in writing in a report, transcript or other document which, if that question had been a question as to the law of England and Wales, could be cited as an authority in legal proceedings in England and Wales.

(6) Section 32(6) of this Act shall apply to notices required to be served by subsection (3) above as it applies to notices required to be served by section 32(4).

PART IV

MISCELLANEOUS AND GENERAL

General interpretation and savings.

45.—(1) In this Act—

    " child " means a person under the age of fourteen;

    " conduct " includes any act or omission, and the possession of any article;

    " court-martial " means a court-martial constituted under the Army Act 1955, the Air Force Act 1955 or the Naval Discipline Act 1957 or a disciplinary court constituted under section 50 of the said Act of 1957;

1955 c. 18.
1955 c. 19.
1957 c. 53.

" proceedings ", except where the context otherwise requires, PART IV means criminal proceedings.

(2) In this Act references to a conviction include references to a conviction by a court-martial; and in relation to a court-martial " conviction "—

    (a) as regards a court-martial constituted under the Army Act 1955 c. 18. 1955 or the Air Force Act 1955, means a finding of guilty 1955 c. 19. which is, or falls to be treated as, a finding of the court duly confirmed; and

    (b) as regards a court-martial or disciplinary court constituted under the Naval Discipline Act 1957, means a finding of guilty 1957 c. 53. which is, or falls to be treated as, the finding of the court,

and " convicted " shall be construed accordingly.

(3) Where in any proceedings the age of any person at any time is material for the purposes of any provision of this Act other than section 17(2), his age at the material time shall for the purposes of that provision be deemed to be or to have been that which appears to the court to be or to have been his age at that time.

(4) For the avoidance of doubt it is hereby declared that in this Act references to a person's husband or wife do not include references to a person who is no longer married to that person.

(5) Any reference in this Act to any enactment is a reference thereto as amended, and includes a reference thereto as applied, by or under any other enactment, including this Act.

(6) Nothing in this Act shall affect the practice as to the reception of evidence in proceedings where, after a person has been convicted of an offence, it falls to any court to determine how he should be dealt with for it.

(7) Nothing in this Act shall prejudice the operation of any enactment which provides (in whatever words) that any answer or evidence given by a person in specified circumstances shall not be admissible in evidence against him or some other person in any proceedings or class of proceedings (however described, and whether civil or criminal).

In this subsection the reference to giving evidence is a reference to giving evidence in any manner, whether by furnishing information, making discovery, producing documents or otherwise.

(8) Nothing in this Act shall prejudice any power of a court, in any proceedings, to exclude evidence (whether by preventing questions from being put or otherwise) at its discretion.

(9) It is hereby declared that where, by reason of any defect of speech or hearing from which he is suffering, a person called as a witness in any legal proceedings (whether civil or criminal) gives his evidence in writing or by signs, that evidence is to be treated for the purposes of this Act as being given orally.

PART IV
Minor and
conse-
quential
amend-
ments, and
repeals.
1957 c. 53.

46.—(1) In section 129C of the Naval Discipline Act 1957 (evidence of proceedings of court-martial), after subsection (3) there shall be added as subsection (4)—

" (4) In this section ' court-martial ' includes a disciplinary court under this Act."

(2) The enactments mentioned in Schedule 1 to this Act shall have effect subject to the consequential amendments specified in that Schedule.

1877 c. 14.

(3) The Evidence Act 1877 (which is obsolete) is hereby repealed.

(4) The enactments and instrument mentioned in Schedule 2 to this Act are hereby repealed to the extent specified in column 3 of that Schedule.

Short title,
extent and
commence-
ment.
1957 c. 53.
1795 c. 7.
(36 Geo. 3).
1949 c. 68.

47.—(1) This Act may be cited as the Criminal Evidence Act 1972.

(2) This Act, except in so far as it amends the Naval Discipline Act 1957 or makes any repeal in the Treason Act 1795 or the Representation or the People Act 1949, shall not extend to Scotland or Northern Ireland.

(3) This Act shall come into force on   ;
and the provisions of this Act shall (so far as applicable) have effect—

(a) in relation to proceedings on indictment for an offence, if (but only if) the person charged with the offence is arraigned on or after that day; and

(b) in relation to proceedings before a magistrates' court acting as examining justices, or proceedings on the summary trial of an information, if (but only if) the time when the court begins to receive evidence in the proceedings falls on or after that day:

Provided that the restrictions imposed by paragraphs (a) and (b) above shall not apply to section 1 (and do not affect section 27) of this Act.

SCHEDULES

SCHEDULE 1

CONSEQUENTIAL AMENDMENTS OF ENACTMENTS

Section 46.

Amendment	Provision of this Act on which amendment is consequential	
The Children and Young Persons Act 1933 Section 42 of the Children and Young Persons Act 1933 shall be amended as follows—	Section 22.	1933 c. 12.
(a) in subsection (1), the words " on oath " shall be omitted;		
(b) after subsection (1) there shall be inserted as subsection (1A)—		
" (1A) A deposition made in pursuance of this section shall be made on oath if made by a young person, but not if made by a child; and the deposition of a child shall not be taken under this section unless in the opinion of the justice taking it the child is possessed of sufficient intelligence to justify the admission of his deposition in evidence and understands the importance of telling the truth in it.";		
(c) after subsection (2) there shall be added as subsection (2A)—		
" (2A) If a person whose deposition is taken otherwise than on oath under this section wilfully makes in it a statement which he knows to be false or does not believe to be true, in such circumstances that he would, if the deposition had been made on oath, have been guilty of perjury, *he shall be treated for the purposes of Part I of the Children and Young Persons Act 1969 as guilty of an offence.*".		1969 c. 54.
The Children and Young Persons Act 1963 In section 16(2) of the Children and Young Persons Act 1963, for the words from " notwithstanding " onwards there shall be substituted the words " notwithstanding that the question falls within subsection (2) or (3) of section 6 of the Criminal Evidence Act 1972 or that the asking of it has ceased to be prohibited under subsection (1) of that section ".	Section 6.	1963 c. 37.

Amendment	Provision of this Act on which amendment is consequential
The Children and Young Persons Act 1963 (continued) In section 28(1) of the Children and Young Persons Act 1963, for the words " child or young person " there shall be substituted 'the words " young person or, except in criminal proceedings, any child ".	Section 22.

1968 c. 19.

| *The Criminal Appeal Act 1968*
Section 23 of the Criminal Appeal Act 1968 shall be amended as follows—
(*a*) in subsection (1)(*b*), for the words from " order " to " lies " there shall be substituted the words " on the application of any party to the appeal order any witness who in the proceedings from which the appeal lies would have been compellable to give evidence for that party ";
(*b*) subsection (3) shall be omitted. | Section 9. |

1968 c. 64.

| *The Civil Evidence Act 1968*
In section 17(2)(*a*) of the Civil Evidence Act 1968, for the words from " the provisions " to " but " there shall be substituted the words " the references in the said section 5 or the said section 4, as the case may be, to any cause pending as mentioned in that section shall be construed as references to any criminal proceedings so pending; ". | Section 15. |

Section 46.

SCHEDULE 2

REPEALS

Acts

Chapter	Short Title	Extent of Repeal
36 Geo. 3. c. 7.	The Treason Act 1795.	In section 1, the words " upon the oaths of two lawful and credible witnesses ".
14 & 15 Vict. c. 99.	The Evidence Act 1851.	Section 13 so far as it applies to criminal proceedings.

Chapter	Short Title	Extent of Repeal
16 & 17 Vict. c. 83.	The Evidence (Amendment) Act 1853.	Section 3, so far as unrepealed.
28 & 29 Vict. c. 18.	The Criminal Procedure Act 1865.	Sections 3 to 6 so far as they apply to criminal proceedings.
34 & 35 Vict. c. 112.	The Prevention of Crimes Act 1871.	Section 18, so far as it applies to criminal proceedings, except so much of the paragraph beginning with the words " A previous conviction in any one part " as precedes the words " and a conviction ".
40 & 41 Vict. c. 14.	The Evidence Act 1877.	The whole Act, so far as unrepealed.
46 & 47 Vict. c. 3.	The Explosive Substances Act 1883.	Section 4(2).
55 & 56 Vict. c. 4.	The Betting and Loans (Infants) Act 1892.	Section 6.
58 & 59 Vict. c. 24.	The Law of Distress Amendment Act 1895.	Section 5.
61 & 62 Vict. c. 36.	The Criminal Evidence Act 1898.	The whole Act, except sections 3 and 7(3).
1 & 2 Geo. 5. c. 6.	The Perjury Act 1911.	Section 9.
4 & 5 Geo. 5. c. 58.	The Criminal Justice Administration Act 1914.	Section 28(3).
15 & 16 Geo. 5. c. 86.	The Criminal Justice Act 1925.	Section 12, so far as unrepealed.
19 & 20 Geo. 5. c. 34.	The Infant Life (Preservation) Act 1929.	Section 2(5).
23 & 24 Geo. 5. c. 12.	The Children and Young Persons Act 1933.	Section 15. Section 26(5). Section 38. In section 42(1), the words " on oath ".
23 & 24 Geo. 5. c. 36.	The Administration of Justice (Miscellaneous Provisions) Act 1933.	In section 2(2)(b), the words " or pursuant to an order made under section 9 of the Perjury Act 1911 ".
12, 13 & 14 Geo. 6. c. 68.	The Representation of the People Act 1949.	Section 146(5).
15 & 16 Geo. 6. & 1 Eliz. 2. c. 55.	The Magistrates' Courts Act 1952.	In Schedule 5, the entry relating to the Criminal Justice Act 1925.
3 & 4 Eliz. 2. c. 20.	The Revision of the Army and Air Force Acts (Transitional Provisions) Act 1955.	In Schedule 2, paragraph 5.
4 & 5 Eliz. 2. c. 69.	The Sexual Offences Act 1956.	Section 2(2). Section 3(2). Section 4(2). Section 12(2) and (3). Section 15(4) and (5). Section 16(2) and (3). Section 22(2). Section 23(2). Section 39.

Chapter	Short Title	Extent of Repeal
4 & 5 Eliz. 2. c. 69.	The Sexual Offences Act 1956 (*continued*).	In Schedule 3, the entry relating to section 15 of the Children and Young Persons Act 1933.
7 & 8 Eliz. 2. c. 25.	The Highways Act 1959.	In Schedule 22, the entry relating to the Evidence Act 1877.
8 & 9 Eliz. 2. c. 33.	The Indecency with Children Act 1960.	Section 1(2).
1965 c. 20.	The Criminal Evidence Act 1965.	The whole Act.
1965 c. 51.	The National Insurance Act 1965.	Section 94(6).
1965 c. 72.	The Matrimonial Causes Act 1965.	In section 43(1), the words from " but a husband or wife " to the end of the subsection.
1967 c. 34.	The Industrial Injuries and Diseases (Old Cases) Act 1967.	Section 11(5).
1968 c. 19.	The Criminal Appeal Act 1968.	In section 23, in subsection (1)(*c*), the words " subject to subsection (3) below ", and subsection (3).
1968 c. 60.	The Theft Act 1968.	In section 27, subsection (3) and, in subsection (5), the words from " and " onwards. In section 30, in subsection (2), the words from " and a person " onwards, and subsection (3).
1969 c. 48.	The Post Office Act 1969.	In section 93(4), the words " the Criminal Evidence Act 1965 and ". In Schedule 4, paragraph 77.

Instrument

Number	Title	Extent of Repeal
1952 No. 1334.	The National Assistance (Adaptation of Enactments) Regulations 1952.	Part II of the Schedule.

ANNEX 2

NOTES ON DRAFT CRIMINAL EVIDENCE BILL

References to paragraphs (except in relation to provisions of the draft Bill or of enactments) are to those of the report.

PART I

PROVISIONS AS TO VARIOUS MATTERS

CLAUSE 1 (CIRCUMSTANCES IN WHICH INFERENCES MAY BE DRAWN FROM ACCUSED'S FAILURE TO MENTION PARTICULAR FACTS WHEN QUESTIONED, CHARGED ETC.)

Clause 1 substantially abolishes the rule (part of the so-called " right of silence ") that, if the accused relies in his defence on some fact which he failed to mention when questioned or charged, the court or jury may not infer from the failure that his evidence on the matter is untrue and may not treat the failure as corroboration of the evidence against him.

Subsections (*1*) and (*2*) provide that the court or jury may draw from a failure of the sort mentioned above such inferences as appear proper and may treat it as corroboration, or as capable of amounting to corroboration, of any evidence given against the accused in relation to which the failure is material. The fact relied on must be one which it would have been reasonable to expect the accused to mention. The provisions will apply to the accused's failure to mention the fact when questioned by a police officer or by any person " charged with the duty of investigating offences or charging offenders " and also to his failure to mention the fact when charged or officially informed (by a police officer or other person such as mentioned above) that he might be prosecuted for the offence. The provisions will apply both to the trial and to committal proceedings; and it will be permissible for the inferences to be drawn (i) at committal proceedings, for the purpose of determining whether to commit the accused for trial, (ii) at a summary trial, for the purpose of determining whether there is a case to answer or whether the accused is guilty, (iii) by the judge at a trial on indictment, for the purpose of determining whether there is a case to answer and (iv) by the jury, for the purpose of determining whether the accused is guilty. The application of the provision as to corroboration will be similar; and the clause refers to treating the failure " as, or as capable of amounting to, corroboration" because it is for the judge to determine whether in the circumstances the failure is capable of amounting to corroboration of the other evidence and for the jury to determine whether it does corroborate the evidence. The failure may corroborate evidence given by the prosecution or evidence given by or on behalf of another accused. The proposals are discussed in paragraphs 32–39 (in relation to the drawing of inferences) and paragraphs 40–42 (in relation to corroboration).

Subsection (*3*) provides that the provisions of the clause are not to be treated as implying that any evidence which is at present admissible as to the silence or other reaction of the accused in the face of anything said in his presence about

211

the offence is no longer admissible (*paragraph* (*a*)) or to preclude the drawing of any inference from this which could be drawn at present (*paragraph* (*b*)). The committee contemplate that the effect will be that the courts will be able to take as liberal a view as to the inferences which it is right to draw in a proper case from the accused's failure to mention some exculpatory matter to a private person as from his failure to do so to a police officer (paragraph 34).

Subsection (*4*) provides that the provisions of subsections (1) and (2) about the consequences of failure to mention a matter when officially questioned, charged etc. shall not apply to a failure before the commencement of the Act. The provision is included because the accused might have remained silent in reliance on his existing immunity from the drawing of adverse inferences from his silence.

Subsection (*5*) is a declaratory provision as to the absence of any legal requirement that a police officer or other person who suspects a person of an offence should caution him before questioning him. The subsection is unnecessary in law, but it is included in support of the committee's recommendation that the administrative requirements in Rules II and III(a) of the Judges' Rules to caution a suspect should be abolished (paragraph 43).

Clause 2 (Confessions)

Clause 2 relaxes, mostly in favour of the prosecution, the present rule that a confession by the accused is inadmissible unless the prosecution prove that it was " voluntary, in the sense that it has not been obtained from him by fear of prejudice or hope of advantage, exercised or held out by a person in authority, or by oppression "[1]. A confession obtained by oppression will still be excluded in all cases (assuming that the question of admissibility is raised), but a threat or inducement will have this effect not, as at present, in all cases but only if it was such as to be likely, in the circumstances, to " render unreliable any confession which might be made by the accused in consequence thereof ".

Subsection (*1*) contains the general rule that a confession by the accused may be given in evidence by the prosecution if it is " relevant to any matter in issue in the proceedings " and is not excluded by the court under subsection (2) or (3). The provisions in the clause as to inadmissibility on account of a threat etc. will apply only if the confession is tendered in evidence by the prosecution[2]. But, if admissible, it will be admissible for all purposes (subject to subsection (4)), and therefore admissible for or against any of the co-accused. The purpose of the provision that the confession shall be admissible " in so far as it is relevant to any matter in issue in the proceedings " is to limit admissibility to where the fact confessed to relates to the offence charged or to some other conduct which is admissible in evidence (e.g. an admission by the accused that he committed some other offence which is admissible under clause 3).

Subsection (*2*) contains the proposed new rule that a confession, in order to be admissible, must not have been obtained by " oppressive treatment " of the accused (*paragraph* (*a*)) or " in consequence of any threat or inducement of a

---

[1] See paragraph 53.

[2] Under the hearsay provisions in Part II of the draft Bill one co-accused will be able to give in evidence a statement made by another co-accused; and even if this contains a confession of guilt, there will be no restriction on admissibility such as is provided for by clause 2.

sort likely, in the circumstances existing at the time, to render unreliable any confession which might be made by the accused in consequence thereof (*paragraph* (*b*)). " Oppressive treatment " is intended to have the same meaning as " oppression " has for the purpose of the present rule as indicated by the Court of Appeal in *Prager*[1](paragraph 60). The proposed test in respect of a " threat or inducement " is described in paragraphs 65–66. The defence will in all cases be able to raise the question of admissibility by representing to the court that the confession was or may have been obtained by a method mentioned, and it will then be for the prosecution to satisfy the court beyond reasonable doubt as to the conditions for admissibility. The requirement to satisfy the court " beyond reasonable doubt " is in accordance with the rule as stated in the English cases, but these are all cases noted only in the Criminal Law Review and without the text of the judgments. The decisions have been disapproved by the High Court of Australia on the ground that it is wrong to apply to questions arising incidentally for decision by the judge the standard of proof required in the case of questions to be decided by the jury[2]; but the committee regard this as right in policy, and the provision is included in order to make the matter certain. The subsection provides that a confession which does not satisfy the conditions mentioned shall not be given in evidence " whether by virtue of this section or otherwise ". This is to avoid any argument that a confession inadmissible under the clause will be admissible under any of the provisions about hearsay evidence in Part II.

Subsection (*3*) enables the court of its own motion to require the prosecution to prove the matters mentioned in subsection (2) on which admissibility depends even if the defence have not raised the question. This seems desirable for the reasons given in paragraph 54.

Subsection (*4*) makes it clear that, where a confession is admissible under the clause, it is admissible as evidence of any fact stated in it, including facts favourable to the accused. Under the present law it is a matter of dispute whether a confession which is admissible when tendered by the prosecution is admissible by virtue of an exception to the rule against hearsay or by virtue of a special rule relating to confessions. But there is a substantial body of opinion to the effect that it is admissible by virtue of an exception to the rule against hearsay[3]; and since clause 30 limits the cases of admissibility of a hearsay statement to the cases provided for by the Bill and the other cases mentioned in the clause, it seems to the committee desirable to say expressly in clause 2 that a confession is admissible as evidence of the facts stated in it. The committee agree in particular with the view expressed by Archbold and Phipson in the passages referred to in the last footnote that under the present law any part of a confession which is favourable to the maker is admissible (subject to weight) as evidence of the facts stated in it. This is supported in particular by the recent case of *McGregor*[4]. It seems to the committee right in policy that this should be so, and subsection (4) provides accordingly. Naturally the weight to be attached to the self-serving parts of a confession will depend

---

[1] (1971), 56 Cr. App. R. 151, 161.
[2] See Cross on Evidence, 3rd edition, p. 59; R. S. O'Regan in [1964] Crim. L.R. 287.
[3] See Archbold, Criminal Pleading, Evidence and Practice, 37th edition, paragraph 1129; Phipson on Evidence, 11th edition, paragraphs 1538–1539.
[4] [1968] 1 Q.B. 371; 51 Cr. App. R. 338. The case is referred to in another connection in paragraph 27.

very much on the circumstances, and it may well be very little. The proviso to subsection (4) contains a particular provision in relation to the self-serving parts of a confession. It provides that the court shall not be required to treat an issue as having been raised (on behalf of the defence) by reason of any statement in those parts. The proviso relates to the provisions of clause 8, and its purpose is explained in the note on that clause. The provision in the main part of clause 2(4) that a confession is admissible as evidence of the facts stated in it will also have the effect that a confession by co-accused A which is admissible for the prosecution under the clause and which implicates co-accused B will be admissible (again subject to weight) against B as well as against A. This is a change from the present law, and it is in accordance with the provision in clause 31(2) by which an out-of-court statement by any of the accused will be admissible against any of the others. Clause 2(4) applies to a statement of opinion in a confession in the same way as to a statement of fact. This will apply, for example, to an admission by a motorist that he regarded his driving as dangerous.

Subsection (5) provides that the fact that a confession is inadmissible under the clause shall not affect the admissibility of any facts discovered as a result of the confession or the admissibility of the other matters mentioned in the subsection. The purpose and effect of the subsection are described in paragraphs 68–69.

Subsection (6) defines " confession " so that it " includes any statement wholly or partly adverse to the accused, whether made to a person in authority or not and whether made in words or otherwise ". By making no difference between a statement " wholly " or " partly " adverse to the accused the subsection preserves the effect of the decision in *Harz and Power*[1] that there is no difference, in relation to admissibility, between a full confession of guilt and an incriminating admission falling short of a full confession. The definition abolishes the rule that a threat or inducement, in order to make a resulting confession inadmissible, must have been uttered or held out by a " person in authority " (paragraph 58). An example of a confession made otherwise than in words would be where the accused nods in reply to an accusation.

CLAUSE 3 (ADMISSIBILITY OF OTHER CONDUCT OF ACCUSED TENDING TO SHOW DISPOSITION)

Clause 3 restates with substantial amendments the law as to when evidence of conduct of the accused other than the offence charged is admissible as tending to show a disposition to commit the kind of offence charged. The provisions of the clause are summarized in paragraph 101 and there are therefore only a few matters to be mentioned here.

In *subsections* (3) and (5) the provisions making previous convictions of the accused admissible for the purposes and in the circumstances specified are limited to convictions by or before a court in the United Kingdom or by a court-martial (defined in clause 45(1)) there or elsewhere. The purpose is to limit the provisions to convictions in courts within the general competence of the Parliament of the United Kingdom. This is because the admissibility of a conviction under clause 3 depends on the facts of the offence to which it

---

[1] [1967] 1 A.C. 760; 51 Cr. App. R. 123. The case is referred to in paragraph 53.

relates and because the provisions in clause 25 making admissible certain documents relating to a conviction for the purpose of identifying the facts cannot appropriately be extended to convictions in courts with which the Parliament of the United Kingdom is not concerned. The conviction will be conclusive evidence that the accused committed the offence to which it relates (paragraph 99).

In the provision in *subsection (4)(c)* that, where the *actus reus* is admitted, evidence of other conduct of the accused is admissible " to prove that there was no lawful justification or excuse for the conduct in respect of which the accused is charged " the phrase "lawful justification or excuse" is intended to cover matters such as lawful authority, self-defence, duress and ignorance (where these are defences). *Paragraphs (a), (b)* and *(c)* overlap to a certain extent.

In *subsection (7)(b)* the saving for the operation of any enactment " contained in this Act " by virtue of which evidence of other conduct or convictions of the accused is or may be admissible relates to the provisions of clauses 6 and 7 concerning cross-examination of the accused and the rebutting of a claim by him to be of good disposition or reputation and those of clause 14 concerning proof of a conviction which is denied.

Subsection (8) applies the provisions of clause 25 to clause 3. This is mentioned above in relation to subsections (3) and (5) of clause 3. The note on clause 25 refers.

CLAUSE 4 (GIVING OF EVIDENCE BY ACCUSED)

Subsection (1) restates the present rule (in s. 1—opening words and paragraph (a)—of the Criminal Evidence Act 1898 (c. 36)) that the accused is competent to give evidence on his own behalf or for a co-accused, but not compellable. The common law rule that he is incompetent as a witness for the prosecution (subject to what is said below in relation to subsection (5)) will remain.

Subsection (2) abolishes the right of the accused to make an unsworn statement instead of giving evidence on oath (paragraphs 102–106).

Subsection (3) restates the rule in s. 2 of the 1898 Act that, if the accused is called as a witness but does not call any other person to give evidence as to the facts (as distinct from evidence of the accused's character), then the accused must be called immediately after the close of the evidence for the prosecution. It is by virtue of this provision that the defence may make an opening statement only if they call a witness to the facts other than the accused. (The rules at committal proceedings and summary trials are different, and depend on Rules 4 and 13 respectively of the Magistrates' Courts Rules 1968.)

Subsection (4) provides that, in the absence of a decision by the court to the contrary, the accused, if he gives evidence, shall do so before any other evidence is called for the defence; but it makes it a matter within the complete discretion of the court whether to allow the defence to postpone calling the accused. This relaxes the present rule that it is only in exceptional cases that the court should allow this (paragraph 107). The subsection will apply both to trials on indictment and to summary trials.

215

Subsection (5) is a declaratory provision, in accordance with the present law, that, if two or more persons have been jointly charged but for some reason any of them (say, A) is not, or is no longer, liable to conviction at the trial of any of the others (say, B), then A is compellable as a witness for the prosecution[1] or for B[2]. This situation might occur if A has been acquitted (perhaps after a decision to offer no evidence against him), if he has received a free pardon, if a *nolle prosequi* has been entered in respect of him or if the court has ordered that he should be tried separately after B's trial. However, the subsection will not affect the rule of practice that the prosecution should not call a co-accused who is still to be tried at a separate trial[3].

Subsection (6) provides that subsection (5) shall not apply to a situation where A and B (in the case supposed in the note on subsection (5)) are husband and wife. This situation is dealt with separately in clause 9(5) because of the limited compellability of the spouse of an accused person as provided for by clause 9.

Subsection (7) repeals s. 12 of the Criminal Justice Act 1925 (c. 86), the only unrepealed provision of which provides that any statement made by the accused at the committal proceedings at the end of the case for the prosecution may be given in evidence at the trial (paragraph 106).

CLAUSE 5 (ACCUSED TO BE CALLED UPON TO GIVE EVIDENCE AT TRIAL)

Clause 5 provides that, if at the trial of the accused the court considers that there is a case for him to answer, then, subject to certain exceptions, the court shall at the appropriate time call on him to give evidence and that, if he then refuses to do so or if he refuses without good cause to answer any question, the magistrates' court or jury may draw such inferences from the refusal as appear proper and may treat it as corroboration, or as capable of being corroboration, of any evidence given against the accused. The clause includes provision for the court to inform the accused at the end of the case for the prosecution that he will be called on to give evidence and to warn him of the effect of the clause if he refuses. No provision is made requiring the court to warn the accused of the effect of the clause if he refuses without good cause to answer a particular question, because the accused has in any event no right to refuse; but it will be open to the court to give the warning if it thinks right.

The provisions of clause 5 are summarized in paragraph 113, where it is mentioned that the present prohibition (in s. 1(*b*) of the Criminal Evidence Act 1898) of comment by the prosecution on the accused's failure to give evidence will cease to have effect with the repeal of s. 1(*b*); but a few other matters are mentioned below.

Subsection (4) is included in order to make it clear that the clause does not override the rule that the accused cannot be compelled to give evidence and also to make it clear that he is not to be treated as guilty of contempt of court if he refuses to do so. Without the subsection it might seem from the provision for the court to call upon the accused to give evidence that he would be guilty of contempt of court by not going into the witness box to give evidence when

---

[1] *Winsor* (1866), L.R. 1 Q.B. 289, 390.
[2] *Boal*, [1965] 1 Q.B. 402, 415; 48 Cr. App. R. 342, 345; *Richardson* (1967), 51 Cr. App. R. 381.
[3] *Pipe* (1966), 51 Cr. App. R. 17.

called upon. To disobey an order by the court to answer a particular question will still be contempt of court.

In *subsection* (5), which specifies the cases in which the accused may have " good cause " for refusing to answer a particular question, the reference in *paragraph* (*a*) to the accused's being entitled to refuse to answer a question " by virtue of . . . any . . . enactment [other than clause 6(1)] or on the ground of privilege" will include (i) his limited right, under clause 15(2)(*b*), to refuse to answer a question on the ground that this would tend to expose him to proceedings for an offence (other than the offence charged) or for the recovery of a penalty or on the ground that it would tend to expose his wife to proceedings for an offence or for the recovery of a penalty, and (ii) the right of a person aged twenty-one or over, under s. 16(2) of the Children and Young Persons Act 1963 (c. 37) (as to be amended by Schedule 1) to refuse to answer a question about a conviction when he was under fourteen. But the enactments mentioned in clause 25(3) which provide that a conviction leading to probation or discharge is to be disregarded except for certain purposes will not entitle the accused to refuse to answer a question about a conviction such as mentioned. This is because clause 25(3) provides that the enactments shall not affect the operation of clause 3 and because clause 6(1) disentitles the accused, if he gives evidence, to refuse to answer a question about a conviction of which evidence is admissible under clause·3. The reference in *paragraph* (*b*) to the court's excusing the accused " in the exercise of its general discretion " from answering a question relates to the general exclusionary discretion preserved by clause 45(8).

The provision in *subsection* (6) concerning the trial of a child for homicide is explained in the note on clause 22(3).

CLAUSE 6 (RESTRICTIONS ON CROSS-EXAMINATION OF ACCUSED)

Clause 6 replaces the greater part of the provisions of s. 1(*e*) and (*f*) of the Criminal Evidence Act 1898 with important changes. These are partly for reasons of policy and partly for the purpose of clarification. The most important change is to restrict the right of the prosecution or of a co-accused to cross-examine an accused about misconduct other than the offence charged on the ground that he has made imputations against the witnesses against him. The provisions of paragraphs (*e*) and (*f*) which are not dealt with in clause 6 are those in paragraph (*e*) and paragraph (*f*)(i) which prevent the accused from claiming any privilege against incriminating himself in relation to the offence charged (dealt with in clause 15(2)) and those in paragraph (*f*)(ii) relating to where the accused seeks to establish his own good character (dealt with in clause 7).

Subsection (*1*) contains the general prohibition of asking the accused in cross-examination any question tending to reveal the fact that he has committed any offence other than the offence charged or that he has been charged with, or convicted or acquitted of, another offence (*paragraph* (*a*)) or that he is of bad disposition or reputation (*paragraph* (*b*)). The subsection corresponds to the prohibition in the opening part of s. 1(*f*) of the 1898 Act. It is substantially similar to this in effect but includes some changes for the purpose of clarification. First, the prohibition of asking a question " tending to reveal to the court or jury " a fact such as mentioned secures that it will apply only

217

to a question which introduces the fact into the evidence for the first time, so that the prohibition will not apply if the fact has already been mentioned by the accused. This settles the law in accordance with the majority view in *Jones v. Director of Public Prosecutions*[1] (paragraphs 116–117). Second, paragraph (*a*) expressly prohibits a question whether the accused has been acquitted of an offence. This is implicit in the prohibition of asking the question whether he has been charged with the offence, but it seems desirable to make the prohibition explicit. Third, paragraph (*b*) replaces the prohibition of asking a question tending to reveal that the accused is of " bad character " with that of a question tending to reveal that he is " generally or in a particular respect a person of bad disposition or reputation ". The substitution of the reference to " disposition or reputation " for the reference to " character " is for the sake of clarity, as explained in paragraph 118. The express provision that the question is prohibited if it tends to reveal the fact that the accused is " generally " or " in a particular respect " a person such as mentioned is included for the sake of clarity and of drafting consistency with clause 7, where the distinction is important for the reason mentioned in the note on the clause.

Subsection (2) removes the prohibition in subsection (1) entirely in respect of any question tending to reveal a fact about the accused if evidence of the fact is admissible for the purpose of proving that he committed the offence charged. This settles the law in accordance with the minority view in *Jones v. Director of Public Prosecutions* of the relation between paragraphs (*e*) and (*f*) of s. 1 of the 1898 Act (paragraphs 116–117). Subsection (2) also makes the removal of the prohibition, in the cases where it is removed, co-extensive with the prohibition itself[2]; that is to say, it allows any question which is prohibited by subsection (1) if the question is admissible for the purpose mentioned. This is a change from the present law, as the prohibition in the opening words of s. 1(*f*) applies to any question which tends to show that the accused (i) has committed an offence, (ii) has been convicted of it, (iii) has been charged with it or (iv) is of bad character, but paragraph (*f*)(i) removes the prohibition only in respect of (i) and (ii). There seems no reason why the removal should not be co-extensive with the prohibition. A question whether the accused has been charged with, or even acquitted of, an offence might be admissible in order to prove that he possessed some particular piece of knowledge which is relevant for the purpose of the offence charged. The prohibition is removed for the benefit of a co-accused as well as for that of the prosecution. Thus, if A and B are tried jointly, A will be able, whether or not B has given evidence against him, to cross-examine B about any matter about which the prosecution could cross-examine him for the purpose of showing that B and not A committed the offence. This is in accordance with the present law; for A is entitled to put questions to B which are relevant to the issue in the hope of strengthening his own case whether or not B has given evidence against him[3], and such questions would be permissible even though they tended to show that B had committed other offences[4]. In *Miller*[5] it was held that one of the accused (X) might, for the purpose of showing that another accused (Y) and not X committed the offence.

---

[1] [1962] A. C. 635; 46 Cr. App. R. 129.
[2] The remaining subsections in clause 6, and clause 7, are similar in this respect.
[3] *Hilton* (1971), 55 Cr. App. R. 466.
[4] *Miller* (1952), 36 Cr. App. R. 169.
[5] Above.

ask a witness for the prosecution a question tending to show that Y had been in prison at a certain time (this being directly relevant in the circumstances). and clearly it would have been equally permissible for X to put the question to Y himself.

Subsection (3) removes the prohibition in subsection (1) so 'as to enable co-accused A to ask co-accused B any question tending to reveal a fact about B if evidence of the fact is admissible in order to prove that A is not guilty of any offence with which A is charged (paragraph 117 n. 1). If B was also charged with the offence, and A was seeking to show that B and not A committed it, the question would be permissible under subsection (2), as mentioned at the end of the previous paragraph. But if A and B are being tried together and the particular offence is one with which A alone is charged, then subsection (2) will not apply. For example, A may be charged with burglary and B with handling stolen goods coming from the theft, and A may wish to cross-examine B in order to show that B and not A committed the burglary, and for this purpose he may wish to cross-examine B about misconduct on B's part which would be admissible under clause 3. Clause 6(3) will allow this.

Subsection (4) contains the proposed new rule as to when the accused is to be liable to cross-examination about his previous misconduct on account of having made imputations against a witness for the prosecution or against a witness for a co-accused. The prohibition in subsection (1) is removed so as to allow this only when the main purpose of the imputation is to raise an issue about the witness's credibility and the cross-examination is relevant to the accused's credibility as a witness (paragraphs 128–129). Apart from limiting the cross-examination to what is relevant to the credibility of the accused and the impugned witness, the subsection departs from s. 1(*f*)(ii) of the 1898 Act in not allowing the cross-examination on account of an imputation against the prosecutor as distinct from a witness for the prosecution and in allowing it on account of an imputation against a witness for a co-accused (paragraph 131). Whether the imputation is made against a witness for the prosecution or against a witness for the co-accused, both the prosecution and the co-accused will (as in the case of cross-examination under subsection (2)) be allowed to cross-examine the former accused as mentioned. Whether this is allowed at present was left open by the Court of Appeal in *Russell*[1], as mentioned in paragraph 131 n. 1 (p. 84).

Subsection (5) removes the prohibition in subsection (1) in a case where the accused has given evidence against any co-accused. It preserves the present rule in s. 1(*f*)(iii) of the 1898 Act except that it allows the cross-examination in any case where the two accused are jointly charged and not only, as at present, when they are charged with the same offence (paragraph 132). As under s. 1(*f*)(iii), the prohibition of cross-examining the accused who has given the evidence will be removed not only in favour of the accused against whom the evidence is given but also in favour of the prosecution and any of the other co-accused. The clause will not alter the present rule that the court has no discretion to prevent cross-examination by the accused against whom the evidence is given but has a discretion to prevent cross-examination by the prosecution[2] (paragraphs 121, 132).

---

[1] [1971] 1 Q.B. 151, 153 A–C, 155 D–E; 55 Cr. App. R.23, 27–28. 31.
[2] *Murdoch v. Taylor*, [1965] A.C. 574; 49 Cr. App. R. 119.

None of the provisions in clause 6 about cross-examination of the accused (or of those in clause 10 about cross-examination of other witnesses) affect the law as to adducing evidence that a witness is unfit to be believed because of mental instability[1] or the law as to discrediting a witness by evidence of bad reputation for, or opinion as to, his veracity[2].

CLAUSE 7 (ADMISSIBILITY OF EVIDENCE AND QUESTIONS ABOUT ACCUSED'S DISPOSITION OR REPUTATION)

Clause 7 replaces the rules as to the right of the accused to set up his good " character " (which expression is replaced, as in clause 6, by " disposition or reputation ") and as to the right of the prosecution or a co-accused to rebut the claim. The present rules depend on the common law except that the right to cross-examine the accused in order to rebut the claim depends on s. 1(f)(ii) of the Criminal Evidence Act 1898.

Subsection (1) states the rule that the accused may cross-examine a witness. or give or call evidence, to show that he is a person of good disposition or reputation, but that the prosecution or a co-accused may rebut the claim by calling evidence to the contrary, by giving such evidence (in the case of a co-accused) or by cross-examining the accused who makes the claim or any other witness in order to show the contrary. The subsection alters the common law rule (ignored in practice) that the meaning of " character " for the purpose of the rule is reputation only and not disposition (paragraph 134). But it preserves the common law rule that the accused may not, by setting up good " character " in one respect only (e.g. as to honesty or sexual probity). prevent the prosecution or a co-accused from showing that the former accused is of bad " character " in other respects. The rule that the accused's character is indivisible for this purpose was laid down in *Winfield*[3] and approved in the third of the six propositions with which Viscount Simon L.C. concluded his speech in *Stirland v. Director of Public Prosecutions*[4]. The rule seems to the committee generally right in policy, and it is preserved by the provision that, if the accused gives evidence that he is " generally or in a particular respect a person of good disposition or reputation ", the prosecution or a co-accused may prove that he is " a person of bad disposition or reputation " (the words " generally or in a particular respect " not being repeated). The subsection also makes it clear that the claim to be of good disposition or reputation may be made directly or by implication. The importance of this is that, if the accused tries to hint indirectly that he is a respectable person, the prosecution will be able to rebut this directly (paragraphs 135–136). The subsection also makes it clear that a co-accused, as well as the prosecution, may rebut the claim (paragraph 136).

Subsection (2) makes it clear that the prosecution or a co-accused may call evidence of an accused's previous convictions in order to rebut his claim to be of good disposition or reputation. This is allowed in practice at present (rightly, in the committee's view), but it seems desirable to make the matter explicit because the authority for the practice seems to rest on a dictum in

---

[1] *Toohey v. Metropolitan Police Commissioner*, [1965] A.C. 595; 49 Cr. App. R. 148.
[2] *Richardson and Longman*, [1969] 1 Q.B. 299; 52 Cr. App. R. 317.
[3] (1939), 27 Cr. App. R. 139, 141.
[4] [1944] A.C. 315, 326–327; 30 Cr. App. R. 40, 54.

Redd[1], although the dictum in fact consists of approving a statement in Archbold misstating the effect of two earlier cases. Consistently with the policy of the clause, subsection (2) disapplies the prohibition in clause 6(1) in relation to cross-examination for the purpose of rebutting the accused's claim to be of good disposition or reputation.

CLAUSE 8 (LIMITS OF BURDEN OF PROOF FALLING ON ACCUSED)

Subsection (*1*) provides that, in any case where by virtue of any rule of the common law or of any existing enactment the defence have the burden of proving any matter, the effect will be that, instead of their having to prove it on a balance of probabilities as at present, they will have only to adduce or elicit some evidence sufficient to raise an issue on the matter and, if they do so, the court or jury will decide by reference to the whole of the evidence whether the prosecution have proved the matter against the accused. If there is no evidence sufficient to raise the issue, the matter will be taken as proved against the accused (*paragraph* (*a*)); but if there is sufficient evidence, the prose-cution will have the ordinary burden of proving it beyond reasonable doubt (*paragraph* (*b*)) (paragraphs 140, 142). It will be for the court to decide, in accordance with the ordinary principles, whether there is sufficient evidence to raise the issue. This will depend on the facts of the particular case; but there is a special provision in the proviso to clause 2(4) that the court shall not be required to treat an issue as raised by reason only of any statement favourable to the accused which is included in a confession and is therefore admissible by virtue of subsection (4) as evidence of the facts stated in it. The proviso is included because the provision in the subsection that a confession admissible under the clause is admissible as evidence of any fact stated in it, including any fact favourable to the accused, might suggest that the court would be bound to treat any statement favourable to the accused, however unconvincing it was, as sufficient to raise an issue in his favour for the purpose of clause 8. The effect of clause 8 will be to change the existing persuasive burdens on the defence to evidential burdens (paragraph 138). The only existing persuasive burden on the defence by virtue of a rule of the common law is that of proving insanity (last part of paragraph 140). There are many such burdens by virtue of enactments, of which paragraph 137 mentions two typical examples. The provision in paragraph (*b*) that the court or jury " shall decide by reference to the whole of the evidence whether the prosecution has proved [the] matter against the accused, drawing such inferences from the evidence as appear proper in the circumstances " follows the language of s. 8 of the Criminal Justice Act 1967 (c. 80), which (changing the rule laid down in *Director of Public Prosecutions v. Smith*[2]) provides that the court or jury shall decide whether the accused intended or foresaw a result of his actions " by reference to all the evidence, drawing such inferences from the evidence as appear proper in the circumstances ".

Subsection (*2*) makes it clear that the alteration made by subsection (1) is to apply to every enactment which has the effect of casting a persuasive burden of proof on the defence. Subsection (2) is included because of the widely different language of the many enactments to which subsection (1) is to apply.

---

[1] [1923] 1 K.B. 104, 106–107; 17 Cr. App. R. 36, 38–39.
[2] [1961] A.C. 290; 44 Cr. App. R. 261.

Subsection (3) defines the " existing enactments " to which subsection (1) is to apply as enactments passed before the commencement of the Bill. But it provides also (in *paragraph (a)*) that, unless the contrary intention appears, future enactments shall be construed as having the same effect as if they were existing enactments. The result will be that, if Parliament decides that any burden which it casts on the defence should be a persuasive one, it will be necessary to make this clear in the enactment casting the burden (for example, by providing that clause 8 shall not have effect in relation to that enactment). *Paragraph (b)* secures that, if any statutory instrument made under an existing or future enactment contains a provision such as is mentioned in the clause casting a burden of proof on the defence, the provision will be construed as if it was contained in the parent enactment.

Subsections (4) and *(5)* provide that the alteration made by subsection (1) shall not apply to enactments providing for " third-party proceedings " under which a person charged with a contravention of a statute may in certain circumstances obtain an acquittal by proving that the contravention was due to the act or default of another person brought before the court (paragraph 141(i)). So far as the committee know, the only existing enactments in question are those specified in subsection (5), but subsection (4) provides that the exception shall apply to any other similar enactment, whether existing or future.

Another exception, relating to the evidential effect of a conviction of a person other than the accused, is made by clause 24(2), as is mentioned in paragraphs 141(ii) and 219(i). The note on clause 24 refers.

CLAUSE 9 (COMPETENCE AND COMPELLABILITY OF SPOUSE OF ACCUSED)

Clause 9 substantially alters the law as to the competence and compellability of the spouse of the accused. (For convenience it will be assumed that the accused is the husband, but the law is and will remain similar whether the accused is the husband or wife.)

Subsection (1) makes the accused's wife competent for the prosecution in all cases, unless she is herself a co-accused (paragraph 148). If a co-accused wife is being tried together with her husband, she will be incompetent as a witness for the prosecution as in the case of any other co-accused who is on trial; but if she is not being tried together with him, she will be competent as a witness for the prosecution under subsection (5) and the proviso to subsection (1), but will not be compellable for the prosecution except in the cases provided for by subsection (3). Subsection (1) also makes the wife competent as a witness for her husband and, whether or not her husband is willing, for his co-accused. In this respect the clause follows s. 1 of the Criminal Evidence Act 1898 except that it does not preserve the provision in s. 1(*c*) that her husband's consent is necessary for her to give evidence for a co-accused (paragraph 155).

Subsection (2) makes the accused's wife compellable as a witness for him unless she is being tried together with him (paragraph 153). If she is being tried together with him, she will be competent as a witness for him under subsection (1).

Subsection (3) makes the accused's wife (unless she is being tried together with him) compellable for the prosecution in the case of any offence consisting

222

of an assault on or a threat of violence to her or to a person under sixteen belonging to the same household as the accused or in the case of a sexual offence against a person under sixteen such as mentioned (paragraphs 149–152). " Sexual offence " is not defined, and therefore the subsection will apply to any kind of sexual offence, whether under the Sexual Offences Act 1956 (c. 69), the Indecency with Children Act 1960 (c. 33) or otherwise. In cases where the wife is compellable as a witness for the prosecution she will also be compellable as a witness for a co-accused (paragraph 155).

Subsection (4) provides that, if the parties are no longer married, they shall be compellable as witnesses as if they had never been married. As a result, they will be compellable to give evidence concerning matters which occurred when they were married as well as evidence concerning other matters (paragraph 157). But the rules as to competence and compellability will not be affected by a judicial or other separation (paragraph 156).

Subsection. (5) declares that, where a husband and wife have been jointly charged but the wife is for some reason not, or no longer, liable to conviction at the trial in question, she is compellable to give evidence on behalf of her husband and, in a case falling within subsection (3), compellable to give evidence for the prosecution or another co-accused. The subsection corresponds to clause 4(5).

Subsection (6) abrogates the rule in s. 1(*b*) of the 1898 Act that the failure of the wife to give evidence shall not be made the subject of comment by the prosecution (paragraph 154).

CLAUSE 10 (RESTRICTIONS ON CROSS-EXAMINATION OF WITNESS OTHER THAN AN ACCUSED)

Subsection (1) provides that a witness other than any person charged in the proceedings shall not be asked any question as to his conduct on any occasion. or as to whether he has committed, or been charged with or convicted or acquitted of, any offence, unless this is relevant to an issue in the proceedings or to his credibility as a witness. The reason for including a provision stating a proposition which would seem to go without saying is given in paragraph 159.

Subsection (2) applies subsection (1) to an accused person who was jointly charged with the person being tried but who is for some reason not, or no longer, liable to conviction at the trial in question and is called as a witness at it. Since the person in question is not being tried, he should be subject, in relation to cross-examination as to his conduct, to the rules in clause 10 relating to ordinary witnesses and not to those in clause 6 relating to a person who is on trial. The situations which subsection (2) contemplates are those referred to in the note on clause 4(5).

The last paragraph of the note on clause 6 relates to clause 10 also.

CLAUSE 11 (CIRCUMSTANCES IN WHICH PARTY MAY CROSS-EXAMINE HIS OWN WITNESS)

Clause 11 replaces the present rule in s. 3 of the Criminal Procedure Act 1865 (c. 18) as to the circumstances in which a party may cross-examine his own witness. It provides that the party may not impeach the witness's credibility by evidence that the witness is a person of bad disposition or reputation but that, if the witness gives evidence adverse to the party or evidence inconsistent with a statement made by the witness on a previous occasion, the party may, with the leave of the court, cross-examine the witness as if he were a witness called by another party (paragraphs 161–165). Leave, if given, will be for cross-examination generally and will not be required for particular questions. From the time when leave is given it will be as if the witness had been called by another party, and the only power of the court to limit cross-examination will be such power as it has to limit ordinary cross-examination.

CLAUSE 12 (RIGHT OF CROSS-EXAMINING PARTY TO PROVE WITNESS'S PREVIOUS INCONSISTENT STATEMENT)

Clause 12 restates, without change of substance, the provision in s. 4 of the Criminal Procedure Act 1865 that, if a witness is cross-examined about a previous statement which he is alleged to have made inconsistent with his present evidence, and does not admit that he made it, the party cross-examining him may prove that he made it (paragraph 166). The clause does not reproduce the provision in s. 4 that, before proof can be given of the previous statement. " the circumstances of the supposed statement, sufficient to designate the particular occasion, must be mentioned to the witness, and he must be asked whether or not he has made such statement ". It seems unnecessary to reproduce this requirement, as the matter referred to would be bound to be shown in the cross-examination. Like s. 4 of the 1865 Act, the clause applies only to permissible cross-examination. For example, the prosecution may not cross-examine the accused about the contents of an inadmissible confession on the ground that it is inconsistent with his evidence[1].

By clause 33(1) the witness's previous statement, if proved by virtue of clause 12, will be admissible as evidence of any fact stated in it of which direct oral evidence by the witness would be admissible.

CLAUSE 13 (USE OF DOCUMENT CONTAINING PREVIOUS INCONSISTENT STATEMENT OF CROSS-EXAMINED WITNESS)

Subsections (1) and *(2)* reproduce, with minor adaptations to fit the structure of the Bill, the provisions of s. 5 of the Criminal Procedure Act 1865 as to the right of a party to cross-examine a witness so as to contradict his evidence by means of a written statement made by the witness and inconsistent with his evidence (paragraph 167).

Subsections (3) and *(4)* adapt the provisions of subsections (1) and (2) to documents not in writing. For example, clause 41(1), as applied by clause 13(4), defines " document " as including a "disc, tape, sound-track, or other device " for reproducing sounds. As a result clause 13 will apply to a case where the witness's previous statement was made orally but recorded by means of one of these devices. The committee considered whether it was necessary or desirable to include any special provision as to documents not in writing. S. 5 of the 1865 Act naturally applies only to documents in writing, and it might be that no provision need be made about other kinds of documents because. in the event that a party cross-examining a witness wished to contradict him from a tape-recording of a statement made by the witness and inconsis-

---

[1] *Treacy* (1944), 30 Cr. App. R. 93.

tent with his evidence, the court would be likely to apply rules similar to those contained in the clause concerning documents in writing; it would in any event scarcely apply the common law rules which s. 5 of the 1865 Act abrogated in the case of documents in writing. But it seemed to the committee that for the sake of clarity it would be best to provide, as does subsection (3), that the clause should apply to documents not in writing " with the necessary modifications ". Subsection (3) also enables the court to direct that a reference in the clause to a document should be construed as, or as including, a copy of a document. As a result of subsection (3), and of the incorporation by subsection (4) of the provisions in clause 41(1) and (2) as to the interpretation of references to documents and copies, the court will be able, if the witness's previous statement which it is proposed to use in order to contradict him was made orally and recorded on a tape, to direct that the witness should be shown a transcript of the relevant part of the tape in a case where, had the statement been made in a document in writing, it would have been necessary, under subsection (1)(b), to draw the witness's attention to the relevant part of the document.

By clause 33(1) the witness's previous statement, if proved by virtue of clause 13, will be admissible as evidence of any fact stated in it of which direct oral evidence by the witness would be admissible.

CLAUSE 14 (RIGHT OF REBUTTAL WHERE CROSS-EXAMINED WITNESS DENIES HAVING BEEN CONVICTED ETC.)

Clause 14 (which corresponds to the opening part of s. 6 of the Criminal Procedure Act 1865) provides that, if any witness (including the accused, if he gives evidence), on being asked in cross-examination a permissible question as to whether he has been charged with or convicted or acquitted of any offence, denies or does not admit this, the cross-examining party may bring evidence to prove it (paragraph 168).

The main part of s. 6 of the 1865 Act, which provides for the manner of proving convictions, is replaced by clause 26.

CLAUSE 15 (PRIVILEGE AGAINST INCRIMINATION OF SELF OR SPOUSE)

Subsection (1) (which corresponds to s. 14(1) of the Civil Evidence Act 1968 (c. 64)) provides that the privilege of a witness (including the accused, if he gives evidence) against self-incrimination shall apply only to incrimination as regards criminal offences under the law of a part of the United Kingdom and penalties provided for by such a law (*paragraph (a)*) and that the privilege shall extend so as to enable the witness to object to incriminating his spouse in this way (*paragraph (b)*) (paragraph 169).

Subsection (2) restricts in two ways the right of the accused, if he gives evidence, to claim the privilege against self-incrimination or against incriminating his spouse. *Paragraph (a)* provides that he shall not be entitled to claim the privilege against self-incrimination in respect of the offence charged (paragraphs 170–171). *Paragraph (b)* provides that, in respect of an offence other than the offence charged, the accused shall have the privilege against self-incrimination only if the offence is one which in the opinion of the court is relevant solely or mainly to the accused's credibility as a witness and is not one about which the accused is liable under clause 7 to be questioned because he has made a claim to be of good disposition or reputation (paragraphs 170–171). Paragraph (*b*) applies to the accused's privilege against incriminating his spouse in the same way as it applies to his privilege against incriminating himself (paragraph 172).

Subsection (3) restricts the privilege of the accused's spouse (if the spouse gives evidence) against incriminating the accused to the same extent as sub-section (2) restricts the privilege of the accused, if he gives evidence, against incriminating himself (paragraph 172).

Subsection (4) relates to proceedings for the recovery of a penalty. All the provisions of clause 15 (except those in subsections (2)(*a*) and (3)(*a*), which relate only to incrimination in respect of the offence charged) concerning the privilege of a witness against incriminating himself or his spouse in respect of the possibility of proceedings for a criminal offence apply also to incriminating himself or his spouse in relation to the possibility of proceedings for the recovery of a penalty. Subsection (4) provides that proceedings for this purpose shall include civil proceedings. Proceedings for a penalty are, as mentioned in paragraph 13 of the Law Reform Committee's 16th report (Cmnd. 3472), obsolete except in revenue cases; but it is clearly right that clause 15 should follow s. 14 of the Civil Evidence Act 1968 in extending the relevant provisions about the privilege to proceedings for the recovery of a penalty.

CLAUSE 16 (ABOLITION OF CERTAIN PRIVILEGES)

Clause 16 abolishes the unimportant privileges specified in the clause. These are described briefly in paragraph 173. As mentioned in that paragraph, the privileges were abolished so far as civil proceedings were concerned by the corresponding s. 16 of the Civil Evidence Act 1968.

CLAUSE 17 (CORROBORATION IN PROCEEDINGS FOR SEXUAL OFFENCES)

Subsection (1) provides that, at a trial on indictment for a sexual offence, the judge shall warn the jury that there will be a special need for caution before convicting the accused on the uncorroborated evidence of the person against whom the offence is alleged to have been committed (paragraphs 186–188). The subsection will apply only where the last-mentioned person was aged fourteen or over at the time of the alleged offence, because subsection (2) makes different provision for where he was under fourteen. Subsection (1) replaces the present common law requirement (mentioned in paragraph 176) to give a warning as to the " danger " of convicting on uncorroborated evidence.

Subsection (2) provides that, in any proceedings (on indictment or summary) for a sexual offence against a person who, at the time of the alleged offence, was a child (that is to say, a person under fourteen: clause 45(1)), the accused shall not be convicted on the uncorroborated evidence of the child (paragraphs 186–188). By virtue of clause 22(2) children under fourteen who give evidence will do so unsworn; and the present provision in s. 38 of the Children and Young Persons Act 1933 (c. 12) that a person cannot be convicted of any offence on the unsworn evidence of a child unless it is corroborated will be replaced by the narrower rule in clause 17(2) applying only to sexual offences (paragraphs 206, 208).

Clause 17 (like clause 9(3)) will apply to any kind of sexual offence, whether under the Sexual Offences Act 1956 (c. 69), the Indecency with Children Act 1960 (c. 33) or otherwise.

CLAUSE 18 (CORROBORATION IN PROCEEDINGS FOR PERJURY ETC.)

Clause 18 substitutes a new section for s. 13 of the Perjury Act 1911 (c. 6). The existing section (quoted in paragraph 189) provides that a person shall not be convicted of perjury or certain other offences " solely upon the evidence of one witness as to the falsity of any statement alleged to be false ". The substituted section will apply only to perjury in judicial proceedings, to the kindred offence under s. 89 of the Criminal Justice Act 1967 (c. 80) of wilfully making a false statement in a written statement tendered in evidence under s. 2 or 9 of the 1967 Act and to the inchoate offences of attempting, inciting or attempting to incite another to commit any of these offences (paragraphs 189–191). For the restriction contained in the words quoted above there will be substituted a restriction of the usual kind that the evidence as to the falsity of the statement must be " corroborated in some material particular by other evidence " (paragraph 192).

By clause 27 a prosecution for any of the offences to which clause 18 applies will require the authority of the Director of Public Prosecutions.

CLAUSE 19 (ABOLITION OF CERTAIN REQUIREMENTS AS TO CORROBORATION)

Subsection (1) abrogates any rule of law or practice by which the evidence of one witness is incapable of corroborating the evidence of another witness (paragraph 194).

Subsections (2) and *(3)* repeal two statutory provisions requiring a second witness for a conviction of certain offences (paragraphs 175(i) and (iv), 195).

Subsection (4) repeals five provisions of the Sexual Offences Act 1956 requiring corroboration in the case of certain sexual offences (mentioned in paragraph 175(v)). The question of corroboration in these offences will be governed by the provisions of clause 17 relating to corroboration in sexual offences generally (paragraph 188). This will involve a minor change in the law (in addition to the larger changes discussed in paragraphs 186–188) in that the five provisions in the Sexual Offences Act apply not only to the ordinary case where the chief witness for the prosecution is the woman or girl concerned but also to the exceptional case where he is somebody else; but it seems quite unnecessary to include any provision to preserve the requirement of corroboration in these cases.

CLAUSE 20 (DIRECTIONS TO JURIES ABOUT CONVICTING ON UNCORROBORATED EVIDENCE)

Subsection (1) provides that, subject to the provisions to be mentioned, at a trial on indictment it shall be for the court to decide in its discretion, having regard to the evidence given, whether the jury should be given a warning about

227

convicting the accused on uncorroborated evidence and, accordingly, that any rule of law or practice making it obligatory in certain circumstances for the court to give the warning is abrogated. The provisions referred to above are (i) the provision in clause 17(1) requiring the giving of a warning in the case of a sexual offence against a person aged fourteen or over, (ii) that in clause 17(2) requiring corroboration in the case of a sexual offence against a child under fourteen and (iii) the existing enactments not repealed by the Bill, and any future enactments, relating to corroboration. Clause 20(1) does not affect the cases where corroboration is required by law. Its effect will be to abolish the requirement to give a warning in every case in relation to the evidence of an accomplice (paragraphs 183–185) or the sworn evidence of children (paragraph 208). In the case of children the requirement to give the warning will in any event be superseded by the provisions of clause 22 that children under fourteen shall give their evidence unsworn. As a result of clause 20(1) the court will have the duty to consider, in all cases, whether a special warning is called for in respect of the evidence of any particular witness, having regard to all the circumstances, including the other evidence given. The discretion will be subject to appeal in the ordinary way. By providing for the abrogation of any rule that it is " obligatory " in certain circumstances (that is to say, in the case of the evidence of an accomplice or the sworn evidence of a child) to give a warning, the clause takes account of the possibility that a warning, of the kind required by the present law, may still be called for in particular cases (paragraph 185).

Subsection (2) makes it clear that the court is not required to use any particular form of words when warning the jury as to the need for caution before convicting the accused on uncorroborated evidence or when directing them as to the effect of any enactment under which corroboration is necessary. The courts have several times stressed that there is no stereotyped formula for giving the warnings or directions required at present; but the subsection is included lest it should be thought that the alteration made by the Bill as to the kind of warning which is to be given involves the use of a particular form of words related to the language of the Bill (paragraph 188).

CLAUSE 21 (DIRECTIONS TO JURIES ABOUT RELIANCE ON DISPUTED IDENTIFICATION OF ACCUSED)

Clause 21 imposes a new particular duty on the court relating to evidence of identification. It provides that, at a trial on indictment, the court shall warn the jury of the special need for caution before convicting the accused where the case against him depends wholly or substantially on the correctness of one of more identifications of him which the defence allege to be mistaken; but the court is not to be required to use any particular form of words in giving the warning (paragraphs 198–199). The warning required by clause 21 is different from that required by clause 17(1) in the case of the uncorroborated evidence of a person aged fourteen or over in respect of whom a sexual offence is said to have been committed in that clause 21 does not refer to corroboration; for clause 21 applies whether or not the evidence of identification is corroborated and applies even when there is more than one identification (paragraph 199). The reason for providing that the court shall not be required to use any particular form of words in giving the warning is similar to that for including clause 20(2).

CLAUSE 22 (EVIDENCE OF CHILDREN)

Clause 22 makes fresh provision as to the giving of evidence by children in criminal cases in place of the present provision in s. 38 of the Children and Young Persons Act 1933 (c. 12). It also makes certain ancillary provisions in relation to other enactments concerning depositions and other written statements of evidence by children.

Subsection (1) introduces the fresh provisions in the other subsections and repeals s. 38 of the 1933 Act, the main provision of which, enabling a child to give unsworn evidence, is quoted in paragraph 204.

Subsection (2) states the new rule that a child (that is to say, a person under fourteen: clause 45(1)) shall not be sworn as a witness but that he may give evidence unsworn " if in the opinion of the court he is possessed of sufficient intelligence to justify the reception of his evidence and understands the importance of telling the truth in [the] proceedings " (paragraph 206). By virtue of clause 45(3) the age of the witness will be deemed to be that which it appears to the court to be. Therefore the court will not have to require evidence of the age, but will be able to require or hear evidence of this if it considers it necessary.

Subsection (3) modifies the provisions of clause 5 in relation to the trial of a child under fourteen, as is mentioned in clause 5(6). These provisions are included because, if Part I of the Children and Young Persons Act 1969 (c. 54) were fully in force, no child under fourteen could be charged with any offence except homicide (s. 4). Clause 5 provides for the accused (if there is a case for him to answer) to be called on to give evidence and for the consequences mentioned to follow if he refuses to be sworn or if, having been sworn, he refuses to answer a particular question; and as clause 22(2) provides that the evidence of a child will always be given unsworn, subsection (3) modifies clause 5 by applying it, in the case of a trial of a child, to the child's agreeing or refusing to give evidence instead of to his being or refusing to be sworn. The latter part of clause 22(3) ensures that the child will not be called on at all to give evidence under clause 5(2) unless he is capable of giving evidence under clause 22(2). The words " for homicide " are in italics because at the time of making this report Part I of the 1969 Act is not fully in force and it is therefore still possible for a child under fourteen to be tried for other offences; and if Part I is not fully in force when the Bill is enacted, clauses 5(6), 22(3) and the other italicized provisions will require adjustment (cf. paragraph 207).

Subsection (4) provides that, if a child gives unsworn evidence (in accordance with subsection (2)) in committal proceedings, and his evidence is put into writing as provided for by the Magistrates' Courts Rules, it shall be treated as a deposition. The subsection replaces (so far as is necessary) the second half of the main part of s. 38(1) of the 1933 Act.

Subsection (5) provides for the event that a child gives false unsworn evidence in such circumstances that, had the evidence been given on oath, he would have been guilty of perjury. At present s. 38(2) of the 1933 Act makes this punishable on summary conviction (assuming that the child is of the age of criminal responsibility, which at present is ten). Since a child under fourteen would not be liable, if Part I of the 1969 Act were fully in force, to be prosecuted for any offence, subsection (5) substitutes for the provision in s. 38(2) of the 1933 Act a provision that the child shall be treated for the purposes of Part I of the 1969 Act as guilty of an offence (paragraph 207). The result will be that he will be liable to care proceedings in juvenile courts under s. 1(2)(*f*) of the 1969 Act. Subsection (5) of the clause, like subsection (3), is drafted on the assumption that Part I of the 1969 Act will be fully in force when the clause is enacted, and will require adjustment if this is not the case.

Subsection (6) makes provision, consequential on subsection (2), in relation to a written statement of evidence by a child under fourteen made under s. 2 or 9 of the Criminal Justice Act 1967 (c. 80) or s. 27 of the Children and Young Persons Act 1963 (c. 37). These enactments provide for written statements to be admissible in evidence in certain cases subject to certain conditions. S. 2(1) and s. 9(1) of the 1967 Act provide that a written statement by a person shall be " admissible as evidence to the like extent as oral evidence to the like effect by that person "; and s. 27(1) of the 1963 Act provides that a statement by a child (under fourteen) shall be " admissible in evidence of any matter of which his oral testimony would be admissible ". As the admissibility of oral evidence by a child will in future depend on the child's fulfilling the conditions mentioned in clause 22(2), and as the court before which the written statement is tendered in evidence will not be able to judge whether the child did fulfil these conditions, subsection (6) provides that the admissibility of the statement shall be determined on the assumption that oral evidence by the child could be received under subsection (2). The clause does not include any requirement to ensure that the child did in fact fulfil these conditions, because ss. 2 and 9 of the 1967 Act and s. 27 of the 1963 Act contain adequate provisions for a party to object to the admissibility of the written statement.

Subsection (7) provides that, where the age of any person at any time is material for the purposes of any of the provisions of ss. 42 and 43 of the 1933 Act, his age shall for those purposes be deemed to be that which appears to the justice of the peace concerned (s. 42) or to the court (s. 43) to be his age at the time in question. S. 42, as it now stands, provides that, on a charge of any of certain offences against a child (under fourteen) or a young person (aged fourteen to sixteen), a justice of the peace, if satisfied on medical evidence that it would involve serious danger for the child or young person to attend before a magistrates' court for the purpose of committal proceedings, may take his deposition in writing on oath. S. 43 (which does not require amendment by the Bill) provides that, at a trial (on indictment) for any of these offences, if the court is satisfied as mentioned above that it would involve serious danger for the child or young person to attend at the trial, a deposition of the child or young person, whether taken in the ordinary way or as allowed by s. 42, shall be admissible in evidence subject to certain conditions. In consequence of the provision in clause 22(2) that a child's evidence shall be given unsworn, s. 42 is amended by clause 46(2) of, and Schedule 1 to, the Bill so that a deposition taken under s. 42 will have to be made on oath if made by a young person but not if made by a child. In order that the justice of the peace shall not have to require proof of the age of the deponent, clause 22(7) provides that for the purpose of s. 42 of the 1933 Act the deponent's age shall be deemed to be that which appears to the justice to be his age. The provision in clause 22(7) corresponds to that in clause 45(3) relating to the Bill generally. Clause 22(7) makes similar provision in relation to s. 43 of the 1933 Act.

CLAUSE 23 (GENERAL RULE, AND COURT'S DISCRETION, AS TO TIME AT WHICH EVIDENCE MAY BE CALLED AT TRIAL)

Subsection (1) gives statutory force to the rule of practice that any evidence given at the trial of a person, whether it is given for the prosecution or for the accused, should be given before the close of the party's case; but in view of the uncertainty, on the present authorities, as to when the court may allow a party to adduce evidence after the close of his case, the subsection makes the matter one for the discretion of the court (paragraphs 209–212). This is subject to the proviso, which provides that the accused shall not be allowed to give evidence after the close of his case unless he has done so in the course of that case (paragraph 212). The subsection is made subject to the provision in clause 3(6) enabling the prosecution to cross-examine a witness for the defence, or to adduce evidence after the conclusion of the case for the defence, about other conduct of the accused which is admissible under the earlier provisions of clause 3 if the court is satisfied that the admissibility of the evidence did not arise or become apparent before that stage. The saving in clause 23(1) for " any other enactment relating to the time when any evidence may be given " covers s. 11(4) of the Criminal Justice Act 1967, which allows evidence to disprove an alibi to be given before or after evidence is given in support of the alibi, or any other enactment which might give a right to adduce evidence at any particular stage.

Subsection (2) enables the court, in the exercise of its discretion under subsection (1), to allow evidence to be given at any time before the delivery of the verdict or the decision of the magistrates' court. This is a change from the existing law so far at least as trials on indictment are concerned (paragraphs 213–216).

Subsection (3) provides that, if at a trial the court has indicated that it will exercise its discretion under the clause so as to allow a party to adduce evidence after the close of his case, any person who, after the court has given this indication, gives evidence on behalf of any other party may be cross-examined about the matter, whether he gives evidence before or after the postponed evidence is given. The subsection is included for the sake of convenience at the trial. If, for example, the court indicates that it will allow the prosecution to call a witness after the conclusion of their case to give evidence on a particular topic about which evidence has not previously been given (perhaps because the witness was not available earlier or the matter arose unexpectedly), it will naturally be convenient that the intervening witnesses who can speak to the matter should be able to be cross-examined about it. But owing to the rule of practice confining cross-examination to questions relevant at the time, the court might be obliged, in the absence of the subsection, to prevent the cross-examination on the ground that, unless and until the postponed witness is called, it is impossible to tell whether the cross-examination is relevant. The subsection will enable the intervening witnesses to be cross-examined about the topic in question at the time when they are called instead of having to be recalled for the purpose after the late evidence has been given.

Subsection (4) provides that the power of the court to call a witness (where exercisable in criminal trials) shall be exercisable up to the same time as that up to which the court will be able under the clause to allow evidence to be given on behalf of a party.

CLAUSE 24 (CONVICTION AS EVIDENCE OF COMMISSION OF OFFENCE BY PERSON OTHER THAN THE ACCUSED)

Clause 24 provides that evidence that a person other than the accused has been convicted of an offence shall be admissible for the purpose of proving that the other committed the offence when this is relevant to an issue in the proceedings against the accused. The effect will be to abolish the rule in *Hollington v. Hewthorn*[1] in its application to criminal proceedings. The clause corresponds to part of s. 11 of the Civil Evidence Act 1968, which abolishes the rule for civil proceedings (paragraphs 217–219). (Provisions corresponding to other parts of s. 11 are in clauses 25 and 45.) The admissibility of convictions of the accused himself will depend on clauses 3(3) and (5), 6 and 7(2).

Subsection (1) provides that the fact that a person other than the accused has been convicted of an offence shall be admissible for the purpose of proving that the other committed the offence of which he was convicted if proof of this is relevant to an issue in the proceedings against the accused (paragraph 218). For example, if A is charged with handling goods stolen by B, evidence that B was convicted of stealing the goods will be admissible in order to prove that they were stolen. Convictions are limited to convictions in the United Kingdom or by a court-martial for the same reason as under clause 3(3) and (5). The words at the end of subsection (1) providing that a person's conviction of an offence shall be admissible " whether or not any other evidence of his having committed that offence is given " are included for the sake of conformity with clause 3(5) and contrast with clause 3(3).

Subsection (2) provides that, where a conviction is proved under subsection (1), the person convicted shall be taken to have committed the offence " unless the contrary is proved " (paragraph 218). But the subsection also provides that clause 8 shall not have effect in relation to the subsection. This is in order that the burden on the defence of disproving the correctness of a conviction which is admissible under clause 24 shall be a persuasive one (to disprove this on a balance of probabilities) as opposed to an evidential one (to adduce evidence sufficient to raise the issue whether the person in question was rightly convicted) (paragraph 219(i)).

Subsection (3) contains two savings. *Paragraph (a)* provides that nothing in the clause shall prejudice the admissibility of any conviction which would be admissible apart from the clause. For example, if a person other than the accused has given evidence and been asked in cross-examination about a previous conviction as allowed by clause 10 but denies it, evidence of the conviction will be able to be given under clause 14. Again, the fact that a person has been convicted of an offence may be directly relevant apart from the fact that he committed it. Thus, a person might be charged with an offence of deception involving a pretence that somebody else had a blameless record, and the prosecution might wish to prove that the accused knew that

---

[1] [1943] K.B. 587.

the other person had been convicted of an offence of dishonesty. *Paragraph* (*b*) provides that nothing in the clause shall prejudice the operation of any enactment whereby a conviction or a finding of fact is made conclusive for the purpose of any other proceedings. The committee have not in mind any public or general enactment under which a conviction or finding of fact is conclusive for the purpose of criminal proceedings; but the saving is included because there may be such provisions in existing local and private enactments or in future public enactments and because there is a similar saving in relation to civil proceedings in s. 11(3) of the Civil Evidence Act 1968.

Subsection (*4*) applies the provisions of clause 25 for the purposes of clause 24. The note on clause 25 refers.

CLAUSE 25 (PROVISIONS SUPPLEMENTARY TO SS.3 AND 24)

Clause 25 contains (as mentioned briefly in paragraph 220) various provisions supplementary to clauses 3 and 24. It corresponds to part of s. 11 of the Civil Evidence Act 1968. The reason why the clause applies only to convictions admissible under clause 3 or clause 24 is that the main purpose of clause 25 is to make certain documents admissible to show the facts of the offence to which the conviction which it is claimed is admissible under clause 3 or 24 relates. Without information about the facts of the offence to which the conviction relates it may be impossible to tell whether the fact that the person in question committed it is or is not relevant. Although the facts of an offence may sometimes be material in relation to a conviction which it is claimed is admissible under clause 6, 7 or 10, this will ordinarily not be so, and it is therefore unnecessary to make any special provision for the admissibility of documents in order to show the facts of an offence to which the conviction relates. The Bill follows the present law in not making general provision for the admissibility of documents showing the facts of an offence when a conviction of the offence may be admissible in evidence (for example, when the accused may be questioned under s. 1(*f*)(ii) of the Criminal Evidence Act 1898).

Subsection (*1*) provides that for the purposes mentioned above the contents of any document which is admissible as evidence of the conviction, and the contents of the relevant information, complaint, indictment or charge-sheet, shall be admissible. The reference to a " complaint " is for the purpose of Scottish convictions and that to a " charge-sheet " is for that of convictions by court-martial. The saving for the possibility of " other admissible evidence " will, for example, allow for a case where oral or other evidence is given of the proceedings at the trial which resulted in the conviction.

Subsection (*2*) provides for the admissibility of duly certified copies of documents admissible under subsection (1).

Subsection (*3*) provides that certain enactments under which a conviction leading to probation or discharge is to be disregarded shall not affect the operation of clause 3 or 24. The purpose of the enactments overridden is to prevent the convictions from counting as part of the accused's criminal record in the sense of making it likely that he will be punished more severely on account of them for later offences; but subsection (3), like s. 11(5) of the Civil Evidence Act 1968, ensures that the convictions will be admissible for the evidentiary purposes specified.

233

Subsection (*4*) limits the admissibility of convictions under clause 3 or 24 to subsisting convictions (so as to exclude convictions quashed on appeal or cancelled by means of a free pardon).

CLAUSE 26 (MANNER IN WHICH CERTAIN UNITED KINGDOM CONVICTIONS AND ACQUITTALS MAY BE PROVED)

Clause 26 is (as mentioned briefly in paragraph 220) a modernized provision for the proof of convictions or acquittals. It supersedes the provisions in s. 13 of the Evidence Act 1851 (c. 99), s. 6 of the Criminal Procedure Act 1865 (c. 18) and s. 18 of the Prevention of Crimes Act 1871 (c. 112).

Subsections (*1*), (*2*) and (*3*) provide that the fact that a person has in the United Kingdom been convicted or acquitted of an offence otherwise than by a court-martial (which for this purpose includes a naval disciplinary court: clause 45(1)) may be proved by means of a certificate purporting to be duly signed by the appropriate officer of the court, together with evidence identifying the person named in the certificate as the person whose conviction or acquittal is to be proved. The clause does not provide for proof of convictions by courts-martial or naval disciplinary courts, because convictions by courts-martial can be proved in any court, including civilian criminal courts, under s. 200 of the Army Act 1955 (c. 18), s. 200 of the Air Force Act 1955 (c. 19) and s. 129C of the Naval Discipline Act 1957 (c. 53) and convictions by naval disciplinary courts will be able to be proved under s. 129C of the 1957 Act as amended by clause 46(1) of the draft Bill. The provisions in subsections (2) and (3) as to the contents and proof of certificates and as to the person to sign them follow s. 199(3) and (4) of the Army Act 1955.

Subsection (*4*) contains a saving for any other " authorised manner " of proving a conviction or acquittal. This includes evidence by a person present in court, proof by means of finger-prints under s. 39 of the Criminal Justice Act 1948, a written statement under s. 2 or 9 of the Criminal Justice Act 1967 or an admission under s. 10 of the 1967 Act.

CLAUSE 27 (INSTITUTION OF PROCEEDINGS FOR PERJURY ETC.)

Clause 27 provides that proceedings for perjury in judicial proceedings or certain kindred offences shall require the authority of the Director of Public Prosecutions (paragraph 221). The offences are the same as those to which the requirement of corroboration in s. 13 of the Perjury Act 1911 is to be limited by clause 18. These are mentioned in the note on clause 18. In consequence of the restriction on prosecutions the clause also abolishes the power conferred by s. 9 of the 1911 Act on judges and certain other authorities to direct a prosecution for perjury.

CLAUSE 28 (DUTY OF MAGISTRATES' COURTS TO HAVE REGARD TO ENACTMENTS ABOUT WARNINGS TO JURIES)

Clause 28 contains a declaration of the duty of a magistrates' court at a summary trial to have regard to all such enactments as would or might in comparable circumstances at a trial on indictment require the court to warn the jury of a special need for caution before convicting (paragraph 222). The effect will be that the magistrates should (as at present) consider whether, had the trial been on indictment, the court would have to give the warning, and, if so, that they should direct themselves accordingly. The relevant provisions are in clauses 17(1), 20(1) and 21.

CLAUSE 29 (ABOLITION OF RIGHT TO MAKE EVIDENCE OF DOCUMENT CALLED FOR AND INSPECTED BY AN OPPONENT)

Clause 29 abolishes the rule in *Stroud v. Stroud*[1] so far as it applies to criminal proceedings. This is the rule that, where party A calls for a document in the possession of party B and B produces the document without putting it in evidence, and A reads it, B can require A to put it in evidence (paragraph 223).

PART II

HEARSAY EVIDENCE

CLAUSE 30 (HEARSAY EVIDENCE TO BE ADMISSIBLE ONLY BY VIRTUE OF THIS ACT AND OTHER STATUTORY PROVISIONS OR CERTAIN RULES OF LAW)

Clause 30 provides that a statement other than one made by a person while giving oral evidence shall be admissible as evidence of any fact stated in it only to the extent that the statement is admissible by virtue of (i) a provision in the Bill, (ii) any other statutory provision (defined in *subsection (2)* so as to include statutory instruments) or (iii) any of the common law rules mentioned in clause 40 (paragraphs 236(vi), 248). By referring to a " statement other than one made by a person while giving oral evidence " the clause covers previous statements made by a person who gives evidence in the proceedings in question as well as statements made by a person who does not (cf. paragraphs 225, 226(i)). In future an out-of-court statement, in order to be admissible as evidence of the facts stated in it, will have to come under one of these heads; and it will be necessary to ascertain under which head it comes, because admissibility by virtue of a clause in the Bill will depend on fulfilment of the requirements stated in the Bill which are applicable to that clause, and similarly in the case of admissibility by virtue of other statutory provisions. Admissibility under the Bill will be mostly under Part II; but in some cases it will be under other provisions, including the case of confessions admissible on behalf of the prosecution under clause 2. Examples of statements admissible by virtue of a statutory provision outside the Bill are written statements admissible under s. 2 or s. 9 of the Criminal Justice Act 1967 (c. 80) and the many kinds of certificates admissible under various enactments relating to particular subjects. By limiting admissibility as mentioned the clause excludes any question of admissibility by virtue of a common law rule other than one mentioned in clause 40 (paragraph 248). For example, all the common law as to admissibility of statements by deceased persons (including dying declarations) will be swept away. Notes on some of the common law rules preserved by clause 40 are given in the note on that clause.

The scheme of clauses 30–40 corresponds to that of ss. 1–9 of the Civil Evidence Act 1968 (c. 64) except that the Act gave quasi-statutory force to the previous common law rules mentioned in s. 9, whereas the Bill preserves the rules mentioned in clause 40 as common law rules. The reason for this difference is that the Act draws certain distinctions between some of the

---

[1] [1963] 3 All E.R. 539.

common law rules which it converts into statutory rules. In particular, it makes the admissibility of statements under some of them subject to the notice and counter-notice procedure provided by the Act, in so far as the statements also fall under provisions of the Act to which that procedure applies. These and other complications which had to be included in s. 9 of the Act are unnecessary for the Bill, because the common law rules which necessitated the complications in the Act are of limited or doubtful application to criminal cases. Therefore the Bill simply leaves the preserved common law rules as they are pending codification of the law of evidence. The clause also differs from s. 1 of the Act in not providing specifically for admissibility of a hearsay statement " by agreement of the parties ". This is because admissibility by agreement is provided for by another " provision of this Act ". This is clause 38, which imposes certain restrictions on admissibility in criminal proceedings which do not apply to civil proceedings.

CLAUSE 31 (ADMISSIBILITY OF OUT-OF-COURT STATEMENTS AS EVIDENCE OF FACTS STATED)

Clause 31 makes a first-hand out-of-court statement admissible as evidence of the facts stated in it provided that the maker of the statement is called as a witness or the party desiring to give the statement in evidence is unable for a reason specified in the clause to call the maker. The clause corresponds generally to s. 2 of the Civil Evidence Act 1968, but with substantial differences which are mainly owing to the differences between civil and criminal proceedings.

Subsection (1) contains the main provision that an out-of-court statement made by a person, whether orally or in a document or otherwise[1], shall, if certain conditions are fulfilled, be admissible as evidence of any fact stated in it of which direct oral evidence by that person would be admissible. The conditions are that the maker has been, or is to be[2], called as a witness (*paragraph (a)*), that he is compellable as a witness but refuses (in court) to be sworn (*paragraph (b)*) or that it is shown that he is dead or cannot be called for any of the other reasons specified in *paragraph (c)* (paragraphs 236(i), 249). The principle is that the party desiring to give the statement in evidence should either call the maker or show why he cannot call him (paragraph 238(ii)). Admissibility is to be subject to the provisions in the later subsections of the clause, to the provisions of clause 2 preventing the prosecution from giving in evidence a confession obtained in the ways mentioned in that clause[3] and to the restrictions imposed by clause 32. The provisions of paragraphs (*b*) and (*c*) specifying the cases in which a party is to be able to give a statement in evidence on account of being unable to call the maker correspond generally to the provisions of s. 8(2)(*b*) ·of the Civil Evidence Act 1968 specifying the cases in which a party to civil proceedings who has received notice of another party's desire to put a statement in evidence is not allowed to require the

---

[1] As to " or otherwise " see the note on subsection (5).

[2] Subsection (3) provides that, if a statement has been received in evidence on the footing that the maker is to be called as a witness, but the maker is not called, the statement shall be disregarded.

[3] As to the relation between clauses 2 and 31, see the last two sentences of the note on clause 2(2).

latter party to call the maker of the statement as a witness[1]; but paragraphs (*b*) and (*c*)(iii) in the Bill have no counterparts in the Act. Paragraph (*c*)(iii), by providing for where the maker of the statement is competent but not compellable on behalf of the party desiring to give the statement in evidence, takes account of the special rules in criminal proceedings which restrict the possibility of calling the accused or his spouse as a witness. It thus covers the case where one accused wishes to give in evidence a statement made by a co-accused or by the spouse of the latter, and it also covers the case where the maker cannot be compelled to give evidence because he has diplomatic or similar immunity from legal process. The clause (unlike clause 34, in the case of records) does not follow the Civil Evidence Act in providing for the case where the maker of the statement cannot reasonably be expected to have any recollection of the matters to which the statement relates. In this case it will be for the party desiring to give the statement in evidence to call the maker, when the party will be able to give his statement in evidence under paragraph (*a*). Unless the statement is a written one amounting to a proof of evidence (when clause 32(3) will apply), there will be no legal obstacle to calling the maker and giving his statement in evidence instead of questioning him with a view to his giving oral evidence about the facts dealt with in the statement; but no doubt the party will try to get the witness to give oral evidence about these facts, in so far as the witness is able to do so, as otherwise the value of the out-of-court statement will be impaired.

Subsection (2) enables the prosecution to give in evidence an out-of-court statement made by one of a number of accused persons and provides that it shall be admissible as evidence of any fact stated in it in relation to each of the accused (paragraphs 236 (last sentence), 251–252). The subsection follows the principle underlying the clause in that the prosecution cannot call the maker of the statement as a witness. It is also, like subsection (1), subject to the provisions in clause 2 restricting the admissibility of a confession when tendered by the prosecution. The express provision that the statement, if admissible, is to be admissible " in relation to each of the accused " is included in order to make it absolutely clear that the subsection overrides the present rule that a confession by one of a number of accused persons is admissible only against the maker.

Subsection (3) provides for the possibility that an out-of-court statement has been received in evidence on behalf of a party under subsection (1)(*a*) on the footing that the party is going to call the maker as a witness but for some reason the maker is not called. Subsection (1)(*a*) makes the intention to call the maker, in addition to his actually being called, a ground of admissibility because it may be convenient for the statement to be received before the maker is called; but subsection (3) provides that, if the maker is not called, the statement shall be disregarded. The situation where the fact that a statement was made is conditionally admissible in evidence, so that evidence of it is given but, if the condition is not fulfilled, the statement has to be disregarded, is one which may arise under the present law (for example, in relation to a statement made in the presence of the accused), and no difficulty seems

---

[1] They also correspond broadly to the conditions specified in the proviso to s. 1(1) of the Evidence Act 1938 (c. 28) (which section was repealed by the 1968 Act) and to s. 1(1)(*b*) of the Criminal Evidence Act 1965 (c. 20) (which is repealed by the draft Bill).

likely to arise from the requirement in subsection (3) to disregard a statement in the circumstances mentioned.

Subsection (*4*) provides for a case where a deposition of a child or young person is received in evidence under s. 43 of the Children and Young Persons Act 1933 (c. 12) and it is also desired to give in evidence an out-of-court statement (other than the deposition) made by the child or young person. S. 43 provides that at a trial for any of certain offences the deposition of a child or young person shall, subject to certain conditions, be admissible in evidence if the court is satisfied (on medical evidence) that the attendance before the court of the child or young person would " involve serious danger to his life or health ". The condition described in the words quoted differs a little from the condition in clause 31(1)(*c*)(i) that the maker of the statement should be shown to be " unfit by reason of his bodily or mental condition to attend as a witness "; for the basis of s. 43 is that the attendance of the child or young person would do him harm, while the basis of clause 31(1)(*c*)(i) is that the maker of the statement is unfit to attend. Subsection (3) of clause 31 therefore extends subsection (1)(*c*)(i) to this case in relation to statements outside the deposition, leaving s. 43 of the 1933 Act to govern the admissibility of the deposition. The clause makes no corresponding provision in respect of a case where a deposition is received in committal proceedings under s. 41 of the Magistrates' Courts Act 1952 (c. 55) on the ground that the maker is " dangerously ill and unlikely to recover " or is received at the trial under s. 6 of the Criminal Law Amendment Act 1867 (c. 35) on the ground that " there is no reasonable probability that [the deponent] will ever be able to travel or to give evidence ". This is because in these cases the condition in clause 31(1)(*c*)(i) that the person in question is " unfit by reason of his bodily or mental condition to attend as a witness " is necessarily satisfied. Nor is any provision made in respect of the special rule made by s. 27 of the Children and Young Persons Act 1963 (c. 37) as to the evidence of children in committal proceedings for sexual offences. S. 27 provides that, subject to certain exceptions, a child shall not be called as a witness for the prosecution in these cases but that a statement in writing by the child shall be admissible instead. To enable the prosecution to give in evidence an oral statement by the child in addition to his written statement would be contrary to the basis of the section; and the section does not prevent the defence from calling the child.

Subsection (*5*) is the provision which in general excludes second-hand hearsay from admissibility under the clause (paragraphs 237(i), 244, 253). The subsection provides that, where a statement made " otherwise than in a document " is admissible under the clause, no evidence other than direct oral evidence by the maker or any person who heard or otherwise perceived it being made shall be admissible for the purpose of proving it. In most cases a statement made " otherwise than in a document " will have been made orally, but it might have been made, for example, by sign language or by nodding in reply to a question. For convenience, in what follows, it will be assumed that any non-written statement has been made orally. The effect of the subsection is that, if A makes an oral statement that, for example, the number of a car which he has just seen involved in an accident was XYZ1, and it is desired to prove that A said this, it will be necessary to do so by oral evidence of A or of somebody (B) who heard him say it. It will not be possible to call C to give evidence that he heard B say that A made the statement. Nor will a written statement by B that he heard A make the statement be admissible, because, although B's statement was made in a document, it is only with A's statement, and not with B's, that the clause is concerned[1]. B's written statement will not be admissible as evidence of the number of the car because B, not having seen the number, could not give oral evidence of it. But if A has written down the number, the subsection will not apply and (provided that the conditions laid down in the clause as to A's being called or as to its being impossible to call him are satisfied) any evidence sufficient to establish that A in fact wrote down the number will be admissible for the purpose of proving what it was. The subsection provides also that nothing in s. 2 or 9 of the Criminal Justice Act 1967 (c. 80) (or in any other enactment passed before the new Act) shall render a written statement admissible for the purpose of proving the making of the oral statement. This provision is included because s. 9(1) (for example) provides that (subject to certain conditions) " a written statement by any person shall . . . be admissible as evidence to the like extent as oral evidence to the like effect by that person ", and this might have had the effect of making admissible a written statement by B that he heard A say the number of the car. The proviso makes an exception for oral evidence given in previous legal proceedings, because in this case there is likely to be reliable evidence (as the result of a shorthand note or otherwise) of what the person who gave evidence said in doing so (paragraph 253). By providing that the fact that the evidence was given may be proved " in any manner authorised by the court " the proviso will enable the court to allow a transcript of the evidence to be read. It will also enable the court, as a condition of giving its authority, to require the party concerned to read all the relevant part of the evidence. The subsection corresponds to s. 2(3) of the Civil Evidence Act.

Subsection (6) is a clarificatory provision. It provides that, if A has made an oral statement in the hearing of B, and B reduces it or its substance into writing at A's instance at the time or reasonably soon afterwards, the resulting statement is to be treated as having been made in the document by A. Whether a documentary statement is to be treated as made by somebody from whose oral statement the document was drawn up is a question which may be important for the purposes of clause 31 (in particular, for that of the provision in subsection (5) restricting the admissibility of a statement made " otherwise than in a document ") and for the purposes of provisions in other clauses (mentioned in subsection (6)) which depend on some factor special to the maker of a statement. The reasons for including subsection (6), and its effect, are discussed in paragraphs 254–255; and in paragraph 255 it is mentioned that even without the subsection the clause would very probably be construed in the way provided by the subsection. The requirement that B should have reduced A's statement into writing " at the instance " of A is not intended to impose a strict test: the provision is intended to cover any case where B has acted on a request, express or implied, or a mere hint, but to exclude a case where B has merely written down of his own motion something which he has overheard. The words at the end of the subsection providing that the statement in the document shall be treated as having been made in it by

---

[1] This is subject to what is said below in relation to subsection (6).

the maker of the oral statement " whether or not it would be so treated apart from this subsection" are included in order to make it clear that the subsection is intended to provide for the special kind of case described in it and is not intended to cover all the circumstances in which a written statement embodying the contents of an oral statement is to be treated as having been made by the maker of the oral statement (for example, where he has expressly adopted the written statement as his). Nor is the subsection intended to throw any doubt on the proposition that an oral statement mechanically recorded, even without the maker's knowledge that this is being done, is to be treated as having been made by him in the document consisting of the tape or other device in which the statement is recorded (see the definition of " document " in clause 41(1)).

CLAUSE 32 (RESTRICTIONS ON ADMISSIBILITY OF STATEMENTS BY VIRTUE OF S. 31)

Subsection (1) restricts the admissibility of a statement made after the accused, or any of them, has been charged with the offence, has been officially informed that he might be prosecuted for it or has been served with a summons in respect of it (paragraphs 237(iv), 240–242, 256). A statement made after any of these happenings will not be admissible on the ground that the maker is absent abroad, non-compellable as a witness, impossible to identify or impossible to find or that, though compellable as a witness, he refuses to be sworn. " Officially informed " is defined in subsection (1) so as to apply to police officers and the other persons mentioned in clause 1(2) in relation to official questioning. The restriction will apply to a statement made after the time when any of the things mentioned has been done in relation to any of the accused, because otherwise the charging of one suspect might prompt an associate to arrange for a false statement to be made exculpating one or both. The provision in *paragraph (c)* to exclude a statement made after the accused was served with a summons may involve revision of Rule 82(2) of the Magistrates' Courts Rules 1968, under which a summons served otherwise than personally is in certain circumstances to be treated as not having been served unless it is proved that it came to the knowledge of the person to be served.

Subsection (2) restricts the right of the prosecution to give in evidence an out-of-court statement made by the wife or husband of the accused (paragraphs 237(v), 245, 252, 256). A statement by (say) the wife is not to be admissible on behalf of the prosecution on the ground that the wife gives or is to give evidence unless she in fact gives evidence for the prosecution; and her statement is not to be admissible on behalf of the prosecution on the ground that she is dead or that it is otherwise impossible for the prosecution to call her unless she is, or would if living have been, compellable for the prosecution under clause 9. The restriction by which the right of the prosecution to give in evidence a previous statement made by a wife who is called as a witness at the trial is to be limited to where she is called by the prosecution is a restriction which will have little application in practice. For the more usual situation will be that the wife is called by the defence and the prosecution wish to contradict her evidence by means of a previous statement which she has made inconsistent with her evidence; and they will be able to do this under clause 12 or 13 without any restriction on account of her being the accused's wife.

The restriction will, however, apply to the occasional case where the prosecution might have wished to give in evidence a statement by the wife not contradictory of anything which she had said when giving evidence in court. The provision that, in a case where the wife does not give evidence, the prosecution may give her statement in evidence only if she is compellable for the prosecution is the more important one. It will apply, for example, where she has made a statement damaging to her husband but is not called as a witness. The restriction will apply only if the parties are still married at the time of the proceedings or, in a case where the wife has died, if they were still married at the time of her death. The restriction will not affect the right of the prosecution under clause 31(2) to give in evidence a statement made by the wife if she is charged jointly with her husband (paragraph 252). There will be no restriction on the right of co-accused A to give in evidence a statement by the wife of co-accused B whether or not she is compellable for A.

Subsection (3) makes it necessary to obtain the leave of the court before giving in evidence a statement contained in a document which is in the nature of a proof of evidence if the person whose proof it is has been or is to be called as a witness in the proceedings in question. It also provides that the court shall not give leave unless it is of the opinion that in the circumstances " it is in the interests of justice for the witness's oral evidence to be supplemented by the reception of that statement or for the statement to be received as evidence of any matter about which he is unable or unwilling to give oral evidence " (paragraphs 237(ii), 239, 256). By requiring the leave of the court in a case where the party wishing to give the statement in evidence has not yet called the maker as a witness but intends to call him the subsection prevents the possibility that a party might say that he intends to call the maker and might argue that his intention to do so entitles him to give the statement in evidence immediately. It will be for the court to determine whether the document is in the nature of a proof of evidence within the principle of the subsection. The subsection corresponds very generally to s. 2(2) of the Civil Evidence Act 1968, but it is limited to proofs, so that (for example) leave will not be necessary in order that the witness may give evidence that he made a previous statement. The clause does not reproduce the provision in s. 2(2)(*b*) of the Act that, with two exceptions, the court may not give leave for the statement to be given in evidence until the conclusion of the witness's examination-in-chief; but the court will be able, in giving leave, to postpone the giving of the statement in evidence till this stage if it thinks fit. Clause 32(3) also differs from s. 2(2) in that the restriction on the right to give evidence of the witness's previous statement applies to all parties and not merely to the party calling the witness. This is because otherwise, where a witness called by co-accused A has failed to come up to his proof and the court has refused leave for the proof to be put in by A, co-accused B could put it in as of right under clause 31(1)(*a*).

Subsections (4)–(6) provide that, at a trial on indictment, a statement shall not be admissible, without the leave of the court, on the ground that the maker is dead or that it is otherwise impossible to call him unless the party seeking to give the statement in evidence has served notice of his intention to do so on the other parties within seven days of the end of the committal proceedings (paragraphs 237(iii), 240–242, 256). If the trial was to begin earlier than this, the court would no doubt give leave or else adjourn the trial. The particulars to be included in the notice are specified in subsection (5). These are designed to enable the other parties to verify the reason why the maker of the statement cannot be called as a witness and the truth of the statement. The provision in *paragraph (c)*(ii) for a case where it is desired to give in evidence a statement contained in a document, and the maker of the document is not the same person as the maker of the statement, relates to the situation provided for by çlause 31(6) where an oral statement made by A is reduced into writing by B. In this case it may be important for another party to check the reliability of B as well as that of A. Subsection (6) provides for the methods by which a notice may be served and is in exactly similar terms to s. 9(8) of the Criminal Justice Act 1967, which relates to the service of a notice of intention to tender a written statement in evidence. The requirements in subsections (4)–(6) of the clause do not apply to summary trials (paragraph 256).

CLAUSE 33 (WITNESS'S PREVIOUS STATEMENT, IF PROVED, TO BE EVIDENCE OF FACTS STATED)

Subsection (1) provides that, where a previous inconsistent statement made by a person called as a witness in the proceedings in question is proved by virtue of clause 12 or 13, or where a previous statement of his is proved (by virtue of the common law) for the purpose of rebutting a suggestion that his evidence given at the proceedings has been fabricated, then the previous statement shall be admissible as evidence of any fact stated in it of which direct oral evidence by the witness would be admissible. The purpose (as mentioned in paragraphs 232 and 257) is to get rid of the complication in the present law that a previous statement by a witness may be admissible for certain purposes but not as evidence of the facts stated in it. It is well established that, when a previous statement is proved under the Criminal Procedure Act 1865 (c. 18), it is not evidence of the facts stated in it but only evidence to neutralize the evidence given in court. The status of a previous statement admitted in order to rebut a suggestion of fabrication is not clear. The subsection corresponds to s. 3(1) of the Civil Evidence Act 1968. (S. 3(1) refers to ss. 3, 4 and 5 of the 1865 Act, which apply to civil as well as criminal proceedings and are replaced, so far as is relevant for the purpose of clause 33, by clauses 12 and 13 of the Bill.) Subsection (1) of clause 33 provides expressly that admissibility shall be by virtue of the subsection, so that the conditions and restrictions in clauses 31 and 32 will not apply.

Subsection (2) provides that nothing in the Act shall affect the common law rules relating to the circumstances in which, when a witness is cross-examined on a document used by him to refresh his memory, the document may be made evidence in the proceedings, but that, if a document or part of it is made evidence in this way, it shall be admissible as evidence of any fact stated in it (as with the documents to which subsection (1) applies). The common law rule referred to is, approximately, that, if the party cross-examining a witness from a document which the witness has used to refresh his memory goes beyond the parts which the witness has used for this purpose, the opponent has the right to require that the document should be treated as evidence[1]. There is no authority on whether a statement in a document

---

[1] *Senat v. Senat*, [1965] P. 172, 177.

used in this way becomes evidence of the facts stated in it; but, in accordance with the principle of subsection (1), subsection (2) provides that it shall do so. The subsection is similar to s. 3(2) of the Civil Evidence Act 1968.

CLAUSE 34 (ADMISSIBILITY OF CERTAIN RECORDS AS EVIDENCE OF FACTS STATED)

Clause 34 provides for the admissibility of evidence contained in records (paragraphs 236(ii), 237(ii), (iv), 258). The clause corresponds to s. 4 of the Civil Evidence Act 1968, but with the important differences mentioned in paragraph 258, which summarizes the provisions of the clause. It supersedes the Criminal Evidence Act 1965 (c. 20) (paragraph 233).

Subsection (1) provides that a statement contained in a document shall be admissible as evidence of any fact stated in it of which direct oral evidence would be admissible if (a) the document is or forms part of a record compiled as mentioned below and (b) the person who originally supplied the information from which the record was compiled is (or is to be) called, or cannot for a reason to be mentioned be called, as a witness. As to (a), the requirements are that (i) the person who originally supplied the information must be a person who had, or may reasonably be supposed to have had, personal knowledge of the matters dealt with in the information, (ii) the person who compiled the record must in doing so have been acting under a duty ("acting under a duty " being given a wide meaning in this connection by subsection (6)) and (iii) either the informant must have supplied the information directly to the compiler of the record or any intermediaries through whom it was supplied must in passing on the information have been acting under a duty. It will not be necessary that the original informant should have been acting under a duty when giving the information to the compiler of the record or to the intermediary. For example, if a person voluntarily gives information to a policeman, and the policeman passes it on in the form of a message to the police station, where an officer on duty records it, the entry in the record will be admissible. The requirement mentioned in (b) above will be referred to under subsection (2). Subsection (1) does not include any requirement corresponding to the requirement in clause 31(1) that the fact contained in the statement must be one of which direct oral evidence *by the maker of the statement* would be admissible. This is because the same effect is secured by the requirement that the person who originally supplied the information contained in the record must be a person who had, or may reasonably be supposed to have had, personal knowledge of the matters dealt with in it. It is therefore unnecessary to provide that the statement should be one of which direct oral evidence *by the supplier of the information* would be admissible; and the possibility that the supplier might have been a person incompetent to give evidence is too remote to be worth taking into account (especially having regard to the provisions of clause 36(4) about the weight to be attached to statements).

Subsection (2) specifies the conditions for admissibility referred to in (b) in the note above on subsection (1) as to the calling of the person who supplied the information or as to its being impossible to call him. The conditions are similar to those specified in clause 31(1) in relation to statements not contained

243

in records except that clause 34(2)(*c*)(vi) gives the extra ground that " having regard to the time which has elapsed since [the supplier] supplied the information and to all the circumstances, he cannot reasonably be expected to have any recollection of the matters dealt with in the statement".

Subsection (3) provides that the provisions of clause 31(3), as to the situation when a statement has been received in evidence under that clause on the footing that the maker is to be called as a witness but the maker is then not called, shall apply to the corresponding situation where a statement in a record has been received in evidence under clause 34 on the footing that the original supplier of the information in it is to be called as a witness but the supplier is then not called. The note on clause 31(3) refers.

Subsection (4) restricts the admissibility of a statement contained in a record if the person who originally supplied the information did so after the accused, or any of them, had been charged with the offence, had been officially informed that he might be prosecuted for it or had been served with a summons in respect of it (paragraphs 237(iv), 258). The subsection corresponds to clause 32(1). A statement made after any of the happenings mentioned will not be admissible on the ground that the person who originally supplied the information is absent abroad, non-compellable as a witness, impossible to identify or impossible to find or that, though compellable as a witness, he refuses to be sworn. There is no similar restriction in respect of a case where the ground for admissibility is that the supplier cannot reasonably be expected to have any recollection of the matters dealt with in the information. In view of the purpose for which the restriction is proposed (avoiding the danger of concocted statements) it seems unnecessary to extend the restriction to admissibility on the ground mentioned.

Subsection (5) provides that, in a case where a document containing a record such as mentioned in the clause is in the nature of a proof of evidence, and the person who originally supplied the information has been or is to be called as a witness, the statement in the record shall not be given in evidence without the leave of the court (paragraphs 237(ii), 258). The subsection corresponds to clause 32(3), and the same restrictions as to the giving of leave are to apply as in the latter provision.

Subsection (6) gives a partial definition of the reference to " acting under a duty " for the purpose of the requirement that the original supplier of the information, or the intermediary between him and the compiler of the record, should have been " acting under a duty ". The subsection provides that this should include " acting in the course of any trade, business, profession or other occupation . . . or for the purposes of any paid or unpaid office ". This is because admissibility under the clause is based on the idea that the compiler or intermediary should have been acting in some official or quasi-official capacity and not merely for personal or other private purposes. In particular, the definition will ensure that the clause will apply to records kept by the owner of a " one-man company ", who without the definition might not be regarded as acting under a " duty ". The definition is not inclusive, so that it will be open to the courts to give a wide meaning to the concept in other respects as well.

244

CLAUSE 35 (ADMISSIBILITY OF STATEMENTS PRODUCED BY COMPUTERS)

Clause 35 makes information derived from computers admissible subject to the conditions specified (paragraphs 236(iii), 259). The requirements are summarized in paragraph 259, where it is mentioned that the clause is similar to s. 5 of the Civil Evidence Act 1968 except in the respect mentioned. *Subsection* (6), which penalizes the intentional giving of a false certificate as to the working of a computer or otherwise as to the conditions on which admissibility is to depend, corresponds to s. 6(5) of the Act.

CLAUSE 36 (PROVISIONS SUPPLEMENTARY TO SS. 31 TO 35)

Clause 36 contains a number of supplementary provisions, mostly corresponding to s. 6 of the Civil Evidence Act 1968 (paragraph 260).

Subsection (1) provides that a statement contained in a document and admissible under clause 31, 34 or 35 may be proved by the production of the document or by the production of a copy authenticated in such manner as the court may approve. The subsection is similar to s. 6(1) of the Civil Evidence Act.

Subsection (2) provides that, for the purpose of deciding whether a statement is admissible under the provisions mentioned above, the court may draw any reasonable inference from the circumstances in which the statement was made, including the form and contents of a document in which the statement is contained. The subsection is similar to s. 6(2) of the Civil Evidence Act, and there is a corresponding provision in s. 1(2) of the Criminal Evidence Act 1965.

Subsection (3) adapts the references in clauses 31(1)(*b*) and 34(2)(*b*) to refusing to be sworn so that, in the case of a child, they will apply to refusing to give evidence. The subsection corresponds to the first part of clause 22(3).

Subsection (4) provides that in estimating the weight, if any, to be attached to a statement admissible under clause 31, 33, 34 or 35 regard shall be had to all the circumstances and in particular to contemporaneity or otherwise and to the question whether any person who was in a position to do so had any incentive to conceal or misrepresent the facts. The subsection corresponds to s. 6(3) of the Civil Evidence Act and to s. 1(3) of the Criminal Evidence Act 1965.

Subsection (5) provides that, for the purpose of any enactment requiring evidence to be corroborated or regulating the manner in which uncorroborated evidence is to be treated, a statement admissible under clause 31 or 33 shall not be capable of corroborating evidence given by the maker and a statement admissible under clause 34 shall not be capable of corroborating evidence given by the supplier of the information. The subsection is similar (except in the respect mentioned below) to s. 6(4) of the Civil Evidence Act, the purpose in each case being to preserve the principle that a witness may not corroborate himself. The difference between the provisions is that s. 6(4) refers to any " rule of law or practice " in relation to corroboration as well as to any enactment, while clause 36(5) refers only to enactments. This is because there are no rules of the common law or rules of practice requiring corroboration in criminal proceedings and the existing rules regulating the manner in which uncorroborated evidence is to be treated (that is to say, requiring the court to give a warning as to the danger of convicting in reliance on it), in so far as not made statutory by the Bill, are abolished by clause 20(1).

Subsection (6) enables the court to act on a medical certificate in determining whether or not a person is fit to attend as a witness for the purpose of clause 31(1)(*c*)(i) or clause 34(2)(*c*)(i). The subsection corresponds to s. 8(5) of the Civil Evidence Act and to the second part of s. 1(2) of the Criminal Evidence Act 1965.

CLAUSE 37 (ADMISSIBILITY OF STATEMENTS MADE AS IMMEDIATE REACTION TO EVENTS IN ISSUE PERSONALLY WITNESSED)

Clause 37 substantially restates the common law rule as to the admissibility of a hearsay statement as forming part of the *res gestae* (paragraphs 236(iv), 261). There is no corresponding provision in the Civil Evidence Act 1968 for the admissibility in civil proceedings of a statement which was admissible at common law under the *res gestae* rule: in civil proceedings the statement must now satisfy one of the other conditions for admissibility stated in the Act.

Subsection (1) is the main provision. Under it the statement (which naturally will have to be made "otherwise than in a document ") will, in order to be admissible, have to be one which " directly concerns an event in issue in [the] proceedings which took place in the presence, sight or hearing of [the maker] " (*paragraph (a)*) and "was made by him as an immediate reaction to that event" (*paragraph (b)*). The clause, like the common law, is based on the proposition that a statement made in these circumstances is likely to be reliable. In addition to redefining the test for admissibility, the subsection will ensure that the statement will be admissible as evidence of any fact stated in it (thus dispelling any remaining doubt under the present law as to the legal status of a statement admissible under the rule). It was mentioned in paragraph 261 that the test for admissibility would be somewhat narrower than that described by the Privy Council in *Ratten v. R.*[1]; for in the committee's opinion the statement in question in *Ratten* would not be admissible under subsection (1) (though it would still be admissible for the purpose for which, as mentioned in the paragraph, the Privy Council held that it was in fact admitted).

Subsection (2) limits admissibility under the clause to first-hand hearsay. The subsection corresponds to clause 31(5).

Subsection (3) prevents a statement admissible under the clause from counting as corroboration of any evidence given by the maker. The purpose is that mentioned in the note on clause 36(5).

CLAUSE 38 (ADMISSIBILITY OF HEARSAY EVIDENCE BY AGREEMENT OF THE PARTIES)

Clause 38 enables the parties, subject to certain conditions and restrictions, to agree that a hearsay statement which would otherwise be inadmissible shall

---

[1] (1971), 56 Cr. App. R. 18.

be admissible as evidence of any fact stated in it (paragraphs 236(v), 262). This right will be new in criminal proceedings. In civil proceedings the existing right of the parties to waive the rule of inadmissibility is preserved by the provision in s. 1(1) of the Civil Evidence Act 1968 that an out-of-court statement shall be admissible " by agreement of the parties " and the provision in s. 18(5)(*b*) saving " the operation of any agreement . . . as to the evidence which is to be admissible . . . in [legal] proceedings ".

Subsection (1) contains the general rule mentioned above that an out-of-court statement shall be admissible by agreement of the parties as evidence of any fact stated in it and lays down the conditions and restrictions referred to. These are (i) that the agreement must be made at a hearing and by all the parties, (ii) that the court may nevertheless exclude the statement if it thinks fit, (iii) that a statement shall not be admissible on behalf of the prosecution unless all the accused are legally represented and (iv) that an agreement made at committal proceedings shall not count for the purpose of the trial. If the agreement is effective at the trial, it will count for the purpose of any appeal or retrial. Since admissibility depends on agreement, it will not be restricted to first-hand hearsay statements.

Subsection (2) provides for the proof of a statement contained in a document. The subsection corresponds to clause 36(1).

Subsection (3) secures that, in a case where a statement is admissible under the clause but might have become admissible under clause 31 or 34 (that is to say, if the conditions in those clauses were satisfied), the statement shall not be capable of counting as corroboration of any evidence given by the maker. The purpose is that mentioned in the note on clause 36(5).

CLAUSE 39 (ADMISSIBILITY OF EVIDENCE AS TO CREDIBILITY OF MAKER ETC. OF STATEMENT ADMITTED UNDER CERTAIN PROVISIONS OF PART II)

Clause 39 provides for the admissibility of evidence as to the credibility of the maker of a hearsay statement which is admitted in evidence under certain of the clauses in a case where the maker is not called as a witness (paragraph 263). The clause corresponds to s. 7 of the Civil Evidence Act 1968 but with the exception mentioned in paragraph 263.

Subsection (1) deals with the case where a hearsay statement is given in evidence under clause 31 and the maker is not called as a witness. *Paragraph (a)* provides that any evidence which, had the maker been called, would have been admissible for the purpose of destroying or supporting his credibility as a witness shall be admissible for that purpose (that is to say, in relation to his statement). The most important cases where evidence is admissible for the purpose of destroying a person's credibility as a witness are the cases (mentioned in paragraph 263) relating to bias on the part of the witness, a previous inconsistent statement made by him[1] or the fact that he has been convicted of an offence. (The rule as to bias depends on common law, that as to previous inconsistent statements will depend on clause 12 (replacing s. 4 of the Criminal Procedure Act 1865), and that as to previous convictions

---

[1] Subsection (2) also applies to this case, as is mentioned below in the note on that subsection.

will depend on clause 14 (replacing s. 6 of the 1865 Act).) In addition, evidence by witness A may be admissible to the effect that witness B is unfit to be believed because of mental instability or because of his bad reputation for veracity or of A's opinion as to this[1]. If a witness's credibility has been attacked in these ways, evidence to the contrary is admissible to support his credibility (although in general evidence of a witness's good character is inadmissible); and evidence of a witness's previous consistent statement is admissible under the common law rule referred to in clause 33(1)(b) in order to rebut a suggestion that his evidence has been fabricated. In all these cases similar evidence will be admissible under clause 39(1)(a) in order to destroy or support the credibility of the maker of the statement which is admitted under clause 31. *Paragraph* (b) of subsection (1) deals with the case where a witness may be cross-examined about a matter in order to destroy his credibility as a witness but where, if he denies the matter put, evidence may not be adduced in order to rebut his denial. This is the usual situation, the exceptions being those mentioned above in relation to paragraph (a). For the reason given in paragraph 263 of the report, paragraph (b) of the subsection provides that, in the cases to which it applies, evidence of the matter which could have been put to the maker of the statement, had he been called as a witness, may be adduced with the leave of the court. The corresponding situation where evidence of a statement is given under clause 34 is dealt with in subsection (3) of clause 39. Except to the extent provided for by clause 39(2) no provision is made as to destroying the credibility of the maker of a *res gestae* statement given in evidence under clause 37, because the fact that admissibility will depend on the statement's having been made as an immediate reaction to the event in question makes it unlikely that there will be any occasion to attack the maker's credibility otherwise than by evidence that he made an inconsistent statement, which will be allowed by subsection (2). No provision is made in relation to a case where the statement is given in evidence by agreement under clause 38, because the likelihood that a party would wish to adduce evidence to discredit a person whose statement he has agreed should be given in evidence is remote.

Subsection (2) deals with the case where a hearsay statement is given in evidence under clause 31 or 37, the maker is not called as a witness but a party wishes to prove that the maker has made a statement inconsistent with the statement given in evidence. This is allowed in all cases. The subsection overlaps to some extent with subsection (1), as is shown by the reference in the note on subsection (1) to cases where evidence may be given to destroy a witness's credibility; but separate provision is made in subsection (2) for the sake of clarity. In particular, evidence may show that a person has contradicted himself without " destroying his credibility as a witness " (he may be a perfectly truthful person and have corrected a mistake in his earlier statement); and, as mentioned towards the end of the note on subsection (1), subsection (2) applies to where the statement is admissible under clause 37 but subsection (1) does not. It is clearly necessary to allow a party to adduce evidence that a person has made a statement contradicting his statement admitted under clause 37. The corresponding situation where evidence of a statement in a record is given under clause 34 is dealt with in subsection (3) of clause 39. For a reason similar to that given in the last sentence of the

---

[1] See the last paragraph of the note on clause 6.

note on subsection (1), subsection (2) makes no provision allowing a party to adduce evidence that the maker of a statement received in evidence by agreement under clause 38 has contradicted himself.

Subsection (3) adapts subsections (1) and (2) to the case of a statement in a record which is given in evidence under clause 34 by applying them to the person who originally supplied the information from which the record was compiled in the same way as they apply to the person who made the statement which is given in evidence under clause 31.

Subsection (4) provides that the provisions of clause 31(6) as to when a statement in a document reproducing an oral statement shall be treated as having been made by the maker of the oral statement shall apply to clause 39 as they apply to clause 31. The result will be that, where the statement in the document is to be treated as having been made by the maker of the oral statement, the provisions of clause 39 as to contradicting or supporting the credibility of the maker of a statement will apply to the maker of the oral statement. (The reason why clause 31(6) does not itself provide for its application to clause 39, as it does for its application to clauses 32, 36 and 41, is that the three last-mentioned clauses " have effect for the purposes of [clause 31] " as clause 31(6) mentions, whereas clause 39, being an independent provision, does not.)

Subsection (5) secures that, where a previous inconsistent statement made by the maker of a hearsay statement is proved by virtue of subsection (2) in order to show that the maker has contradicted himself, the previous statement shall be admissible as evidence of any fact stated in it in the same way as a previous inconsistent statement made by a witness is admissible for this purpose by virtue of clause 33(1).

CLAUSE 40 (SAVING FOR CERTAIN COMMON-LAW EXCEPTIONS TO RULE AGAINST HEARSAY)

Clause 40, which is to be read with clause 30, preserves the admissibility of hearsay statements admissible under the common law rules mentioned in *subsection (2)* (paragraph 264). The clause corresponds to s. 9 of the Civil Evidence Act 1968, but with the differences mentioned in the note on clause 30—in particular, the difference that the Act gives quasi-statutory force to the rules preserved. Since clause 40 preserves the rules only to the extent of their present application to criminal proceedings (which in some cases is limited or doubtful, as mentioned in the note on clause 30), and since subsection (3) provides that the words in which a rule is described in subsection (2) are intended only to identify the rule and not to alter it, it is unnecessary to go into the rules fully in this note. But a few matters are mentioned below.

Admissibility under the common law rules will be free from any of the restrictions provided for by the Bill. Therefore, in the absence of any common law restrictions, there will be no restriction under these rules as preserved on the admissibility of second-hand or remoter hearsay or on that of a statement made by a person incompetent to give evidence or by the spouse of the accused.

249

The provision in *subsection (2)(a)* describing the common law rule by which certain admissions adverse to the accused but made by a person other than the accused are admissible differs from the provision in s. 9(2)(a) of the Act, which refers only to the rule that in civil proceedings " an admission adverse to a party to the proceedings, whether made by that party or by another person " is admissible. The difference is because in the Bill the most important case of an admission—that of one made by the accused himself—is dealt with in clause 2. A statement adverse to the accused but made by somebody else may be admissible under the hearsay provisions of the Bill—in particular clause 31(1) or (2)—subject to any applicable conditions or restrictions; but in these cases the statement will be received in evidence not as an admission but simply as admissible hearsay. Subsection (2)(a) preserves the admissibility of what are thought to be the only cases of vicarious admissions of the accused which are or may be admissible in evidence against him at common law. Sub-paragraph (i) refers to an admission " by an agent of the accused acting within the scope of his authority "[1]. Sub-paragraph (ii) refers to an admission " by a person engaged with the accused in a common enterprise, if made in pursuance of their common purpose "[2]. Sub-paragraph (iii) refers to an admission " by one person to another where the maker is a person to whom the other was referred by the accused for information "[3].

Subsection (2)(e), which refers to the rule by which " evidence of a person's reputation is admissible ", differs a little from the reference in s. 9(4)(a) of the Act to the civil rule by which " evidence of a person's reputation is admissible for the purpose of establishing his good or bad character ". Paragraph (e) is included in clause 40(2) as a precaution in order to save the rules (mentioned at the end of the note on clause 6) as to the admissibility of evidence of a witness's reputation for veracity and the rule as to the admissibility of evidence of reputation for the purpose of criminal libel.

For the reasons given in paragraph 264 the clause does not include any provision as to the admissibility of evidence of things said at identification parades.

CLAUSE 41 (INTERPRETATION OF PART II)

Subsection (1) defines certain expressions for the purposes of Part II of the draft Bill, and *subsection (2)* gives a partial definition, in relation to certain special kinds of " documents " (devices for reproducing sounds or visual images), of the references in Part II to copies of documents (paragraph 265). Those subsections follow exactly s. 10(1) and (2) of the Civil Evidence Act 1968.

---

[1] *Hall* (1838), 8 C. & P. 358, 360; *Edwards v. Brookes (Milk) Ltd.*, [1963] 1 W.L.R. 795, 798; [1963] 3 All E.R. 62, 64. In the latter case Lord Parker C.J. said, at the beginning of the report of his judgment, that one of the questions was whether an employee of the accused company was " an agent of the status who prima facie would be entitled to make statements and admissions on behalf of the company ".

[2] *Blake and Tye* (1844), 6 Q.B. 126. This head of admissibility may fall under sub-paragraph (i), because, as Dixon C. J. said in *Tripodi* (1961), 104 C.L.R. 1, 7, " the basal reason for admitting the evidence of the acts or words of one against the other is that the combination or preconcert to commit the crime is considered as implying an authority to each to act or speak in furtherance of the common purpose on behalf of the others ".

[3] *Mallory* (1884), 13 Q.B.D. 33.

Subsection (3), which has no counterpart in the Civil Evidence Act, allows a " protest, greeting or other verbal utterance " to be treated for the purposes of Part II of the draft Bill as " stating any fact which the utterance implies ". An example of a protest would be that suggested by Cockburn C.J. in *Bedingfield*[1] where the victim of an assault cries out " Don't, Harry! " An example of a greeting would be " Hullo, Bill! " The subsection is intended to make it clear that these utterances are to be capable of being treated as implying, for example, that Harry was doing something unwelcome to the alleged victim or that Bill was in the presence of the speaker. Without the provision it might be argued that the utterance was not a " statement " and was therefore incapable of being evidence of the fact which it implied. Whether an utterance is in fact to be treated as implying and stating a particular fact will naturally depend on the circumstances.

PART III

OPINION AND EXPERT EVIDENCE

CLAUSE 42 (APPLICATION OF PART II TO STATEMENTS OF OPINION)

Clause 42 adapts the provisions of Part II of the draft Bill for admissibility of hearsay statements of fact to hearsay statements of opinion (paragraphs 266–267). The clause is in nearly the same terms as clause 1 of the draft Civil Evidence Bill annexed to the Law Reform Committee's report mentioned in paragraph 266[2].

Subsection (1) is the main provision. It provides that Part II (except the inapplicable clause 35 dealing with computer evidence) shall apply to statements of opinion as it applies to statements of fact with the necessary modifications (paragraph 267)[3]. It mentions specifically the principal modification that references in Part II to a fact stated in a statement shall be construed as references to a matter dealt with in it. The general provision for " the necessary modifications " will, inter alia, enable references to a representation of fact to be read as references to an expression of opinion and references to the accuracy of a statement to be read as references to its reliability.

Subsection (2) makes two particular provisions as to the way in which the provisions of clause 34 for the admissibility of statements contained in records are to apply in relation to statements of opinion contained in records. The two provisions are needed because of the difference between what an expert witness and what a non-expert witness may say by way of expressing his opinion when giving his evidence. If the witness is giving expert evidence, his opinions are admissible even if not based on personal knowledge, and he may be asked to give his opinion on the basis of assumed or hypothetical facts; but if he is not speaking

---

[1] (1879), 14 Cox 341, 342.

[2] A Civil Evidence Bill in terms of the Law Reform Committee's draft Bill, but with small differences, was introduced in the House of Commons on 20th December 1971.

[3] Subsection (4) of clause 2 makes provision as to expressions of opinion in a confession by the accused admissible under clause 2, as is mentioned at the end of the note on that subsection.

as an expert, the rule (as declared by clause 43(2)) is that he may express his opinion only as a way of conveying facts personally perceived by him. Since one of the conditions stated in clause 34(1) for the admissibility of a statement of fact contained in a record is that the supplier of the information should have had (or supposedly have had) personal knowledge of the matters dealt with in it, and since clause 42(1) provides that the provisions of clause 34(1) as to statements of fact shall apply in relation to statements of opinion, it follows that the admissibility of a statement of opinion contained in a record must be made to depend on whether the person who expressed the opinion recorded in it would have been able to express the opinion had he been giving oral evidence. Therefore the first part of subsection (2) provides that clause 34, as applied by clause 42(1), shall not render a statement of opinion contained in a record admissible unless oral evidence to the same effect by the person who originally supplied the information contained in the record (that is to say, who expressed the opinion recorded in it) would have been admissible. As a corollary to this, the second part of the subsection, in order to take account of the fact that an expert's opinion is admissible even if not based on personal observation and may be given on the basis of assumed or hypothetical facts, provides that in the case of expert evidence the provision in clause 34(1), as applied by clause 42(1), requiring personal knowledge on the part of the supplier shall not apply. If the statement of opinion contained in the record was made by a person not qualified to give expert evidence on the matter, the statement will be admissible only if the maker made it as a way of conveying relevant facts personally perceived by him. The result will be that, in the case of a statement by a non-expert, clause 42 will not enlarge admissibility beyond what is provided for by clause 34 read with the declaratory provision in clause 43(2).

CLAUSE 43 (ADMISSIBILITY OF EXPERT OPINION AND CERTAIN EXPRESSIONS OF NON-EXPERT OPINION)

Clause 43 contains two provisions intended to clarify the law as to the admissibility of expert and non-expert opinion evidence respectively (paragraphs 266, 268–270). The clause is similar to clause 3 of the draft Civil Evidence Bill referred to at the beginning of the note on clause 42 of the present draft Bill except that clause 3 of the former Bill does not include the equivalent of subsection (4) of clause 43 of the present Bill (which the committee decided to include after the publication of the Law Reform Committee's report and which (as mentioned in paragraph 269) the committee think is desirable for criminal proceedings).

Subsection (1) provides that the opinion of an expert witness on any relevant matter on which he is qualified to give expert evidence shall be admissible in evidence. This provision, read with subsection (3), will make it clear that an expert is not to be prevented from giving his opinion on a matter on the ground that this is the ultimate issue which the court or jury has to decide (paragraphs 268–269).

Subsection (2) is a declaratory provision that a statement of opinion by a non-expert witness on a relevant matter (including, by virtue of subsection (3), any issue in the proceedings), if made " as a way of conveying relevant facts personally perceived by him ", is admissible as evidence of what he perceived. The purpose of the subsection is shown in paragraph 270.

Subsection (*3*) defines " relevant matter " for the purposes of subsections (1) and (2) as including " an issue in the proceedings in question ". The main purpose is shown in paragraph 268 and the note on subsection (1), but the definition applies to subsection (2) also.

Subsection (*4*) declares that nothing in the clause is to be taken to affect the rules of law as to the topics on which expert evidence is or is not admissible. The purpose, as mentioned in paragraph 269, is to prevent any possibility of misunderstanding as a result of the provision in subsection (1), read with subsection (3), that an expert witness may give his opinion on the ultimate issue. Subsection (4) is included to make it clear that in order that the provision in subsection (1) may apply the topic under consideration must be one on which expert evidence is admissible under the ordinary rules of law.

CLAUSE 44 (EVIDENCE OF FOREIGN LAW)

Clause 44 makes the two provisions for the proof of foreign law which are described in paragraph 271. The clause is similar, except in two minor respects, to clause 4 of the draft Civil Evidence Bill referred to at the beginning of the note on clause 42. The first difference relates to the requirement in *subsection* (*3*) of each clause that a party intending to adduce a finding by an English court in previous proceedings on a question of foreign law shall give notice of his intention to the other parties. Clause 4(3) of the Civil Evidence Bill provides that the notice shall be given in accordance with rules of court. In the present Bill *subsection* (*3*) of clause 44, read with *subsection* (*6*), provides that notice shall be served in the way provided by subsection (6) of clause 32 in respect of notice of intention to give a hearsay statement in evidence under subsection (4) of that clause. The second difference is that *subsection* (*4*) of the present draft clause departs a little from the corresponding subsection (4) of the civil clause as to the courts whose findings or decisions on questions of foreign law are to be admissible under the clauses (in particular, in order to include the since-established Crown Court):

PART IV

MISCELLANEOUS AND GENERAL

CLAUSE 45 (GENERAL INTERPRETATION AND SAVINGS)

Clause 45 defines certain expressions for the purposes of the draft Bill generally (in addition to the special definitions in clause 41 for the purposes of Part II) and makes certain savings. Notes on some particular matters follow.

Subsection (*1*) includes the provision that in general in the Bill the expression " proceedings " without more means criminal proceedings.

Subsection (*3*) provides that, where the age of any person at any time is material for the purpose of any provision other than clause 17(2), his age shall be deemed to be that which it appears to the court to be or to have been at that time. The subsection will operate in relation to clauses 9(3), 22[1],31(4)

---

[1] Clause 45(3) does not apply to subsection (7) of clause 22, but the latter subsection makes similar provision in relation to the taking and admissibility of depositions of children and young persons under ss. 42 and 43 of the Children and Young Persons Act 1933. The note on clause 22(7) refers.

and 36(3). The effect will be (for example) that, if a boy or girl is to give evidence, the court will be able to judge from his or her appearance or any information given to the court whether the evidence has to be given on oath or unsworn under clause 22; and if a question arises whether the spouse of the accused is a compellable witness for the prosecution under clause 9(3) on the ground that the victim of the offence charged was under sixteen at the time of the offence, the court will be able to decide the question similarly. Clause 45(3) is similar to s.126(5) of the Magistrates' Courts Act 1952 (c. 55) except that under the latter provision the court has to determine the age " after considering any available evidence ". Subsection (3) of the clause leaves this requirement out as unnecessary. The subsection does not apply to the requirement in clause 17(2) that on a charge of a sexual offence against a child the evidence of the victim must be corroborated. Here if it is necessary to establish that the victim was aged fourteen or over, so that corroboration is not required by law, the age will have to be proved by evidence other than appearance alone.

Subsection (4) makes it clear that references to a person's husband or wife do not include references to a person no longer married to that person. The subsection corresponds to the last provision in s. 18(2) of the Civil Evidence Act 1968. It will operate in relation to clauses 9 and 15. The provision in clause 32(2) restricting the admissibility of an out-of-court statement by the spouse of the accused is itself so framed as to secure the same result.

Subsection (6) contains a saving for the practice when, after conviction, it falls to a court (the court of trial, the court to which the accused is committed for sentence or an appellate court) to determine how the accused should be dealt with. At this stage, when it becomes the duty of the court to inform itself of all relevant matters for this purpose, the strictness of the rules of evidence is relaxed and, in particular, hearsay evidence is admitted freely and evidence is often received without an oath. The Bill leaves the present practice completely unaffected. In particular, the court may still require strict proof if, for example, there is a dispute about the facts of an offence of which the accused has pleaded guilty; nor will the Bill affect the rule that a police witness giving evidence about the accused's previous history must not make general allegations against him which cannot be proved if necessary[1].

Subsection (7) saves the operation of enactments which provide that any answer or evidence given by a person in specified circumstances shall not be admissible against him or some other person in other proceedings (civil or criminal). The subsection corresponds to s. 18(4) of the Civil Evidence Act 1968. Both provisions relate to enactments under which a person is compelled to give information for certain purposes even though it might incriminate him but is, in return, protected from having it referred to against him in any proceedings. An example is the provision in s. 31(1) of the Theft Act 1968 (c. 60) that (i) in certain proceedings, such as proceedings for the recovery or administration of any property, a person shall not be entitled to refuse to answer a question on the ground that this would reveal that he or his wife has committed an offence under the Act but (ii) the answer may not be given in

---

[1] *Van Pelz* (1942), 29 Cr. App. R. 10; *Robinson* (1969), 53 Cr. App. R. 314.

evidence against that person or his wife in proceedings for an offence under the Act. There are also several enactments of this kind relating to particular subjects which are among the enactments set out in the Schedule to the Civil Evidence Act (being amended verbally by s. 17(3) to conform with the provisions in s. 14 of the Act relating to the privilege of a person against incriminating his wife).

Subsection (8) saves any power of a court to exclude evidence at its discretion notwithstanding that the evidence may be relevant and admissible in law (paragraph 278). The subsection is similar to s. 18(5)(*a*) of the Civil Evidence Act. The reference to excluding evidence " by preventing questions from being put *or otherwise* " includes cases where the court excuses the witness from answering a question already put to him and cases where the judge directs the jury that they should ignore the evidence or where the magistrates' court itself decides to ignore it. As mentioned in paragraph 278, the subsection leaves any question of the extent of the discretion, and as to the principles on which it should be exercised, to the common law. In addition to the general saving in clause 45(8) the draft Bill refers specifically to the discretion in clause 5(5)(*b*), which provides that it shall be a " good cause " for a refusal by the accused to answer a particular question if " the court in the exercise of its general discretion excuses him from answering it ".

Subsection (9) is a declaratory provision that, where because of a defect of speech or hearing a witness has to give his evidence by writing or signs, the evidence is to be treated as given orally. The subsection is similar to s. 18(6) of the Civil Evidence Act.

CLAUSE 46 (MINOR AND CONSEQUENTIAL AMENDMENTS, AND REPEALS)

Subsection (1) adds a new subsection (4) to s. 129C of the Naval Discipline Act 1957 (c. 53). S. 129C (which was inserted in the 1957 Act by s. 57(1) of the Armed Forces Act 1971 (c. 33)), provides (as mentioned in the note on clause 26(1)) for the proof, in civilian courts, of the result of proceedings at naval courts-martial. The new subsection (4) extends these provisions to naval disciplinary courts.

Subsection (3) repeals the Evidence Act 1877 (c. 14). The 1877 Act, as it stands at present, provides that on the trial of an indictment for a nuisance to a public highway, river or bridge, or of any other indictment " for the purpose of trying or enforcing a civil right only ", the defendant and his spouse are to be competent and compellable witnesses. As mentioned in the report in relation to clause 9[1], criminal proceedings for these purposes are in practice obsolete. This is partly as a result of statutory remedies established since 1877. There is therefore no purpose in preserving the 1877 Act.

CLAUSE 47 (SHORT TITLE, EXTENT AND COMMENCEMENT)

Subsection (2) restricts the Bill to England and Wales except in relation to the enactments referred to. As the committee are concerned with the law

---

[1] Paragraph 143 n. 1.

administered by the ordinary criminal courts in England and Wales only, it will be for consideration whether and how far the Bill, when introduced, should apply to trials by courts-martial (to which in general the English law of evidence applies).

Subsection (*3*) leaves a blank for the date of commencement of the Act and provides that, except as mentioned in the proviso, the Act shall apply only to proceedings begun on or after that date. Clearly some time will have to elapse between the passing of the Act and its commencement in order to give time for it to be studied and the necessary administrative arrangements to be made. The provisions excluding proceedings in progress is necessary because of the rule that, in the absence of provision to the contrary, changes in the law of evidence apply to proceedings in progress when the changes take effect. No problem arises in relation to the Bill (except as mentioned below in relation to the proviso) so far as concerns proceedings begun on or after the commencement of the Act: but in the case of proceedings in progress at the date of commencement it would not be practicable to change over to the new rules in the middle (for example, on account of the changes in clauses 5 and 9). The proviso excludes clause 1, because of the special provision made by subsection (4) of that clause, and indicates that clause 47(3) does not apply to clause 27 (because the requirement that the Director of Public Prosecutions should have authorized the proceedings will in any event apply only to the institution of proceedings after the commencement of the Act).

SCHEDULE 1 (CONSEQUENTIAL AMENDMENTS OF ENACTMENTS)

Children and Young Persons Act 1933 (*c. 12*)

S. 42 (as mentioned in the note on clause 22(7)), provides that, on a charge of any of certain offences against a child (under fourteen) or a young person (aged fourteen to sixteen), a justice of the peace may, if satisfied on medical evidence that it would involve serious danger for the child or young person to attend before a magistrates' court for the purpose of committal proceedings, take his deposition in writing " on oath ". In consequence of the provision in clause 22(2) that a child under fourteen shall give evidence unsworn (and subject to the conditions mentioned as to his being of sufficient intelligence and understanding the importance of telling the truth) the Schedule amends s. 42 so that (i) only the deposition of a young person will be made on oath and that of a child will be made unsworn (and subject to the conditions mentioned) and (ii) a child who wilfully makes a false statement in the deposition will be liable to be dealt with in the way provided by clause 22(5) in the case of a child who gives false unsworn evidence in court.

Children and Young Persons Act 1963 (*c. 37*)

S. 16(2) includes a provision that in any proceedings against a person for an offence committed when he was of or over the age of twenty-one the accused shall not be asked any question relating to any offence of which he was found guilty while under the age of fourteen " notwithstanding that the question would otherwise be admissible under section 1 of the Criminal Evidence Act 1898". The Schedule replaces the words quoted so as to make the prohibition apply notwithstanding that the question would otherwise be ad-

256

missible under any of the relevant provisions of clauses 6 and 7 (clauses 6(2)–(5) and 7(2)) corresponding to the relevant provisions of the 1898 Act (s. 1 (*f*)).

S. 28(1) includes a provision that in an oath taken by a child or young person in any court other than a juvenile court the words " I promise before Almighty God " shall be used instead of " I swear by Almighty God ". Since clause 22(2) provides that in criminal proceedings a child shall give evidence unsworn, the Schedule restricts s. 28(1) to evidence given by a young person in any proceedings and to evidence given by a child in civil proceedings.

Criminal Appeal Act 1968 (*c. 19*)

S. 23 provides for the hearing of evidence by the Court of Appeal. Subsection (1)(*b*) empowers the court to order the attendance of " any witness who would have been a compellable witness in the proceedings from which the appeal lies ". Since under the present law a witness who is compellable for any party at the trial is compellable for all parties, s. 23 does not distinguish between compellability on behalf of the appellant and compellability on behalf of the prosecution. But now that clause 9 of the draft Bill differentiates between the parties at the trial in relation to compellability of the accused's spouse, the Schedule amends s. 23(1)(*b*) of the 1968 Act so that the Court of Appeal will be able to order the attendance of a person who would have been a compellable witness at the trial on behalf of the party who is seeking the attendance of that person at the appeal. S. 23(3), which provides for the case where, as a result of the restriction in s. 1(*a*) of the Criminal Evidence Act 1898, the appellant's spouse could not have been called to give evidence at the trial except on the application of the accused, is repealed as a result of the abolition of the restriction mentioned.

Civil Evidence Act 1968 (*c. 64*)

S. 17(2) deals with the application of the provisions of the Act concerning the privilege of a witness against self-incrimination to cases where the evidence of the witness is being taken under an order made by a court or judge in England and Wales for the purpose of legal proceedings pending in a court outside England and Wales. Orders may be made under the Foreign Tribunals Evidence Act 1856 (c. 113) for the purpose of proceedings in foreign countries and under the Evidence by Commission Act 1859 (c. 20) for the purpose of proceedings in Her Majesty's dominions. The power to order the taking of evidence under the 1856 Act was extended to criminal proceedings by s. 24 of the Extradition Act 1870 (c. 52); but the power is rarely exercised for the purpose of criminal proceedings, as evidence for this purpose is ordinarily taken by a magistrate in accordance with an order by the Secretary of State under s. 5 of the Extradition Act 1873 (c. 5). Theoretically, it seems that an order might be made in England and Wales under the 1859 Act for the purpose of criminal proceedings in British courts abroad[1], but in fact this is not done. In respect of the privilege against self-incrimination and other privileges s. 5 of the 1856 Act and s. 4 of the 1859 Act provide that the

---

[1] This was mentioned in paragraph 277, in relation to the possibility of obtaining evidence for the purpose of criminal proceedings in England and Wales.

witness shall have the same rights as a witness would have in a cause pending before the court or judge in England and Wales by whom the order for the examination of the witness was made. These two sections made no distinction, in relation to privilege, between examinations for the purpose of civil proceedings and those for the purpose of criminal proceedings, as the privileges were similar in both cases; but when s. 14 of the Civil Evidence Act (corresponding to clause 15 of the draft Bill) declared the extent of the privilege against self-incrimination in civil proceedings in England and Wales, it became necessary to amend s. 5 of the 1856 Act and s. 4 of the 1859 Act so as to distinguish between civil and criminal proceedings. Therefore, s. 17(2)(a) provided that in the case of an examination for the purpose of criminal proceedings the provisions of the 1968 Act relating to privilege should be disregarded in determining the rights of the person being examined (so that the existing law as to privilege would continue to apply); but s. 17(2)(b) provided that in the case of examination for the purpose of civil proceedings the witness's rights should be those to which he would be entitled in civil proceedings in England and Wales (so that the new provisions in the Act should apply). Now that clause 15 of the draft Bill makes provisions as to privilege for the purpose of criminal proceedings (corresponding, as mentioned, to those of s. 14 of the 1968 Act), the Schedule amends s. 17(2)(a) of the 1968 Act so that in the case of examination for the purpose of criminal proceedings the witness's rights shall be those to which he would be entitled in criminal proceedings in England and Wales. Thus in either kind of proceedings the witness will have the same rights as in the corresponding proceedings in England and Wales. The Schedule makes no provision as to the rights of a witness who is being examined by a magistrate under s. 5 of the Extradition Act 1873 for the purpose of foreign criminal proceedings, because s. 5 is itself framed so as to secure that the witness shall have the same rights as in committal proceedings before the magistrate and the Bill will apply to these.

Produced in England for Her Majesty's Stationery Office by Commercial Colour Press, London E.7.
Dd.0593220 K2 9/80